Applied
Cross-Cultural
Psychology

IN

CROSS-CULTURAL RESEARCH AND METHODOLOGY SERIES

Series Editors

Walter J. Lonner, *Department of Psychology, Western Washington University (United States)*
John W. Berry, *Department of Psychology, Queen's University, Kingston, Ontario (Canada)*

Volumes in this series:

Volume   4 Myerhoff/Simić LIFE'S CAREER-AGING
Volume   5 Hofstede CULTURE'S CONSEQUENCES
Volume   6 Williams/Best MEASURING SEX STEREOTYPES, Revised Edition
Volume   7 Pedersen/Sartorius/Marsella MENTAL HEALTH SERVICES
Volume   8 Lonner/Berry FIELD METHODS IN CROSS-CULTURAL RESEARCH
Volume   9 Cushner/Brislin INTERCULTURAL INTERACTIONS (2nd edition)
Volume 10 Dasen/Berry/Sartorius HEALTH AND CROSS-CULTURAL PSYCHOLOGY
Volume 11 Bond THE CROSS-CULTURAL CHALLENGE TO SOCIAL PSYCHOLOGY
Volume 12 Ward ALTERED STATES OF CONSCIOUSNESS AND MENTAL HEALTH
Volume 13 Williams/Best SEX AND PSYCHE
Volume 14 Brislin APPLIED CROSS-CULTURAL PSYCHOLOGY
Volume 15 De Vos/Suárez-Orozco STATUS INEQUALITY
Volume 16 Nsamenang HUMAN DEVELOPMENT IN CULTURAL CONTEXT
Volume 17 Kim/Berry INDIGENOUS PSYCHOLOGIES
Volume 18 Kim/Triandis/Kagitçibasi/Choi/Yoon INDIVIDUALISM AND COLLECTIVISM

Applied Cross-Cultural Psychology

edited by
Richard W. Brislin

Cross-Cultural Research and Methodology Series
Volume 14

SAGE PUBLICATIONS
The International Professional Publishers
Newbury Park   London   New Delhi

For information address:

SAGE Publications, Inc.
2455 Teller Road
Newbury Park, California 91320
E-mail: order@sagepub.com

SAGE Publications Ltd.
6 Bonhill Street
London EC2A 4PU
United Kingdom

GN
270
. A67
1990
C.2

SAGE Publications India Pvt. Ltd.
M-32 Market
Greater Kailash I
New Delhi 110 048 India

Printed in the United States of America

Library of Congress Cataloging-in-Publication Data

Applied cross-cultural psychology / edited by Richard W. Brislin
    p.   cm. — (Cross-cultural research and methodology series ;
  vol. 14)
   Includes bibliographical references.
   ISBN 0-8039-3785-7. — ISBN 0-8039-3786-5 (pbk.)
  1. Ethnopsychology—Cross-cultural studies. 2. Psychology,
Applied—Cross-cultural studies. I. Brislin, Richard W., 1945-
II. Series: Cross-cultural research and methodology series ; v. 14.
GN270.A67 1990
155.8—dc20   90-8296
                                       CIP

99 00 01 10 9 8 7 6

Sage Production Editor: Susan McElroy

2161216 x

CONTENTS

About the Series   7

1. Applied Cross-Cultural Psychology:
   An Introduction
   Richard W. Brislin   9

2. Theoretical Concepts That Are Applicable to the
   Analysis of Ethnocentrism
   Harry C. Triandis   34

3. An Overview of Cross-Cultural Testing and Assessment
   Walter J. Lonner   56

4. Interventions for Development Out of Poverty
   Durganand Sinha   77

5. Cross-Cultural Psychology and the Formal Classroom
   Kenneth Cushner   98

6. Family and Home-Based Intervention
   Çigdem Kâgitçibaşi   121

7. Indigenous Psychology: Science and Applications
   Uichol Kim   142

8. International Students: Cross-Cultural Psychological
   Perspectives
   R. Michael Paige   161

9. Work Attitudes, Leadership Styles, and Managerial
   Behaviors in Different Cultures
   C. Harry Hui   186

10. Dispute Processing: A Cross-Cultural Analysis
    Kwok Leung and Pei-Guan Wu   209

11. Psychology of Acculturation: Understanding Individuals
    Moving Between Cultures
    John W. Berry   232

12. The Environment, Culture, and Behavior
      Janak Pandey   254

13. Culture and Health
      Lisa Marie Ilola   278

14. Applications of Cross-Cultural Psychology in the
      Field of Mental Health
      Juris G. Draguns   302

15. Cross-Cultural Orientation Programs
      D. P. S. Bhawuk   325

Author Index   347

Subject Index   357

About the Authors   363

ABOUT THE SERIES

The Sage Series on Cross-Cultural Research and Methodology was created to present comparative studies on cross-cultural topics and interdisciplinary research. Inaugurated in 1975, the series is designed to satisfy a growing need to integrate research method and theory and to dissect issues from a comparative perspective; a truly international approach to the study of behavioral, social, and cultural variables can be done only within such a methodological framework.

Each volume in the series presents substantive cross-cultural studies and considerations of the strengths, interrelationships, and weaknesses of its various methodologies, drawing upon work done in anthropology, political science, psychology, and sociology. Both individual researchers knowledgeable in more than one discipline and teams of specialists with differing disciplinary backgrounds have contributed to the series. While each individual volume may represent the integration of only a few disciplines, *the cumulative totality of the series reflects an effort to bridge gaps of methodology and conceptualization across the various disciplines and many cultures.*

When Richard Brislin was corresponding with the contributing chapter authors shortly after he had invited them to prepare manuscripts for this volume in the series, he asked them to keep two audiences in mind. The first audience, he said, should be undergraduate students. He correctly assumed that the very broad base represented by chapters in this volume would be appealing to many college and university faculty who might select it as a text, or a supplement to a text, in undergraduate courses dealing with cultural factors in human behavior. For this reason, the book contains the *basics* and not complex theoretical issues. Brislin identified the second audience as practitioners who would benefit from a review of the concepts being presented. For instance, clinical and counseling psychologists would benefit from Juris Draguns's chapter; industrial/organizational psychologists, from the overview of Harry Hui; those interested in culture and epidemiology, by Lisa Ilola's chapter; and so forth. The title, *Applied Cross-Cultural Psychology*, is, therefore, appropriate. We believe that the book will be attractive to a variety of relative newcomers as well as seasoned cross-culturalists, and especially to those who are looking for a fairly comprehensive and clearly written sketch of current knowledge with a cross-cultural focus in several different areas of the social and behavioral sciences.

As series editors, we want to point out two things that may help in understanding the nature of this volume. First, this is not the first book with the title Applied Cross-Cultural Psychology. The first book carrying that title was the collection of readings resulting from the second international conference of the International Association of Cross-Cultural Psychology (that book was edited by Berry and Lonner, and was published by Swets and Zeitlinger in 1974). The current book, however, is much more *applied* (in the real sense of that word) than the 1974 book. Second, this current book is somewhat of a companion to Volume 8 in the series *Field Methods in Cross-Cultural Research* (edited by Lonner and Berry, and published by Sage in 1986). In combination, these two books would provide the cross-cultural researcher with specific methodologies and information on how they may be used in different applied areas.

We want to express our thanks to Rich Brislin for doing a characteristically excellent job of organizing and editing the book as well as convening the 1989 workshop at the East-West Center's Institute of Culture and Communication. We also want to thank Helen de Leon Palmore, Program Officer at ICC, for the key role she played in making the workshop a successful and pleasant experience. At the workshop, drafts of all chapters were presented and discussed, and the whole process was a productive and smooth operation resulting in this very welcome addition to the series.

—Walter J. Lonner
John W. Berry

ACKNOWLEDGMENTS

Rich would like to acknowledge a number of people whose efforts were indispensable. The unwavering support of Dr. Victor Hao Li, president of the East-West Center, and Robert Hewett, Director of the Center's Institute of Culture and Communication, made the entire project possible. A number of people took on tasks at various stages during the book's preparation. These tasks included reading chapters and suggesting sentences in need of clarification, assisting at the conference that brought the chapter authors together, assisting in the preparation of indices, and identifying places were examples would help in the exposition of theoretical points. Heidi Denecke, Tamara Echter, Sharon Gorman, John Howe, Fran Mularski, Shakti Rana, Vasanthi Ranganathan, and Tammy Stein involved themselves in these tasks, and the authors join Rich in expressing their gratitude.

1

APPLIED CROSS-CULTURAL PSYCHOLOGY
An Introduction

RICHARD W. BRISLIN

Although forecasts about the future are often cautiously made, one prediction can be made with certainty. There will be extensive contact among people from quite different cultural backgrounds, contact that could have been avoided in the past if people had wished. The reasons are plentiful. Increased air travel has brought tourists to heretofore rarely visited places. Because these tourists sometimes become interested in investing money in the newfound places, they contribute to an internationalization of the world's economy. Schools and neighborhoods can no longer be the fortresses of one privileged group that makes a point of excluding those with a different skin color or different customs. Immigrants, refugees, and minorities in a country often refuse to become part of a homogeneous melting pot and instead make requests of schools, employers, and governments to respect many of their cultural traditions (Berry, this volume). Increases in the amount of education available to people lead to greater sophistication about many aspects of everyday life such as their consumer behavior. People want reliable and affordable products such as electronic equipment and automobiles. If these are made in other countries, they will be bought.

Contact brings both advantages and disadvantages. Adult refugees and immigrants may find far more opportunities for good-paying jobs, but their children may learn attitudes in school that challenge traditional authority patterns at home (Cushner, this volume). International students may bring in needed money to universities whose traditional student body is declining (Paige, this volume), but these newcomers may experience considerable stress when adjusting to the differences they encounter (Draguns, this volume). Overseas business people may find new marketplaces in other countries, but they will surely encounter differing attitudes about work and leadership when they interact with decision makers in those countries (Hui, this volume). Extensive contact also brings with it the threat to people's physical health (Ilola, this volume). The scientist who discovered the retrovirus that causes AIDS,

Robert Gallo, argues that international contact played a central role in the spread of the disease:

> I suspect that until the 1950's the AIDS virus was probably isolated in small pockets of Central Africa. But when people started moving from rural communities to large cities, they brought the virus with them. And by the 1960's, technological advances like the passenger jet began to bring people around the world into closer contact. By then, also, the medical use of blood had become global. Blood products for hemophiliacs, for example, were being sent from the United States to Japan. As a result, a virus that might once have remained relatively rare and isolated became common and global. (Gallo, 1989, p. 32)

A common thread running through all these examples is that the people involved are originally from quite different cultural backgrounds and are engaging in extensive intercultural contact and negotiation. Because "culture" is so central to an understanding of such contact, as well as to an understanding of all the chapters in the book, an introduction to its importance is warranted.

Identifying Culture's Influence on Behavior: Culture Contact

Consider people who have traveled to many parts of the world. They will have observed (a) recurring patterns of behavior that (b) differ from place to place but that (c) within those places are observable generation after generation. Indeed, (d) adults have the responsibility of ensuring that members of new generations adopt those recurring patterns of behavior that mark people as well-socialized individuals. The term that best summarizes the recurring patterns of behaviors is *culture*. The "place" referred to in the second sentence is often a country, or it is a locale with its own norms that exists within a large and highly factionalized country. One of the best ways to observe culture and cultural differences is for people from one country to live in a culture other than the one in which they were socialized. There, they will observe proper, effective behavior that meets the goals established by citizens in those other cultures. The most memorable will be those behaviors that are clearly different, ranging from the odious to the delightful, from the point of view of the observers from elsewhere. Such observations have been made for thousands of years by travelers, merchants, missionaries, military personnel, and (more recently) anthropologists and psychologists (Brislin, Cushner, Cherrie, & Yong, 1986).

To use slightly more technical language, culture refers to widely shared ideals, values, formation and uses of categories, assumptions about life, and goal-directed activities that become unconsciously or subconsciously accepted as "right" and "correct" by people who identify themselves as members of a society. That society is an entity larger than one's family with which people identify themselves as members and/or that *others* use to categorize them as members. A society is sometimes a country (e.g., Japan), sometimes a more delimited segment of society (e.g., the middle class in the United States), and sometimes an ethnic group within a large country (e.g., Polish Americans, or Palestinian Arabs living in Israel). With these examples as prototypes, there are other large groups with which people have strong emotional ties that can also be analyzed using the concept "culture." These include one's organization ("organizational culture"), religion (e.g., Roman Catholicism), and profession (e.g., academic culture). When interacting across cultural boundaries, there are often clashes if the "right and correct" behaviors differ. As Walter Lonner (this volume) points out, Americans and Europeans feel they have a correct view about the value of standardized tests in schools. The improper use of the tests, however, can be an unethical imposition on immigrant students whose cultural background does not include familiarity with tests. A key to understanding culture, and this example, is that people do not think that they are imposing themselves or their views on others. Cultural practices, like testing in some countries, is so common and has such a long history that people do it without much thought concerning its impact on others from a very different background.

Identifying Cultural Variables: Analyzing Observable Differences

Culture can be distinguished from other important concepts, such as "individual differences," by examining a number of features. When a concept is considered, the more of the following indicators that can be applied, the more likely the concept is an example of a cultural variable rather than an individual-differences variable. The latter type of variable, of course, describes some people in a society but not all and often marks a concept on which people *in* a given society can be placed along a range. Intelligence is a frequently mentioned example. There is a range in this variable from high, through average, to low. Conceptualization of variables in terms of a wide range *within* a culture marks an individual-differences variable. I am unaware of any widely accepted arguments that place one culture or another higher versus lower on the dimension of intelligence. Some features of a culture are as follows: (1) Culture consists of the part of the environment that people make (Herskovits, 1948). Typhoons are not part of a culture. They are part of the physical environment to which people must react. Houses that are built in reaction to frequent typhoons, on the other hand, are part of the culture. Culture consists of both visible and physical elements, such as houses and superhighways, as well as less visible norms associated with the physical elements. Examples are norms concerning who is allowed to build houses, taboos that determine how houses are built and used, guidelines concerning who (if anyone) pays for the construction, reputations concerning who is an especially good house builder, and so forth. The less visible concepts, values, categories, norms, and assumptions about life, or what Triandis (1972) calls subjective culture, that affect behavior are of most interest to psychologists and consequently will be emphasized here. A number of authors in this volume refer explicitly to elements of subjective culture (e.g., Kim, Pandey).

(2) Culture is indicated by ideas that are transmitted generation to generation, rarely with explicit instruction, by members of the older generations. Key people to observe are parents, teachers, bosses, and widely respected elders. The value placed on formal education in Japan is a good example (see Cushner, this volume). I do not believe parents say, "Our culture places a premium on people obtaining as much formal education as possible." Rather, this cultural value is transmitted from parents to children less directly. For instance, parents make sure children do their homework. They deny television privileges to children if poor grades are received, and they point to others in the community who have risen above their status at birth because of their education. Parents pay for after-hours additional schooling and often buy an extra set of school textbooks so that they can help their children with their homework. One reason for the success of Asian Americans in American schools is that they bring a respect for education from their cultural background. This value is widespread enough in Japan, Korea, and other Asian countries to be called "cultural." In the United States, a value placed on formal education is more an individual-differences variable: Some children and parents have this value and some do not.

(3) The fact of transmission generation to generation means that there will be identifiable childhood experiences that lead to the internalization of cultural values. Some such experiences have already been introduced: Japanese children will remember being denied privileges because of mediocre grades and will remember the study area their parents set aside for them. Another example is the sort of memories that

children in individualistic societies recall, such as memories about the first time they stood alone and addressed a large audience (e.g., in school or at a church-sponsored meeting). Triandis (this volume) discusses individualism and collectivism at length, and this important cultural dimension is also featured in the chapters by Hui and Kâgitçibaşi. A major distinction is that individualists pursue their own goals, whereas collectivists are willing to subordinate their own goals to those of a group. Taking care of elderly parents provides an example. An individualist would be more likely to move 1,000 miles to accept a good job, leaving parental care to others (siblings, a nursing home). Collectivists would be more willing to downplay their own goal of the good job and would stay near their parents. But if they are constantly to pursue their own goals, the cultural expectation is that individualists (found, for example, in the United States and Canada) have to "stand on their own two feet." They have to learn to fend for themselves in the job market, for instance, because they only infrequently have members of a collective (e.g., uncles, cousins) who can secure employment for them. Consequently, they have to learn how to move out from the nuclear family into the larger society. Many individualist adults remember being invited to a party when they were 10, 11, or 12 years old. They did not particularly want to go because they did not know everyone who would be there, or they simply wanted to do something else. Their mothers, however, said, "You really should go. You've got to learn to meet people." These sensitive and concerned mothers realized the importance of a social skill necessary for success in an individualistic society.

A troublesome aspect of distinguishing culture from individual differences is to answer the question, "How many people have to do it or have it before it is cultural?" There is no perfect answer. I suggest the following when my students ask: 70% to 80% either behave according to the cultural value or are familiar with the value even though they may reject it at the moment. Voting in a democratic manner is certainly a cultural value in the United States, even if less than 50% of eligible voters take advantage of their privilege during a specific election year. People beyond that 50% are familiar with democratic voting, and they can take advantage of their right to participate in future years if issues are brought before the public that interest or concern them. Another good indicator is to consider childhood experiences in a slightly different manner. Consider the question, "If this experience did not happen, *could it well have happened*?" The experiences that a child could well have had, like being shooed out of the house to go to a party, are an indicator of culture. A Japanese adult may not remember her parents buying an extra set of school textbooks to help with homework, but she can say that it well could have happened if she had even slight problems with her grades.

(4) The successful result of myriad socialization experiences is that children eventually become accepted members of adult society. A helpful image is to imagine a room full of 18- to 20-year-olds. The elders in a community consider these people young adults and make the summary judgment about each, "Yes, that person is one of us," or "No, that person is not one of us." The people identified as "one of us" have internalized the culture into which they were born. Often, the elders can give only a few reasons for their judgments, and the expressed reasons often refer to visible factors such as dress, participation in ceremonies, diet, and use of language. Less visible factors such as internalization of values go undermentioned, but these are nevertheless taken into account when making the summary judgment.

(5) Cultural factors are not discussed frequently within a society. Rather, culture is taken for granted, much like the air we breathe if we happen to live in rural areas of North America. If a factor is taken for granted, it is not discussed very much. Or, if a cultural value is widely shared, it is rather uninteresting to talk about it because people taking part in the conversation will quickly begin to repeat what everyone already knows. A good exercise to demonstrate this point involves asking groups of people who were socialized in the same society to consider a number of concepts and to ask, "Is this part of our culture?" Examples follow:

—freedom of speech that does not put others in direct danger
—equal justice under the law
—women's right to an abortion on demand
—the right to own handguns
—working as hard as possible during one's formal schooling
—accepting employment in one's own choice of jobs

One person records the amount of time the group takes to come to a decision. If *little* time is needed, this is an indication that the concept is culturally determined. If people take longer (e.g., on the issue of women's right to an abortion), this is an indication that the concept is looked upon differently by various individuals within a society. Some concepts will provoke almost no discussion, for instance, accepting employment of one's own choice. Yet there are cultural differences when other countries are considered. One of the demands for democratic reform expressed by Chinese students in the Beijing demonstrations (in May 1989) is the right to choose one's own employer rather than to accept government directives.

(6) Concepts and practices strongly influenced by culture remain despite mistakes and slipups. Most Americans will agree that "equal justice under the law for the rich and the poor" is a cultural value. Are there slipups and mistakes in the application of this value? There certainly are! Wealthy individuals can hire the most clever and experienced lawyers to represent them when they are accused of transgressions. They have a greater chance of lenient treatment compared with indigent individuals who have to depend on younger, overworked, and less experienced public defenders. But does the cultural value remain? I believe that the answer is "yes." Is "tolerance of people of different skin colors" an American cultural value? Some might argue that it is, but my feeling is that it does not pass the test of slipups and mistakes (Blauner, 1989). There are too many and too diverse deviations from the value (e.g., neighborhood segregation, continuing challenges in courts to school integration plans, use of racial epithets and ethnic slurs even in polite society) for tolerance of skin color differences to be considered cultural.

(7) When cultural factors are considered, there are likely to be feelings of bewilderment and even helplessness when attempts at planned cultural change are considered. If culture is transmitted generation to generation, this means that values, ideas, and concepts exist for long periods of time. They are not likely to change quickly despite the most massive interventions. Through Supreme Court decisions in the early and mid-1950s, the United States attempted to change long-standing practices, then an accepted part of the culture, that separated Blacks and Whites. The continuing existence of Black-White tensions in neighborhoods, schools, and the workplace attest to the difficulties of change. The educational system in different countries provides other examples. I believe that there are cultural differences in the respect given to members of the teaching profession. Respect is higher in Japan and other Asian countries than it is in the United States (see Kim, this volume). A reasonable part of attempts to improve public education in the United States would be to encourage far greater respect for the teaching profession so that the best, brightest, and most committed consider it for their life's work. But when attempts to change the level of respect for teachers are considered, the conclusion will be that "this is extremely difficult." Salaries will have to be increased considerably because Americans respect money. Parents will have to point with as much pride to their sons and daughters studying for a teaching career as they do to their offspring studying medicine or law. Guests at cocktail

parties will have to seek out members of the teaching profession instead of avoiding them with bored shrugs of the shoulders. Politicians will have to stop using the schools as convenient targets for criticism in their quest for votes. None of these changes will occur quickly.

An example of cross-cultural research: Moral development. In addition to analyzing features and dimensions, cross-cultural understanding can also be advanced by examining *tasks* that all cultures must undertake (Aberle, Cohen, Davis, Levy, & Sutton, 1950). Examples include survival into future generations, regulating people's sexual appetites, controlling intrasocietal violence, and preparing a culture's youth to eventually take responsible places in adult society. To expand upon the latter example, part of this preparation includes moral education. Individuals have to accept a system of right and wrong, and they must take the viewpoint of others into account and must not act solely on their own instincts and preferences. For example, at some point in their lives, people must give up individual temptations (e.g., striking people when angry) for the smooth functioning of society. Frequently, conceptual frameworks developed in one society can be used as starting points for investigations elsewhere when the framework is concerned with a clear universal concept. Moral development is clearly such a concept, and there is a well-developed framework for its study. Cross-cultural research often leads to modifications and improvements in conceptual frameworks that were largely developed in one society, and research on Kohlberg's (1971) model of moral development is a good example.

Kohlberg proposed that all people proceed through an identifiable set of stages in their moral development. There are certainly culture-specific aspects within each stage, such as the types of behavior that are punished when performed by children, but on a conceptual level the steps in the Kohlberg system summarize the stages of moral development through which individuals will pass.

The six stages (summarized by Snarey, 1985) are

(1) obedience and punishment—avoid breaking those rules that are punished;

(2) instrumental purpose—following rules when there is a personal interest involved; to do "right" brings benefits to oneself;

(3) interpersonal accord—living up to what is expected of a person; acting in accordance with one's role that is given by respected others;

(4) social accord and system maintenance—fulfilling the duties to which a person has agreed; laws are to be upheld except in extreme cases; "right" includes making contributions to others;

(5) social control, individual rights—knowledge of pluralism in societal standards; most values should be upheld in one's own group because of social contracts but some nonrelative rights such as life and liberty must be upheld in any society; and

(6) universal ethical principles—self-chosen ethical principles, such as universal principles of justice; the equality of human rights and respect for the dignity of human beings as individual persons; when laws violate these principles, one acts in accordance with one's own judgments regarding ethics and morals.

Cross-cultural research using the Kohlberg framework has been reviewed by Snarey (1985). He concluded that the stages represent useful summary positions in the development of moral standards, and that the original scoring system (that compares respondents' answers with the six stages) can be improved if some of the cross-cultural data are taken into account. For example, there was more expressed concern for nonhuman animal life in India than researchers have found in the United States. Arguments about morals based on this concern are not well handled by the scoring system. A number of researchers (Dien, 1982; Wu, 1989) have suggested that inadequate attention has been given to moral thinking based on concern for the collective. Put another way, the scoring system handles the moral thinking of individualists better than the thinking of collectivists. Tietjen and Walker (1984) discussed a collectivist's arguments that are difficult to score according to guidelines in the instrument's manual. One moral dilemma in the Kohlberg instrument involves a man who steals a drug to save his dying wife. Some village leaders in New Guinea pointed to the community's role: "If nobody helped him [save his dying wife] and so he [stole to save her], I would say *we* had caused that problem" (Tietjen & Walker, 1984, p. 21). Modifications in the Kohlberg framework to handle these concerns brought on by cross-cultural data should not prove to be a difficult task.

If I had written this chapter a year ago, I would have also pointed to the influence of European philosophers on the thinking behind stages five and six. Snarey suggests Immanuel Kant and John Rawls, and I add John Locke, Edmund Burke, and Thomas Jefferson. I would have argued that this limited the usefulness of these stages for cross-cultural research. Yet the ideals referred to in these stages can be readily found in the thoughts of today's young intellectuals in various parts of the world: China, Poland, Burma, the Soviet Union, Israel, East Germany, and so forth. Of course, there has been extensive media coverage of their activities, with the tearing down of the Berlin Wall providing one of the most memorable news stories since World War II. There may be more universality in concerns about individual freedoms than cross-cultural researchers would have admitted a year ago. The variables associated with the role of individual freedom in moral arguments will undoubtedly be the focus of future research. Candidates include urbanization, formal education, overseas experience or exposure to diversity through the mass media, and so forth. The eventual combination of individualistic and collectivist thinking (Kâgitçibaşi, 1988, and this volume) is also an important area for research.

One road to more concern with individual freedom involves a weakening of the collective. As people move to urban areas, they leave many others from their influential collective behind. Apartments or flats in the cities can provide attractive housing given the standards to which they were accustomed. But there is no room in these flats for parents, not to mention grandparents and other extended family members. Going away to college involves some break from the family, individual achievement marked by grades, and individual thought going into term papers, theses, and dissertations. Collectivist students in individualist countries find that they can disagree with their professors without censorship. These individualistic experiences become attractive, and traditional practices of the collective such as nepotism in hirings and promotions rather than decisions based on ability become frustrating. The individualistic moral ideals that are well integrated into the Kohlberg framework become an extension of one's formal education and a development from one's experiences independent of the collective.

THEMES FOUND THROUGHOUT VARIOUS CHAPTERS

A number of themes are addressed in different ways by different authors, and an understanding of them can assist in attempts to integrate the points made across the various chapters.

Ethnocentrism

If people are "ethnocentric," they use standards from their own cultural background to judge and to make conclusions about people from other cultures. Looking at the roots of the word is helpful: People view their own *ethnic* group as *central* and judge the rest of the world according to its standards. Breaking down ethnocentric thinking is the goal of Harry Triandis's chapter. He points out that if people understand the reasons other people behave as they do, then ethnocentric thinking diminishes. He presents a number of concepts, such as individualism and collectivism as already introduced, that are extremely helpful in understanding other cultures. An important goal of sophisticated cross-cultural thinking (the opposite of ethnocentrism) is to understand behavior from the point of view of people in the other culture. To use a more technical term, the goal is to make *isomorphic* attributions (see the chapter by Bhawuk). If people in a certain culture interpret the causes of behavior in a certain way (their attribution), then people from another culture are said to make isomorphic attributions if they can interpret behavior in the same way.

Juris Draguns presents an interesting example in his chapter on mental health. People who exhibit odd or strange behavior *from a therapist's viewpoint* are sometimes labeled "schizophrenic." If the people are from a different cultural background than the therapist, the chances of such an attribution increase because more behavior will seem odd and even bizarre to the therapist. If the therapist makes special efforts to understand the behavior from the other people's viewpoint, there is less chance that all differences will be seen as strange. Put another way, if the therapist learns to understand the reasons for the seemingly strange behaviors, he or she will be making more isomorphic attributions.

If people can become less ethnocentric, they can benefit from ideas that are imported from other cultures. Rather than dismissing ideas from elsewhere as unusable (because they seem odd and unworkable according to people's familiar standards), a lack of ethnocentrism can lead to the conclusion that "there may be some ideas worth considering." Examples abound throughout the book. Çigdem Kâgitçibaşi points out that interventions aimed at benefiting children are much more effective if they involve the entire family rather than just the children themselves. Such family-oriented interventions, some of which have taken place in her native Turkey, are well worth considering as educators design programs aimed at increasing the reading skills of schoolchildren (see the chapters by Kim and Cushner). Kwok Leung and Pei-Guan Wu argue that people in certain Asian countries have had long experience with different methods of resolving disputes. Their wisdom should be of benefit to groups in other countries (e.g., Neighborhood Justice Centers in the United States) whose members are interested in resolving disputes without the costly and time-consuming interventions of the formal court system.

Lisa Ilola points out that research carried out in certain countries and among certain religious groups has documented the medical benefits of altering people's life-styles. These contributions have been made in a country (Finland) and as a result of work in a religious organization (Seventh-Day Adventists) that do not spring immediately to mind when the conclusions of health-oriented research are mentioned. But a great deal of wisdom about such factors as diet, alcohol and tobacco use, and the presence of support groups will be lost if the relevant research is ignored. Given the certain increase in everyday intercultural interaction (discussed at the beginning of this chapter), Michael Paige argues that it will be very unwise if people fail to benefit from interactions with foreign students. Such interactions can be some of the most affecting and memorable experiences that take place during people's formal education. Such interactions can also benefit people who live near universities and who make the effort to involve foreign students in community affairs (e.g., as guest speakers in schools, at service club gatherings, and as invited contributors to local newspapers).

Culture-General and Culture-Specific Concepts

A major goal of cross-cultural psychology is to document concepts that are useful in comparing cultures as well as documenting concepts that are specific to a culture (see the chapter by Kim). Parental responsibility to socialize children so that they become accepted members of a culture is a general concept useful in comparing cultures. The exact manner in which parents socialize their children is culture specific. As part of the same research program reviewed by both Kim and Cushner in their chapters, Jordan and Tharp (1979) found that Hawaiian adults involve older siblings in the socialization of the youngest members of the family. The culture-general goal of socialization for responsible adulthood is common to Hawaii and to more individualistic cultures such as middle-class Canada, the United States, or Great Britain. The amount of responsibility given to older children for the care of younger siblings is culture specific.

Culture-general concepts are sometimes called "etic," and culture-specific concepts are sometimes called "emic." This terminology leads to the often-heard phrase *the emic-etic distinction* (e.g., Berry, 1969; Brislin, 1983). The terms are freely adapted from phon*etic* and phon*emic* analysis in linguistics. The goal of phonetics is to develop a systematization of sounds that are part of at least one of the world's languages. Different languages can then be compared using such a system. The goal of a phonemic analysis is to document the sounds that are meaningful within any one language, with no explicit attempt to compare that phonemic system with any other. Considering the initial "l" versus the initial "r" sounds helps make the distinction. Such a distinction is part of a phonetic analysis, because it is an important distinction within a large number of languages (e.g., the English "lock versus rock"). But it is not part of a Japanese phonemic analysis because the distinction does not led to differences in meaning within that language. This leads to difficulties when Japanese adults learn English. They have to put a good deal of time and effort into making an initial "l"/initial "r" distinction: right versus light. Their difficulty often leads to jokes by comedians who specialize in humor based on the way different people use the English language (dialectical humor).

Borrowing the idea of "difficulty with other people's phonemics" is useful in understanding one aspect of the emic-etic distinction. If people are unfamiliar with another culture's emics (e.g., older siblings with major responsibilities for their younger siblings, permitting their presence in what a teacher from another culture thought would be a parent-teacher's conference), they will seem puzzling and special efforts will have to be made to understand them. As discussed in the previous section of this chapter, the less ethnocentric people are, the more willing and able they should be to learn another culture's emics.

It is important to keep in mind that the emic-etic distinction will be frequently encountered when trying to understand culture and cultural differences. Another example may be useful. Individualism and collectivism have been introduced (above), and the concepts will be discussed further by Triandis in the next chapter. Some concepts are common (etic) to both individualist and collectivist cultures. One common goal is that adults be able to branch out from their families so that they can seek benefits offered by the larger society. This is an important goal for everyone, but especially for people who want to maintain close interpersonal ties with others from their same cultural background (e.g., immigrants from a small to a very large country) and who also want to secure good jobs that are available in the larger society. This type of desired culture contact is analyzed by John Berry in his chapter on acculturation. The behaviors necessary for branching out into the larger society are different for individualists and collectivists.

To transcend the distance between self and others, people in individualistic societies have to develop a certain set of social skills. These include public speaking, meeting others quickly and putting them at ease (see previous discussion), making a good first impression, and being well mannered, cordial, and verbally fluent during initial encounters with others. These skills are not as necessary for collectivists. When it comes time for a person to meet unknown others in the larger society, members of the collective act as go-betweens and make introductions, describe the person's accomplishments and abilities, and so forth. In short, individualists have to rely on themselves and to develop skills that allow them to branch out in society. Collectivists have a supportive group that assists in this same goal. Individualism and collectivism can both lead to happiness if certain conditions are met. Individualism works well if people are physically attractive, intelligent, and well educated, have resources to offer to employers, and have well-developed social skills. Collectivism works well if people are members of a group that has many members who possess high status in the larger society, if they are willing to be loyal and to maintain lifelong commitments, and if they can act in expected ways (subservient to superiors, bossy with subordinates) depending upon their own place in the status hierarchy. In his chapter on work attitudes and managerial behavior, Harry Hui elaborates on this point in his discussion of relations between superiors and subordinates in collective societies.

Cultural Awareness During Interventions

Another theme present in a number of chapters is that an awareness of culture and cultural differences is extremely important in interventions into people's lives. *Intervention* is used in a broad sense to refer to various change attempts whether they be the improvement of preventative health behaviors (Ilola), the delivery of nutritional supplements (Kâgitçibaşi), attempts to start new businesses (Hui), attempts to resolve conflicts (Leung and Wu), efforts to introduce change in the schools (Cushner), or programs to ameliorate poverty (Sinha).

One cultural difference centers on the importance of the family in one's life, especially the role the family might play in maintaining changes introduced elsewhere. In his chapter, John Berry points out that some societal institutions can introduce changes that conflict with traditional norms. Immigrants to Canada and the United States might come from cultures where parental authority is respected and where children rarely argue with their parents. This deference to authority can clash with a teacher's expectation that children will speak up in a class, will defend their own opinions, and will even disagree with the teacher at times. When children do indeed take a position different from that of their teacher, similar behavior does not go over well when parents are challenged at the dinner table. In her chapter, Çigdem Kâgitçibaşi recognizes the importance of the family and realizes the possibility of conflict and confusion if ideas introduced in one place (e.g., the school or after-hour programs attached to the school) are not supported by the family. She found that efforts to encourage autonomy in children were successful if parents understood the intervention and felt involved in it. At times, interventions into the lives of one child, if supported by the family, transferred to the child's brothers and sisters even when they were not part of the formal program. Future research will undoubtedly focus on structural characteristics within families that make interventions like those reviewed by Kâitçibaşi, Sinha, Cushner, and Kim possible. Unfortunately, there are families with such severe problems (e.g., spouse and child abuse, alcohol and drug addiction) that their involvement in change attempts will lead to barriers rather than to improvements.

Lisa Ilola reviews important research on government interventions into preventative health care. Important cultural differences that are involved include respect for government and the appropriateness of governmental interventions into people's lives. The government of Finland has placed more restrictions on tobacco advertisement and liquor sales than most countries. People's health has improved, but it is important to realize that governmental interventions such as these are much more acceptable in some countries than in others. In the United States, both citizen and industry groups representing consumer interests would either generate support against the passage of necessary legislation, or they would take such legislation to the courts if it happened to be signed into law. Ilola is quite accurate when she draws a parallel with seat belt usage and mandatory helmets for motorcycle riders. Rather than accepting these reasonable protections of their health and safety, many Americans resent intrusions into their freedom of choice. The latter is a prime American cultural value, and intervention efforts that ignore it are certain to face difficulties. Other practices in other countries seem odd to Americans who value personal freedom and choice. In Australia, citizens can be fined if they do *not* vote in elections. In Germany, students accepted for entrance into universities have far less choice than Americans concerning the exact university that they attend. In Japan, there are much more stringent requirements for immigrants to attain citizenship and to secure the right to vote. The fact that these practices seem odd is explainable by reference to the discussion of culture presented previously. Cultural practices unthinkingly become accepted as "the way things are done around here," and there is no need to explain the reasons for the practices. Deviations from the familiar practices, as found in other countries, seem odd, strange, and unreasonable.

Some culturally supported interventions are quite subtle. The people who introduce or maintain an intervention should be highly respected members of a culture or else the intervention may not receive enough attention to become widely accepted. Both Ilola and I have followed the intervention program in Hawaii that encourages citizens to obtain free blood pressure readings from firefighters. In Hawaii, firefighters are members of a highly respected profession. In fact, public opinion polls have documented that they are members of Hawaii's most respected profession, higher than (prepare yourself, gentle reader) college professors and medical doctors (T. Brislin, 1989). Just a few reasons are that they are very visible in Hawaii's communities. They have an active program in elementary schools centered on fire safety presentations. They entertain school field trips to fire stations. They are very active in community service activities, especially the coaching of both young girls and boys in such sports as soccer, baseball, basketball, and volleyball. They are residents of virtually all communities in Hawaii, even those that attract the most wealthy. Because many firefighters are members of families in Hawaii that go back five and six generations, members of those extended families bought into various neighborhoods before they became the state's most expensive areas. Consequently, firefighters have day-to-day contact with all segments of Hawaii's society. Given this familiarity and respect, they volunteered to oversee a blood pressure check program. Anyone in Hawaii can receive a free blood pressure check by simply presenting him- or herself at one of Hawaii's fire stations. Because there is a station in every neighborhood, it is easy to receive such a check, and the concept "blood pressure" is a part of people's everyday thinking about their health.

Differences and Deficits

When people from another culture seem to have a problem, judgments about reasons for the "problem" often come from outsiders. People within the culture often complain that the outsiders' label is little more than a product of their ethnocentrism. The label "problem" often leads to the conclusion that people in the other culture have some sort of deficit that decreases their chances of success in the school or workplace. Or the deficit is seen as interfering with such culture-general goals as good health.

An alternative approach, widely recommended by cross-cultural psychologists (e.g., Kim, this volume), is to look behind behaviors that lead to the attribution of "deficit." Often, the behaviors will be seen as reflecting a difference rather than a deficit. If the guidance in Triandis's chapter is accepted, the difference will not always be seen as automatically undesirable. Further, the willingness to put ethnocentrism aside allows people to put time and effort into identifying opportunities that build upon cultural differences. In his chapter, Cushner reviews research into cultural differences as found in schools. Children from collective cultures are much more likely to look after each other's needs and to downplay their own goals in favor of goals set by the group. An important caveat is that the children must be from the same collective or the teacher must have generated a sense of collectiveness (see the chapter by Hui). Rather than labeling such collective behavior as some sort of deficit in the quest for autonomy (a labeling difficulty also recognized by Kâgitçibaşi), a sensitivity to group goals can be viewed as an important difference. Further, it may be possible to build upon the difference in the pursuit of other goals. A major development in education over the last 20 years has been the use of cooperative learning groups. As Cushner points out, the formation of such groups has been an important component of programs to increase the reading level of Hawaiian schoolchildren. During their out-of-school free time, Hawaiian children play in groups more than their individualistic counterparts (e.g., people originally from the continental United States). Teachers, then, can benefit from the natural tendency of some collective children to form work groups, and the teacher can guide the groups to goals (e.g., reading) that benefit them as individuals.

At times, there will not be a cultural difference that can be of assistance in interventions. Durganand Sinha reviews efforts to ameliorate the effects of poverty in India, effects that include malnutrition, apathy, low achievement, poor linguistic skills, and a sense of helplessness. A casual reader might conclude that Sinha is focusing on a set of cultural deficits for these problems. A more careful reading, however, reveals great sensitivity to the children of poverty, a sensitivity reflected in a distinguished career of research, education, and intervention efforts. Never does Sinha blame children or their families. He is quite explicit in his call for social and economic reform. But such reforms take years if not decades and are dependent upon a multitude of factors such as politics and industrialization—so what should be done in the interim? Sinha suggests a number of possible interventions aimed at nutrition, linguistic skills, self-confidence, and teacher expectations of students. These are important targets that call for intervention, but the focus does not have to be concerned with underlying cultural deficits for which the people are to blame. Sinha's suggestions for interventions into people's thought processes are especially interesting. If people can learn to think in self-confident terms, and can view themselves as able to overcome obstacles, then behavior will be directed toward attainable goals and will not become lost to apathy.

The distinction between obvious problems and underlying deficits, I believe, is central to an appreciation of Walter Lonner's chapter on testing and assessment. The use of tests in cross-cultural settings can identify problems, such as a deficiency in mathematics achievement among members of a recent immigrant group. But there is no necessity of going beyond the identification of a problem to a list of explanations that focus on deficiencies. Rather, tests can be seen as diagnostic aids that can identify needed changes in a school's curriculum, preparation of teachers, involvement of parents, and so forth. The real difficulties surrounding the use of tests arise when they are taken too seriously. Instead of a properly limited use, such as identifying children from one cultural background that can use assistance in adjusting to a school system designed for children from another culture, tests are taken as unchangeable measures of underlying abilities such as intelligence. Lonner presents a number of guidelines for the culturally sensitive use of tests, such as the recommendation to consider broader views of intelligence. Traditional intelligence tests are associated with the tasks schoolchildren are expected to perform. Broader views, reviewed by Lonner, look at a larger number of skills valued by society, such as people's interpersonal sensitivity. Lonner also makes the important suggestion that many research projects will benefit if existing tests are *not* used. Rather, the researchers may discover many more important results if they develop new tests or alternative assessment procedures that are sensitive to the cultural background of those being tested or assessed.

The Chapters and the Future

Given the previous arguments that there will surely be more extensive intercultural contact in years to come, it is useful to preview the chapters to determine what insights into the future they can offer.

In addition to his call for a recognition of and reduction in ethnocentrism, Harry Triandis presents advice for culturally sensitive behavior when interacting with people from very different cultural backgrounds. For instance, individualists should recognize the importance of developing long-term relationships with collectivists. The type of short-term interaction typical of an individualist's "network" of useful "contacts" is seen as offensive by collectivists. When working in organizations in an individualistic country, collectivists must learn to be less modest and to communicate their potential contributions to projects in a forthright manner.

Walter Lonner points out that standardized tests are frequently encountered in highly industrialized nations. Their frequency of use has *almost* led them to achieve "cultural" status according to the criterion that test use no longer needs a constant defense (see the discussion above). The fact that test use has not quite achieved the status of a cultural practice is due to people like Lonner who remind us of its limits. Still, many parents look forward to the day that they receive scores on the standardized tests that their children take in schools. Further, employers regularly give tests to applicants for jobs, and it is a rare psychological or psychiatric clinic that does not use one personality assessment device or another. An understanding of the use of tests is important for people from "non-test-frequent" cultures who decide (or are forced) to settle in industrialized nations. Further, such an understanding is important for people from "test-wise" cultures who should become more sensitive to needs of others who are less familiar with the role of tests.

An understanding of culture and cultural differences can lead to self-insights concerning what people in certain cultures are more and less able to do well. Individualism has its benefits: People can rise according to their abilities and can harness their talents in the pursuit of their goals. Individualistic cultures, however, are less skillful in addressing the needs of the less fortunate given the strong cultural value that "people should be able to take care of themselves." In the United States, for instance, problems of the inner city, homelessness, and poverty are national disgraces for a country that claims to have one of the world's highest living standards. Durganand Sinha makes a number of suggestions for interventions into the lives of children affected by poverty. The fact that the majority of programs he reviews were carried out in India should *not* be a reason for automatic dismissal of his insights. A major question for the future, however, is whether or not the trend toward industrialization found in all parts of the world will interfere with a collective concern for others. If it does, then the difference between "haves" and "have-nots" will become even more distinct than it is today.

Formal and informal schooling. A major meeting place for people from different cultures has long been the school classroom (Hakuta,

1986). Children from minority cultures have had to make stress-inducing adjustments when adapting to the expectations of teachers and classmates from the dominant culture in a society. As culture contact increases, Kenneth Cushner argues that teachers must become aware of the discontinuities between a child's home culture and the culture of the school. For some children, there are few adjustments: the sorts of behaviors expected at home are quite consonant with the expectations of the schools. Similar books, games, tasks, and adult-child interactions are found in the home and the school. For other children, the expectations are so different that success in school can actually interfere with the child's family relations.

Realizing this potential set of problems, Çigdem Kâgitçibaşi recommends interventions that take the child's support group into account. She reviews a number of studies that report far more benefits for children when the parents become involved. She also identifies an important combination of individualistic and collective orientations that can ameliorate stress during times of social change. Kâgitçibaşi points out that urbanization and industrialization may lead to an individualistic orientation when the material aspects of life are considered but that people can remain quite collective in the emotional realm. The emotional support provided by a collective can act as a buffer against the stresses and strains faced by people in the process of acculturation.

If people are aware of cultural variables and take pains *not* to impose their own preconceived views, they can become sensitive to unique insights into human behavior, such as this combination of individualistic and collective orientations. Uichol Kim argues that a sensitivity to indigenous psychologies, or behavior as seen from people's own viewpoints, is necessary for cross-cultural understanding. Several of his examples deal with school-related behaviors. His detailed review of why Japanese children demonstrate a high degree of proficiency in mathematics is especially instructive. In addition to the greater amounts of time that they spend in school, Japanese children are exposed to very ambitious expectations that are set by their mothers. Further, the mothers engage in a great deal of self-sacrifice and spend a great deal of time monitoring their children's progress. To please their parents, children work toward the high expectations set in the family. Characteristics such as being *hard working, diligent,* and *persistent* become the norm. These terms sound strangely old-fashioned in some countries, even though they must have at one time been prominent parts of such complex concepts as "the value of hard work" (see Hui's treatment of the work ethic). The key point is that behavior of Japanese schoolchildren, as well as that of productive Japanese workers in business and industry, cannot be understood without a detailed knowledge of their socialization. Much of this knowledge has been gathered through methods known as "the indigenous approach." Much of the knowledge is summarized in Japanese concepts familiar to all children, concepts that become accepted parts of the children's view of the world.

How are people to obtain firsthand knowledge of the indigenous views as experienced in other cultures? An excellent approach, suggested by Michael Paige, is to involve foreign students in the educational curriculum at the elementary, high school, and college levels. Foreign students can offer real-life, affecting examples of the sometimes abstract concepts students read in books. I have asked foreign students to give guest presentations in my classes. The presentations can be even more effective if students prepare questions beforehand. For instance, knowing that a Japanese national will be coming to class, students might review Kim's summary of childhood socialization in Japan and ask questions about it. Knowing that they will receive firsthand examples of the concepts presented in their reading, students are likely to become more interested in the materials.

The world of work. Since the devastation of World War II, a number of countries such as Germany and Japan have experienced stunning success in the rebuilding of their businesses and industries. Today, there is no longer one country that can impose its views in the global world of business. Rather, many countries are "players" in the international marketplace. Given the amount of cross-country investments, and the number of multicountry joint ventures, it is becoming more and more probable that the workplace will rival the school as a meeting place for people from different cultural backgrounds. C. Harry Hui reviews differences in the way people look at the workplace and at their jobs. One interesting concept he reviews is that some aspects of work-related theories developed from research in North America and Europe are even more important when considering Asia. Many theories of leadership look at people's "task orientation" and "social orientation" (Landy, 1989). Leadership training programs in Europe and North America aim at encouraging the development of both: a task orientation to increase productivity, together with a social orientation so that subordinates feel needed and valued. Hui argues that leaders in Asia have to be even more sensitive to this combination. In India, for instance, a nurturant task leader is the desired model. Such a person is much like a stern but loving father who sets high goals but who also communicates an appreciation that the workers are part of the "organizational family." As part of joint ventures, managers from one country frequently accept assignments in another. If they cannot modify their managerial behavior as appropriate in the other country, they increase the chances of business failure.

In any extensive intercultural contact, in the business world or elsewhere, there will inevitably be conflicts. Kwok Leung and Pei-Guan Wu review methods that allow people to deal with the conflict while maintaining long-term relationships. This emphasis on relationship maintenance is important because people use quite different methods to deal with conflicts depending upon whether or not they will interact in the future. For example, the formal courts are likely to be avoided when long-term relationships are important. Courts often implicitly label one side a "winner" and the other a "loser" when rendering decisions. This fact can cause more ill will than the initial reason for bringing the case to court. A better approach is to think in terms of "win-win" solutions in which both parties set aside their dispute and agree that they have benefited from the conflict-reduction negotiations. The metaphor of the "orange" is useful to keep in mind. Two people may both want the same orange. During attempts to mediate the conflict, it may be discovered that the people have different needs. If one wants the rind for a cookie recipe, and the other wants the fruit to make juice, then both people can emerge as winners.

Stress and health. Extensive intercultural contact can lead to stresses that affect people's physical and mental health. John Berry focuses on processes of psychological acculturation, or the changes that individuals undergo as they react to other cultures with which they come into contact. A major contribution of this chapter is the placement of psychological variables in a broader context that includes historical, economic, political, and demographic issues. Historical factors include the amount of experience a country has had integrating new immigrant and refugee groups. Economic factors include the types of jobs newcomers to a culture can expect to find. Politics include the policies that governments have established to encourage or to discourage multiculturalism. Demographic factors include the number of people in urban versus rural areas and (especially) the move from small communities to big cities.

All over the world, there is a move from rural to urban areas that puzzles people familiar with urban problems. Are people really going to improve their lives by moving away from rural areas? After all, cities in many parts of the world have housing shortages, pollution problems, high levels of unemployment, inadequate transportation facilities, and other ills of urbanization. A key to understanding the move is not to romanticize rural village life. How much food do people consume there? How much abuse do tenants have to endure from landowners? What is the level of drudgery people can expect in their work? Are traditional power hierarchies stifling to ambitious but modestly born individuals? Are their more opportunities for children, especially access to schools? People moving to cities do not always expect to turn their lives around completely. If they feel that they can improve their lot in life by a small but noticeable amount, they may make the move.

Such moves, however, can contribute to the environmental problems that Janak Pandey reviews. He analyzes the effects of crowding, natural catastrophes (greater effects with larger populations), energy conservation, and dangers to the long-term equilibrium between humans and the environment established over a number of centuries. Cultural factors cannot be forgotten. Even though these environmental problems are found all over the world, within any one country, cultural factors will play a role. Similar to a theme found in other chapters, lessons learned in one country may help planning efforts in another. The perceived problems due to overcrowding, for example, may be lessened if people develop coping skills for dealing with large numbers of others. Pandey reviews an interesting example drawn from research carried out in Mexican slums. People have a need for both interaction with others (some of the time) and for privacy (at other times). In the slums, an informal norm became established that socializing should take place in open areas but that privacy was guaranteed when people went into their own homes.

Acculturative stress and environmental problems can affect people's health. Dividing up a large amount of research according to an admittedly imperfect distinction, Lisa Ilola focuses on studies of physical health and Juris Draguns reviews the literature on mental health. Certain health issues reviewed by Ilola and Draguns are so much a part of people's culture that any person who has extensive intercultural interaction will encounter the issues at one time or another. Ilola points out that people from many cultures somatize their problems, that is, mental problems are communicated through physical complaints. If they have a psychological stressor in their lives (e.g., an immigrant who is forced to accept a lower-status job in the new country), they will experience the stressor in physical terms. Typical complaints include headaches, difficulties sleeping, stomach pains, and diarrhea. This phenomenon of somatization is so widespread that it should be understood by teachers, medical doctors, employers, governmental officials, and others who work with people undergoing the acculturation process.

Juris Draguns points out that people who try to assist others undergoing acculturative stress can build upon universal aspects of the "formal helper" role. No matter what people's exact specialty (e.g., native healer or psychiatrist), interventions that take a number of factors into account will probably have a greater chance of success. These include a shared framework between helper and client concerning why people have difficulties as well as a culturally acceptable interpretation of the specific problem, the trappings of status and expertise, client expectations of implicit or explicit suggestions for improvement, and a view of the helping effort as "special" and as more intense and emotionally charged than behaviors in the client's everyday routine. If such culture-general factors are ignored, clients may be unable to label the helper as credible enough to be taken seriously.

Another formal helper role is carried out by the experienced person who helps others to benefit from intercultural interactions. When the helper leads formal efforts to prepare people to live and to work in other cultures, that helper is drawing from the area known as "cross-cultural orientation programs." D. P. S. Bhawuk reviews various types of programs, accomplishable goals, and evaluation efforts. He presents a helpful model, based on three concepts, that organizes a large number of program descriptions and research studies. His three concepts are (a) the level of involvement of the helper or trainer, (b) the involvement level of the trainees, and (c) the cultural generality or cultural specificity of the program's focus at any one time.

An important point is that virtually any research finding from the various chapters in this book can be communicated according to one or more of the training methods that Bhawuk reviews. Research findings do not have to be limited to people who possess the same familiarity with and access to scholarly journals. One of the "helper" roles in cross-cultural psychology is to communicate research findings to a broad audience. This has been the purpose of the entire book, and it is a specific goal of cross-cultural training programs.

For many years, hundreds of cross-cultural psychologists have been doing research across cultures, often using abstract concepts and usually testing hypotheses within the context of the "science" of psychology. These efforts have resulted in significant gains in modifying and improving psychological theory (Triandis et al., 1980-1981). The intent of this book was to take a number of these abstractions and complex details and to explain them to college students, practitioners, and others who may not have as much interest in the details as they do in the applications or benefits of such study. The prominent psychologist George Miller (1969) advocated "giving psychology away." By this he meant giving to the people and to the common welfare those findings derived in the laboratories and in the ivory tower of academia. In this sense, this book is "giving away" cross-cultural psychology by summarizing some basic findings and showing how they can be used in applied settings.

REFERENCES

Aberle, D., Cohen, A., Davis, A., Levy, M., & Sutton, F. (1950). The functional prerequisites of a society. *Ethics, 60,* 100-111.

Berry, J. (1969). On cross-cultural comparability. *International Journal of Psychology, 4,* 119-128.

Blauner, B. (1989). *Black lives, White lives: Three decades of race relations in America.* Berkeley: University of California Press.

Brislin, R. (1983). Cross-cultural research in psychology. *Annual Review of Psychology, 34,* 363-400.

Brislin, R., Cushner, K., Cherrie, C., & Yong, M. (1986). *Intercultural interactions: A practical guide.* Newbury Park, CA: Sage.

Brislin, T. (1989, February 23). "Want lots of respect? Become a firefighter." *Honolulu Advertiser,* p. A-1.

Dien, D. S. (1982). A Chinese perspective of Kohlberg's theory of moral development. *Developmental Review, 2,* 331-341.

Gallo, R. (1989). My life stalking AIDS. *Discover, 10*(10), 30-36.

Hakuta, K. (1986). *Mirror of language: The debate on bilingualism.* New York: Basic Books.

Herskovits, M. (1948). *Man and his works.* New York: Knopf.

Jordan, C., & Tharp, R. (1979). Culture and education. In A. Marsella, R. Tharp, & T. Ciborowski (Eds.), *Perspectives on cross-cultural psychology* (pp. 265-285). New York: Academic Press.

Kâgitçibaşi, Ç. (1988). Diversity of socialization and social change. In P. Dasen, J. Berry, & N. Sartorius (Eds.), *Health and cross-cultural psychology* (pp. 25-47). Newbury Park, CA: Sage.

Kohlberg, L. (1971). From is to ought: How to commit the naturalistic fallacy and get away with it in the study of moral development. In L. Mischel (Ed.), *Cognitive development and epistemology* (pp. 151-284). New York: Academic Press.

Landy, F. (1989). *Psychology of work behavior* (4th ed.). Belmont, CA: Brooks/Cole.

Miller, G. (1969). Psychology as a means of promoting human welfare. *American Psychologist, 24,* 1063-1075.

Snarey, J. (1985). Cross-cultural universality of social-moral development: A critical review of Kohlbergian research. *Psychological Bulletin, 97,* 202-232.

Tietjen, A., & Walker, L. (1984). *Moral reasoning and leadership among men in a Papua New Guinea village.* Unpublished manuscript, University of British Columbia, Vancouver, British Columbia, Canada.

Triandis, H. (1972). *The analysis of subjective culture.* New York: John Wiley.

Triandis, H., Lambert, W., Berry, J., Lonner, W., Heron, A., Brislin, R., & Draguns, J. (1980-1981). *Handbook of cross-cultural psychology* (6 vols.). Boston: Allyn & Bacon.

Wu, D. (1989). *Explicit and implicit moral teaching of preschool children in Chinese societies.* Paper presented at the International Conference, "Moral Values and Moral Reasoning in Chinese Societies," Taipei, Taiwan.

2

THEORETICAL CONCEPTS THAT ARE APPLICABLE TO THE ANALYSIS OF ETHNOCENTRISM

HARRY C. TRIANDIS

When people come into contact with individuals from other cultures, they observe differences in dress, customs, behavior patterns, language, and more. Most people react to such differences "ethnocentrically," that is, they use their own ethnic group (an in-group) as the standard and judge others favorably if they are like in-group members and unfavorably if they are not. This human tendency is so widespread that we must do something about it if we are to get along with people from other cultures. In this chapter, we will discuss theoretical ideas that help us reduce ethnocentrism.

Getting along means being effective in our interactions with others. If we must negotiate with people from another culture, either as tourists or as business people, if we are to act as advisers, counselors, clinicians, or social workers, we must understand what makes them tick. We need to be able to put ourselves in their shoes and look at the world the way they see it. But to do that we must know *how* they are different.

Of course, people are different in a myriad of ways. In this chapter, several major factors that underlie differences across cultures will be discussed. In addition, we will examine a way of thinking about culture that should help us look at these differences with more tolerance, and less ethnocentrism. To do this well, it is useful to consider first what ethnocentrism does to us.

SOME CONSEQUENCES OF ETHNOCENTRISM

Our own culture provides us with a cognitive framework for thinking about the world. It is a ready-made *Weltanschauung,* as the Germans say, that is, a worldview, a philosophy that helps us evaluate what is going on around us. The philosophy guides judgments on what is an acceptable religion, who is a good marriage partner, what is a good job, and many other aspects of everyday life. For those of us who have been exposed to only one culture, there is no other *Weltanschauung.* We are stuck with it. Even if we have had contact with people from other cultures, if these cultures were similar to ours, we may not have experienced a really different culture. So it is natural to use our own culture as the standard and judge other cultures by the extent they "meet the standard." People all over the world do the same.

Studies of ethnocentrism carried out by psychologist Donald Campbell and his associates (Brewer & Campbell, 1976; Campbell & LeVine, 1968) have shown that all people have tendencies to

(1) define what goes on in their own cultures as "natural" and "correct" and what goes on in other cultures as "unnatural" and "incorrect";

(2) perceive in-group customs as universally valid; that is, what is good for us is good for everybody;

(3) think that in-group norms, roles, and values are obviously correct;

(4) believe that it is natural to help and cooperate with members of one's in-group;

(5) act in ways that favor the in-group;

(6) feel proud of the in-group; and

(7) feel hostility toward out-groups.

In fact, many cultures define the word *human* with reference to their own cultural group, so that people of other cultures are not perceived as fully human. The ancient Greeks made the distinction between those who spoke Greek and those whose language was incomprehensible and sounded like "barbar" (a repetitive chatter), and so they called them *barbarians*. The ancient Chinese referred to themselves as "the central kingdom." In many languages, the word for *human* is the same as the name of the tribe.

For example, in a study (Brewer & Campbell, 1976) of the way people in 30 African tribes perceived each other, there was a tendency for similar tribes to be perceived as "good" and likable, and dissimilar tribes to be seen as "bad" and disliked. A major determinant of attraction was whether the behavior of the tribe was "predictable" and the tribe could be trusted. When the other group behaves in ways we find surprising, or unpredictable, we are likely to dislike it. Because many "strange customs" are perceived when we interact with people from very different cultures, we are quite likely to dislike members of that culture. But it is common sense that, when we dislike them, we would not want to be in their shoes to see the world the way they see it. So, in essence, our dislikes are barriers to understanding and effective communication and interaction.

THEORETICAL FRAMEWORK

A helpful way to think about cultural differences is to consider a particular theoretical framework. In this framework, the ecology (resources available, the way one can make a living, the climate, the geographical environment) influences the culture, which in turn influences the people's social behavior.

Culture is the human-made part of the environment. It has two major aspects: objective (e.g., roads) and subjective (e.g., beliefs). In fact, subjective culture has many elements, such as beliefs, attitudes, norms, roles, and values. Social behavior is a consequence of many factors. There is quite a lot of research that supports the idea that the ecology is a determinant of culture, and culture is an important determinant of social behavior. It is also important to think of ecology-culture-behavior links for a very practical reason. When we see a behavioral pattern that we find exotic, different, or even offensive, it is desirable to try to think of the rewards that may be behind it. What is it in the ecology that is likely to have caused it? If we can find the links between ecology and behavior, we will be more understanding and tolerant of the behavior we do not like. We will also be able to change our moral judgments, and that is very important when we are dealing with other cultures.

It is very difficult to think about behaviors that are different from the ones we are used to and not judge them as wrong. Difference invites comparison and evaluation. Yet, if we see that the ecology of the other culture is different from our ecology (e.g., a difference in population density), we can find the difference understandable and even say to ourselves: "If I lived in that ecology I probably would do exactly the same." This can lead to tolerance for other cultures.

There are different kinds of ecologies. Geographical features, such as climate, land fertility, and available resources, shape these ecologies. One aspect that is most important is the way people make a living. There have been changes over time, from hunting, food gathering, and fishing as one type of life-style, to agriculture, to industrial activities, to societies characterized by services and information processing. In the advanced economies of Europe, North America, and Japan, "information processing" is now an important activity. That does not mean that there are no cases of hunting, fishing, agriculture, or industrial production. Rather, what happens is that, as societies evolve, they engage in *additional* activities, that is, they became more complex. Complexity can be indexed by many objective factors, such as the presence of writing, multiple levels of social and political organization, complex transportation systems, large cities, and so on. The Romans and ancient Chinese were already very complex. But modern technology creates additional complexity. We now have complexity in almost every domain—for example, compare a farmer's market, which does not differ from a market in many agricultural cultures, with the Sears catalogue, which contains thousands of items. Or think of the 250,000 or so occupations that are listed in the *Dictionary of Occupational Titles*. Cultures are shaped by such structural factors (e.g., how many different groups there are) but also by historical factors, such as wars and the acquisition of values from other cultures.

There are certain cultural attributes that covary with changes in ecology. These attributes constitute cultural syndromes.

CULTURAL SYNDROMES

A cultural syndrome is a pattern of values, attitudes, beliefs, norms, and behaviors that can be used to contrast a group of cultures to another group of cultures. In this section, we will describe several of these syndromes such as cultural complexity, individualism versus collectivism, and tight versus loose cultures. There is not enough research on the relationships among these syndromes. It may be the case that complexity is related to individualism, and to looseness, but we cannot be sure at this time.

Cultural Complexity

The more complex the culture, the more people must pay attention to *time*. If you have a few things to do, you can do them in any sequence, and at any time. If you have many things to do, and especially if what you do must be coordinated with what other people do, then you must pay attention to time. There is evidence (Levine & Bartlett, 1984) that the more industrial/technological the culture (e.g., Japan, Sweden, the United States), the more people pay attention to time. Time is used more tolerantly in South America, though in places like Brazil, especially in the large cities, there is considerable attention paid to time. One example will illustrate the cultural differences on the time dimension. When asked, "If you have an appointment with a friend, how long will you wait before deciding that the friend will not come?" people in industrial/technological cultures give answers in *minutes,* in cultures intermediate in complexity, in *hours,* and in technologically less complex cultures, in *days.* Conceptions of time are also different. In the West, we think of time as linear—past-present-future. In many cultures time is circular, that is, it occurs in recurring cycles. Also, we consider it correct to do one thing at a time, such as carry on a conversation with one person, then with another. In some cultures, such as Saudi Arabia, it is perfectly correct to carry on several conversations simultaneously.

Another variable characteristic of complexity is "specificity" as opposed to "diffusion." The more complex the culture, the more "roles" (what people are supposed to do, because of their position in a social group) become specific. Therefore, a janitor can be the head of a church, because the role system of the workplace is completely specific to the workplace and unrelated to the role system of the church. In less complex cultures, there is diffusion of roles. Another way to put it is that in simple cultures most roles are like the spouse-spouse role (diffuse) in our culture, rather than like the customer-salesperson role (specific) in the United States. In specific roles, we care only that the person is doing what is expected and do not care about the other person's religion, politics, or aesthetic tastes. But we do care about the religion, politics, and aesthetic preferences of spouses. What we find in less complex cultures is that people care very much about the religion, politics, and aesthetics of others, even in roles of little significance, such as salesperson. Most Western cultures are specific, but many middle-Eastern cultures are diffuse. Thus in the Arab world and Iran, a person's religion is a major determinant of social behavior.

Related to the ideas of specificity-diffusion is the dimension of "field independence-field dependence." *Field independence* means that people can extract a stimulus pattern from its context. For instance, field independent hunters can perceive a distant brown animal even when it is surrounded by a similarly colored environment. *Field dependence* means that people are strongly influenced by the context when making perceptual judgments, so they have greater difficulty extracting a stimulus pattern from its context. In hunting and gathering ecologies, people are field independent, whereas in agricultural ecologies they are field dependent (Berry, 1979). Child-rearing patterns in hunting/gathering cultures emphasize the child's autonomy and self-reliance, whereas in agricultural cultures they emphasize the child's obedience and conformity.

Practical implications of cultural complexity. Misunderstandings can easily occur when people use time differently (e.g., feel that the other's lateness implies disrespect or object to the other person carrying out several conversations simultaneously). Also, differences on the specificity dimension produce misunderstandings. For example, it is difficult to criticize a person in a diffuse culture, because the distinction between "your ideas" and "you as a person" does not exist. In diffuse cultures, people often act nicely but think that the other person is a jerk. In the West, such behavior is considered hypocritical. But it must be understood in the context of the culture. The person is acting correctly, even if we do not like what we see. Conversely, Americans are seen as abrasive and arrogant by people from diffuse cultures.

Individualism Versus Collectivism

A number of dimensions of cultural variation have been proposed (Triandis, 1984). Of the score of such dimensions, the most promising, in the sense that it is likely to account for a great deal of social behavior, is individualism and collectivism. People in every culture have both collectivist and individualist tendencies, but the relative emphasis is toward individualism in the West and toward collectivism in the East and South (e.g., Africa). The construct has been popular in most of the social sciences for about a century. For example, the terms *Gemeinschaft* and *Gesellschaft* in sociology, or relational versus individualistic value orientation in anthropology, have been used for some time. However, there has not been systematic work at the individual level until relatively recently. Hofstede (1980) identified this dimension in a study of several thousand IBM employees in 66 countries. Since then, others, such as Bond (see the Chinese Cultural Connection, 1987) working with the values of college students in 21 countries, have found it. We (Triandis, Bontempo, et al., 1986) replicated some of Hofstede's results with 15 samples from different parts of the world. In addition, as we probed with a more refined focus, we found four factors that are related to individualism-collectivism in the same way as certain mental factors, such as verbal and quantitative abilities, are related to a general intelligence measure, such as IQ. They were *family integrity* (typical item: Children should live at home with their parents until they get married) and *interdependence* (e.g., I like to live close to my good friends), representing aspects of collectivism; and *self-reliance with hedonism* (e.g., If the group is slowing me down, it is better to leave it and work alone; the most important thing in my life is to make myself happy) and *separation from in-groups* (e.g., agreement with items indicating that what happens to extended family members, such as cousins, is of little concern to the person), representing aspects of individualism.

Over the years, we have worked with many different items, and both within culture and across cultures, to refine the measurements (e.g., Triandis, Leung, Villareal, Clack, 1985; Triandis, Bontempo, Villareal, Asai, Lucca, 1988). As a result, we have arrived at a number of "defining attributes" of the construct. First, collectivists pay much more attention to some identifiable in-group and behave differently toward members of that group than they do toward out-groups. The in-group can best be defined by *the common fate* of members. In many cases, it is the unit of survival, or the food community. If there is no food, all members of the in-group starve together. In different cultures, the in-group can be different. For example, in most cultures, the family is the main in-group, but in some other cultures, other in-groups such as the tribe or the country (in the case of the patriot) can be just as important. The work group is an important in-group is some countries (e.g., Japan) that have achieved stunning economic success since World War II. Collectivism also influences different aspects of social life. For example, in theocracies, or Mao's China, the state had much to say about art, science, politics, religion, truth, and social life. In the West, the state has less to say (but note the debate over abortion, which suggests that some people want the state to have more to say).

In collectivist cultures, in-group goals have primacy over individual goals. In individualist cultures, personal goals have primacy over in-group goals. For example, in a collectivist culture, people may live near their parents, to help them during old age, even when they do not like the town or cannot find good jobs; in an individualistic culture, they may move to a place with a nice climate, even if that is very far from their parents. People from collectivist cultures often interpret the behavior of people from individualist cultures as "selfish."

In collectivist cultures, behavior is regulated largely by in-group norms; in individualist cultures, it is regulated largely by individual likes and dislikes and cost-benefit analyses. Thus for "traditional" behaviors (e.g., having children), norms should be more important in collectivist and attitudes more important in individualist cultures. Consistent with the notion that lower-class groups, in most societies, are more collectivist than upper-class groups, Davidson, Jaccard, Triandis, Morales, and Diaz-Guerrero (1976) found that, among lower-class Mexican women, norms determined whether they wanted to have one more child, whereas among upper-class Mexican and also among U.S. women, their own attitudes predicted whether they were going to have one more child. For "nontraditional" behaviors (e.g., whether or not to attend school), this difference between the two kinds of cultures will not necessarily occur. Formal schooling of children, it must be remembered, is a relatively recent development in many cultures.

Collectivists emphasize hierarchy. Usually the father is the boss and men are superordinate to women. This is not nearly as much the case among individualists. Furthermore, harmony and saving face are important attributes among collectivists, who favor homogeneous in-groups and insist that no disagreements should be known to out-groups. In individualistic cultures, confrontations within the in-group are acceptable and are supposed to be desirable because they "clear the air."

In-group fate, in-group achievement, and interdependence within the in-group are emphasized by collectivists. Personal fate, personal achievement, and independence from the in-group are emphasized by individualists. But *self-reliance* has a different meaning in these two kinds of cultures. In collectivist cultures, it means "I am not a burden on the in-group"; in individualist cultures, it means "I can do my own thing." In collectivist cultures, there is great concern about what happens in the in-group and to in-group members. This is also true in individualist cultures, but the in-group in that case is narrow, consisting only of first-degree relatives and a few "best friends," and there is more emotional detachment from the larger in-group.

The *self* is defined as an appendage of the in-group in collectivist cultures and as a separate and distinct entity in individualist cultures. Thus when asked to write 20 statements that begin with "I am . . .," collectivists used in-group-related responses (e.g., I am a son; I am Roman Catholic) whereas individualists used personal attributes (I am kind; I am hardworking). The percentage of responses that have relevance to some "social entity" can vary from zero to 100% from person to person. The mean for collectivists samples was as low as 29% (Hawaiians of East Asian background) and as high as 52% (students from the People's Republic of China), whereas the means of individualistic samples was as low as 15% (Hawaiians of Portuguese descent; Greek students from Athens) and as high as 19% (Illinois students). In collectivist cultures, people are members of one or a few stable in-groups and are influenced very much by these in-groups. Behavior in individualistic cultures is rarely greatly influenced by any one in-group, because there are so many in-groups and they often make contradictory demands. The *individual* decides which group to pay attention to, "picks and chooses" in-groups, and forms new in-groups when that is convenient.

Vertical relationships, such as parent-child, that are in conflict with horizontal relationships, such as spouse-spouse, take priority in collectivist cultures and vice versa in individualistic cultures. Certain values such as achievement, pleasure, and competition are emphasized by individualists more than by collectivists, whereas family integrity, security, obedience, and conformity are valued more by collectivists.

Antecedents of individualism. The major determinant of the shift from collectivism to individualism is affluence. Hofstede (1980) found correlations of the order of .80 between the rank of a country on his individualism score (based on responses to values) and gross national product (GNP) per capita. As people become affluent, they become financially independent and also independent from their in-groups. Of course, we know that industrialization and technological developments are related to affluence. Thus "cultural complexity," as discussed above, is linked to individualism.

In individualistic cultures, child-rearing practices emphasize the child's autonomy, self-reliance, and independence. In collectivist cultures (remember that these tend to be agricultural), we find emphasis on obedience, duty, and sacrifice for the in-group (Berry, 1979) because it is more functional to conform to authorities while public works (e.g., building of irrigation canals and storage bins) are being performed. In complex industrial cultures (the United States, Italy, Poland, Japan), the upper classes emphasize self-reliance and independence and are individualistic, whereas the lower social classes emphasize obedience in their child rearing and tend to be conforming (Kohn, 1969, 1987). There are also regional differences (e.g., more collectivism in the South than in the North of Italy).

Social mobility and geographical mobility also contribute toward individualism. The upper classes are more individualistic than the lower, and those who have migrated to other countries are more individualistic than those who have never moved. Movement from rural to urban centers is also correlated with individualism. One reason is that social mobility includes leaving behind many members of the in-group, as people move to places with better jobs or improve their social status.

Consequences of individualism. Collectivists behave very differently toward their in-groups and their out-groups. Of course, individualists also behave differently, but the difference is not so large. For example, collectivists are extremely hospitable, cooperative, and helpful toward their in-groups but can be rude, exploitative, and even hostile toward their out-groups. If you are invited to the home of a traditional collectivist, the best food will be served. An individualist may serve the best when "a few people are around" and serve more ordinary food when many guests are present. But an individualist will be polite to strangers, when waiting in line, or in the subway, whereas a collectivist can treat strangers like objects who can be pushed around and who can be cheated in business transactions.

Collectivists behave toward their friends and coworkers with more intimacy, and toward their out-groups with less intimacy, than do individualists. Collectivists prefer to resolve conflicts amicably, to a greater extent than do individualists (Leung, 1987). Because individualists must enter and leave many in-groups, they develop superb skills for superficial interactions but do not have very good skills for intimate behaviors (see Triandis, 1989; Triandis, Bontempo, et al., 1986; Triandis, Brislin, Hui, 1988).

Communication in collectivist cultures tends to be associative, that is, people rely on the associations of the listener. This also happens in individualistic cultures, but less so. For example, when acronyms are used by Washington bureaucrats (e.g., BIA, OMB, ONR), they rely on the listener's knowledge of what the acronym means. Or when physicians talk with other physicians and nurses, they use terminology that relies on the other's knowledge. The difference is that, when the bureaucrats or physicians talk to people who are not likely to understand those terms, they switch to definitions of their terms. In collectivist cultures, people habitually talk associatively, and only if they were educated in the West are they likely to define their terms. In short, collectivists pay much more attention to the context of the communication, that is, everything that is associated with the message, such as verbal associations, gestures, body posture, and the face muscles of the other person. Some specialists think that Switzerland is the country where communication is least dependent on context and Japan is the country where communication is most dependent on context. The United States is supposed to be closer to Switzerland than to Japan.

There is also a tendency for collectivist cultures to rely on an ideological framework when they communicate. That is, they use a framework from a religious system or Marxism or some other ideological framework as part of their communication. They assume that the listener shares that framework. Of course, if the listener does not share that framework, the communication will be very obscure. However, if the listener shares the framework, such use of the framework improves communication.

Measurement. Multimethod strategies have been used to measure individualism, including observations, responses to attitude (e.g., Hui, 1988) and value items, reactions to scenarios (e.g., "Suppose you won a lottery. Would you share 0% . . . 100% with your parents?"), studies of the self-concept, judgments about the distance of self from in-groups and out-groups, studies of the perceived homogeneity of in-groups and out-groups, and psychophysical judgments concerning social distance and its relationships to the appropriateness of social behaviors having particular attributes. Limitations of space preclude discussion of these studies, but interested readers can find them in Triandis (1989).

Practical implications of differences between collectivism and individualism. Triandis, Brislin, and Hui (1988) discuss the kinds of training that are appropriate for individualists interacting with collectivists and for collectivists interacting with individualists. They make a total of 46 recommendations for such training. A summary of these recommendations is provided below. Interested readers should consult the original publication.

Individualists interacting with collectivists should learn to pay attention to group memberships. This is important because the collectivist's behavior will follow the norms of the in-group more than the individualist's. One should be particularly concerned about the attitudes of the authorities in the collectivist's in-groups, because the collectivist's behavior will reflect their attitudes, beliefs, and norms to a much greater extent than the individualist is used to seeing.

One should expect to see changes in the behavior of the collectivist when this person changes groups. The individualist is well advised to learn much about the way the collectivist's in-groups function, the norms they have, the duties they assign to their members. Furthermore, they should avoid using themselves as the standards of how much time people are likely to spend in their in-groups. Collectivists are more committed to their groups and will spend more time with their in-group members.

When a conflict occurs between vertical and horizontal members of the collectivist's in-group, the probability is that the vertical members will win the contest. In a collectivist culture, it is OK to break a prior engagement with a friend of the same sex and age if you have received an invitation from a high-status person. Your friend will understand. This is less likely in an individualistic culture.

To get a collectivist to do something, one of the more effective methods is to convince his or her superiors that such behavior is desirable. One of the more convincing arguments for behavior change is to argue that a desired behavior will advance the in-group's goals. The collectivist is likely to be uncomfortable in competitive situations, will want to emphasize harmony within the in-group, and will be concerned that in-group members "save face." Public criticism is a "no-no" to a greater extent in collectivist than in individualist cultures.

The collectivist will expect a long-term relationship. Business is not conducted as soon as people meet for the first time but after trust has been established over a relatively long time period. One of the disappointments of collectivists is that individualists do not become intimate with them. Individualists do not become as committed to their social relationships as do collectivists. Money-making opportunities have been lost because individualists wanted to "get down to business" whereas collectivists wanted to develop good interpersonal relationships.

Collectivists from East Asia are unjustifiably modest. They often do not take credit for their accomplishments, and they do not boast. This can cause problems, because individualists are more boastful and do not mind mentioning their accomplishments.

When resources are to be distributed, the collectivist tends to use equity (to each according to his or her contribution) with out-group members and equality (to each equally) or need (to each according to need) with in-group members. The individualist tends to use equity with everybody. This can cause misunderstandings, because there will be many situations in which the collectivist will want to distribute the resources equally while the individualist will insist on the use of the equity principle. This can be particularly difficult if the collectivist sees the individualist as a member of the in-group, and the individualist does not. It becomes a clear signal of "rejection" for the collectivist that the individualist insists on using equity as the principle for the division of resources.

Collectivists are comfortable in unequal status relationships. They feel it is right to show respect to people in authority and to be bossy when dealing with subordinates. Many individualists feel uncomfortable with unequal relationships. They are likely to suggest: "Call me by my first name," or, what is even worse, to call the collectivist by a first name, much before the collectivist feels ready for it. In fact, there are studies about the success of colonial powers that indicated that the British and Germans in the nineteenth century were more successful with some collectivist populations than the Americans because they were more comfortable when dealing with their hierarchies.

Collectivists pay attention to "who the other is," that is, to family, tribal group, or social class memberships. Individualists pay attention to "what the other does, or has done." This leads to fundamental differences in social behavior, such as what information they seek and want to have, and how they evaluate this information. First meetings with collectivists tend to be very formal. Only when you become an in-group member will the behavior of the collectivist become really friendly and intimate. But a high-status outsider (e.g., a visiting American professor in Asia) can become an in-group member in a collectivist culture rather quickly. Status means a lot, and it facilitates in-group membership.

Gift giving is especially important in collectivist cultures. Interactions tend to be in kind and not monetary. In fact, collectivists who see you as an in-group member will be offended if you offer them money for a service they have performed. It is a clear signal to them that you do not consider them in-group members. The proper repayment is for you to do a service for them. Let the other guide your intimacy. Be willing to disclose information, when the other discloses information, in order to establish intimate relationships. For example, people in collectivist cultures are very likely to ask you how much money you make. If you turn them down in horror, you have lost your chance to establish a good relationship. You do not have to tell them if you do not want. You can instead tell them about the high cost of living and refer to your income indirectly, for example, "I pay a quarter of my income on housing."

A wise piece of advice for any intercultural interaction is this: Do not jump to conclusions when the other makes what appear to be strange suggestions. "Play along" until you understand the other's culture. For example, in many collectivist cultures, people do not deal with "customers" the way they do in individualistic cultures. They expect that some money will be given to them personally by the customer to facilitate the transaction. For example, a customs officer may expect some money to clear a shipment. Individualists are likely to see this as a bribe, but it is quite normal in collectivist cultures. In collectivist cultures, people have many obligations to an extended in-group, and resources tend to be limited. So what appears as a bribe must be seen in context.

In collectivist cultures, people expect to accompany their in-group members and to do many tasks together with them. Privacy is valued in individualistic cultures and togetherness in collectivist cultures. This can cause problems for the individualist who wants to "be alone." Similarly, the collectivist might be offended because you do not stick with the group. A related problem is that, when you make a date with a collectivist, the chances are that a whole group will show up, accompanying your date! That is probably not what you had in mind. Also, the number of people that accompany a collectivist constitutes an index of status. An individualist may go to a meeting alone but risks that the collectivist may see him as a "nobody." Important people are always accompanied. Conversely, the collectivist may show up with a lot of others, not to put pressure on the individualist but simply to indicate his or her importance.

Now we turn to the opposite case: when collectivists have to be trained to interact effectively with individualists. Collectivists have to be taught to pay less attention to in-groups and not to expect behavior to be a function of norms nearly as much in individualistic cultures as in their own cultures. This means that they should be taught to pay attention to attitudes, beliefs, and individual cognitions. This also means that demographic attributes, such as gender, age, and the like, carry less weight in individualistic cultures than they do in collectivist cultures. The collectivist must learn to pay less attention to them.

The collectivists should expect the individualists to be proud of past and current behavior, such as their accomplishments. Individualists value being distinguished, important, competent. These are important aspects of their self-concept. At the same time, they are not too emotionally attached to their in-groups. Collectivists must learn to pay less attention to the in-groups of individualists and more to what the individualists have accomplished. If conflict occurs between vertical and horizontal relationships, the individualist is likely to favor the horizontal. This will appear strange to collectivists, who cannot conceive that one might, for instance, not do what one's father wants and instead do what one's closest friend wants.

The individualist may be very competitive, particularly in situations where comparisons with others are salient. This is not an indication of nastiness, or hostility, but a response to a lifetime of conditioning to act competitively.

A collectivist who tries to persuade an individualist will do well to make the argument personal, complimenting the other. Stress on the idea of harmony within the in-group, cooperation, and avoidance of confrontation will not carry much weight with individualists.

Expect individualists to be strongly attached to the nuclear but not the extended family and to feel few obligations toward extended family members. Expect interactions with individualists to be very friendly but superficial and short term. You can do business with an individualist very soon after you meet. Time is money for the individualist, and too many preliminaries are seen as a waste of time. Expect your relationship with the individualist to last only as long as it "pays off" in some way. That is, the rewards from the relationship must exceed the costs of the relationship at all times.

Pay much attention to contracts. Signatures mean a lot. Students from collectivist cultures have been known to visit several apartments and to sign what appeared to them as an indication of interest, so they could later decide which of the apartments to rent! A signature in many collectivist cultures is worth nothing. What really matters is the person's word. One can tentatively look around, and there is no commitment until one says "I will rent this." Not so in individualist countries.

Individualists will be more comfortable with equal status relationships than with hierarchical relationships. This requires some fine distinctions. When a professor says "call me by my first name," he does not really mean "we are now buddies."

When resources are to be distributed, individualists will use the principle of equity, using equality and need much less than you will. The use of equity does not mean that you are an out-group member. It is just the way things are done in individualist cultures. Do not expect to receive respect just because of your position, for example, because you are male or upper class. You have to earn respect by what you do. It is all right to talk about your accomplishments. Do not be too modest. If you do not "blow your own horn," no one else will. But one does this indirectly and subtly. Avoid behaviors that are extremely superordinate (bossy) or subordinate (servile). Individualists do not expect or like them. Expect individualists to suspect authority and to prefer horizontal relationships. Also, expect them to be less tolerant of illicit behavior (e.g., not paying taxes) than you are. In many collectivist cultures, a personal relationship is so powerful that a person can confess an illicit behavior and the other "will understand." That is particularly the case when dealing with impersonal entities, like "the government." Do not assume that this is so in individualistic cultures. Do not expect to be accompanied by a lot of people when you go somewhere. Individualists do many things alone. This is actually desirable. Many intellectual activities, such as solving a mathematical problem, can best be done alone; so it is good for you to learn to do things alone. Individualists will prefer to work in situations where their individual effort is noted and recognized. They will not like group work, where the group gets rewarded but individuals remain anonymous.

Some values seem to be especially emphasized by individualists. Specifically, they feel that humans should be masters over nature rather than be subjugated to nature or live in harmony with nature. Subjugation and harmony are more likely to be emphasized by collectivists. The future is the dominant time orientation of individualists, whereas collectivists many times emphasize the past (e.g., their ancestors, the major historical figures of their cultures).

Tight Versus Loose Cultures

In tight cultures, people are expected to behave according to norms, and there is very little tolerance for deviation from norms. Loose cultures give people a good deal of freedom to deviate from a norm. A discussion of the tight-loose dimension was first presented by Pelto (1968). Hofstede's (1980) "uncertainty avoidance" dimension has much in common with "tightness."

In tight cultures, norms are clear and deviation from them is punished. Thus people are more likely to engage in covert (fantasy) behaviors, such as humor, art, and music, than in loose cultures. In tight cultures, people feel anxious and insecure (Hofstede, 1980) because their behavior can easily be found to be improper. Japan has been described as the prototypical tight culture, though it is not tight in every aspect of social life (e.g., when the Japanese are drunk, they are excused of more transgressions than those who are drunk in the United States), and Thailand as the prototypical loose culture. A friend of mine in Japan, who can definitely afford a car, told me that he does not have one because he does not want to risk having an accident. He would rather pay for taxis, because he would not have the responsibility for an accident should one occur.

Antecedents. A probable antecedent of tightness is cultural homogeneity. Hofstede found Japan and Greece to be very high on that dimension (which he called " uncertainty avoidance"), and certainly these are cultures that are culturally homogeneous. Looseness is probably linked to cultural heterogeneity as well as cultural marginality. For example, Thailand is marginal because it is located between the colossal cultures of India and China. Hofstede found looseness (low uncertainty avoidance) in Hong Kong and Singapore, two cultures where East (China) meets West (Britain).

Consequences. Tight cultures expect people to behave exactly as the norms of the culture specify. In ancient Japan, a samurai would kill a commoner who did not behave exactly as expected. Loose cultures are quite tolerant of behavior that does not conform to expectations. In tight cultures, people want clarity of instructions or a clear instruction to "do what makes sense to you." In loose cultures, people are used to "playing by ear" in their relationships.

Practical implications of the tight-loose dimension. People from tight cultures enjoy predictability, certainty, and security. They like to know what the other is going to do and get quite upset if the other does what they do not expect. They are likely to reject people from loose cultures on the grounds that they are undisciplined, childlike, and unpredictable. People from loose cultures are likely to see those from tight cultures as rigid, inflexible, obstinate, and uncompromising. Above all, they are likely to see them as authoritarian, if they detect emphases on both hierarchy and tightness.

It would help people from loose cultures to see those from tight cultures as products of their ecology. They come from homogeneous cultures, where norms are clear and can be imposed by authority figures with little difficulty. Conversely, it would help people from tight cultures to see those from loose cultures as products of their ecologies. They come from heterogeneous cultures or ones that are marginal between two great cultural traditions. If one is to do well in such cultures, one must be loose. Looseness is also related to creativity. If one is allowed to deviate from norms, one might hit on a new design for living that works better than previous designs. Students who take risks in a "loose" college course, whose professor is tolerant of diversity, may write truly original and creative term papers.

MORE SPECIFIC DIMENSIONS OF CULTURAL DIFFERENCES

Cultures differ in many specific ways, but limitations of space preclude their discussion. However, three of these specific dimensions will be mentioned: masculinity-femininity; emotional control versus expressiveness; and contact versus no contact. Differences can be found (a) in values and (b) in behavior. In what follows, we will discuss one of the value differences (preference for values favored by men more than by women) and two of the behavior differences (acceptability of showing one's emotions and preference for body contact or no contact).

Masculinity Versus Femininity

There is little doubt that men and women are different even in cultures that underemphasize this difference. Eagly (1987) discussed the social behavior of the two genders and indicated many similarities as well as differences. An interesting similarity is between masculine and individualistic behaviors and feminine and collectivist behaviors. Hofstede (1980) identified masculinity-femininity differences in terms of work-related goals. In Hofstede's study, Japan was masculine and Sweden feminine.

Masculine cultures emphasize getting the job done, achievement, progress, advancement. Feminine cultures emphasize the quality of life, good interpersonal relationships, nurturing, concern for others. Being strong and effective matters to people in the masculine cultures; being kind and caring matters to people in the feminine cultures.

Practical implications of the masculinity-femininity dimension. People from masculine cultures will see people from feminine cultures with some disdain because they are not "tough" enough; people from feminine cultures will see people from masculine cultures with disdain because they are not caring enough. Consistent with this cultural dimension, Sweden tops the world in the proportion of its GNP given to the poor countries of the world, whereas Japan is one of the lowest givers. Being aware of the position of one's culture on this dimension (see Hofstede, 1980, for the data) can help one anticipate differences and moderate one's behavior to make it more acceptable to people from the other culture.

Emotional Control Versus Emotional Expressiveness

Cultures differ in the way they deal with emotions. In cultures where people are expected to express mostly pleasant emotions, even in situations that are unpleasant, such as in Japan, people do very well in controlling their emotions. In cultures where people are not expected to control their emotions, such as in Southern Europe, people often feel good about expressing themselves openly. There is some evidence that people in Africa and places near Africa express their emotions freely, and the further people are from where humans first developed, the more control they have over their emotions. The hypothesis that has been offered to explain this phenomenon is that humans first developed in Africa and expressed their emotions freely. But as they migrated to remote corners of the globe, they had to learn to control the unfriendly environment as well as themselves. Self-control became a value, and emotional control was a manifestation of that value.

Practical implications of the emotional control dimension. Those who control their emotions are seen by those who do not control them as "cold fish," "well-oiled machines," efficient, but unlovable. Those who control their emotions look to those that do not as charming, but too emotional and likely to be unreliable when their emotions overtake them. From a mental health point of view, those who do not control their emotions have the edge. *Catharsis* is the technical term for talking about your concerns, expressing your emotions without reservation, and becoming "clean" of your repressed hostilities. But those who do not show their emotions must be admired for their ability to control themselves and not expose their negative feelings. It is important to know that this dimension exists and to see it nonevaluatively.

Contact Versus No-Contact Cultures

Hall (1959) has described contact cultures as those that use much touching, small distances between the bodies, and loud voices. Cultures around the Mediterranean and their derivative cultures (e.g., Latin America) are contact cultures, whereas cultures in East Asia are no-contact cultures. North Europe tends toward the no-contact and North America tends toward the contact side of the neutral point on this dimension. A demonstration of these differences was provided by Sussman and Rosenfeld (1982). They asked students from Venezuela and Japan to carry on a conversation and measured the distances between their bodies. The distances that males used when placing their chairs in position for the conversation were larger than the distances used by females. The distances used by Japanese talking in Japanese were larger than the distances used by Venezuelans conversing in Spanish. Americans were in between. However, when the foreign students conversed in English, the cultural differences disappeared.

Practical implications of the contact difference. When people from a contact culture interact with people from a no-contact culture, there is a high probability that they will be misunderstood. For example, touching and holding hands with a member of the same gender can be misunderstood as homosexual advances. Conversely, the behavior of the no-contact persons can lead to the perception that they are cool, aloof, and stuck up. The high-contact person often sees the no-contact person as excessively formal and remote.

CULTURAL TRANSITIONS

Over time, certain segments of each society converge. The convergence seems especially clear when people do the same job. For example, airline personnel show many similarities, no matter what their ethnic background. Individualism is spreading around the world as cultures become affluent. Students in Japan are now more on the individualistic than the collectivist side of the neutral point (see Triandis, Bontempo, et al., 1988).

Many other cultural transitions can be identified. For example, when moving from a traditional to a modern culture, when migrating to another culture, or when experiencing social mobility (either upward or downward), in-groups are left behind, and hence there is a shift toward individualism. When this happens, certain cultural elements show accommodation, that is, the person who emigrates acquires the cultural attributes of the host culture. Other elements show overshooting, that is, people from a collectivist culture may acquire some individualistic traits that are even more individualistic than the host culture. And on some elements there is ethnic affirmation, that is, the person who emigrates emphasizes his or her own culture more in the new setting than in the original setting (Triandis, Kashima, Shimada, & Villareal, 1986). We hypothesized that, on the most visible cultural elements (e.g., dress), there is overshooting; on the moderately visible (food habits), there is accommodation; and on the not visible (e.g., religious beliefs, values concerning loyalty to parents), there is ethnic affirmation. The evidence was consistent with this hypothesis, but more research is needed to test it. From a practical point of view, this means that we must not expect the various elements of culture to move together during a cultural transition. Some will move in one direction and other elements will move in another direction.

CONCLUSION

There are myriad cultural differences that can bother us when we interact with people from other cultures. However, we can learn to tolerate them, and even enjoy them, if we understand them better. When we realize that if we had been raised in the ecology of the other cultural group we would probably be acting just as they act, we can begin fitting into their shoes. An essential aspect of empathy with the other culture is to learn to assign causes to events the same way *they* assign causes to events (more technically, to make isomorphic attributions). This we can do much better if we understand the specific ways we are different from them. The analysis of the cultural syndromes described in this chapter suggested what specific information we must consider when interacting with people from other cultures. We did, of course, cover only some of the relevant information. One could spend a lifetime discussing cultural differences, and even then one would not have covered all of them. We have discussed what I think are the most important differences that must be understood if we are to relate effectively to members of other cultures.

REFERENCES

Berry, J. W. (1979). A cultural ecology of social behavior. In L. Berkowitz (Ed.), *Advances in experimental social psychology* (Vol. 12, pp. 177-207). New York: Academic Press.

Brewer, M. B., & Campbell, D. T. (1976). *Ethnocentrism and intergroup attitudes.* New York: John Wiley.

Campbell, D. T., & LeVine, R. A. (1968). Ethnocentrism and intergroup relations. In R. Abelson et al. (Eds.), *Theories of cognitive consistency: A sourcebook.* Chicago: Rand McNally.

Chinese Cultural Connection. (1987). Chinese values and the search for a culture free dimension of culture. *Journal of Cross-Cultural Psychology, 18,* 143-164.

Davidson, A. R., Jaccard, J. J., Triandis, H. C., Morales, M. L., & Diaz-Guerrero, R. (1976). Cross-cultural model testing: Toward a solution of the etic/emic dilemma. *International Journal of Psychology, 11,* 1-13.

Eagly, A. H. (1987). *Sex differences in social behavior: A social-role interpretation.* Hillsdale, NJ: Lawrence Erlbaum.

Hall, E. T. (1959). *The silent language.* Greenwich, CT: Fawcett.

Hofstede, G. (1980). *Culture's consequences.* Beverly Hills, CA: Sage.

Hui, C. H. (1988). Measurement of individualism-collectivism. *Journal of Research on Personality, 22,* 17-36.

Kohn, M. L. (1969). *Class and conformity.* Homewood, IL: Dorsey.

Kohn, M. L. (1987, August). *Cross-national research as an analytic strategy.* Presidential address to the American Sociological Association.

Leung, K. (1987). Some determinants of reactions to procedural models of conflict resolution: A cross-national study. *Journal of Personality and Social Psychology, 53,* 898-908.

Levine, R. V., & Bartlett, K. (1984). Pace of life, punctuality, and coronary heart disease in six countries. *Journal of Cross-Cultural Psychology, 15,* 233-255.

Pelto, P. J. (1968, April). The difference between "tight" and "loose" societies. *Transaction,* pp. 37-40.

Sussman, N. M., & Rosenfeld, H. M. (1982). Influence of culture, language, and sex on conversational distance. *Journal of Personality and Social Psychology, 42,* 66-74.

Triandis, H. C. (1984). A theoretical framework for the more efficient construction of culture assimilators. *International Journal of Intercultural Relations, 8,* 301-330.

Triandis, H. C. (1989). Cross-cultural studies of individualism and collectivism. In *Nebraska Symposium on Motivation.* Lincoln: University of Nebraska Press.

Triandis, H. C., Bontempo, R., et al. (1986). The measurement of the etic aspects of individualism and collectivism across cultures. *Australian Journal of Psychology, 38,* 257-267.

Triandis, H. C., Bontempo, R., Villareal, M. J., Asai, M., & Lucca, N. (1988). Individualism and collectivism: Cross-cultural perspectives on self-ingroup relationships. *Journal of Personality and Social Psychology, 54,* 323-338.

Triandis H. C., Brislin, R., & Hui, C. H. (1988). Cross cultural training across the individualism-collectivism divide. *International Journal of Intercultural Relations, 12,* 269-289.

Triandis, H. C., Kashima, Y., Shimada, E., & Villareal, M. (1986). Acculturation indices as a means of confirming cultural differences. *International Journal of Psychology, 21,* 43-70.

Triandis, H. C., Leung, K., Villareal, M., & Clack, F. L. (1985). Allocentric vs idiocentric tendencies: Convergent and discriminant validation. *Journal of Research in Personality, 19,* 395-415.

3

AN OVERVIEW OF CROSS-CULTURAL TESTING AND ASSESSMENT

WALTER J. LONNER

The field of psychological testing and assessment is well established in "mainstream" psychology, which has a strong Euro-American origin and orientation. Much of the history and literature on testing and assessment has to do with the extent to which techniques developed in the "mainstream" can be, or even *should* be, extended to other cultures or ethnic groups.

Nearly all research projects in cross-cultural psychology have a measurement component. Most of the these projects involve tests and related assessment devices that either (a) use the original versions of tests or (b) use devices borrowed or copied from techniques widely available in countries where psychology is highly developed. Such borrowing or adapting can cause significant problems; this tendency has been lamented by psychologists from countries where psychology is not yet fully developed. For instance, Sinha (1983) suggested that many concepts that are important in India (and by implication elsewhere) may be missed if tests and procedures are not developed from *within* a country by its *own* psychologists. Sinha noted that all too often in the past most tests used in India were "imperfect translations or adaptations of Western tests." Although Indian (Kulkarni & Puhan, 1988) and Chinese (Zhang, 1988) psychologists, among others, are currently showing great sophistication in analyzing assessment in the context of their countries, Sinha's bleak assessment is likely a recurrent theme around the developing or so-called Third World. Applied cross-cultural psychologists need to take appraisals such as Sinha's seriously if they are to avoid duplicating the mistakes of others. Thus this chapter carries an admonition: Although hundreds of tests and assessment procedures work reasonably well in the Western world, it must be proven and not assumed that they will work equally well in cultures where they were not developed.

The Nature and Purpose of Psychological Assessment

The main purpose of *any* assessment procedure is to sort persons into a specific category (or categories) so that they can be described and understood better. Once such description and understanding is established, the assessor is in a position to help make decisions about people such as academic or job placement or for possible clinical intervention. Another reason to assess is simply to be more aware of how people around the world cut up and contemplate their psychological worlds. At the aggregate or group level, the assessment of personality, attitudes, and values might be done to describe entire communities or cultures. For instance, aspects of subjective culture (Triandis, 1972) and values (Schwartz & Bilsky, 1987; Zavalloni, 1980) might be assessed in an effort to help explain how people in various cultures differ on such matters as social justice, morality, the perception of time or social distance, and other important dimensions of human interaction. In the Schwartz and Bilsky study, the Rokeach Value Survey, which measures instrumental and terminal values, was used in Israel and Germany as a means to help develop a universal psychological structure of human values.

A definition. According to Anastasi (1988, p. 23), a psychological test is an "objective and standardized measure of a sample of behavior." The key terms in this definition are *objective* (meaning unbiased and not influenced by someone's subjective valuing system), *standardized* (meaning that the same uniform procedure of test administration must apply to all), and *sample of behavior* (meaning a representative and unbiased sample of some specific aspect of the person's *behavior,* which perhaps encompasses both observable behavior such as actions as well as unobservable behavior such as attitudes and values but that are nevertheless part of cognitive activity). If all the elements in this definition prevail, then we have an objective and formal testing procedure.

Ethical, legal, and scientific responsibility strongly suggests that formal courses in testing or assessment are *mandatory* before the tests are used. Moreover, it is recommended that the reader consult recent texts to obtain a comprehensive view of the total field of psychological testing and all the constraints that may currently exist in using them. Four current texts in the area that give broad and generally similar coverage are Anastasi (1988), Cohen, Montague, Nathanson, and Swerdlik (1988), Cronbach (1984), and Kaplan and Saccuzzo (1989). Although all of these texts cover the essentials of psychological testing, they are oriented to the English-speaking world, and only Anastasi and Cronbach give any attention to cultural factors. A quick search in nearly any country where psychology is highly developed will probably result in finding a current text or resource on testing that is oriented to local needs and priorities. For instance, Kulkarni and Puhan (1988) give an excellent account of present and future trends of psychological assessment in India; their extensive reference list is rich with Indian resources that may well be helpful elsewhere.

Major Issues in Testing and Assessment Across Cultures

The proper development (or adaptation) of measurement devices for cross-cultural use has been a major methodological concern among cross-cultural psychologists for years. A number of books, book chapters, and journal articles have served as useful guides and resources, and they warrant consultation when planning and implementing cross-cultural research. These resources include Brislin, Lonner, and Thorndike (1973); Cronbach and Drenth (1972); Irvine and Berry (1983, 1988); Irvine and Carroll (1980); Lonner and Berry (1986); Lonner and Ibrahim (1989); and Samuda (1975). Most of these resources deal with several recurring issues in cross-cultural testing and assessment. In the following pages, each of these issues will be explained briefly before turning to specific domains of testing.

Issue 1: How familiar is testing and assessment to people in the culture or ethnic group in question? In much of the Western world, there seems to be a test for just about everything, including grade placement, clinical diagnosis, marital happiness, and so forth. Probably no other country can match the United States in test usage, where most current tests were developed (but many other highly "psychologized" countries, such as Australia, Canada, Great Britain, the Netherlands, New Zealand, and West Germany are not far behind). Because of such familiarity, the typical Western citizen is unfazed when he or she is required to take a test. In most of the world, however, testing is not part of the cultural landscape. Thus when tests are modified for use elsewhere, especially in the developing world, one must take these differentials of familiarity into account. Similar differentials may exist between different socioeconomic classes *within* cultures.

Trimble, Lonner, and Boucher (1983) noted that three assumptions are made by the researcher or experimenter when an individual is subjected to psychological measurement. The first assumption is that individuals can order or rank stimuli along linearly constructed stimuli, and that this is a universally valid procedure. Example: A person is asked to rate another person, place, or thing on a seven-point scale (where 1 = good, 4 = neutral, and 7 = bad). The second assumption is that all subjects can readily produce judgments about social and psychological stimuli that are representative of the way that judgments are made on an everyday basis by members of a particular group. Example: An individual is asked to compare and contrast three or more objects, selecting the two that are most similar. Such processes may be foreign to many cultures. The third assumption is that all individuals are capable of self-assessment and self-reflection, and that people do not mind disclosing these excursions into the self. Example: Subjects are asked to report on their satisfaction with their spouses. Although these processes and assumptions are nearly automatically valid in the highly psychologized cultures, it may be unwarranted to assume their presence in all cultures. Moreover, these assumptions are used more for the convenience of the researcher so that his or her data can be tidy than they are for the convenience of the subject. The subject, after all, may consider the tests to be so trivial or meaningless as to provide random or nonsense responses, if he or she responds at all.

Issue 2: Are all psychological constructs and concepts universally valid? Popular psychological concepts that are taken for granted in the Western world, and for which many tests may have been developed for their measurement, may not exist in many cultures. Or, if the concepts do exist elsewhere, their behavioral manifestations may vary considerably. The Western concept of intelligence is a good example. Mainstream Western psychologists "know," for instance, that intelligence exists, and that someone who has a lot of intelligence knows many things and can produce responses very quickly. Thus in the West, one is intelligent if one is both smart and fast. As reported by Wober (1974), however, among the Baganda people of Uganda, their concept of intelligence, *obugezi,* is associated with wisdom, slow thoughtfulness, and saying the right thing. Thus slow and ponderous thought and a great desire to be socially correct are indicators of intelligence among the Baganda; in the academically supercharged Western world, however, where knowing many things and being able to recall them fast is often a meal ticket to better education and jobs, such behavior may be viewed as dim-witted (see the chapter by Kâgitçibaşi in this volume).

The issue here is the extent to which a concept or construct developed in *one* culture can be (or should be) transported to another culture as if its parameters will not change in the process of extending it elsewhere. According to today's standards in conducting cross-cultural research (Lonner & Berry, 1986), to do so is considered to be a major methodological mistake as well as a certain sign of ethnocentrism or cultural insensitivity.

Issue 3: How do we know that the bases of comparison are equivalent across cultures? If the bases of comparison are not equivalent across cultures, then valid comparisons across cultures cannot be made. For instance, if one wanted to measure and compare "politeness" across cultures, one would want to be sure that politeness is understood *on each culture's terms* before attempting any comparisons. One culture's notion of politeness may be based on how many questions were asked about family members, whereas politeness in another culture may be gauged according to how quiet and *nonintrusive* one is during conversation (see the chapter by Bhawuk, this volume).

A similar problem exists at the level of translation. This type of equivalence concerns the meaning that persons attach to test or questionnaire items. Literal translation is usually inadequate. For example, in the United States, it is common to see such items as this on tests: "Republicans are more patriotic than Democrats" (to measure political attitudes, for instance). But it would be illogical to use such an item in a culture whose people have little or no familiarity with what *Republican* and *Democrat* (the two major political parties in the United States) mean. To solve such problems, the researcher must be concerned with translating such items so that they are conceptually equivalent. For example, suppose it is determined that the core characteristics of "republicanism" are conservative fiscal restraint and limited government intervention into the rights of the states and individuals. On the other end of the spectrum, suppose that the key characteristics of being a democrat include massive support to the people in the form of liberal fiscal policies. Thus instead of using the culture-loaded item "Republicans are more conservative than Democrats," a somewhat more neutral item for use in making comparisons might be this: "People who do not intervene in the rights of others are more patriotic than those who believe in substantial control by the government." Key operative phrases in this rendering are *intervene in the rights of people, patriotic, government,* and *control.* These are much better "culture-common" concepts than Republican and Democrat, therefore, lending themselves better to comparative research.

Acceptable cross-cultural research involving language differences usually must include rather sophisticated translation procedures, such as those outlined by Brislin (1986). Many hours of careful, dedicated research may be needed to make even a brief questionnaire appropriate for culture-comparative research.

A number of rival hypotheses may account for differences more convincingly than true differences at the level of constructs. For instance, experimenter effects (such as the presence of an imposing authority figure, who is often foreign and a curiosity item) may cause anxiety or excitement, which would affect test performance. Wide differentials in motivation may account for differences in scores. Also, response sets, or tendencies to respond to the *form* of the item or the way it was asked, may be the reason for differences rather than the actual *content*. "Acquiescence" (the tendency to agree with just about everything), "social desirability" (responding in socially approved directions), or "positional" (responding to items in the middle) are three common response sets. Any number of many types of response sets (Fiske, 1970) may interact with cultural factors to produce results that may be meaningless or at least misleading.

Issue 4: Should test stimuli be in the verbal or the visual mode? Items on psychological tests can appear either in the verbal mode (written or spoken language) or in the visual mode (pictures or figures, for instance). It has often been assumed that the comprehension of language is more culturally variable than the comprehension of nonlinguistic stimuli. Therefore, the reasoning goes, if one wants to develop a test that is "culture fair," it should be purged of as much verbal content as possible. In other words, stimuli in the nonverbal mode would constitute a "common denominator" approach to developing test items. This assumption may be unwarranted, however. Bagby (1957), for instance, showed in an experiment concerned with binocular rivalry (presenting two "rival" scenes briefly, one to each eye, and forcing the subject to describe what was seen) that Mexican subjects chose Mexican scenes such as a bullfight over American scenes such as a baseball game, whereas the reverse was true for U.S. subjects. This supported the theory that says that perception is strongly influenced by previous experience (see also Deregowski, 1980). Thus simply "purging" verbal stimuli from assessment devices will not necessarily give quick solutions to the problem of equivalence of stimuli. Equivalence should be proven rather than assumed.

Issue 5: How does one avoid using "deficit" language when inter-preting test score differences between cultures? When interpreting test score differences between individuals or groups in any culture, there is a natural tendency to interpret differences by using language that suggests that one individual or group is "better" than another individual or group. This is logically consistent; after all, appropriate within-culture norms are typically established in such a way that roughly half the group will indeed perform "better." There is a similar tendency, when interpreting test score differences *between* cultures (at either the individual or the group level), to use language suggesting "superordination-subordination." For instance, in comparing achievement test scores between John and James, two citizens of the same country, it would normally be acceptable to say something like "John has a higher achievement test score than Jim, and is therefore better equipped for university." This suggests, and rightly so, that James's lower score is the result of some "deficit"—in actual abilities, in quality of education, in motivation, and so on. However, unless one has developed impeccable cross-cultural norms on some test that has been carried to some other culture and translated for use there, it could be a serious error to say, for instance, that "Mujafi scored lower on Test X than John, and therefore is not as well equipped for something" (college, a job, further training, or whatever). It may simply be that there is only a quantitative difference (caused by the sort of methodological difficulties reviewed earlier) that is inappropriately overinterpreted as a qualitative difference. It has been said that nature abhors a vacuum. Test interpreters may abhor uninterpreted test score differences, but to do so cross-culturally by using deficit language is to be avoided. The individual or group for whom the translated test may be unfamiliar should always be given the benefit of the doubt (see Irvine & Berry, 1988, for further discussion).

The issues discussed on the previous pages do not exhaust the concerns that shroud testing and assessment in different cultural contexts. Others could easily have been discussed in some detail. For instance, many researchers decry studies involving only one researcher who may be using only one method or one test. This matter prompted a call for the use of *multiple researchers* and *multiple methods* in psychological research (Campbell & Fiske, 1959). This classic paper suggested that anything short of a multitrait, multimethod matrix could easily lead to uninterpretable or ambiguous results. Written *before* cross-cultural research experienced substantial growth, its message takes on even more important dimensions for our present purposes. A single researcher using one method to measure a solitary concept in an isolated culture may signal problems.

SPECIFIC DOMAINS OF
TESTING AND ASSESSMENT

Although psychological tests exist for nearly every human attribute or dimension, the two largest areas are concerned with the assessment of intelligence and abilities and the assessment of personality. Some major cross-cultural perspectives and concerns will be presented for both of these areas.

Intelligence and Ability Testing

Variations in mental abilities and reasons for them have intrigued psychologists for many years; questions about intelligence abound and proliferate. One standard inquiry concerns the relative contributions of nature (are we born with it?) and nurture (are we taught to be intelligent?). Another concerns the range of human abilities: How can we explain the peaks of genius represented by people of Einsteinian endowment as well as the broad range of abilities that lie in the valleys below? The most basic question of all is this: What is intelligence?

A popular view is that there is a general factor in human intelligence and that it is universal. Frequently abbreviated as simply "g," this general factor is equivalent to horsepower in an automobile engine: The more "power" one has, the more adept one is intellectually. This conception has broad appeal because it seems to accord with more observable ranges of human attributes such as height, weight, running speed, and general endurance, and it tends to correlate highly with educational achievement. The position also has been attacked as elitist. Coming from a British tradition (Spearman, 1927), it essentially implies that those with more "g" are "better" or at least better off. Vernon (1969) was among the leaders in popularizing "g" and how it may vary across cultures. The Raven Matrices (see any testing text), probably the most widely used "intelligence" test across cultures, is purportedly a "pure" measure of "g."

Another popular view is that intelligence consists of two major components: verbal and nonverbal. Thus individuals will be assessed as higher in one area than the other or, perhaps, equally able in both areas. The Wechsler method of intelligence testing (again, consult any testing text) is the most widely used procedure for estimating intelligence of this type; the procedure has been adapted for use in many cultures. Other approaches have used factor analysis to identify specific components of intelligence. Factor analytic procedures developed by Thurstone, Cattell, Guilford, and others will normally be explained in texts on psychological testing as will other perspectives on the assessment of intelligence and abilities. A general finding is that the factor structure of intelligence is complex and varies considerably across cultures. As reported by Zhang (1988), Confucius (551-479 B.C.) classified people into three categories: those of "great wisdom," those of "average intelligence," and those of "little intelligence." Considering that factor analysts have identified dozens if not hundreds of intellectual factors in their search for the underlying, complex structure of human abilities, the simplicity of the Confucian approach is appealing.

Universalism versus cultural relativism. Two of the most hotly debated issues in the domain of intelligence are these: (1) Is it useful to think in terms of "intelligence quotients"? (2) Is intelligence best viewed as some universal human attribute or should it be conceptualized and measured in culture-relative terms only?

Despite its popularity, many believe that the concept of the IQ has done a disservice to many people and has actually become a tool used by the elite to suppress those in less powerful positions in society (Kamin, 1974). In the United States, for instance, one of the more striking contemporary examples of this is the well-known *Larry P. v. Wilson Riles* case (Riles was then California's Superintendent of Public Instruction). It was ruled that Larry P. was erroneously classified as mentally retarded. As a result, the California Supreme Court issued an order banning the use of all IQ tests for the placement of Blacks in special education programs. There likely are parallels of this controversy over misclassification in other cultures.

Many believe that the concept of *intelligence,* as psychology has used the term for the better part of a century, is dying or is already dead (Mercer, 1988). On the other side of the coin are the many statisticians, measurement specialists, and theoreticians who believe that the IQ paradigm should be dealt with in the scientific community rather than in the legislative world, where the acceptance of concepts might depend more upon the latest court ruling than on the canons of objective science. Thorndike (1988) reminds us that there are two basic premises by which science operates.[1] The first, he says, is that there is "a universe outside the human mind that exists independent of our awareness of it."

The second is that "there is a set of principles, at least in theory discoverable, by which that universe operates, and that these principles do not depend on our belief systems." The assumption is, of course, that human intelligence is a real entity and, because it is real, it can be measured. Implicit in this assumption is that intelligence as a human characteristic transcends culture, that intelligence is as "knowable" and as "demonstrably evident" in Paris as it is in Beijing or Calcutta.

Obviously, the contextualists or relativists contend that "intelligence," however it is defined or measured, is best understood in culture-relative terms. In support of this position, a number of "culture-sensitive" intelligence tests have appeared. Done more with tongue in cheek than as advances in the scientific measurement of intelligence, such tests usually prove a point rather effectively: One cannot perform very well on an "intelligence" test unless one is familiar with the culture in which it originated. In the United States, one such creation is the Cumberland Test, which, like similar devices, emerged as a response to the widespread belief that most tests are biased in favor of dominant Whites. The Cumberland gets its name from the Cumberland Mountains, where many "hillbillies" (with the stereotype of backward and uneducated people) live. A multiple-choice item on the Cumberland asks what "popskull" is. Of four alternatives, the correct answer is "white lightning," which is another name for locally (and illegally) distilled spirits. It is quite likely that every country in the world has subgroups with their own legacies and vernacular, the content of which could be the basis for "culture- or context-relevant" tests. But are these intelligence tests or tests of cultural adaptation? Or is intelligence nothing more than adaptation—the more "adapted" one is, the more "intelligent" one is?

Serpell (1982) describes a number of "emic," or culture-relative, measures of intelligence. For instance, among the Chi-Chewa (of Zambia), the concept of *nzelu* is an indigenous term involving what they would term "intelligent behavior." *Nzelu* intelligence apparently involves wisdom, cleverness, and a social responsibility factor. This concept may be equivalent to the Ugandan concept of *obugezi* (Wober, 1974), mentioned earlier.

Gardner (1983) developed a popular theory of multiple intelligences. Gathering information from many sources, and not just the results of standardized tests and other formal procedures, Gardner proposed the existence of different kinds of intelligence, with the implication that they are all equally important when used in their proper, respective contexts. Instead of asking: "How smart is he?" Gardner would prefer to ask, "How is he smart?" The specific intelligences Gardner has proposed are (a) linguistic, (b) logical-mathematical, (c) spatial, (d) musical, (e) body-kinesthetic, (f) interpersonal (sometimes called "social" intelligence), and (g) intrapersonal intelligence, or insight into oneself. The first three or four of these "intelligences" almost always emerge as dominant factors in traditional, standardized intelligence tests. This has been so pervasive in Western psychology that it is routine for psychologists to think of people in terms of how much verbal, logico-mathematical, or spatial intelligence they have. However, perhaps different social and cultural demands, interacting with different biological endowments, result in the formation of intelligences of the type Gardner has proposed. Thus one could think in terms of a culture that emphasizes proprioception and kinesthetic awareness (e.g., hunters) or one that requires high degrees of interpersonal (for instance, a charismatic leader) or intrapersonal (a great philosopher) skills *rather than* putting all people on the same continua that have been doggedly used for so many years. Of course, it is one thing to speculate about other types of intelligence that may be on par with some of the more traditional approaches, but quite another to document these as cross-culturally useful through careful and systematic study.

The *triarchic theory of intelligence* proposed by Sternberg (1985, 1986, 1987) is another recent formulation. Similar to but more heavily documented than Gardner's views, the triarchic model allows for three different types of intelligence. *Componential* intelligence is closely related to traditional views of intelligence. The basic unit is the *component,* which is involved with information processing and the storage of information that is necessary for a person to make plans, solve problems, and translate thoughts into action. A person high on componential intelligence should do well in traditional academic settings.

Experiential intelligence focuses, of course, on experience; an individual high in this area may not do so well on tests but may shine when it comes to insight and creativity—being able, on the basis of experience, to see the quickest and most creative solution to a problem. The third part of the triad is called *contextual* intelligence. It involves being skilled in staying out of trouble ("street smarts"), how to solve real-life problems such as family budget crises, and how to get along with people. Also called *tacit knowledge,* it is this kind of everyday knowhow that may be much more important than "book" knowledge in terms of simply getting along in the world. This is the sort of knowledge that is necessary to have if one is to pass such "context-loaded" tests as the Cumberland Test, which, as explained above, are better described as indices of cultural adaptation than they are of "raw" ability.

THE ASSESSMENT OF PERSONALITY

The domain of personality assessment, which is generally concerned with the assessment of *typical* (as opposed to *maximum*) performance, is large and the issues complex, especially cross-culturally. For assessment purposes, Cohen, Montague, Nathanson, and Swerdlik (1988, pp. 286-287) offered a workable definition of personality: "Personality [is] an individual's unique constellation of psychological traits and states." This "unique constellation" may consist of the person's characteristic mode of behaving, of his interests, values, attitudes, tendencies toward psychopathological conditions, fitness for certain kinds of work and not others, and so on. One's "personality" is largely a reflection of how one has been shaped by culture, or has adapted to it. Thus even though allowances would have to be made for intracultural variation, it is convenient (but simplistic) to think in terms of every specific culture or ethnic group fostering the development of an ideal, adaptive "personality"—that prototypical person who has all the characteristics that are consistent with that culture or ethnic group. Sometimes this has been called *modal personality,* or *national character,* terms that imply that there is a personality that is a good representative of a particular culture (such as the thrifty Swiss, the cold Swede, or the superficial American). These "snapshots" or stereotypes, however, even if they do contain a kernel of truth, obscure wide individual variations that will be found in any culture.

Universalism Versus Particularism in Personality Assessment

Although the many terms and constructs used in the field of personality are usually ill-defined, they are heuristic devices that are necessary in the development and construction of the thousands of devices that are available at any given time for their measurement. A scale or inventory can be developed to measure any term or concept that is used in a specific culture. This assumption carries with it the likelihood that a reasonably accurate and meaningful description of the range of variation within that culture is possible. Take, for instance, the concept of conformity. Conformity and how it may relate to other facets of behavior has been studied extensively by Western psychologists. In the Euro-American tradition, conformity (and its opposite, nonconformity) has been the focus of extensive study and has been linked to submis-

siveness, authoritarianism, lowered self-confidence, obedience, shy-
ness, dependence, lack of creativity, and many other variables. Because
of extensive convergent validation, it is reasonably well understood
what it means to be described as a "conformed individual" in the
individualistic Western world. However, in what sense can the concept
of conformity be successfully extended to other cultures? Here we have
a very important issue, one that parallels cross-cultural concerns in the
measurement of intelligence and abilities: To what extent can the
dimensions of personality that are valid for one culture be useful in
other cultures? Continuing with the example of conformity, can we
assume that the concept as a reference to personality or behavior exists
everywhere? Is it possible that *conformity* and *conformity behavior* are
meaningless terms in other cultures? If so, then it is obvious that any
attempt to measure conformity elsewhere, with measures developed in
the West, will result in misleading and probably useless data. The same
concerns exist for any term or concept that is used to describe individuals. However, we can assume that a number of personality concepts
are so important that any human group will have terms for them. For
instance, Goldberg (1981) has developed a convincing case for the
existence of lexical universals. If they are indeed universals, measuring
them and comparing them within and across cultures can lead to interesting and meaningful data.

Examples of the Cross-Cultural Use of
Specific Personality Scales

For the purpose of giving the reader a "feel" for the problems and
prospects associated with the cross-cultural assessment of personality
variables (and *not* for the purpose of *endorsing* or *recommending* their
use), three specific devices will be briefly described: the Minnesota
Multiphasic Personality Inventory (MMPI), the State-Trait Anxiety
Inventory (STAI), and the Locus of Control Scale. A consideration of
some of the major issues associated with the cross-cultural use of these
procedures should "sensitize" the reader to the many issues that pervade
the cross-cultural assessment of personality.

The MMPI is the most widely used device of its kind in the world.
In its full form, it consists of 566 self-referenced statements to which
the subject or client responds either "true," "false," or "cannot say." It
contains items like these: "I like to take long walks" and "When I was
in school I was considered a student leader." It is assumed that different
"types" of people will respond in similar ways to such items, and on

this basis one's personality dispositions can be understood better using the folk wisdom captured by the saying, "Birds of a feather flock together," which assumes that people come in "bunches" or as "types."

The MMPI was constructed by using the empirical method of test construction: Contrast criterion groups to "control" groups at the item level, then develop scales around those items that discriminate between the groups and discard the remainder. Using the previous procedure since its inception in the 1940s, the MMPI has been used primarily to assess what can best be described as "psychopathological tendencies." This is so because the criterion groups typically consist of individuals who have been clinically diagnosed as paranoid or schizophrenic—two of ten "clinical" scales that are included on the standard profile sheet. Nowadays, however, the syndromes associated with the clinical scales are not nearly as important as what is called "configural" scoring. With configural scoring, and consequently the interpretation (often done by sophisticated computer programs) that follows, the *pattern* of scores and their various elevations are much more meaningful than the frequently ambiguous names that were originally associated with the scales.

The MMPI has been used extensively in other cultures (it has been estimated that 125 translations are available). It will no doubt be used cross-culturally into the indefinite future, and perhaps for defensible reasons. For example, it has an enormous literature, making comparisons and contrasts possible nearly anywhere with any type of abnormal pattern. This may be especially fruitful for widely researched conditions, such as schizophrenia and depression, that are good candidates for universality (see the chapter by Draguns in this volume). Also, the rather straightforward, atheoretical, and open-ended technique afforded by the empirical strategy permits the construction of any number of criterion groups, for any condition or syndrome, in nearly any country.

There are, however, several reasons why the MMPI should be viewed with caution when contemplating its use cross-culturally. For instance, it is decidedly a creation of the "Western" view of etiology and psychiatric classification (and is, therefore, culture-bound); its original normative samples came from small, rural parts of Minnesota (in the United States); and there is little or no "theory" guiding its cross-cultural use. Moreover, many (e.g., Colligan, Osborne, Swenson, & Offord, 1983) have cautioned against its use with ethnic minorities in the United States on the basis of there being inadequate norms. Dana (1988, p. 490) has gone further in suggesting that "culturally determined thought processes, including ethnocentrism, world view, and etic preoccupation predispose interpretation of the MMPI to unintentional bias as a result of minimization of consistent group differences in responding."

Those who are charting the future use and growth of the MMPI are aware of its many shortcomings but argue that it has considerable promise for cross-cultural use (Butcher & Keller, 1984). It recently went through a major "face-lift" and renorming process. The nature of the revision resulting in MMPI-2 is explained in detail in the 1989 manual.[2] Its continued cross-cultural use, however, should be firmly stamped with a warning: Caveat emptor (buyer beware), for its misuse can lead to terrible errors and tragic consequences.

Spielberger, Gorsuch, and Lushene (1970) developed the STAI to assess both *state* anxiety (situational or transitory anxiety) and *trait* anxiety (a generalized and enduring characteristic of the person), both of which are very likely universals, but with causes and symptoms that are culturally variable. The 20 A-State items describe current feelings (e.g., "I feel nervous"); the 20 A-Trait items are phrased more generally (e.g., "I lack self-confidence").

The STAI has been used extensively in other cultures (Spielberger & Diaz-Guerrero, 1976, 1983, 1986), and a general bibliography is available (Spielberger, 1984). The typical other-culture use of the STAI is simple and straightforward: Translate the scale into another language, administer it to samples of individuals from another culture, and then determine how it relates to or explains nontest variables such as job performance, interpersonal competence, or success in therapy. This is a defensible *within*-culture strategy, but the way it has typically been used has not contributed much to an understanding of the phenomenon of anxiety *across* cultures. Like other attractive devices that have been used to measure the dimensions of personality across cultures, including the MMPI, the STAI suffers from an absence of some kind of coherent theoretical structure in which to put the culturally diverse accumulated findings.

The STAI can be used as an example of a potentially serious psychometric problem in culture-comparative research. The problem is as important and as cautionary for nearly any paper-and-pencil device designed to measure any dimension of personality as it is for the STAI's intent to measure the construct of anxiety. The problem is this: No one has yet found a way to calibrate anxiety *scale* values with levels of *actual* anxiety. If comparisons of anxiety levels (STAI scores) are done within one cultural group or ethnic community (as Spielberger et al. have done), this would probably not be particularly troublesome; such a procedure is, of course, done all the time, and perhaps should stop there. But if used *across* cultures for *comparative* purposes, the absence of a common reference point (equivalent to the contrast between 0 degrees Celsius and 32 degrees Fahrenheit to measure freezing level, for instance) can lead to serious errors. Is an anxiety scale score of 8 in Mexico the same or different as a score of 8 in Japan or Canada? None of the culture-comparative research with the STAI has been convincing in this regard. Lonner and Ibrahim (1989, pp. 258-259) summarized this problem as follows:

> For tests or scales to be directly interpretable on mean scale values across culture-linguistic groups, several things must be achieved: (a) each item's validity as an indicator of the underlying trait should remain unchanged; (b) the scale values and probability of endorsement at the item level should be the same; and (c) all the items taken together should have the same average validity, the same average absolute scale value, and the same operating characteristics in all cultures to which the inventory is extended. It is most unlikely that all of these conditions can be met in an absolute sense.

These are formidable requirements to be met, if indeed they can ever be satisfied even within the culture where a particular scale originated. Measuring the ephemeral dimensions of personality is not easy to do; the widely differing subjective evaluations of statements contained in personality scales and inventories will *always* create uncertainties about where a person's or a group's "real" level is. It is one of the paradoxes of cross-cultural research that so many truly interesting personological dimensions that we intuitively *know* to be different to some degree across cultures cannot be assessed with the same degree of accuracy with which botanists can measure regional differences in pollen count or meteorologists can pinpoint annual differences in rainfall between regions.

The widely studied concept of locus of control originated within a social learning framework (Rotter, 1966). It has been hypothesized that the nature of the social environment, and generalized expectancies from it, contributes to the development of "internally controlled" individuals (independent, self-sufficient, and autonomous people) who believe in the value of their own efforts as well as to the development of those who are "externally controlled" (by luck, fate, or chance, feeling that they are victims of a capricious and unpredictable environment). Where one falls on this hypothesized continuum is usually measured by the Locus of Control Scale, or the I-E Scale. It consists of oppositional statements such as these:

a) How far one gets in life depends a lot on whether one is at the right place at the right time.

b) Success in life is determined almost entirely by how hard one works.

The "a" option is, of course, the "external" item, and one's score is simply the sum of items answered in that direction.

There is a general rule in the assessment of personality dimensions across cultures that one must proceed with extreme caution and not fall prey to simplistic notions or "quick fixes." The I-E Scale (and its various versions, including forms designed for children) is no exception to this rule. There has been an avalanche of published reports concerning various facets of control and its correlates, with a unifying, clear statement yet to emerge from all this activity (Phares, 1976). A fairly recent book is concerned with the numerous methods to assess locus of control (Lefcourt, 1981), and it seems to be one of the favorite techniques to use across cultures if for no other reason than the fact that it concerns important psychological and geopolitical realities. A companion book published more recently (Lefcourt, 1984) concerns extensions and limitations of this construct; a very useful chapter in that book reviews the extensive literature on the locus of control concept across cultures (Dyal, 1984).

A Lingering Issue:
Standardized Versus Nonstandardized Assessment

The last several pages have been concerned with the possible cross-cultural use of three "ready-made" old standbys in the assessment of personological dimensions: the MMPI, the STAI, and the I-E Scale. One can feel a certain level of comfort in using these devices and many others that could have been summarized. After all, many have used them, more or less successfully, in a very large number of research projects; there is security in numbers and in tradition. The accumulated data alone on these three devices give one confidence that he or she is contributing to the overall understanding of the construct(s) underlying these measures and their sociocultural correlates. In addition to these three devices, one could select any number of "off-the-rack" devices by consulting texts on psychological testing, by examining test manuals, or by following the lead of what others have done. For instance, many continue to use various tests of "cognitive style" in extending Witkin's theory of psychological differentiation across cultures (Berry, 1976; Witkin & Berry, 1975). This is safe, prudent, and may minimally indicate that one has selected the right "instrument" for the right "job" from among the available alternatives.

Yet there is another option, one that may require considerable work and is fraught with potential problems. But this option also contains the promise of creativity, of exploration, of carving out new territory. Instead of using ready-made measures, this option would capitalize on fresh ideas afforded by the unlimited potential of nonstandardized assessment. Maybe cross-cultural psychologists, fearful of creating yet another layer of error variance and inviting unpleasant criticism from the orthodox masses (worse yet, from their peers), have been too cautious. Perhaps cross-cultural psychologists, or indeed anyone who desires to assess any of the many facets of human behavior, should feel unconstrained in trying out new things. Maybe cross-cultural psychologists should get bolder in their attempts to design new ways to measure old (or new) constructs. In a comment that can only encourage exploration and creativity, Burrisch (1984, p. 219) said that "it cost me two hours and a bottle of wine to write an aggression and a depression scale that turned out to be of equal or superior validity, compared to much more sophisticated instruments." (He failed to mention, however, the considerable time it usually takes to establish the validity and reliability of these scales.) The cross-cultural researcher often has ample contact with local colleagues as well as plenty of free time in places with interesting and inexpensive wine. These conditions suggest that there may be no reason why he or she could not follow Burrisch's lead and construct a device suited to the immediate needs of the research project, provided, of course, that suitable levels of validity and reliability are achieved.

CONCLUSIONS AND RECOMMENDATIONS

The main goal of this chapter has been to sensitize the reader to some key issues and problems in cross-cultural assessment. For the student or applied researcher who may require more detail, most of the references that have been cited in this chapter should be consulted. In particular, several edited books—Cronbach and Drenth (1972) and Irvine and Berry (1983, 1988), for instance—will be especially helpful because the ideas and efforts of many researchers and practitioners from various cultures are included in them. Two sources should aid in the actual administration of tests and other measures to people from diverse backgrounds. They are Brislin et al. (1973) and Sundberg and Gonzales

(1981). These latter sources cover such factors as getting to know how people in other cultures perceive testable problems, deciding which test (if any) to use, determining efficient ways to motivate those who take tests, identifying and solving problems that might emerge during test administration, and so forth.

The careful cross-cultural researcher who contemplates the need to use tests and scales will have to answer three important questions: (1) Is testing or assessment absolutely essential in each particular case? (2) What is the best way to approach assessment in the particular cultural context? (3) How should the results be interpreted so that maximum benefits to the people who were assessed and to the research project, and minimum errors to both, can be achieved? We should expect and accept no less.

NOTES

1. The source of Mercer's and Thorndike's perspectives (Lonner & Tyler, 1988) will not be easy to find in a library. This small book is available at cost (roughly $5.00 per copy). It is suitable as a text or supplemental text for any class that concerns cultural factors in learning and motivation. Similarly, the article by Zhang (1988) will be difficult to find. Please write W. J. Lonner for more information about either of these references.

2. The manual is available from the University of Minnesota Press, Minneapolis, Minnesota 55455.

REFERENCES

Anastasi, A. (1988). *Psychological testing* (6th ed.). New York: Macmillan.

Bagby, J. W. (1957). A cross-cultural study of perceptual dominance in binocular rivalry. *Journal of Abnormal and Social Psychology, 54,* 331-334.

Berry, J. W. (1976). *Human ecology and cognitive style: Comparative studies in cultural and psychological adaptation.* Beverly Hills, CA: Sage.

Brislin, R. W. (1986). The wording and translation of research instruments. In W. J. Lonner & J. W. Berry (Eds.), *Field methods in cross-cultural research.* Newbury Park, CA: Sage.

Brislin, R. W., Lonner, W. J., & Thorndike, R. M. (1973). *Cross-cultural research methods.* New York: John Wiley.

Burrisch, M. (1984). Approaches to personality inventory construction: A comparison of merits. *American Psychologist, 39,* 214-227.

Butcher, J. N., & Keller, L. (1984). Objective personality assessment: Present status and future directions. In G. Goldstein & M. Hersen (Eds.), *Handbook of psychological assessment.* New York: Pergamon.

Campbell, D. T., & Fiske, D. (1959). Convergent and discriminant validity by the multi-method, multi-trait matrix. *Psychological Bulletin, 56,* 81-105.

Cohen, R. J., Montague, P., Nathanson, L. S., & Swerdlik, M. E. (1988). *Psychological testing: An introduction to tests and measurements.* Mountain View, CA: Mayfield.

Colligan, R. C., Osborne, D., Swenson, W. M., & Offord, K. P. (1983). *The MMPI: A contemporary normative study.* New York: Praeger.

Cronbach, L. J. (1984). *Essentials of psychological testing* (4th ed.). New York: Harper & Row.

Cronbach, L. J., & Drenth, P. J. D. (Eds.). (1972). *Mental tests and cultural adaptation.* The Hague, The Netherlands: Mouton.

Dana, R. H. (1988). Culturally diverse groups and MMPI interpretation. *Professional Psychology: Research and Practice, 19,* 490-495.

Deregowski, J. (1980). Perception. In H. C. Triandis & W. J. Lonner (Eds.), *Handbook of cross-cultural psychology* (Vol. 3). Boston: Allyn & Bacon.

Dyal, J. A. (1984). Cross-cultural research with the locus of control construct. In H. Lefcourt (Ed.), *Research with the locus of control construct: Vol. 3. Extensions and limitations.* New York: Academic Press.

Fiske, D. (1970). *Measuring the concepts of personality.* Chicago: Aldine-Atherton.

Gardner, H. (1983). *Frames of mind: The theory of multiple intelligences.* New York: Basic Books.

Goldberg, L. (1981). Language and individual differences: The search for universals in personality lexicons. In L. Wheeler (Ed.), *Review of personality and social psychology* (Vol. 2). Beverly Hills, CA: Sage.

Irvine, S. H., & Berry, J. W. (Eds.). (1983). *Human assessment and cultural factors.* New York: Plenum.

Irvine, S. H., & Berry, J. W. (Eds.). (1988). *Human abilities in cultural context.* London: Cambridge University Press.

Irvine, S. H., & Carroll, W. K. (1980). Testing and assessment across cultures. In H. C. Triandis & J. W. Berry (Eds.), *Handbook of cross-cultural psychology: Vol. 2. Methodology.* Boston: Allyn & Bacon.

Kamin, L. (1974). *The science and politics of I.Q.* New York: John Wiley.

Kaplan, R. M., & Saccuzzo, D. P. (1989). *Psychological testing: Principles, applications, and issues.* Pacific Grove, CA: Brooks/Cole.

Kulkarni, S. S., & Puhan, B. N. (1988). Psychological assessment: Its present and future trends. In J. Pandey (Ed.), *Psychology in India: Personality and mental processes* (Vol. 1). New Delhi: Sage.

Lefcourt, H. M. (Ed.). (1981). *Research with the locus of control construct: Vol. 1. Assessment methods.* New York: Academic Press.

Lefcourt, H. M. (Ed.). (1984). *Research with the locus of control construct: Vol. 3. Extensions and limitations.* New York: Academic Press.

Lonner, W. J., & Berry, J. W. (Eds.). (1986). *Field methods in cross-cultural research.* Newbury Park, CA: Sage.

Lonner, W. J., & Ibrahim, F. (1989). Assessment in cross-cultural counseling. In P. Pedersen, J. G. Draguns, W. J. Lonner, & J. E. Trimble (Eds.), *Cross-cultural counseling* (3rd ed.). Honolulu: University of Hawaii Press.

Lonner, W., & Tyler, V. (1988). *Cultural and ethnic factors in learning and motivation: Implications for education: The Twelfth Western Symposium on Learning.* Bellingham, WA: Western Washington University.

Mercer, J. (1988). Death of the I.Q. paradigm: Where do we go from here? In W. J. Lonner & V. O. Tyler (Eds.), *Cultural and ethnic factors in learning and motivation: Implications for education: The Twelfth Western Symposium on Learning.* Bellingham, WA: Western Washington University.

Phares, E. J. (1976). *Locus of control in personality.* Morristown, NJ: General Learning Press.

Rotter, J. (1966). Generalized expectancies for internal versus external locus of reinforcement. *Psychological Monographs* (Whole No. 609).

Samuda, R. J. (1975). *Psychological testing of American minorities*. New York: Dodd, Mead.

Schwartz, S. H., & Bilsky, W. (1987). Toward a universal psychological structure of human values. *Journal of Personality and Social Psychology, 53,* 550-562.

Serpell, R. (1982). Measures of perception, skills, and intelligence: The growth of a new perspective on children in a Third World country. In W. W. Hartup (Ed.), *Review of child development research* (Vol. 6). Chicago: University of Chicago Press.

Sinha, D. (1983). Human assessment in Indian context. In S. H. Irvine & J. W. Berry (Eds.), *Human assessment and cultural factors*. New York: Plenum.

Spearman, C. (1927). *The abilities of man: Their nature and measurement*. New York: Macmillan.

Spielberger, C. D. (1984). *A comprehensive bibliography for the State-Trait Anxiety Inventory*. Palo Alto, CA: Consulting Psychologists Press.

Spielberger, C. D., & Diaz-Guerrero, R. (Eds.). (1976). *Cross-cultural anxiety* (Vol. 1). Washington, DC: Hemisphere.

Spielberger, C. D., & Diaz-Guerrero, R. (Eds.). (1983). *Cross-cultural anxiety* (Vol. 2). Washington, DC: Hemisphere.

Spielberger, C. D., & Diaz-Guerrero, R. (Eds.). (1986). *Cross-cultural anxiety* (Vol. 3). Washington, DC: Hemisphere.

Spielberger, C. D., Gorsuch, R. L., & Lushene, R. G. (1970). *The State-Trait Anxiety Inventory*. Palo Alto, CA: Consulting Psychologists Press.

Sternberg, R. J. (1985). *Beyond I.Q.: A triarchic theory of intelligence*. New York: Cambridge University Press.

Sternberg, R. J. (1986). *Intelligence applied*. San Diego: Harcourt, Brace, Jovanovich.

Sternberg, R. J. (1987). *The future of intelligence testing*. Paper presented at the meeting of the American Psychological Association, New York.

Sundberg, N., & Gonzales, L. (1981). Cross-cultural and cross-ethnic assessment: Overview and issues. In P. McReynolds (Ed.), *Advances in psychological assessment* (Vol. 5). San Francisco: Jossey-Bass.

Thorndike, R. M. (1988). Commentary on a paper by Mercer. In W. J. Lonner & V. O. Tyler (Eds.), *Cultural factors in learning and motivation: Implications for education*. Bellingham, WA: Western Washington University.

Triandis, H. C. (1972). *The analysis of subjective culture*. New York: John Wiley.

Trimble, J. E., Lonner, W. J., & Boucher, J. (1983). Stalking the wily emic: Alternatives to cross-cultural measurement. In S. Irvine & J. W. Berry (Eds.), *Human assessment and cultural factors*. New York: Plenum.

Vernon, P. E. (1969). *Intelligence and cultural environment*. London: Methuen.

Witkin, H. A., & Berry, J. W. (1975). Psychological differentiation in cross-cultural perspective. *Journal of Cross-Cultural Psychology, 66,* 4-87.

Wober, M. (1974). Towards an understanding of the Kiganda concept of intelligence. In J. W. Berry & P. R. Dasen (Eds.), *Culture and cognition*. London: Methuen.

Zavalloni, M. (1980). Values. In H. C. Triandis & R. W. Brislin (Eds.), *Handbook of cross-cultural psychology: Vol. 5. Social psychology*. Boston: Allyn & Bacon.

Zhang, H. (1988, October). Psychological testing and China's modernization. *Bulletin of the International Test Commission,* No. 27.

4

INTERVENTIONS FOR DEVELOPMENT OUT OF POVERTY

DURGANAND SINHA

Large tracts of the globe, often characterized as the Third World, suffer from acute poverty. Even in the most prosperous nations of the world, there are pockets of poverty in which a sizable proportion of people are underfed, underclothed, badly housed, and lacking in basic amenities of life. Studies on the psychological dimensions of poverty and their impact on individual functioning have been conducted not so much as academic exercises but with the specific purpose of devising measures for ameliorating their harmful effects. It is in no way implied that psychological dimensions exhaust the universe of poverty and constitute its main cause. It is generated and sustained by economic systems and social structures. Radical transformations are required for its eradication. But the condition of poverty does not restrict itself simply to the economic domain. Its spread is visible in social, psychological, health, and other areas affecting human existence and behavior patterns. Therefore, while recognizing the central role of economic and structural determinants, it is contended that outcomes of poverty include social and personal effects, including the coping processes of the individual. Understanding these processes is useful in devising strategies and programs for persons and groups to develop out of poverty and enjoy a life free from unnecessary and avoidable miseries and deprivations.

CONCEPTUALIZATION OF POVERTY

In the psychological literature, poverty has many conceptual nuances, and there is often confusion about the criteria used to classify groups as poor. Ignoring sophisticated measurement procedures, psychologists have preferred working with categorical-level variables, examining marginal groups like Blacks, Chicanos, Harjans, or those designated, as in India, as "weaker sections" of society.

Apart from purely economic factors, sociocultural indices have been frequently used for designating "poor" and "disadvantaged" groups. In addition to using a single criterion, investigators have used a whole catalogue of objects and possessions in the home (e.g., books, electrical appliances) or neighborhood (e.g., playgrounds), occupation, residence, educational facilities, and activities engaged in by the person. A standard procedure has been to develop a socioeconomic status (SES) scale or specific scales of poverty, like the "deprivation index" of Whiteman and Deutsch (1968) and the Prolonged Deprivation Scale of Misra and Tripathi (1980), taking into account the aspects of environment in relation to which individuals are impoverished.

Thus psychologists have conceptualized poverty as a situation with a number of attendant conditions that individually or collectively influence the development of people, rendering them less capable of overcoming poverty by personal efforts. The sequence of processes representing the relationship between poverty and its psychological and behavioral consequences is illustrated in a schematic model (Figure 4.1).

Poverty is associated with low income, low caste and class status, poor housing, overcrowding, lack of public amenities, various degrees of malnutrition, and high susceptibility to diseases. Further, the poor are exposed to a less stimulating environment, inadequate school facilities, lack of parental support, and the like. These attendant conditions individually or collectively affect people's psychological functioning. The common psychological effects are inappropriate perceptual and cognitive skills, attentional problems, learning disabilities, inadequate linguistic skills, stagnant aspirations, sense of helplessness, low self-esteem, and mental health problems. These, in turn, result in coping strategies that are dysfunctional for academic and other situations in life. The behavioral outcomes in the form of low competencies, low academic performance, high rates of dropout and wastage, low school attendance, stagnation, failure, and withdrawal imply that people are not able to successfully cope with their problems. All these, in turn, accentuate the condition of poverty. In other words, psychological processes operate as mediators between the condition of poverty and its detrimental impact on behavior. It would be wrong to suggest that one is poor because of psychological limitations. But it is also true that a life of poverty produces many psychological ill effects rendering the individual less capable of coping with problems. A kind of vicious circle is created. What is emphasized is that, rather than being its cause, psychological consequences accentuate the situation of poverty.

Psychology as a discipline is most competent to deal with behavioral dimensions, the understanding of which is likely to be helpful in devising action programs and policies for eradicating poverty. It is also emphasized that ignoring psychological variables may lead ameliorative programs to unexpected and at times undesirable consequences.

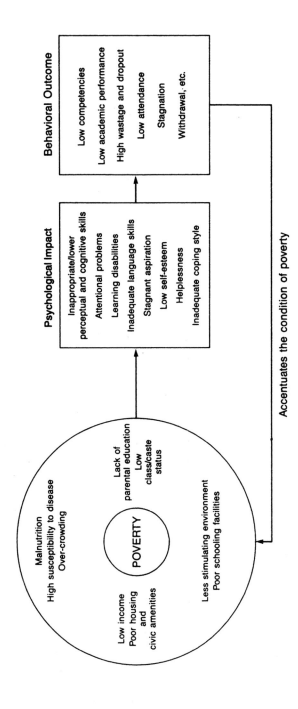

Figure 4.1. Schematic Model of the Relationship Between Poverty, Its Psychological Consequences, and Their Outcomes

Understanding the psychological characteristics of the poor is no less important than the analysis of the system that brought in the condition of poverty.

PSYCHOLOGICAL IMPACT OF POVERTY

Psychological research on poverty can be classified under three broad headings: (a) malnutrition and its impact on development, (b) cognitive dimensions of poverty, and (c) personality and motivational dimensions. The areas of mental health and personal style including self-concept, success-failure orientation, time perspective, and coping behavior have been integrated with (c) in the present chapter. Moreover, (d) studies of self-fulfilling prophesies and (e) attribution processes have led to new insights. Each of these are discussed briefly, and policy and action implications of the major findings are spelled out.

Malnutrition and Its Impact on Development

Malnutrition of various degrees is a condition most frequently prevalent in poor populations living under adverse socioeconomic and environmental circumstances. Although early and severe malnutrition occurs with considerable frequency in the poorer populations of developing countries (up to 20% in some instances), the most widespread type of malnutrition is that of mild-to-moderate, chronic undernutrition, which is most readily noted in some retardation of physical growth and development. Severe protein-calories malnutrition (PCM) includes the conditions of nutritional *marasmus* (starvation) and *kwashiorkor* (protein deficiency) typically occurring as a rather acute illness toward the end of the first or in the second year of life. Severe nutritional deficits alter the child's attentional competencies and responsiveness to the environment (Ricciuti, 1981) and lead to reduced activity and apathy. It has been observed that, although malnourished infants and toddlers seem less responsive to low or moderate levels of stimulation, they appear to be hyperactive at higher stimulus levels. It is highly probable that attentional deficiencies underlie the learning disabilities that are reflected in poor performance in school and various real-life settings. Although this aspect of malnutrition needs to be investigated more systematically, it is obvious that what gets affected adversely is attentional strategies and competence, or learnability, and not basic intellectual capacity. It should be kept in mind that attentional strategies affect IQ *scores*. This is one example of how IQ tests should not be taken as perfect measures of intellectual capacity. Therefore, if, in an intervention program, food supplementation is used along with measures to enhance responsiveness and learning competencies, the adverse effects of early malnutrition can be largely countered.

Mild-to-moderate malnutrition is more widespread. Studies conducted in India, Latin America, and other parts of the world have yielded considerable evidence that the physical development of children, particularly height and weight, go hand in hand with the development of other areas such as language and cognition. There were significant differences in head circumference and growth rate, in intelligence, and on measures of visual-motor development between adequately and inadequately fed lower-class nursery school children from New Delhi (Werner & Murlidharan, 1970). A comparison of 1,336 undernourished rural children at school entry (6-8 years) in Varanasi, India, with a sample of normal children demonstrated impairments of IQ, fine motor coordination, and immediate memory. The former were also slow in verbal reasoning, comprehension, and perceptual ability and displayed inadequacies in social competence and communication. Even for those undernourished children with normal IQ, 16.3% had poor achievement indicating learning difficulties (Agarwal, Agarwal, & Upadhyay, 1988).

Many studies have tried to assess the relative influences of malnutrition and social factors on mental development. Findings are not always consistent. Among Barbadian children of 5-11 years who had suffered moderate to severe degree of malnutrition during the first year of life, IQ was reduced, which was independent of socioeconomic factors. They also showed attention deficit, impaired memory, easy distractibility, poor school performance, and restlessness resembling the syndrome of attention deficit disorders (Galler, Ramsey, Solimano, & Lowell, 1983). On the other hand, the importance of social influence was brought out by the fact that an acute episode of malnutrition in the first two years of life did not affect the intellectual development of children growing in favorable circumstances. In contrast, if the child was in an unfavorable environment for intellectual development, an early bout of malnutrition had marked effects on later mental attainment (Richardson, 1976). In fact, the role of long-term environmental stimulation on Korean orphans adopted in supportive American homes and social environment has indicated that observed behavioral effects of severe malnutrition disappear and children show higher IQ and better school performance as compared with those who returned to their existing environment (Lien, Meyer, & Winick, 1977).

There is ample evidence that unfavorable early child-care practices and dysfunctional patterns of caregiver-infant interaction may contribute to an increased risk of malnutrition, growth retardation, and suboptimal behavioral development (Ricciuti, 1980). The importance of maternal intelligence, attitude, and socioeconomic status of the family for the nutritional well-being of preschool children has been emphasized. Early disturbances in mother-child interactions and inadequate mothering increase the risk not only of malnutrition but also of inadequate psychological development (Vazir, Bhogle, & Naidu, 1988). When mothers were exposed to training in child care, food supplementation produced substantial acceleration in development in rural infants (Bhogle, 1979). A study of very poor tribal children from remote areas of Madhya Pradesh, India, indicated that a suitable educational intervention with mothers brought about marked improvement in language and cognitive development, no matter how poor the children were in their physical environment (Murlidharan & Kaur, 1987).

Many nutritionists and pediatricians concerned primarily with the effects of biological conditions like postnatal malnutrition upon the child's mental development often have tended to underestimate the degree to which mental development may be directly influenced by adverse social and learning experiences prevalent in environments characterized by endemic malnutrition (Ricciuti, 1977). There is a need to examine more precisely the manner in which unfavorable aspects of the child's early social and learning environment and various adverse biological influences interact in jointly shaping the course of the young child's psychological as well as physical growth and development.

Even though the exact mechanisms of influence are yet to be understood, the findings do provide a base for planning appropriate types of intervention concerned with facilitating the child's growth and development. There is strong evidence that the mother's role and the social environment have significant mediating influences. Adverse intellectual consequences of undernutrition and low birth weight are very much attenuated in favorable social environments. Therefore, provision of both nutritional supplementation and enhancement of the child's social, family, and learning environments is essential to promote both physical and psychological development (Ricciuti, 1977).

There are serious doubts about a direct causal and unidirectional relationship between malnutrition and cognitive development. By and large, the findings indicate that the effects of malnutrition are not irreversible if appropriate measures are taken early. This provides a note of optimism and has obvious implication for action programs in that if nutritional treatment, rehabilitation, and enrichment occur early, say, in the first year, the chances of recovery of normal or near-normal intellectual functioning appear quite good.

Cognitive Dimensions of Poverty

There has been extensive research on the impact of poverty on various perceptual and cognitive processes. There is overwhelming evidence from cross-cultural studies and from those conducted on animals and children that environmental deficiencies adversely affect the acquisition of perceptual and cognitive processes. Adverse conditions associated with poverty operate as detrimental influences on intelligence, proficiency in pictorial perception, concept formation, learning, memory and mediational processes, linguistic skills, and academic performance.

Though the evidence is at times confusing, it has generally been observed that children growing in substandard environmental conditions are lower in intelligence than comparison children growing up under more favorable circumstances. Deprivation indices have been found significantly related to performance on both Lorge-Thorndike intelligence and vocabulary tests even within groups homogeneous in race and socioeconomic levels. More disadvantaged groups showed decreasing IQ with age (Whiteman & Deutsch, 1968). Further, socioeconomic status was positively correlated with scores on reading tests. These deficiencies, if left unchecked at early stages, caused irreparable damage to the cognitive and intellectual growth of children and resulted in the "cumulative deficit phenomenon," rendering them progressively more incapable of successful performance in classroom settings. As a result, the longer such children remained in school, despite equal facilities available to them, the further behind they fell in relation to the norms of their age and grade. Though some studies conducted in India (Rath, Dash, & Dash, 1979) have failed to establish a clear-cut relationship between sociocultural disadvantage and performance on various kinds of intelligence tests, the trend of the findings is one of negative relationship between the two (Singh, 1976; Werner & Murlidharan, 1970).

The adverse effects of impoverished circumstances like (a) low economic class and caste status, (b) unsatisfactory school facilities, and (c) residence in unstimulating environments and remote rural areas have been observed on a large variety of perceptual and cognitive tasks. It has also been observed that, although better school facilities do enhance the performance level of disadvantaged children, the differential between advantaged and disadvantaged groups tends to become accentuated with an increase in age and grade, causing a cumulative deficit phenomenon (Sinha, 1977).

Sociocultural disadvantage is associated with general impairment of learning, memory, and mediational abilities (Agarwal et al., 1988; Klein, Freeman, Kagan, Yarbrough, & Habicht, 1972; Sahu & Mahanta, 1977). This occurs similarly with problem solving, concept formation, and conservation skills (Dasen & Colomb, 1982; Misra & Tripathi, 1980). Although disadvantaged background interfered with the acquisition of these skills, provision of training (Rao, 1977) appeared to bring about considerable improvement, which remained stable (Mishra, 1987).

Bernstein (1973) has observed a close association between social class and linguistic skills. Though his contention is controversial, it has stimulated many studies related to sociocultural disadvantage and language development. The findings in general indicate the language skills ranging from basic structural aspects like speech articulation and grammatical usage to more complex functions such as descriptions and classifications were retarded in lower-class disadvantaged children (Chazen, Laing, Cox, & Jackson, 1977). They also scored lower on word reading and verbal conditioning tests (Panda & Das, 1970). A study of scheduled caste (formerly called "untouchable") children in India revealed their "dialect" to be deficient and deviant from the standard language of upper-caste children (Suresh, 1984). Lower-caste 2- to 3-year-old children performed poorly on grammar comprehension, word meaning, and expression skills. The linguistic environment of the family associated with class status operated as a significant moderator variable. Verbal stimulation received in the family, especially from grandparents, exerted a positive influence and could counteract the adverse effect due to lower-class status (A. Singh, 1987).

Linguistic skills and the discontinuity between the language spoken by disadvantaged children and the one used in schools are of vital significance to scholastic performance. Because general language ability is the major differentiating characteristic between class groups, and is a central element in information processing, it is highly essential to give language training a central place in the intervention program framework (Ryckman, 1966).

With cognitive skills, learning and mediational processes, and linguistic abilities being highly relevant to the performance of the child in school, what adverse socioeconomic circumstances seem to do is to increase the discontinuity between skills possessed by the disadvantaged and attentional, cognitive, and linguistic skills requisite to school success. Children, therefore, encounter difficulties in the classroom generating progressive alienation between them and the teacher.

Studies lend ample support to the above contention. In India, at all levels of educational performance, difficulties encountered by the scheduled castes and scheduled tribes in comparison with the general population are reflected in their very low enrollment, irregularity in attendance, high dropout rates, and poor academic records. Specific studies designed for the purpose have demonstrated that the greater the degree of disadvantage, the more inferior the academic performance (Singh, 1980). Even when intelligence is matched, disadvantaged children displayed poorer academic performance. In the United States, it has recently been observed that, although Blacks and Mexican Americans have achieved the largest gain among all SAT takers, a corresponding improvement in their college performance has not taken place (Educational Testing Service [ETS], 1988, p. 2).

Family and social factors are significant in this regard. The family education index for scheduled castes and scheduled tribe groups with poor academic attainment was lowest, and their parents had the lowest aspiration for their children (Rath et al., 1979). Among the disadvantaged tribal and nontribal children, a combination of high intelligence and parental support favorably affected academic achievement. Parental support compensated for lower intelligence, offset adverse effects of low socioeconomic status, and encouraged academic achievement (Singh, 1983, p. 9).

Policy implications are obvious. The point of entry for improving the educational attainment of the disadvantaged is the family (see also Kâgitçibaşi, and Kim, in this volume). If, due to sheer poverty, correctives for disrupted homes, separation from parents, and lack of parental support may take long to be effective, the alternative strategy is to provide the child in the school what he or she lacks at home (Singh, 1983). Because, even at a very early age and much before they enter schools, disadvantaged children lack many of the skills essential for success (ETS, 1988, p. 7), intervention has to occur early to constitute an effective "antidote" to deprived circumstances. School "enrichment" has to be supplemented by appropriate intervention at the level of the family to maximize the outcome.

Personality and Motivational Dimensions

A number of studies have demonstrated, although not in unambiguous terms, the association between other indices of poverty and feelings of insecurity, anxiety, rigidity, conformity, emotional instability, mental health difficulties, lower self-image, extroversion, and some personality characteristics (see Sinha, 1976). The impact of sociocultural disadvantage on motivational variables is more marked. Pareek (1970) has elaborated the motivational syndrome induced by poverty. Apart from helplessness and powerlessness, he considers it as a structural component that produces a threefold motivational pattern characterized by low need for achievement, low need for extension (extending the ego to the society or concern for the common welfare of all), and high need for dependency. The latter is expressed in the form of lack of initiative, shifting responsibility to others, excessive fear of failure, seeking favors from superiors, overconformity, and aggressive rejection of authority.

The picture is ambiguous with regard to the need for achievement. But studies conducted in the West (Hess, 1970) and in India (Misra & Tripathi, 1980) have reported low aspirations on the part of the disadvantaged. It is traced to mother-child interaction, which has been described as a socialization of apathy and underachievement. Harsh authoritarianism of parents with emphasis on positive control, emotional and social distancing between themselves and their children, and early relaxation of close parental supervision generating feelings of unworthiness are factors responsible for it. Low aspirations of disadvantaged children seem like nothing else but the internalized projections of similar aspirations of their parents (Rath, 1973).

There is also evidence that typical adaptation techniques, such as time orientation, self-concept, success-failure orientation, reinforcement systems, sense of control over environment, and coping strategies generally, become adversely affected by the conditions of poverty. A negative relationship between deprivation and self-perception has been noted (Misra & Tripathi, 1980). As for time orientation, unlike the middle and upper classes, the poor hardly display a plan of future action and tend to live in the present or have fanciful ideas about the future (Sinha, 1969). An absence of clear-cut time perspective among the poor has been observed (Agarwal & Tripathi, 1980). They are oriented to the past and are vague about the future, displaying an indefinite, unstructured, and diffuse time orientation without consensual markers—a perspective that has little motivational value.

There are differences on incentive systems, reaction to success and failure, locus of control, and coping style generally. For disadvantaged lower-class children, immediate, material, and concrete reinforcers have been found more effective than verbal ones (Sharma, 1986). Analysis of control strategies used revealed that unskilled working-class mothers relied more on physical feedback, preferred control through implied threat, and seldom showed the child how to do various tasks (Hess, 1970). Lower-class Black and White children displayed significant improvement in performance under praise and approval rather than disapproval (Rosenham, 1966).

Rotter's concept of locus of control has frequently been studied with respect to various castes in India. The disadvantaged tend to display a passive orientation and are more inclined to believe that external forces exclusively control the rewards that they receive. On the other hand, high-caste, advantaged children tend to be more internal (Das & Panda, 1971). In fact, analysis of reactions to success and failure of underprivileged university students has revealed that there is a strong tendency in them to refer success to external "uncontrollable" factors as God, luck, and teacher's kindness, and not to "controllable" factors like one's own effort, thereby failing to take adequate pride in accomplishments that would have a reinforcing effect. This appeal to externality produces a fatalistic outlook and superstitious ritualism, that is, performing some rites before undertaking a big task. Whereas success was externalized, failure was often attributed to oneself. With an unfavorable self-concept and a stringent standard for evaluating one's performance, students' self-image was lowered and their feelings of personal inadequacy were accentuated. They had, in fact, built a mechanism of self-discouragement that was entirely dysfunctional (Sinha, 1980).

The findings indicate that through parent-child interaction and socialization, the disadvantaged develop a pattern of motivation and coping style that is not functional to meet the demands of school settings and various life situations. Because a large part of this mechanism is learned in the family, intervention has to be focused on the family of the disadvantaged child (see Kâgitçibaşi, this volume). As many of the processes are learned early, the action program for development of effective coping strategies has to be forged in family situations before children enter schools.

Rosenthal-Type Studies on Poverty

Rosenthal and Jacobson (1968) have suggested the possibility of the operation of a "Pygmalion effect" or "self-fulfilling prophesy" in the classroom so far as the poor and disadvantaged students are concerned. The teacher quite frequently regards those belonging to disadvantaged groups as possessing lower abilities. Students then perform poorly in examinations (Rath et al., 1979, pp. 93-96). Because teachers' expectations are to a large extent formed on the basis of social factors like class (Dusek & Joseph, 1983) and caste (Sharma & Tripathi, 1988), and because teachers mostly belong to the middle-class and upper castes, their expectations have serious implications for the academic performance of disadvantaged pupils. The essence of the position is that teachers get less from the disadvantaged because they expect less.

One can only guess about how the mechanism of expectation operates in influencing academic performance. It may affect the amount of attention and time that the pupil receives from the teacher; or, through nonverbal cues, the teacher may encourage or dampen the enthusiasm and motivation of the disadvantaged student. It is also possible that the phenomenon may influence the social-emotional climate of the institution, which has a very powerful impact on school performance.

These findings have definite policy implications. Because poor academic performance by disadvantaged students can be ascribed at least partly to the kind of expectations the teachers entertain about them (Panda & Behera, 1985; Rosenthal & Jacobson, 1968), the place of intervention is on the attitudinal plane. If teachers are, during the period of their training, made aware of how the poor performance of disadvantaged students is a demonstration of "self-fulfilling prophesies," and how one has to guard against this *unintentional* bias, it is likely to counteract the adverse influence and help improve academic behavior of pupils from disadvantaged groups.

Attributional Studies

The search for causal explanations of social and natural events is an indispensable part of the human thinking process. Weiner's (1986) conceptualization of attribution behavior has influenced many studies on poverty. He suggests that causal attributions of success and failure significantly influence self-esteem and future expectations, and that success is generally attributed to internal, and failure to external, causes. The nature of causal attribution shows interesting cross-cultural as well as ethnic and social class variations. It has generally been observed that Whites judge internal causes to be more important than external in the case of success and take greater credit for success. They attributed failure to external causes like luck and chance. On the other hand, Asians and Blacks attributed success to external causes but assumed more personal responsibility for failure (Friend & Neale, 1972; Fry & Ghosh, 1980). Analysis of causal attribution of poverty in general revealed that low-income respondents attributed success more to fate and luck than high-income people. This tendency acts as an impediment in successfully meeting the challenges of various life situations.

Further, the success of students identified as "good" and "bright" was attributed by the teachers to family, ability, and effort, and failure to chance and nature of the task. But, for those considered as "not good," failure was ascribed to their family, ability, and effort. When a student's performance was not in congruence with teacher's expectations, more attribution was made to external categories (Sharma & Tripathi, 1988). It is highly probable that teachers' attributions (both with regard to the advantaged and disadvantaged) are somehow communicated to the students so that there is often a high congruence between teachers' attributions and those of the students. It is obvious that attributions help in improving the performance of higher-class, advantaged students but prove detrimental to the performance of the disadvantaged. Thus any intervention program aimed at improving the performance of students coming from disadvantaged circumstances should aim at developing strategies to modify attributions made by teachers and students.

Attributional analysis has its practical utility. There is evidence to suggest that attributional dimensions of locus of control, controllability, and stability are linked with important properties of behavior (Hewstone, 1983) in that they are systematically related to affective reactions and future expectations. Internal (ability) attributions are related to expectations, persistence, and other aspects of achievement behavior. Because attributions made by the disadvantaged involve cognitions, they are more flexible and manipulable; there is greater possibility of changing them as compared with personality traits (Misra & Jain, 1988).

Attributional analysis is relevant in yet another way. Experience with poverty eradication programs, especially in India, has revealed that they have underplayed or missed altogether the subjective reconstruction of poverty by people that helps them to maintain feelings of self-worth along with a sense of control over their lives (Y. Sinha, 1988). The meaning thus construed by the person has behavioral implications, which, in turn, influence the extent of participation in, and the efficacy of, antipoverty programs. The type of attributions of achievement usually made by the disadvantaged subjects, that is, failure is due to lack of ability and effort (internal factors) and success due to fate, chance, or God's will, generate an attitude of dependency on some external agency (government or private). This dependency must be eliminated or at least reduced, and achievement (in this case, development) must be regarded as a result of one's effort and ability (internal attribution). With this pattern of attributions, the process of poverty eradication has a greater chance of being self-generating and self-sustaining. A suitable strategy, therefore, has to be worked out to bring about the necessary cognitive transformation in attributions that reduces dependency and generates initiative and independence in people.

Attributional analysis can also be used to monitor and evaluate poverty alleviation programs. As it is implied that an individual or a group can successfully develop out of poverty if success is attributed to internal causes like personal endeavor, effort, and hard work, periodic analysis of attributions made by the beneficiary groups would be an index of whether the development programs are inducing the appropriate kind of psychological transformation in the people. If development continues to remain "externalized" in the minds of the people, sooner or later it is bound to run into difficulties.

SOME INTERVENTION PROGRAMS

The United States

Studies conducted in different parts of the world indicate that, as a result of being disadvantaged, children have acquired such cognitive and linguistic skills and patterns of motivation that, when they first arrive at school, they already have certain limitations for pursuing school programs successfully. Therefore, if education is to be an equalizer and a factor to help disadvantaged children to grow out of poverty, intervention has to be made before they enter school. Encouraged by the initial success of many small-scale compensatory educational projects in the early 1960s, an elaborate and ambitious intervention program called Operation Head Start was started by the federal government. It was an eight-week program at 2,500 child centers involving over half a million children. Its goal was to equip economically deprived children with skills that they would need when they entered public school. Although there were variations, most of the programs emphasized all aspects of the child's early development. In addition to educationally oriented activities, health and nutritional requirements and emotional and social concerns were considered. Some programs focused only on the schools, others were home based, and some were a combination of the two.

Evaluations of the program consistently showed that children made significant gains in IQ, vocabulary, and school readiness skills such as understanding letters, numbers, and concepts. The gains were large, especially among children with initially low IQ. A disturbing finding, however, was that the early benefits were deceptive in that short-term gains tended to fade out during elementary school years. Little long-term good could be evidenced unless a high-quality educational environment was maintained.

To reexamine the effectiveness of the programs of the 1960s, a consortium of 11 investigators from different parts of the country was formed in 1976. Follow-up data were gathered on those who had participated in programs and who were then 10 to 17 years old, more than 90% being Black from low-income families. Comparison with matched control groups revealed that they had fulfilled the achievement requirements of their schools. They less often repeated a grade or were assigned to a special class for slow learners. They performed better on reading, mathematics, and intelligence tests. They more often completed high school and were more likely to be employed thereafter. Preschool also had some desirable noncognitive outcomes. Mothers' aspirations for their children were raised relative to the children's own aspirations. They were more likely to give achievement-related reasons for being proud of themselves. They rated themselves as better students than their peers and tended to have more realistic vocational aspirations (Lazar & Darlington, 1979, p. 14). The general conclusion was that "children who participated in preschool intervention programs were more likely than control children to meet at least the minimal standards of their schools" (p. 8). Rather than entertaining early disillusionment with the project, the findings suggested that carefully designed early education programs can produce lasting benefits for economically disadvantaged children and can be a powerful factor in their development out of poverty (Lazar & Darlington, 1982).

Latin America

A World Bank review of 15 projects mostly from Latin America, with emphasis on one of the three aspects of service delivery, caregiver education, and community development, revealed that the effect of the intervention on psychosocial development was positive. When compared with children outside the project, those who participated tended to become "more alert," sociable, and curious. There was evidence that those from lower-income and marginal families benefited more, cognitively and socially, than their more privileged peers, and that supplementary nutrition was effective in motivating school attendance (Myers & Hertenberg, 1987, p. 36). Though no attempt was made to look at long-term effects, the evaluations supported the contention of Halpern and Myers (1985, p. 28) that early childhood intervention yields a picture of modest positive effects on initial adjustment to the demands of primary school. Particular factors enhancing this adjustment appeared to be some combination of earlier age of enrollment, improved school readiness, and improved health and energy levels.

A program of intervention through infant stimulation conceived on a national scale for the systematic development of human intelligence was organized by the government in Venezuela from 1979 to 1983. Its main constituents were (a) the "Learning to Think" project, directed mainly at primary school students; (b) the "Instrumental Achievement" project, aimed at increasing the levels of cognitive development and hence the capacity for learning and school achievement among socioculturally underprivileged children; (c) "Project Chess," aimed at developing a problem-solving way of thinking among schoolchildren; and (d) the "Family Project," directed at children from 0 to 6 years and their families. The last project, which was the largest, consisted of a program of integral stimulation for the development of the child in which audiovisual and printed materials were used on 150,000 mothers conveying information on how to attain optimal development of the newborn and how to stimulate speech and different sensory processes.

The program has been received with different degrees of enthusiasm, approval, humor, skepticism, and downright rejection. The main objection to it has been that it did not give sufficient importance to structural variables like living conditions and health (Salazar, 1989). The program operated in a political context and was discontinued with a change in the government. Due to its political overtones, no objective evaluation of its effectiveness has come forth. However, it constitutes an important step in the development of intelligence and cognitive skills by providing enrichment to millions of underprivileged children and bringing them to the level of the rest of the children. It is an important and unique attempt to use psychological technology for accomplishing national goals of human development in a developing country (Salazar, 1984, p. 121).

India

Facing widespread poverty, it is not surprising that the main thrust, especially of the recent five-year national plans, has been the eradication of poverty. Because the main concern has been with disadvantaged children, some details of the Integrated Child Development Services (ICDS) in India will be discussed as another intervention program of enrichment and infant stimulation conceived on a national scale.

ICDS is a massive intervention program concerned with urgent nutritional, health, and other developmental problems faced by the Indian child. It has been conceived to provide adequate services both before and after birth and through the period of growth to ensure children's full physical, mental, and social development. Apart from improving health and nutritional status of children in the age group 0 to 6 years, it aims to lay the foundation for proper psychological, physical, and social development; to reduce the incidence of mortality, morbidity, malnutrition, and school dropout; and to enhance the capability of the mother to look after normal health and nutritional needs through proper nutrition and health education. This package of early childhood services is delivered through *aganwadi* (a grass-roots institution organized in the village or the city), which acts as a focal point for delivery of child development services such as immunization, health checkup, referral, supplementary nutrition, nutrition and health education for expectant mothers, nonformal preschool education, and water and sanitation services. Because women have a key role in the development and welfare of the child, expectant and nursing mothers as well as other women have been brought into the scheme.

Independent evaluations sponsored by UNICEF (Krishnamurthy & Nadkarni, 1983) have shown that it has been making a dramatic impact on malnutrition, infant mortality and morbidity, immunization coverage, school enrollment, and reduction in school dropout rate. From a small beginning, the ICDS now involves more than 200,000 people in 1,738 centrally sponsored and 136 state-sponsored projects, each covering about 18,000 children and 2,000 pregnant and nursing mothers. The focus is mainly on nutrition and health aspects. Psychological facets have so far been neglected mainly due to resource constraints. But it is a colossal intervention program calculated to encourage the development of disadvantaged and underprivileged children so that they are able to combat the situation of poverty.

EPILOGUE

Research on the psychological impact of poverty and its associated variables has considerably enhanced our general understanding of the concomitants of poverty. A general point that emerges is that the detrimental effects of poverty on academic achievement are mediated by a number of intervening processes that are generated on the cognitive, motivational, social, and family planes. These adverse effects are accentuated in the unfavorable proximal environment of the child in which the place of the family is vital. Therefore, intervention strategies have to be targeted not only on specific cognitive, linguistic, or motivational drawbacks but also on the family setting of the disadvantaged if maximal outcome is desired. To ensure that the gains of the intervention are lasting, improvements in the family setting and the educational environment of the child have to be enduring.

What poverty seems to do is not to adversely affect the basic abilities and intelligence but rather to arrest greatly the acquisition of certain skills that are relevant to proper functioning in school. Therefore, interventions have to be directed at the removal of these learning disabilities and incompetencies. What the disadvantaged child lacks in his or her learning environment has to be provided either by the enrichment of the environment or the school setting.

In general, findings indicate that the deficiencies generated due to the circumstances of poverty are not irreversible. It should, however, be noted that no less than 33% of the scholastic attainment profile of children is already decided when they start the first year of primary school (Bloom, 1964); Therefore, appropriate action has to be taken early in order to attenuate most of the effects of disadvantage.

In conclusion, the findings indicate that the psychological damage caused by acute malnutrition and disadvantaged circumstances can be largely counteracted provided that remedial action is taken early and provided that the improved environment is an enduring one. If proper intervention is made at the appropriate time, the disadvantaged child need not remain in the condition of poverty but can acquire appropriate cognitive, linguistic, and other skills to develop out of it.

REFERENCES

Agarwal, K. N., Agarwal, D. K., & Upadhyay, S. K. (1988). Malnutrition and mental functions in school children. In K. N. Agarwal & B. D. Bhatia (Eds.), *Update growth.* Varanasi: Institute of Medical Sciences, Department of Pediatrics.

Agarwal, A., & Tripathi, K. K. (1980). Temporal orientation and deprivation. *Journal of Psychological Researches, 24,* 144-152.

Bernstein, B. (1973). *Class, code and control: Vol. 2. Applied studies towards sociology of language.* London: Routledge & Kegan Paul.

Bhogle, S. (1979). Effects of supplementary food on motor development of rural infants. *Social Change, 9,* 18-22.

Bloom, B. (1964). *Stability and change in human characteristics.* New York: John Wiley.

Chazen, M., Laing, A., Cox, T., & Jackson, S. (1977). Development of children from deprived home background. In *Studies in infant school children: Vol. 2. Deprivation and development.* New York: Basil Blackwell.

Das, U. C., & Panda, K. C. (1971). *Effects of certain non-intellective variables on cognitive performance.* Unpublished manuscript, Regional College of Education, Bhubaneshwar.

Dasen, P. R., & Colomb, E. (1982). The use of Piagetian original scales in the assessment of the impact of malnutrition on cognitive development. In R. Rajalakshmi (Ed.), *Nutrition and development of the child.* Baroda, India: M. S. University, Biochemistry Development.

Dusek, J. B., & Joseph, G. (1983). The base of teacher expectancies: A meta analysis. *Journal of Educational Psychology, 75,* 327-346.

Educational Testing Service. (1988). Minority students in higher education. *Focus* (Princeton, NJ: ETS), *22.*

Friend, R. M., & Neale, J. M. (1972). Children's perceptions of success and failure: An attributional analysis of the effects of race and social class. *Developmental Psychology, 2,* 124-128.

Fry, P. S., & Ghosh, R. (1980). Attribution of success and failure: Comparison of cultural differences between Asian and Caucasian children. *Journal of Cross-Cultural Psychology, 11,* 343-346.

Galler, J. R., Ramsey, F. Solimano, G., & Lowell, W. E. (1983). The influence of early malnutrition on subsequent behavioral development, I. Degree of impairment in intellectual performance. *Journal of American Academy of Child Psychology, 22,* 8-15.

Halpern, R., & Myers, R. (1985). *Effects of early childhood intervention on primary school progress and performance in the developing countries* (mimeo). Ypsilanti, Michigan: High/Scope Educational Research Foundation.

Hess, R. D. (1970). The transmission of cognitive strategies in the poor: The socialization of apathy and under-achievement. In V. L. Allen (Ed.), *Psychological factors in poverty.* New York: Academic Press.

Hewstone, M. E. (1983). *Attribution theory: Social and functional extensions.* London: Basil Blackwell.

Klein, R. E., Freeman, H. E., Kagan, J., Yarbrough, C., & Habicht, J. P. (1972). Is big smart? The relation of growth to cognition. *Journal of Health & Social Behavior, 13,* 219-225.

Krishnamurthy, K. G., & Nadkarni, M. V. (1983). *Integrated child developments services: An assessment.* New Delhi: UNICEF Regional Office for South Central Asia.

Lazar, I., & Darlington, R. (1979). *Lasting effects after preschool: Summary report* (A report of the Consortium for Longitudinal Studies). Washington, DC: U.S. Department of Health & Human Services, Office of Human Development Families.

Lazar, I., & Darlington, R. (1982). Lasting effects of early education: A report from the Consortium of Longitudinal Studies. *Monograph of the Society for Research in Child Development, 47*(2-3, Serial No. 195).

Lien, N. M., Meyer, K., & Winick, M. (1977). Early malnutrition and later adoption into American families. *American Journal of Clinical Nutrition, 30,* 1734-1739.

Mishra, R. C. (1987, December 25-27). *Cognitive stimulation, training and perceptual-cognitive task performance by socially deprived children.* Paper presented to the U.G.C. National Seminar, "Strategies for the Development of Deprived Sections of Indian Society," Department of Psychology, M.K.P. (P.G.) College, Dehradun.

Misra, G., & Jain, U. (1988). Achievement cognitions in deprived groups: An attributional analysis. *Indian Journal of Current Psychological Research, 1*(2), 77-88.

Misra, G., & Tripathi, L. B. (1980). *Psychological consequences of prolonged deprivation.* Agra, India: National Psychological Corporation.

Murlidharan, R., & Kaur, B. (1987). A study of the relationship between physical development and language and cognitive development of tribal preschool children. *Bombay Psychologist, 9*(1/2), 7-17.

Myers, R., & Hertenberg, R. (1987). *The eleven who survive: Toward a re-examination of early childhood development program options and costs.* Washington, DC: World Bank, Education & Training Development.

Panda, K. C., & Behera, H. P. (1985). Perceived attitude of parents and teachers towards exceptional children. *Journal of Orissa Association of Educational Science and Research, 2,* 6-18.

Panda, K. C., & Das, J. P. (1970). Acquisition and reversal in four subcultural groups generated by caste and class. *Canadian Journal of Behavioral Science, 2,* 267-273.

Pareek, U. (1970). Poverty and motivation: Figure and ground. In V. L. Allen (Ed.), *Psychological factors in poverty.* New York: Academic Press.

Rao, S. N. (1977). *Concept development in children* (Monograph I). Tirupathi, India: Sri Venkateswara University.

Rath, R. (1973, December 27-29). *Teaching and learning problem of primary school children: A challenge to Indian psychologists and educationists.* Presidential address, 14th Annual Conference of the Indian Academy of Applied Psychology, University of Calcutta.

Rath, R., Dash, A. S., &.Dash, U. N. (1979). *Cognitive abilities and school achievements of the socially disadvantaged children in primary schools.* Bombay: Allied Publishers.

Ricciuti, H. N. (1977). Adverse social and biological influences on early development. In H. McGurk et al. (Eds.), *Ecological factors in human development.* Amsterdam: North-Holland.

Ricciuti, H. N. (1980, May 5-7). *Effects of adverse environmental and nutritional influences on mental development.* A working paper prepared for P.A.H.O. Conference.

Ricciuti, H. N. (1981). Developmental consequences of malnutrition in early childhood. In M. Lewis & L. Rosenblum (Eds.), *The uncommon child: The genesis of behavior* (Vol. 3). New York: Plenum.

Richardson, S. A. (1976). The relation of severe malnutrition in infancy to intelligence of school children with differing life histories. *Pediatric Research, 10,* 57-61.

Rosenham, D. L. (1966). Effects of social class and race on responsiveness to approval and disapproval. *Journal of Personality & Social Psychology, 4,* 253-259.

Rosenthal, R., & Jacobson, L. (1968). *Pygmalion in the classroom.* New York: Holt, Rinehart & Winston.

Ryckman, D. B. (1966). *Psychological processes of disadvantaged children.* Unpublished doctoral dissertation, University of Illinois. (University Microfilms No. 66-12, 417)

Sahu, S., & Mahanta, J. (1977). Socio-cultural factors, intelligence and mediational abilities. *Indian Journal of Psychology, 52,* 164-168.

Salazar, J. M. (1984). The use and impact of psychology in Venezuela: Two examples. *International Journal of Psychology, 19*(1/2), 113-122.

Salazar, J. M. (1989). Psychology and social change in Latin America. *Psychology & Developing Societies, 1*(1), 91-104.

Sharma, M. (1986). The effects of types of reward on performance of deprived and non-deprived children. *Journal of Psychological Researches, 30*(1), 40-44.

Sharma, R., & Tripathi, R. C. (1988). Teachers' expectations and attributions: The self-fulfilling prophesy cycle. In A. K. Dalal (Ed.), *Attribution theory and research* (pp. 33-59). New Delhi: Wiley Eastern.

Singh, A. (1987). *Certain deprivational factors in language development in children.* Unpublished doctoral dissertation, University of Allahabad, Allahabad, India.

Singh, A. K. (1976). *Social disadvantage, intelligence and scholastic achievement* (Report on the Developmental Norms Project). New Delhi: NCERT.

Singh, A. K. (1980). Social disadvantage and academic achievement. *Social Change, 10,* 15-18.

Singh, A. K. (1983). Parental support and scholastic achievement. *Social Change, 13*(1), 9-14.

Sinha, D. (1969). *Motivation of rural population in a developing country.* Bombay: Allied Publishers.

Sinha, D. (1976). Study of psychological dimensions of poverty: A challenge and necessity. *Journal of Social & Economic Studies, 4*(1), 167-220.

Sinha, D. (1977). Some social disadvantage and development of certain perceptual skills. *Indian Journal of Psychology, 52,* 115-132.

Sinha, D. (1980). Some cognitive and motivational concomitants of poverty. *Social Change, 10,* 3-8.

Sinha, Y. (1988). Subjective explanations of poverty. In A. K. Dalal (Ed.), *Attribution theory and research* (pp. 115-128). New Delhi: Wiley Eastern.

Suresh, J. (1984). *Language socialization of scheduled caste children in India.* Paper presented at the National Seminar on Psycholinguistics in a Multi-Lingual Society, Centre of Advanced Study in Psychology, Utkal University, Bhubaneshwar, India.

Vazir, S., Bhogle, S., & Naidu, N. (1988). Influence of psycho-social factors on the nutritional status of preschool children. *Journal of the Indian Academy of Applied Psychology, 14,* 1-8.

Weiner, B. (1986). *An attribution of motivation and emotion.* London: Springer-Verlag.

Werner, E., & Murlidharan, R. (1970). Nutrition, cognitive status and achievement motivation of New Delhi nursery school children. *Journal of Cross-Cultural Psychology, 3,* 271-181.

Whiteman, M., & Deutsch, M. (1968). Social disadvantage as related to intellective and language development. In M. Deutsch, I. Katz, & A. R. Jensen (Eds.), *Social class, race, and psychological development.* New York: Holt, Rinehart & Winston.

5

CROSS-CULTURAL PSYCHOLOGY AND THE FORMAL CLASSROOM

KENNETH CUSHNER

Psychology has had more influence on our understanding of the social nature of the school than any other discipline in the behavioral and social sciences. It has helped us to understand such processes as stereotyping, attitude formation and attitude change, in-group and out-group formation, and intergroup interactions. Cross-cultural psychology is becoming increasingly relevant today as, more than ever before, many nations of the world face increasing cultural, ethnic, and social diversity. At the same time, these nations seek to prepare their citizens for an interdependent, global society. The latter becomes essential not only to those in nations composed of diverse populations, but in predominantly homogeneous nations as well, as they emerge as participants in a global society.

It is the premise of this chapter that the primary objective of school success for all is rarely achieved because teachers, curriculum writers, administrators, and institutions do not consider the cross-cultural context in which teaching and learning occurs. Appropriate programs and curricula can and have been designed for schools confronting issues related to cultural and ethnic diversity as well as for those wishing to address the present and future needs of an interdependent world. This chapter, although of general interest to the student of cross-cultural psychology, speaks also to teachers, school administrators, and curriculum developers confronting such issues. It focuses on the applications of cross-cultural psychology and training to the improvement of educational achievement and interactions in the formal educational context by looking at three specific areas: (a) the teaching and learning process that occurs as teachers and students of different backgrounds come together; (b) the relationship that exists between schooling and cognition; and (c) the curricular implications for preparing people to live and work in a growing international and interdependent world.

The past 20 years have seen tremendous diversification of students in the public schools in the United States as well as in many other nations of the world. In 1976, 24% of the total student enrollment in U.S. schools was non-White. By 1984, this figure jumped to 29% (Center for Education Statistics [CES], 1987). It is projected that, by the year 2000, 30%-40% of students in schools across the United States will be those traditionally considered as cultural or ethnic minorities.

Britain, too, as another example, has experienced tremendous diversification in population makeup. Success of schoolchildren from Caribbean and South Asian origins has been the focus of considerable concern and research. In schools across Britain, 25% of all children would be expected to be in the top quartile in mathematics, English, and verbal reasoning at the end of their primary education. Among Black children fully educated in the United Kingdom, roughly half the expected number, or 12%-13%, actually achieved this level of school success (Mabey, 1981). Certainly all do not achieve equally in the school setting.

Accompanying cultural and ethnic diversity is the increasing number of children entering school from minority language backgrounds who have little or no competence in the language used in the school. While Spanish is the predominant first language of many children in the United States, an increasing number of students are entering the schools speaking such languages as Arabic, Chinese, Hmong, Khmer, Lao, Thai, and Vietnamese.

This trend, too, appears to be similar in many nations of the world, including Great Britain, France, the Netherlands, Australia, Canada, and Israel. Half of Australia's 16 million people, for instance, were themselves born outside the country or have one parent who was. While one-third of Australia's immigrants are from England or Ireland, two-thirds represent various Eastern European countries, Greece (Melbourne boasts the second largest Greek community in the world, surpassed only by Athens), Italy, Spain, Malta, Yugoslavia, Turkey, Southeast Asia, and Central and South America. In Australia, one person in eight cannot speak English.

A disturbing correlate to the increasing student diversity is the relative homogeneity of most national teaching forces. In the United States, 88% of the teaching force is Anglo and Caucasian; 67%-68% is female (CES, 1987). It is projected that, well into the next century, new teachers in the United States will increasingly be female and White. As a result, certain populations in the schools are missing important role models due to the relative paucity of cultural and ethnic representation in the teaching force. Of equal concern is the fact that most teachers have little experience with members of other cultural backgrounds, thereby hindering their ability to understand, learn, and perhaps effectively teach those who are different from themselves.

Whether we like it or not, educators will be faced with individuals who display a range of attitudes, values, behaviors, and linguistic backgrounds that cannot be ignored. It is suggested that, as people can learn to be bilingual and function effectively in two languages (or become multilingual for that matter), so, too, can people become bicultural or multicultural and learn to function effectively in diverse cultural settings. Cross-cultural psychology can help us look both for universals as well as culture-specific aspects in learning processes, cognitive development, and intercultural interaction.

Differentiating Formal from Informal Learning Environments

The moment a child enters the world, he or she begins the task of learning the requirements of a particular family, cultural group, and society. Learning in this broad sense occurs in both formal and informal settings.

The differences between formal and informal learning are quite distinct (Scribner & Cole, 1973). Informal learning occurs through such forces as the family, media, peers, and siblings and tends to be integrated throughout one's daily activities. It is characterized by observation and imitation and has little or no explicit curriculum. The responsibility for learning falls mainly on the learner, making it rather personal, with extended family members often playing a critical role in the act of instruction. In informal learning, change, discontinuity, and innovation are highly valued.

Formal education, on the other hand, is set apart from the context of everyday life and is typically carried out in the institution we know as the school. It is characterized by intense verbal interchange (lecture in most contexts and questioning in some) and has an explicit and highly structured curriculum. Teachers are usually responsible for imparting knowledge, resulting in a relatively impersonal relationship between teacher and student. In formal educational contexts, maintenance of continuity and tradition are highly valued. Consider this unique feature of formal learning—material is learned from a book that may or may not be useful at a later time. In no other situation is this demand made upon people.

An Historical Context

According to the Laboratory of Comparative Human Cognition (1986), cross-cultural psychology has influenced formal education through three distinct periods during the past 40-45 years. During the first 10-15 years, Euro-American practices in education and cross-cultural psychology were "simply transferred wholesale to other cultures" (Laboratory of Comparative Human Cognition, 1986, p. 1050). The European or Western model of the school, with all its Western ideals and methodologies, was simply copied and rebuilt elsewhere in the world, bringing with it its standard curricula and texts. Educational practices were merely transferred lock, stock, and barrel. This included the use of instructional material and processes that did not consider specific context or culture of origin. Further, methods of psychological testing (see the chapter by Lonner) and decision-making processes concerning the evaluation of material (content) to be taught were imposed on other cultures.

The middle 10-15 years found researchers seeking to identify culture-specific barriers to school success while attempting to understand cognitive processes across cultures. This led to considerable analysis of cognitive development and cognitive style across cultures. Numerous major achievements occurred at this stage. It was recognized that studies of culture and cognition must consider the local framework, both psychological and ecological. Multidisciplinary methodologies, it was found, must be employed when seeking insight into specific problems or conditions (i.e., Was poor school performance the result of delayed development and cultural deprivation or of cultural differences and weak teaching methodology?). The realization that the act of schooling is a distinct form of cultural practice was advanced, that is, that schooling itself demands and brings about unique forms of cognitive processing with, perhaps, limited generalizability to nonschool settings. In other words, there may exist a culture of the school that is consistent across national boundaries.

Currently, we are in a phase whereby knowledge gained from earlier cross-cultural research and curricular innovations can be applied as practical solutions to educational problems faced in a variety of contexts. That is, educators can become culture sensitive in their approach to teaching and learning; sensitive not to the extent that the focus of their teaching is on cultural content (as is the ethnic emphasis so common to many multicultural education efforts) but in that consideration be given to the more subtle, subjective aspects of culture that affect instructional interaction and learning (see Sinha, this volume).

The concept of culture shock may shed some light on this situation. People adjusting to new cultures and different environments call upon a wide range of strategies in their attempts to make sense out of, and work within, a new setting. One characteristic of individuals successfully able to make changes and accommodate diversity is that they can tolerate a certain amount of ambiguity while maintaining a certain degree of flexibility. When individuals can modify their behavior, orientation, or perspective while experiencing a change, the chance of successful adaptation and task effectiveness is increased (Brislin, Cushner, Cherrie, & Yong, 1986). Those unable to make the necessary adjustments become debilitated and stressed and are generally unable to function smoothly or attain their goals. A similar situation can be found at the institutional level, except it is often more difficult to change the system.

Culture shock implies a disorientation that occurs whenever an individual moves from his or her immediate, known, comfortable surroundings to an environment that is substantially different. A significant number of children from many backgrounds experience the equivalent of culture shock when they enter the classroom from a home or social environment that is different from that of the school. For instance, some children grow up in a home environment that demands young people listen to and do not question the authority of the father with regard to social issues. Teachers, however, often demand that children discuss their views openly with other students and adults. Incongruencies such as this can be quite disconcerting to young people. An added difficulty these children face is that they have entered an institution that itself is highly resistant to change, relatively inflexible in its approach to differences, and subsequently discriminating in its actions.

INDIVIDUAL LEARNING STYLES IN
THE SCHOOL CONTEXT

Students of psychology have long studied the relationship between a given stimulus and an organism's response. Two general approaches have emerged: the stimulus-response (S-R) and the stimulus-organism-response (S-O-R) models. The S-R model suggests that behavior is best predicted by studying the functional relationships between stimuli and responses. The S-O-R model suggests that relationships between stimuli and responses are best predicted from information about the mediating processes that occur within an organism. Learning style, proposed as one such mediating process, is seen as individual variations in how people perceive, think, solve problems, learn, and absorb and retain information and/or skills.

Kolb (1976) suggests there are four preferred learning styles, which can be applied to an experiential learning cycle (see discussion by

Bhawuk in this volume). Hughes-Weiner (1986) relates the phases of this cycle to learning in an intercultural context. One preferred mode of learning, *concrete experience,* refers to the experiences people bring with them from the "real world." People from different cultures are likely to have different background experiences and may, therefore, vary in their readiness for academic learning. *Reflective observation,* a second preference, involves perception of and response to information. Because of different behavior patterns, socialization demands, and institutional experiences, people from different societies are likely to make different assumptions about what is true and thereby acquire different bodies of knowledge. A third preference, *abstract conceptualization,* includes the formation of concepts and generalizations based on the inferences people make about distinct pieces of information. People oftentimes have different cognitive frameworks and as such may focus on irrelevant information and make incorrect interpretations in a given situation. *Active experimentation,* a final preference, includes learning through practical manipulation of concrete objects or interaction with people. Behavioral differences in cross-cultural contexts may result in misinterpretations and misattributions as to the meaning of particular acts, thus causing confusion and frustration (see Triandis, this volume).

Considerable differences in learning styles, evident in individuals' needs for quiet or sound, in seating arrangements, mobility preferences, desired temperature, degree and kind of structure required, motivation, and in conformity versus nonconformity have been identified across cultural groups. Jalali (1989) compared the learning characteristics of 300 culturally different fourth, fifth, and sixth graders. She found distinct differences in the learning styles of Afro-, Chinese-, Greek-, and Mexican-Americans. Afro-Americans preferred quiet, warmth, bright light, mobility, routine and patterns, frequent feedback from an authority figure, kinesthetic (action-oriented) instructional experiences, and afternoon or evening learning sessions rather than morning. Chinese-Americans preferred sound, bright light, morning, variety (rather than routines), and peer learning. Greek-Americans preferred learning alone, mobility, variety, and auditory instructions. Mexican-Americans preferred low light, structure, learning alone, tactile and visual instruction, and feedback from an authority figure.

Some propose that the closer the match between a student's learning style and the accompanying instructional style of the teacher, the greater the student's success in school. Hilliard (1976) identified distinct school-related behaviors displayed by students identified as analytical learners and by those considered to be relational learners. Students whose strengths lie in the analytical are more stimulus centered and parts specific, can extract information embedded in text, can find linear relationships rather easily, have long attention and concentration spans, and have greater perceptual vigilance. Students whose preference is relational work to find special or personal relevance in content; are more global in focus; find meaning in text; have greater difficulty finding direct, linear relationships; are emotional; have short attention and concentration spans; and exhibit strong, emotional expressions.

Schools stress the memorization of specific facts, demand a logical and linear approach, emphasize the cognitive domain, are highly scheduled, and are task and rule oriented. Analytical thinkers tend to be rewarded in the school context. Chiu (1985), studying the relationship between learning style, academic achievement, and emotional responsiveness in 50 analytic and 50 nonanalytic Chinese fourth and fifth graders living in Taiwan, found that academic achievement of analytic students was significantly higher than that of nonanalytic students. At the same time, nonanalytic students scored higher on measures of anxiety than did their analytic counterparts. These finding are consistent with observations made in American culture among both White and Black populations (Kagan, Moss, & Sigel, 1973) as well as among students in India (Sharma & Tripathi, 1982). Students displaying relational traits tend not to be reinforced in the school culture and may suffer as a result.

The Culture of the School

The school, as any other institution or organization, has a culture of its own. The roots of Western education can be found in the Greek tradition. In order to succeed in the school context, one must learn to think and communicate by understanding and using words and symbols that have been collected from chosen bodies of previously agreed-upon knowledge. There is nothing innately correct or best about this system; it has merely been found to be a convenient method for carrying out a range of complex tasks in our society. The important point is that the particular symbols used, the knowledge made accessible to others, and the preferred method of imparting that knowledge have been agreed upon by the majority of the members of a particular culture; in the case of the United States and Great Britain (and in many other countries)— the dominant White middle class.

Schools tend to be characterized as being decontextualized. That is, they are structured to teach information in a context-free setting. Teachers talk about what is to be learned, generally in the form of statements, deductions, and samples of short segments of the skill or task to be learned. It is assumed that the skills talked about or studied in school will be generalized to other situations and used at a later time. Children thus learn the skill of addition with the assumption that they will later apply it to a variety of settings. This is called out-of-context teaching and learning. For some students, schools function well in translating concepts into later action.

Schools were not originally established to meet the particular needs of the individual. From early on, attempts were made to socialize young people into adult life and the society at large by striving to have the individual "fit" into the group. The primary role of the teacher in this regard was to unify the individual students in the class. To achieve this end, the child must satisfactorily develop loyalties outside the family and transfer some of them to the classroom teacher, thus encouraging independence from the primary family group.

The characteristics that exist within the school are, as in any culture, maintained by teachers who are themselves successfully socialized into the profession. Those children who are socialized by a culture whose values, beliefs, and behaviors are congruent with the culture of the school stand a better chance of success within the system. LeCompte (1980) suggests that there are baseline conditions that reflect the social and structural demands of schools and transcend the idiosyncrasies of individual teachers. Children who are successful in school learn the whole range of tasks presented to them. Others may learn some of what is required, but not all. In essence, there is a culture particular to the school that must be learned and successfully manipulated.

Compared with some cultural and ethnic groups, middle-class Caucasian children are, in many ways, socialized to be ready for school. Certain values articulated by the school, as well as certain skills that are expected for school success, are instilled in the child by the home and family of many middle-class Americans. LeCompte (1980) cites evidence that middle-class children beginning kindergarten have expectations that are congruent with those of the school. Preschool children from middle-class families expect teachers to structure and organize their day, anticipate that they will learn to "work," and assume that teachers will control and discipline the classroom. In other words, young children from middle-class backgrounds are aware of the cognitive and authority demands of school before coming into actual contact with the institution.

The family may also have such an influence on school readiness and achievement that some children can outperform the so-called majority culture. This may help explain the success many Japanese students experience in mathematics when compared with their American counterparts. A longitudinal study of Japanese and American mothers with their preschool children found distinct differences in parental socialization and teaching style practices (Hess et al., 1986). Japanese mothers work with their children to promote the internalization of adult norms and standards, encourage children to emphasize correct procedures in order to understand, and place greater emphasis on persistence and hard work with the idea that the responsibility for achievement lies with the individual. American mothers, on the other hand, promote deference to external authority and direction, are less oriented toward an internal source of achievement, place greater blame on the school for the child's failure, and place more emphasis on the role of parents in school success.

An Example of Culture Clash: Home Versus School

For many, a congruent transition occurs between home and school, thus encouraging academic success. This does not, however, appear to be the same for all groups in a society. Children from many cultural backgrounds may enter the educational process having been socialized in a manner that is in conflict with the expectations of the school. In this regard, schools often fail due to the cultural incompatibility between the culture of the school and the culture of the child.

The cultural incompatibility approach has been the basis of considerable research at the Center for Development of Early Education (formerly the Kamehameha Elementary Education Program—KEEP), a privately funded, multidisciplinary, educational research and development program attempting to remedy academic underachievement of Native Hawaiians (Vogt, Jordan, & Tharp, 1987). As with many other ethnic minorities in American schools, poor school performance among Hawaiians had been attributed by some to a variety of cultural and home deficiencies. This cultural deficit model, implying a superior-inferior dichotomy, is unfounded, unhelpful, and oftentimes rightfully labeled as racist. All neurologically normal children have already learned a substantial amount of relatively complex material that is specific to their culture by the time they are of school age.

Employing a cultural incompatibility model as opposed to a cultural deficit model implies that all children can learn prerequisite skills for any future need, including school readiness, if given the opportunity.

Researchers at Kamehameha schools proposed that a school environment that was compatible with the child's home culture could be developed, and that this culturally compatible classroom would elicit from children those skills, attitudes, and behaviors that would contribute to the desired learning. Children would thus achieve early school success.

Although research findings are numerous and complex (Vogt et al., 1987), some summary can be made here. The Hawaiian family socializes children to be interdependent and to contribute to the overall family group. The sibling care system, whereby children as young as two or three years of age are cared for by older siblings, promotes a high degree of interdependence and responsibility by enabling children to have early experience caring for younger children and carrying out many important family chores. In this social pattern, adults tend to structure their relationships so they can relate to the sibling group as a whole, not to individuals on a one-to-one basis.

Personal independence is not a sought-after goal. Rather, interdependence or a collective orientation develops (see the chapter by Triandis in this volume). This has implications for motivation and instructional strategies as well as for the reward structure in the classroom. For instance, the Hawaiian child may not be motivated by individual rewards (gold stars, grades) to the extent that his or her Caucasian counterpart may be. Nor would he or she desire to achieve independence from the group. In addition, because Hawaiian children learn from peers from an early age and in turn pass on this knowledge to others, they are as comfortable in the role of teacher as in the role of learner.

Certain conditions found in typical classrooms may not be sufficient to elicit and sustain appropriate learning strategies from children of Hawaiian descent. Sibling care and interdependence may diminish the degree of authority a child may give to any one adult. Children are not accustomed to directing all their attention to one adult for a prolonged period of time. They, therefore, may not learn as effectively in the typical teacher-directed classroom. Peer orientation and affiliation, although frowned upon in the traditional classroom, have been found to contribute to school success with Hawaiian children. Learning stations, or cooperative work groups that enable children to assist one another, do facilitate learning.

Another instance where the culture of the child has become the basis for a modified instructional approach can be found in the small group reading lesson. Common to many Hawaiian families is the activity known as "talk-story." This practice typically is carried out by a small group of adults who come together and verbally re-create memories of past events. These group discussion sessions regularly produce verbal patterns of fluid, overlapping speech and complex word usage. The small classroom reading group, restructured in such a manner to reflect the familiar talk-story event, has resulted in reading instruction that is more inviting and encouraging to children. Reading skill and comprehension have improved dramatically since using this approach.

Indications are that, at an early age, modification of instructional practice, classroom organization, and motivation management that takes into consideration the culture of the child make a significant difference in the educational achievement of Hawaiian children. Concern, however, is mounting as a cumulative deterioration has been observed as children progress to grade three. Current research efforts are seeking to explain, and hopefully remedy, this situation. It is quite possible that efforts to involve the child's entire family (see Kâgitçibaşi, this volume) will prove to be a good approach.

Teachers should realize that students bring a variety of motivation, learning styles, and cognitive patterns with them to the classroom. Culture can explain some of the variation; social class can also have an impact. Yet, there may be more within-group differences than between-group differences and educators are warned against making sweeping generalizations.

Research suggests that there are preferred learning styles and particular patterns of behavior among many cultural and ethnic groups that may be in conflict in the traditional school setting. The school tends to encourage certain groups and individuals by catering to certain preferred strengths. This is unfortunate because, as a society, all kinds of thinkers and doers are needed. The school must learn to serve and reinforce a variety of individuals equally well. Although efforts are under way to address this issue (KEEP is one such example), many minority students find difficulty in the standard classroom. Frustrating the situation is the fact that relatively few teachers receive adequate cross-cultural or multicultural preparation in undergraduate training or while on the job. If educational achievement for all is truly the goal, this situation must radically change.

THE RELATIONSHIP BETWEEN
SCHOOLING AND COGNITION

What does it mean to introduce schooling into the daily experience of individuals? What do we know of school's influence on cognitive development? Although there is a lack of empirical research, most studies say there is "something" about schooling that promotes cognitive development or that results in differences in the manner in which people can use their minds. Early studies of human capacity and cognition often reported that nonliterate or semiliterate people were deficient in basic cognitive skills. In other words, cultural differences were thought to be responsible for different cognitive abilities. This does not, however, appear to be the case. The fundamental capacity of individuals to think and reason is not likely to be affected by cultural differences. Increasingly, studies conducted under culturally appropriate conditions suggest that unschooled individuals are capable of rigorous abstract thinking.

Research analyzing the relationship between schooling and cognition has looked at perception, memory, and classification and concept development and has been reviewed by Rogoff (1981). In addition, schooling's impact on cognitive style and information processing has been investigated across cultural groups.

Perception

Studies of perception look at depth perception in two-dimensional pictures, illusions involving perspective cues, and perceptual analysis. Typically, Western graphic conventions are assessed that indicate depth using size, superimposition, overlap, or perspective cues (parallel lines converging in the distance). Generally speaking, schooling seems to have a profound effect on the individual's ability to read depth cues in two-dimensional pictures. Studies in the area of perceptual analysis and discrimination also suggest that schooling may facilitate representational transfer and analytical discrimination of a stimulus. The results are undoubtedly due to extensive practice deriving information from two-dimensional sources (e.g., drawings, photographs, and television images).

Memory

Studies of memory, the deliberate remembering of unrelated bits of information, look specifically at five areas. (1) *Eidetic imagery* assesses visual images that remain after stimulation. Slight, but not significant, differences in favor of nonschooled individuals have been found, probably due to an overdependence on visual memory. (2) *Paired-associate learning* involves a tester providing a stimulus and the subject repeating a learned response. For instance, students learn to associate "food" with "hunger," or "water" with "book." The greatest schooling effect was found when no relationship existed between the words, as in the "water-book" example. That is, nonschooled children were not at a disadvantage when asked to remember related word pairs such as *black-white* or *up-down,* but were at a disadvantage when asked to remember unrelated word pairs such as *foot-tree.* (3) *Free recall* assesses the ability of subjects to repeat a list in any order. Inconsistent results tend to be found with young children and the nonschooled. However, with older students, literacy seems to be an important factor as individuals impose their own order and meaning to the lists. (4) *Serial recall* tests memory span (in everyday terms, how much people can memorize in the order the material was presented) with words or digits. Schooled subjects show greater recall, suggesting they have more strategies to apply to memory tasks. Finally, studies of (5) *recognition memory,* the ability to recognize previously seen patterns in new contexts, seem to report conflicting results.

In summary, there appears to be a general difference in schooled versus nonschooled ability on memory tasks, but, when some organizational strategy is made explicit, the unschooled make use of it. Reported differences may be due to problem-solving strategies, not memory per se, as, once learning is achieved, retention across groups appears to be equal. Scribner and Cole (1973) suggest that, when information is culturally important, memory can be quite impressive. Readers might find it interesting to identify content areas for which they now have seemingly extraordinary memories (e.g., names of high school classmates, books read, TV and movie stars recognizable on sight).

Classification and Concept Development

Classification and concept development studies look at the organization subjects impose on collections of objects. *Classification* refers to the sorting of objects and pictures. Individuals can classify by perceptual categories (color, number, size, or shape), functional relationships (based on being used together), or taxonomic category—the most advanced—which demonstrates some genus-species-type relationship (i.e., classifying house cats, lions, and tigers together because they are all members of the feline family). The preferred dimension used by an individual or group is taken as the level of abstraction of their thinking.

Populations vary in their preferred dimensions of classification as well as the ease with which they change dimensions. Generally, no differences in classification abilities are found when subjects use familiar objects (for instance, Liberians can differentiate more categories of rice than U.S. students but not as many as the U.S. students can with cards). Classification of geometric figures shows that, with increased schooling, subjects tend to sort more by form than by color, are better able to shift dimensions, and can give more reasons for their sorts.

Concept learning is similar to classification tasks in that the subject's use of various dimensions is considered. Concepts learned by color are learned equally well by schooled and nonschooled subjects; those learned by function are typically only accomplished by schooled children. *Free association* refers to the response individuals make with the first word that comes to mind. In the United States, with increasing age and schooling, there is a general shift from syntactic responses (where the response word follows the stimulus word as with *red-house*) to paradigmatic responses (where the response word is in the same grammatical form as the stimulus, as with *red-blue*). This is attributed to an early emphasis on conceptual and associative relationships among words.

In summary, schooled individuals generally classify by taxonomic group rather than function and by form over color. Schooled subjects also find it easier to shift dimensions. The reported differences, however, may be due to understanding the task, identifying two-dimensional stimuli from years of practice looking at printed material, and familiarity with materials rather than a cognitive propensity to classify more in the abstract.

One's cultural background itself, however, may act to predetermine the approach one takes to any given subject matter that may be taught in the schools. Erickson (1986) points out that cultural background and orientation may determine the manner in which a student approaches a given subject—in his case, science. Assumptions about the nature of the world and one's belief in spiritual versus physical control can have a profound effect on how one approaches the study of science.

Yet, certain school experiences have been found to be affecting enough to have similar effect across cultural groups. Tamir (1983), using a cognitive preference inventory with Jewish and Arab Israeli high school biology students, showed similar patterns of relations between cognitive preferences and achievement after completion of an inquiry-based biology curriculum. He concluded that, despite substantial cultural and home differences, the study of an inquiry-oriented biology curriculum had significant effects on cognitive style relating to information processing in both groups. Even when Arab society stresses rote learning and memorization of facts, students who studied inquiry-oriented science became as strongly oriented toward fundamental principles and critical questioning as their Jewish counterparts who came from a different social milieu with less emphasis on rote learning.

As is being recognized, schools and curricular experiences may exert a significant effect not only on achievement but also on cognitive development and cognitive style as related to information processing. Different from most other activities, schooling does tend to emphasize certain cognitive processes that render individuals able to think and manipulate information in a different manner from those who do not have formal educational experience. Schools stress a search for general rules and principles by focusing on classification of knowledge and the use of a formal symbol system. Children are taught to look for rules from which specific instances can be understood and practiced, such as the application of common operations in the immediate environment. Instruction tends to be in the verbal mode, that is, out of context as opposed to learning through informal observation and hands-on participation. Schooling also emphasizes the learning of "scientific concepts" and the scientific method of analysis, which may result in a tendency to reason in a particular manner.

PLANNING TOMORROW:
AN APPROACH TO INTERNATIONAL AND
INTERCULTURAL EDUCATION

An increasing number of theoreticians are suggesting that, if we are ever to live cooperatively with one another, efforts directed at change must focus on young people. It is here that changes in perception, attitude, and behavior have the potential to have the greatest impact upon the future course of the human race. Concepts and processes learned through our investigations in cross-cultural psychology can become the cornerstone for educational efforts to improve people's interactions and ability to work together. Such efforts can be found under the labels of "global education," "international education," "multicultural education," "intercultural education," and the like. All these labels suggest a similarity of purpose. Schools are beginning to recognize the obligation and opportunity they have to effect change in people's knowledge, attitudes, and behavior about others and their world. That is, schools can become social reconstructionist on a global scale.

Before looking closely at curriculum efforts, a brief overview of an education that is international or intercultural in scope is in order. Hoopes (1980) viewed the world community as being divided into three distinct social groupings. At one level are found local-traditional communities, those societies that require minimal interaction with others in order to satisfy their needs. Few of these communities exist today, but it can be assumed that many have existed in the past. At the next level, the national-modern level, people have the need for services, goods, and knowledge that can only be obtained from others. Finally, the global-postmodern level reflects the situation many find themselves in today. People and nations are so inextricably bound that mere survival becomes dependent upon the smooth, interdependent functioning of the many governments, economies, and technologies.

Many agree that a critical skill in understanding and interacting effectively with others is the attainment of a certain degree of empathy— the ability to project oneself into the mind of another and understand the world from his or her perspective or point of view (see Triandis, this volume). Hoopes suggests that the skill of empathy is critical in the advancement from the local-traditional level to the national-modern level. Because interactions with others rarely occur at the local-traditional level, empathic reasoning is not necessary. The skill of empathy becomes essential at the national-modern level when people must begin to understand others in order to consummate bilateral trade agreements and the like.

The global world, however, involves many players, each coming from a different perspective, having distinct wants and needs, and having diverse ways of thought and expression. A functioning global society demands that individuals have the ability to think, perceive, communicate, and behave in completely new and different ways. It is in preparing human beings for these kinds of interactions that we can apply concepts from cross-cultural psychology and training and thus become proactive in nature and scope (see Bhawuk, this volume). Efforts at prejudice reduction have demonstrated that effective curricular experiences can modify people's thoughts and behaviors.

Prejudice and Prejudice Reduction

Allport (1954) spoke of prejudice as a hostile attitude toward a person who belongs to a group simply because he (or she) belongs to that group and is, therefore, presumed to have the objectionable qualities ascribed to that group. Prejudice and its related "isms" (racism, sexism, and so on) imply a subjective belief in the superiority of one's own group (or gender) over another. But the mere perception of differences with the ascribed superiority is not the most harmful. Prejudicial attitudes held by individuals, groups, and systems can lead to institutional racism, sexism, and discrimination.

Although prejudice is not an inborn trait among human beings, it does seem to be a universal characteristic. For a long time, we have known that prejudice is learned behavior that is expressed very early in a child's life. Although prejudice serves certain functions for people and satisfies certain needs (Katz, 1960), evidence suggests that structured change efforts can reduce its occurrence and perhaps even decrease the likelihood that such negative attitudes will develop (Byrnes, 1988).

School-based efforts to reduce prejudice generally fall into four categories. The first category comes directly from cross-cultural psychology's work in intergroup relations. Although early versions of the contact hypothesis suggested that bringing people of diversity together would result in improved relations and positive attitude change, this was not always found to be the case. The conditions under which contact occurs seem to be critical. Extensive effort in many different contexts (integrated housing, classroom interaction, bilingual education) has resulted in recommendations concerning the best circumstances under which to improve social contact between different groups of people. In general, these include the following:

(1) *Equal status contact,* meaning that individuals coming together have equal access to any rewards available (Amir, 1969). Using bilingualism as an example, in Switzerland, speakers of diverse languages are equally recognized, supported, and accommodated at all levels of society. German, French, and Italian are all considered national languages. In the school context, equal access to knowledge and grades becomes critical (therefore, demanding culturally compatible and effective instruction), as is the encouragement for all students to participate in the various extracurricular activities offered by the school. In the "natural" course of events, this does not often occur. Social class, for instance, often determines the kind of school experiences individuals have. Children from lower socioeconomic groups tend to participate in fewer after-school or extracurricular activities, resulting in less exposure and fewer experiences in working with others. As adults, these individuals show less empathic understanding of others.

(2) Participants come together to achieve some superordinate goal or common task that could not be satisfied without participation of all members of all groups (Sherif, 1958). In the school context, the above recommendations can be implemented not only through sport and music programs but in the classroom setting as well. In the teaching of a second language, immediate and continued use of that new language will encourage and hasten its adoption. Structuring classroom instruction in order to achieve superordinate goals underlies much of the cooperative learning group work finding its way into classrooms today (Slavin, 1986). Cooperative learning approaches structure interaction and instruction in such a manner that completion of an assigned task cannot be accomplished without the effort and application of all group members. This strategy of cooperative learning simultaneously serves many ethnic group members, learning style preferences as well. Such efforts applied to classroom instruction stand to have double payoff.

(3) The social norm must encourage intergroup interaction and the reduction of prejudice. This means that teachers and school administrators must actively encourage and show their support for such activity. Change efforts must be seen as relevant to those at the top as well as to those on the bottom of a hierarchy. In this regard, the system controls much of our ability to make significant change. Official support and status for bilingualism, as in the case of Canada, seems to be a promising example of this on a national level.

(4) High acquaintance potential must exist, thus encouraging intimate contact between individuals in the contact situation. In the school context, this means heterogeneous-ability classroom configurations and mixed sports teams and school clubs. The important consideration here is that individuals have repeated opportunities to get to know others on a rather intimate and personal basis so they become more than mere names and labels.

A second category of activities aimed at reducing prejudice within the school context includes efforts to increase cognitive sophistication or flexibility. Pettigrew (1981) cites numerous studies that suggest that the more inflexible individuals are in their thinking, the greater their degree of prejudice. That is, those who have a tendency to view things in a rather dogmatic or narrow manner tend to be more prejudiced and act in discriminatory ways. Curricula that encourage individuals to identify stereotypes, overgeneralizations, and biases in their own as well as in others' thinking may reduce the occurrence of prejudice.

A third category consists of efforts aimed at improving students' self-esteem. A strong negative correlation between self-esteem and prejudice exists; that is, the higher the self-esteem, the lower the degree of prejudice. Studies have shown that programs and activities that increase self-esteem result in a decrease in prejudice (Cook, 1972). School guidance and counseling programs have served this area well.

A final category consists of attempts to improve empathic understanding of other groups. Cognitive efforts alone seem to have limited impact on people's subsequent thinking and behavior. Integrating cognitive efforts with an affective component that elicits empathy seems to be the most effective way of reducing prejudice. Such activities include having students write their own stories and dramas that present situations in which prejudice and discrimination are actively presented. Some readily available films, books, and plays facilitate this effort. Similarly, some cognitive cross-cultural training strategies that engage the emotions can serve this purpose. The culture-general assimilator (Brislin et al., 1986) and the various culture-specific assimilators that are available may work well here (see Bhawuk, this volume).

Internationalizing the Curriculum

Most discussions of global or international education refer to Hanvey's (1979) classic work, *An Attainable Global Perspective.* Five elements of a global perspective presented by Hanvey include (a) perspective consciousness—the recognition that one's own view of the world is not universally shared; (b) state-of-the-planet awareness—understanding prevailing world conditions and development needs; (c) cross-cultural awareness—recognition of the diversity of ideas and practices found in human societies around the world; (d) knowledge of global dynamics—understanding the key traits and mechanisms of a world system in change; and (e) awareness of human choices—introducing the problems of choice confronting individuals, nations, and the human species as knowledge of the global system expands. Those elements that emerge directly from discussions in the cross-cultural literature are perspective consciousness and cross-cultural awareness. To a lesser degree, awareness of human choices suggests an understanding of the attitude-behavior change literature and the fact that people, if skilled and able to take the initiative, can make a significant difference in their immediate world.

Curricular efforts, as already discussed, have been designed to address change efforts related to prejudice and prejudice reduction in young people. The fact that positive impact can result should encourage the further development of curricula and programs designed to address the five dimensions outlined by Hanvey. Cushner's (1989) study of the impact of a culture-general assimilator (Brislin et al., 1986) on knowledge, cross-cultural adjustment, and behavior among adolescents is of particular interest to those seeking to introduce intercultural interaction concepts in both multicultural and homogeneous school settings. In this study, critical incidents from the culture-general assimilator were modified to be consistent with the experiences and expectations of youths. These materials then became the basis for an orientation program for a multinational group of secondary school students preparing to live in New Zealand for a period of one year. Students were assessed on a number of measures immediately after training and twice during the following six months. Results indicated that trained individuals were better able to identify dynamics that mediate cross-cultural interaction and overseas adjustment, were better able to apply those concepts to their own intercultural interactions, experienced less culture shock, and were more efficient in their interpersonal problem-solving abilities. These results suggest that the culture-general assimilator provides a sound framework and methodology for introducing concepts that are important in a global, interdependent world. Educators should consider further work with this cross-cultural training approach.

As time goes on, the schools are asked to take on more and more responsibility. The result of such pressure is that, increasingly, teachers find they are expected to fit more and more into the already busy school day. Resistance to adding international and/or intercultural courses is understandably high. The preferred approach, which, in turn, also has the potential of having the greatest impact, is to add an international or intercultural component across the courses that already exist. Infusing an international or intercultural perspective across the curriculum helps students understand the interdependent role and dimension of whatever is being taught while helping to realize Hanvey's dimensions. Courses taught with cross-cultural awareness help students see the different manner in which people approach problems and solutions. This, in turn, helps develop perspective consciousness on the part of students. Understanding cross-cultural awareness will, in turn, assist students in understanding global dynamics as they explore how people can come together to solve common problems.

Curricula designed to develop an international or intercultural perspective may go a long way in preparing individuals so they can effectively address problems and prospects that are of global concern. Many problems the world faces today are so multidimensional and interconnected that they cannot be solved from any unilateral, or even bilateral, approach. People must be prepared to accept and work with many others whose ways of thinking, acting, and communicating are quite different. Problems such as the environment (see the chapter by Panday, this volume), world health (see the chapter by Ilola, this volume), and conflict prevention and resolution (see the chapter by Leung, this volume) can only be addressed if people are skilled and trained to use this broader perspective.

SUMMARY

This chapter has attempted to introduce the reader to major ways in which cross-cultural psychology has affected the formal classroom setting. The individual relationship between teacher and student with regards to learning and teaching style was addressed. The relationship between schooling and cognition was reviewed. Finally, efforts to introduce some of the major concepts from cross-cultural psychology and training through international and intercultural curriculum efforts were presented. It was suggested that it is only through a concerted effort at transferring some of this knowledge to young people through various curricular efforts will we ever be able to solve the very difficult problems that face the world today.

SUGGESTIONS FOR FURTHER READING (REFERENCES WITH EXTENSIVE BIBLIOGRAPHIES)

Learning Styles

Lonner, W., & Tyler, V. (1988). *Cultural and ethnic factors in learning and motivation: Implications for education: The Twelfth Western Symposium on Learning.* Bellingham, WA: Western Washington University.

Multicultural Education

Banks, J. (1988). *Multiethnic education: Theory and practice* (2nd ed.). Boston: Allyn & Bacon.
Lynch. J. (1987). *Prejudice reduction and the schools.* New York: Nichols.

Bilingual Education

Ramirez, A. G. (1985). *Bilingualism through schooling: Cross-cultural education for minority and majority students.* Albany: State University of New York Press.

Global Education

Global Perspectives in Education. (1987). *Internationalizing undergraduate education: Resources from the field.* New York: Author.

REFERENCES

Allport, G. (1954). *The nature of prejudice.* New York: Doubleday.

Amir, Y. (1969). Contact hypothesis in ethnic relations. *Psychological Bulletin, 71,* 319-343.

Brislin, R., Cushner, K., Cherrie, C., & Yong, M. (1986). *Intercultural interactions: A practical guide.* Beverly Hills, CA: Sage.

Byrnes, D. A. (1988). Children and prejudice. *Social Education, 52*(4), 267-271.

Center for Education Statistics. (1987). *Digest of education statistics.* Washington, DC: Government Printing Office.

Chiu, L. (1985). The relation of cognitive style and manifest anxiety to academic performance among Chinese children. *Journal of Social Psychology, 125*(5), 667-669.

Cook, S. W. (1972). Motives in a conceptual analysis of attitude-related behavior. In J. Brigham & T. Weissbach (Eds.), *Racial attitude in America: Analysis and findings in social psychology.* New York: Harper & Row.

Cushner, K. (1989). Assessing the impact of a culture-general assimilator. *International Journal of Intercultural Relation, 13*(2), 125-146.

Erickson, F. (1986). Culture difference and science education. *Urban Review, 18*(2), 117-124.

Hanvey, R. G. (1979). *An attainable global perspective.* New York: Global Perspectives in Education.

Hess, R., Azuma, H., Kashiwaga, K., Dickson, W., Nagano, S., Holloway, S., Miyake, K., Price, G., Hatano, G., & McDevitt, T. (1986). Family influences on school readiness and achievement in Japan and the United States: An overview of a longitudinal study. In H. Stevenson, H. Azuma, & K. Hakuta (Eds.), *Child development and education in Japan.* New York: Freeman.

Hilliard, A. (1976). *Alternatives to IQ testing: An approach to the identification of gifted minority children* (Final report). Sacramento: California State Department of Education.

Hoopes, D. (1980). Intercultural education. *PDK Fastback,* No. 144.

Hughes-Weiner, G. (1986). The "learning-how-to-learn" approach to cross-cultural orientation. *International Journal of Intercultural Relations, 10,* 485-505.

Jalali, F. A. (1989). *A cross-cultural comparative analysis of the learning styles and field dependence/independence characteristics of selected fourth-, fifth-, and sixth-grade students of Afro, Chinese, Greek and Mexican-American heritage.* Unpublished doctoral dissertation, St. John's University, New York.

Jordan, C., & Tharp, R. (1979). Culture and education. In A. Marsella, R. Tharp, & T. Ciborowski (Eds.), *Perspectives in cross-cultural psychology*. New York: Academic Press.

Kagan, J., Moss, H., & Sigel, I. (1973). Psychological significance of styles of conceptualization. In J. Wright & J. Kagan (Eds.), *Basic cognitive processes in children*. Chicago: University of Chicago Press.

Katz, D. (1960). The functional approach to the study of attitudes. *Public Opinion Quarterly, 24*, 164-204.

Kolb, D. (1976). *Learning style inventory*. Boston: McBer.

Laboratory of Comparative Human Cognition. (1986). Contributions of cross-cultural research to educational practice. *American Psychologist, 41*(10), 1049-1058.

LeCompte, M. (1980). The civilizing of children: How young children learn to become students. *Journal of Thought, 15*(3), 105-128.

Mabey, C. (1981). Inner London Educational Authority, RS. 776/81.

Pettigrew, T. F. (1981). The mental health impact. In B. Bowser & R. Hunt (Eds.), *Impacts of racism on White Americans* (pp. 97-118). Beverly Hills, CA: Sage.

Rogoff, B. (1981). Schooling and the development of cognitive skills. In H. Triandis & A. Heron (Eds.), *Handbook of cross-cultural psychology: Vol. 4. Developmental psychology*. Boston: Allyn & Bacon.

Scribner, S., & Cole, M. (1973). Cognitive consequences of formal and informal education. *Science, 182*, 553-559.

Sharma, S., & Tripathi, H. (1982). A study of field dependence-independence in high school students as a function of sex, academic achievement, and rural-urban habitation. *Personality and Group Behavior, 2*, 11-14.

Sherif, M. (1958). Superordinate goals in the reduction of intergroup tension. *American Journal of Sociology, 63*, 349-356.

Slavin, R. E. (1986). *Using student team learning* (3rd ed.). Baltimore, MD: John Hopkins University, Center for Research on Elementary and Middle Schools.

Tamir, P. (1983). Cognitive preferences of Jewish and Arab high school students who studied an inquiry oriented biology curriculum for several years. *Research in Science and Technological Education, 1*(1), 17-26.

Vogt, L., Jordan, C., & Tharp, R. (1987). Explaining school failure, producing school success: Two cases. *Anthropology and Education Quarterly, 18*, 276-286.

6

FAMILY AND
HOME-BASED INTERVENTION
ÇIGDEM KÂGITÇIBAŞI

This chapter is about the family and home-based intervention, and these two topics constitute its main parts. In the first part of the chapter, we study the family from a cross-cultural perspective as the core context of human socialization. The emphasis here is mainly theoretical, based on empirical research. We deal with questions of diversity and unity in family interaction patterns. We also examine how families change with social change and development. Home-based intervention is then taken up in the second part of the chapter as an applied area that contributes to both human development and socioeconomic development efforts in the Third World. It also constitutes an important example of cross-cultural applied psychology.

THE FAMILY IN CROSS-CULTURAL PERSPECTIVE[1]

Why Cross-Cultural Psychology of the Family?

The family is of crucial importance for human development. It is, in turn, an integral part of the community and society in which it exists. It reflects society's values and norms. Thus the family can be expected to show much variation across societies. Indeed, a great deal of anthropological research has drawn attention to family diversity. However, such work has had little influence upon psychological study of the family and human development. Psychologists have chosen to underestimate diversity in family patterns. American middle-class family interaction patterns are often considered prototypical of "the family." Yet, in line with variations in social norms and values, family interactions and the meanings attributed to them vary. Thus the same family behavior patterns may mean different things in different cultures. A series of studies by Rohner and his associates on parental acceptance-rejection provide a good example of culturally determined shifts in the meaning of family processes.

Research conducted in the United States (cited in Pettengill & Rohner, 1985) and Germany (Trommsdorf, 1985) showed perceived parental control to be associated with perceived parental hostility and rejection. In other words, children and adolescents who thought that their parents used restrictive discipline (high level of control) also perceived them as hostile and rejecting. However, in Korea (Rohner & Pettengill, 1985) and in Japan (cited in Trommsdorf, 1985), the same parental control is found to be associated with parental acceptance and warmth. Thus "Japanese adolescents even feel *rejected* by their parents when they experience only little parental control and a broader range of autonomy" (Trommsdorf, 1985, p. 238; emphasis in the original).

Such differences may become acutely apparent in culture-contact situations of migration. Thus Pettengill and Rohner (1985) found that Korean American adolescents were similar to American adolescents (in associating parental control with parental hostility) rather than to Korean adolescents. Obviously, the *relevant* sociocultural context in which the individual exists influences his or her experiences and the meanings he or she attributes to them. It is because the Korean American adolescents compare themselves and their parents with the dominant society (American adolescents and parents), and adopt the majority culture's values, that they think this way. Often, intergenerational conflicts arise in such culture-contact situations because the immigrant first generation (parents) continue to have their original cultural group as their reference group and don't change as readily as the second generation. What continues to be "normal" to them, therefore, appears to their children "abnormal" compared with the host society's norms. Thus socially approved ways of doing things and cultural values, together with the more immediate effects of the behavior and expectations of significant others, form a general context into which any event or behavior is embedded and according to which it acquires meaning. Cross-cultural psychological study of the family can examine these complex relations and develop an understanding of diversity as well as commonality in family patterns.

Cross-cultural psychology of the family can also throw light on the variations in child-rearing orientations that form the context of human development across cultures. Families socialize children in line with their beliefs and values. For example, Dasen (1988) has shown that the Baoule people in Africa define intelligence primarily in terms of social skills and manual dexterity (see Kim, this volume). They, therefore, stress these skills in their child-rearing orientation rather than cognitive skills such as abstract reasoning, which we associate closely with intelligence. Such folk theories reflect parents', and society's, view of the nature of the child, which again shows cross-cultural variation.

Both ethnicity and social class influence beliefs, attitudes, and behaviors. This is because people of different ethnic background and socioeconomic status have different experiences, life-styles, and so forth, which determine their worldviews. Often, ethnicity and social class work in combination, because, especially in the context of recent ethnic migration, ethnicity and lower class status overlap. For example, in Australia, differences in child-rearing orientation were found between Anglo-Australian and Italian Australian families. However, when social class standing was controlled, these ethnic differences disappeared (Cashmore & Goodnow, 1986). Similar results were obtained in Canada (Lambert, 1987). It appears that the effects of lower social class standing, especially as characterized by low income and education, can cut across different ethnic groups in the same society or even in different societies.

Earlier work on social class analysis of parental values and child-rearing orientations (Kohn, 1969) focused on parents' expectations about future occupational demands on their children. Middle-class parents stressed autonomy, which they expected to be adaptive to the requirements of individual decision making in middle-class executive positions. Working-class parents stressed obedience and conformity to external constraints in their child-rearing orientations because they considered these characteristics to be more adaptive to their children's future occupations. These expectations are based on parents' current occupational experiences. Following up on this work, Bernstein (1971) showed how class-related living conditions and family communication structures affect children's development. The negative impact of restricted verbalization on cognitive development was especially noted in lower social class families together with restrictive work experiences and unfavorable living conditions.

Extensions beyond social class and ethnic variation are seen in ecological orientations to the cross-cultural study of the family. For example, it is found that, in hazardous environments and in subsistence-level agricultural societies, compliant behavior is encouraged in child rearing because compliance is more adaptive in such ecological contexts (e.g., Berry, 1967; LeVine, 1974).

Independence-Interdependence

A basic dimension along which family patterns show variation is independent-interdependent human relations, which is also known as the individualistic-collectivistic orientation (see Triandis, this volume). The degree of separation and individuation among family members is a key factor in family interactions, and it shows cross-cultural variability. In societies with an individualistic ideology, independence, separation, and individuation are more likely to be seen in the family than in societies that do not have this ideology. In the latter, family relations are characterized by closely knit relatedness and interdependence. This interdependence is especially noticeable through the family life cycle, first as the dependence of the child on the parents, and then, in old age, as the dependence of the elderly parents on the grownup offspring. Thus in a cross-cultural study on the value of children for parents,[2] the "old-age security value" of children was found to be a very important reason for wanting to have a child (or another child) in countries such as Indonesia, the Philippines, Thailand, and Turkey. In Germany and the United States, however, this was not considered to be an important reason at all (Kâgitçibaşi, 1982a, 1982b).

In Western individualistic societies, children are raised to be self-sufficient and self-reliant, and they are encouraged to be independent of their parents. Parents, in turn, want to be independent of their adult offspring in old age. This situation has been noted by many as especially characteristic of the American family and society. For example, Kagan (1984) states: "In American families, the primary loyalty is to self—its values, autonomy, pleasure, virtue and actualization."

In most societies in the non-Western world where traditional family patterns prevail, however, group loyalties rather than individual loyalties are important, and interdependent rather than independent family relations are prevalent. In such a family context, children are reinforced for compliance rather than for autonomy. As mentioned previously, this pattern is functional in hazardous ecological contexts or where cooperative group (family) action is needed for survival or in lower social class settings where job characteristics require compliance. Apart from being adaptive to ecological requirements, however, closely knit relatedness rather than individual separation is a basic cultural value in these societies. Thus in the aforementioned Value of Children Study, when reporting expected future dependence on their grownup offspring, Turkish parents did not express any regret about having to depend on their children. Instead, they gave such responses as, "If our son is worthy of his family, of course he is going to take care of us in old age"; or "A loyal son would never let down his parents." Interdependence is thus a requisite for family honor as well as for family survival. Objective socioeconomic conditions necessitating interdependence (e.g., lack of old-age pensions and social security systems) seem to be associated with cultural values of interdependence.

In Western technological societies, on the other hand, independence is such a cherished value that individuals do not like (or admit) being dependent on anyone, particularly on their children. Thus in the Value of Children Study, a common American response was "I don't want anything from my children, if they can take care of themselves, I'd be glad."

Psychological theorizing in the Western world, and especially in the United States, reflects the individualistic cultural values stressing independence and autonomy. "Separation-individuation" (Mahler, Pine, & Bergman, 1975) is considered necessary for healthy human development, and the development of autonomy is seen as a prerequisite for optimal personality, moral, and cognitive development. Much emphasis is, therefore, given to early independence training of children. Psychologically healthy family interactions are conceived as those among separated individuals with clearly defined personality boundaries. Families in which individual boundaries are blurred and overlapping are considered to be "enmeshed" (unhealthy) families (Minuchin, 1974).

When such a psychological conceptualization is applied cross-culturally, a misfit may occur. As described before, child socialization in the collectivistic society emphasizes relatedness, not separation. For example, the Japanese mother's message to the child has been described as, "I am one with you; we can be and will be of the same mind" (reported in Kornadt, 1987, p. 133). This is exactly the definition of a "symbiotic" relationship, which is an expression of pathological "enmeshment" according to Western psychology. Here we see another contrast between two different meaning systems such that the same pattern of family relations becomes normal in one and abnormal in the other.

The independence-interdependence dimension is basic to understanding family diversity in the world. *Independence* or *interdependence* can refer to material, or emotional, family relations, or both.

Assumption of Decreasing Diversity

As mentioned earlier, psychology has not dwelt very much on the existing diversity in family patterns. This is mainly because, unlike anthropology, psychology is less interested in describing variety than in reaching unifying generalizations. Cross-cultural diversity is difficult to integrate into a general pattern or theory. Therefore, the existing cross-cultural variety is somewhat undermined and is considered transitory. The assumption is that, with modernization, industrialization, and Westernization, the different family patterns will be modified to resemble the Western family. In other words, a unidirectional change is expected toward the Western model. This is also the thesis of modernization theory (Inkeles, 1969).

Even though modernization theory is not as popular today as it was in the 1960s and early 1970s, its claim of unidirectional change is implicitly assumed by both the layperson and the social scientist. Thus many of the Third World countries are considered "transitional" societies. Through this transition, the family is also expected to change from a closely knit, interdependent unit toward the nucleated Western family, characterized by independence, individualism, and separation from kin. Together with structural nucleation in terms of household type, emotional nucleation and individuation are expected to take place with industrialization and urbanization—in short, modernization.

Underlying this expectation of change are two basic assumptions. One is the so-called deficiency hypothesis, which considers that which is different (from the prototypical Western model) to be inferior. One example is that collectivistic orientations are considered to be incompatible with economic development (see Sinha, 1988). This assumption is being challenged today by the examples of Japan and the "four tigers of Asia"—Korea, Taiwan, Hong Kong, and Singapore. The great economic growth in these collectivistic societies shows that closely knit interpersonal and familial relations can be compatible with economic development and that individualism is not a necessary component of industrialization.

The other assumption underlying the expectation of unidirectional change is that the Western family, and society, was itself also collectivistic but became individualistic as a necessary outcome of industrialization. Therefore, as other countries industrialize, they will inevitably go through the same process. This assumption is also being challenged today by the findings of historical demographers. Historical evidence, based on court records and other documents, shows that individualism and the nuclear family existed in Western Europe and especially in England before industrialization (Lesthaeghe, 1983; Lesthaeghe & Surkyn, 1988; Thornton, 1984), even before the rise of Protestantism (Macfarlane, 1978). This evidence has to do, for example, with individual ownership and inheritance of property, individual control of sexuality, age at marriage, and fertility. In the United States also, family patterns similar to current ones are noted in travelers' observations and magazine articles of the preindustrial period (1800-1850) (Furstenberg, 1966; Lantz, Keyes, & Schultz, 1975).

Given this historical evidence, it is not warranted to assume that industrialization *necessitates* individuation. It appears that Western European society had an individualistic culture base and that industrialization capitalized on it. In different societies with a different culture base, industrialization may capitalize on different cultural elements. One such element may be familism and group loyalties, which are being utilized in countries like Japan in forming "company spirit" and in other industrializing Third World societies in forming family businesses. There is, in fact, a great deal of evidence showing the continuity of the basic family culture in many parts of the developed urban industrial sectors of the Third World (e.g., Sinha & Kao, 1988; Yang, 1988). Convergence toward the Western model may, nevertheless, occur. If it does, however, it will probably be due more to cultural diffusion from the West through the mass media and increased intercultural contact rather than being required by industrialization.

The Changing Family

The above discussion does not conclude with the claim that no changes occur in the family with socioeconomic development. Research results show, in fact, that some important modification in family relations take place with urbanization and development. For example, in the aforementioned cross-cultural Value of Children Study, the salience of the old-age security value of children decreased as parents' socioeconomic status increased. Similarly, with increased parent education, the importance of the economic value of children for parents decreased (Kâgitçibaşi, 1982a). This is because, in urban centers, children do not contribute significantly to family income unlike peasant children who work in the field, tend animals, and so forth. In urban living conditions, children become economic costs rather than economic assets for the family. Also, urban parents who participate in organized labor often benefit from old-age pensions and social security systems, and so they are less dependent on their children for their livelihood. As children's economic and old-age security values decrease, and as their costs increase, fewer children are desired and fertility decreases (Kâgitçibaşi, 1982b). Also, son preference decreases because parents no longer need old-age security, a task traditionally expected to be accomplished by sons.

These changes show that, with increased education, urbanization, and socioeconomic development, elderly parents are less dependent on their children for financial benefits. However, these decreasing dependencies are in the *material* domain, *not* in the *emotional* domain. When such a distinction is made between these two domains, we find that most of the evidence refers to the decreasing material dependencies, as exemplified above by the Value of Children Study findings, not to decreasing emotional dependencies.

In fact, there is some evidence that emotional dependencies continue to be important, if not increasing in importance, through economic development. For example, in the Value of Children Study, the psychological value of the child for parents is found not to change with economic development levels, and, in Turkey, it is found to increase with development (Kâgitçibaşi, 1982a). Similarly, Yang (1988, p. 109) reports the continuing importance of "familism" in China in spite of government policies undermining its role. She also finds close relations among the elderly and their adult children even though the elderly do not depend on their children for their livelihood. In fact, the elderly parents may continue contributing financially to their adult children, which Yang (1988) considers "indicative of the traditional parental protection of children until their death."

Other research also points to decreased material dependencies without corresponding decreases in emotional dependencies with modernization. Erelcin (1988) compared modern (young and urban) and traditional groups in Turkey. She found that, whereas traditional groups were willing to give both material and emotional support to those close to them, modern groups showed this willingness more for emotional support. Anthropological observations with urban groups in the more developed areas of the Third World also point to close relations (frequent visits and so on) and emotional support among family and kin (Neki, 1976; Sinha, 1988; Sinha & Kao, 1988). Similar closely knit human networks are also reported for ethnic groups in posttechnological societies, for example, for Asian American and Hispanic families in the United States and various ethnic groups in Australia (see Storer, 1985).

On the basis of research evidence, it can be concluded that material family interdependencies weaken with urbanization and modernization, but emotional interdependencies probably do not change much. It is important to note that family interdependencies do not necessarily relate to household structures; they can exist in nuclear as well as in extended households. Often, families and kin living in nuclear households function as if they were extended families. For example, they may share household chores, child care, leisure time, and so forth. Thus they have been called "functionally extended" (Kâgitçibaşi, 1985) or "modified extended" (Cohler & Geyer, 1982) families.

We have been examining the changing family in modernizing societies. How about the family in posttechnological societies? We have already referred to the high value put on individual freedom and autonomy in the Western, especially American, family. This is a culturally cherished value; it refers to self-reliance and individuation-separation of both the family members from each other and also of the nuclear family from other kin.

Recent observations of the American family, however, have noted a difference between professed values and everyday behavior. Specifically, substantial interdependence is actually found in spite of commitment to independence and self-sufficiency (Bronfenbrenner & Weiss, 1983; Fu, Hinkle, & Hanna, 1986; Keniston, 1985). For example, Cohler and Geyer (1982) present a great deal of evidence for mutual support between married adults and their parents, among close relatives, and among nonkin neighbors in terms of economic help with child care, health care, and moral support. This is found to be especially strong among women and among lower-income groups. Such mutual support, however, is often accompanied by ambivalent feelings if not, at times, discomfort (Cohler & Geyer, 1982), because self-sufficiency is a cultural ideal. Nevertheless, the need for support and relatedness also seem to be present in the families of posttechnological societies.

Recent evidence from Europe further points to this need as expressed in alternative communal life-styles. For example, in the Netherlands, unrelated persons or families are seen to choose shared living arrangements (Saal, 1987). In Israel, proximal households function as "joint families" among the Bene Israel, who migrated to Israel from India (Weil, 1987). Swedish parents are found to value group relations even more than Indian parents because the former miss them more (Ekstrand & Ekstrand, 1987).

On the basis of the above, it may be possible to say that, although on the one hand there is great diversity in family patterns in the world, there may also be some common threads based on the human need for relatedness. Such a basic need has, in fact, been recognized by some psychologists such as Angyal (1951), Bakan (1966), and Otto Rank (1945). These personality theorists stressed the two conflicting needs for autonomy and dependence. They proposed that, though in conflict, both of these needs have to be satisfied for healthy personality development. Bakan, especially, warned against denying the need for union (dependence), probably in reaction to the prevalent individualistic ideology in America. A similar emphasis is also seen in the study of gender, where a relatedness orientation is proposed to characterize female sex-role development more than individualistic autonomy, which characterizes male sex-role development.

Implications for Application

Examination of research results across cultures points to both diversity and similarity in family patterns. It appears that, even though they are basic human needs, dependence and independence (autonomy) may be more or less dominant in different societies. Thus in the Western family and society, independence is the more dominant tendency even though interdependence also exits. In much of the non-Western world, interdependence is the dominant pattern.

There is concern among social scientists and educators in developing countries that strong family and group loyalties suppress individual autonomy. Yet, there is also concern that, with modernization, human support systems may be weakening (e.g., Sinha, 1988). Thus new syntheses are being searched for to integrate interdependence and autonomy (Kâgitçibaşi, 1985, 1987; Sinha, 1985; C. Yang, 1988; K. S. Yang, 1986).

There are important implications of such an ideal synthesis for development programs in general and for education in particular. This is because development efforts and models for the Third World are based on an implicit "model of man," often deriving from Western experience. Such a model provides a framework about how human behavior and human relations are understood and how they can be improved. Thus assumptions about which types of individual and group relations are more conducive to economic growth may underlie the kinds of economic policies proposed to Third World governments by Western governments, banks, international organizations, and so forth. For example, because entrepreneurial individual achievement motivation was considered more conducive to economic growth than cooperative group loyalties, programs to promote achievement motivation were instituted in India in the 1960s (McClelland & Winter, 1969). It turned out that such an individualistic model of man did not quite fit the Indian context.

Alternative approaches to promoting economic development have been formulated that capitalize on collectivistic cultural elements. For example, Sinha (1980) has proposed the "nurturant task leader" for effective management in India (see also Hui, this volume). This is a combination or a synthesis of the nurturant human-relations-oriented leadership and the objective task-oriented leadership styles that have been considered to be opposing styles in Western research.

HOME-BASED INTERVENTION

Any applied work involving intervention benefits from a knowledge of the cultural context. This is even more important where the intervention program is brought in from another cultural context. Intervention attempts in the developing countries need to be sensitive to collectivistic interdependent human relations—"the culture of relatedness" (Kâgitçibaşi, 1987)—prevalent in these societies. This is crucial for any applied work involving the family, for, as we have seen, it is at the level of the family that human interdependencies are strongest.

We have mentioned earlier, for example, that there is concern among Third World psychologists and educators that autonomy is not promoted in the closely knit family and society. Yet, in an attempt to develop autonomy in the child, if the individualistic model is used and the family culture of relatedness is undermined, such an intervention may not be effective. For example, if competition, individual achievement, and separation from the in-group are encouraged without regard for family welfare, there might be resistance to such an intervention. What needs to be done is to work through the closely knit family system to introduce autonomy into it. We will examine such intervention work in this section.

Nonformal Education and the Family

A great deal of education takes place outside the school. Especially in developing countries where a substantial proportion of the adult population has had little or no formal schooling, nonformal adult education assumes great importance. Such education may be designed to teach new marketable skills, better agricultural methods, better health practices, family planning, and the like. Parent education has been gaining an increasing importance in adult education programs. It is designed to sensitize parents to the needs of the growing child as well as providing them with information about child care, health, and nutrition.

Another form of nonformal education that has direct relevance for the family is noninstitutional preschool education. Formal preschool education is provided in an institutional setting, such as a nursery school, kindergarten, or child-care center. Such institutions are often rather expensive to run, and developing countries cannot afford to provide these services to large numbers of children. Providing universal primary schooling and literacy often takes precedence over preschool education. Yet it is generally agreed that the early years in a child's life are crucial for development, and especially in deprived environments it is important to provide children with early stimulation and enrichment. Therefore, alternatives to institutional preschools have been developed in more informal settings, including the family.

In addition to being more cost-effective, providing early enrichment to a child in the home/community context rather than in an institution has other advantages. First of all, such an approach avoids the creation of two different and possibly conflicting environments for the child—the preschool setting and the home/community setting. Second, and more important, home-based education can change the home environment while changing the child. If a child receives cognitive stimulation only in a program carried out at a child-care center, at the completion of the program, she or he is left on his or her own resources. Because his or her home environment has not changed, it cannot help support the child to sustain the cognitive skills gained from the program. In fact, there is evidence that the gains from cognitively oriented programs at child development centers dissipate over time (Smilansky, 1979). It is important, therefore, to support the immediate human environment of the child, which could, in turn, provide the child with continuous support. A great deal of research shows that, when parents are involved in enrichment programs for children, the programs make a greater impact (Kâğitçibaşi, Sunar, & Bekman, 1989; Myers & Hertenberg, 1987; Smilansky, 1979). This is especially the case where parents have low levels of formal education and when the home environment provides inadequate cognitive stimulation for the child. Specifically, helping the mother build self-esteem and competence, so that she can engage in cognitively oriented communication with her child, can help to foster the child's sustained cognitive development. In this way, noninstitutional preschool education and parent education are integrated into a home-based nonformal education.

Especially in sociocultural contexts where close-knit family, kinship, and community ties exist, it makes sense for an educational intervention program to build on these ties as support mechanisms. Such an approach would be more likely to succeed than an individualistic orientation that treats the child separately from his or her environment and ignores the existing family and community ties.

Third, a holistic approach that includes support of the child's immediate environment capitalizes on the child-family-community interaction and can be beneficial not only to the child but also to the family and to the community. This is because such an approach can help build up competence in the child's caregivers as well as mobilizing family and kin-community resources to sustain such competence. Competencies and skills developed in such home-based educational interventions may be expected to generalize to other individuals in the family, particularly younger siblings of the target child, and possibly to neighbors and other members of the community. Such vertical (younger siblings) and horizontal (neighbors) effects are positive by-products of home-based education programs.

Home-based nonformal education can integrate different topics and target groups in a single intervention program. For example, in a home and community-based literacy training program, family planning and health education can be included. Or even an intervention program designed to provide supplementary nutrition directly to children at home or in a feeding center in the community can include a component of creative play activities for the children while they are waiting to be fed. It can also get the mothers involved in such creative play in order to sensitize them to the importance of play for the cognitive development of their children and in order to encourage them to continue it at home. All these home-based nonformal education activities and many others have, in fact, been tried out in various intervention programs around the world (see Myers & Hertenberg, 1987).

At this point, it may be fruitful to remind ourselves of some of the discussion in the first part of the chapter, especially the changing family and its implications for application. There we stressed family diversity in the world and showed the inappropriateness of generalizing from the Western experience to the rest of the world and especially imposing an implicit "model of man" in Third World development programs. Home-based nonformal education can circumvent this problem, because it utilizes a holistic contextual approach. It allows for both diversity and commonality in family patterns and it is a bottom-up rather than a top-down approach to intervention and change. This is because it does not aim to promote change in behaviors and life-styles imposed from outside and *in spite of* people's desires but rather works with them in a cooperative fashion to introduce change. It fits in with the existing reality of the situation even if its aim is to change that situation. Such an approach is more conducive to promoting growth at individual, family/community, and societal levels.

Two Case Studies

We will now briefly review two examples of home- and community-based educational intervention programs conducted as applied research projects involving psychological elements. One of these case studies is from rural Thailand, the other is from urban Turkey; they both involve work with mothers and combine different educational aims.

The Thai study. This study involved the integration of psychosocial components (in the form of mother-infant interaction) in nutrition education in 48 northeastern Thai villages (Kotchabhakdi, Winichagoon, Smitasiri, Dhanamitta, & Valyasevi, 1987). As a part of a large-scale health and nutrition intervention program, interactive video education was used in the villages together with the provision of food supplements for infants. The nutritional status of the infants and young children was initially assessed, and malnutrition was found to be common. Interviews with mothers and home observations provided baseline data about mothers' knowledge of early infant development and child-rearing attitudes.

What made this particular nutrition program different from others was the focus on the psychological aspects of mother-infant interaction. It is based on an interactive conceptualization of nutrition, health, and psychosocial development, each acting on the other two. This is a different conceptualization than a commonly assumed linear model of nutrition leading to health and health leading to psychosocial development. It is based on cross-cultural research with infants and their caretakers. For example, Brazelton, Tronick, Lechtig, Lasky, and Klein (1977) showed that subsequent malnutrition could be predicted with 70%-80% accuracy for Guatemalan infants who had low interactive ability. This points to the fact that babies who have a lower activity level get less food. Because malnourished babies are less active, malnourishment breeds more malnourishment in a vicious circle. In contrast, healthy babies who actively demand food do, in fact, get more food from their caretakers. Similarly, reluctant babies can be fed more if mothers stimulate them during breast-feeding, whereas a nonstimulating psychosocial environment is less conducive to both nutrition and health and psychosocial development of the child.

Other evidence comes from a Mexican study (Carvioto, 1981) where the mothers of malnourished children were found to have less exposure to the radio, to provide lower-quality home stimulation, and to be less responsive to their children than the mothers of normal children living in the same village. Recent reviews (e.g., Jolly, 1988) have stressed the key role of closely knit family ties and environmental support systems for *positive deviance*. This is a term referring to the fact that some children thrive in adverse conditions whereas others cannot make it. Mother(care-taker)-child interaction appears to be particularly important in promoting resilience in the child.

Accordingly, in the Thai village study, optimal mother-child interaction was a goal. Mothers were provided information and feedback through video showings coupled with discussion sessions at home and in groups. Among the topics covered were information about infants' capacity to see, hear, and interact within the first week of life (not originally known by the mothers); the importance of early stimulation of and interaction with the infant for better nourishment and health, and techniques of continuing feeding in spite of the infant's tongue-thrusting reflex or turning away.

As a result of the home-based educational intervention program, the mothers in the experimental villages, compared with those in the control villages, demonstrated more effective feeding and more interaction with their babies; they also allowed the babies more direct visual exposure (by opening up the top of their cribs) and more manipulation of play materials that the mothers made from local plants (as suggested in the education program). In effect, the program empowered the mothers to realize "their capacity to make a difference in their children's growth and development and to make the most use of their potential and existing resources in creating a more nurturing environment for their children" (Kotchabhakdi et al., 1987, p. 21).

The Turkish study. This was a four-year longitudinal study involving intervention in early childhood enrichment and mother training in the low-income areas of Istanbul (Kâgitçibaşi et al., 1989). The aim was to foster the overall development of the child by working through the mother. A holistic model of human development was used, focusing on the interaction of the growing child with his or her family (especially the mother) and the interaction of the family with its own environment (the community). Specifically, mothers were encouraged to develop a positive self-concept and feelings of competence as well as specific cognitive skills and positive orientations to provide their children with more cognitive stimulation and enrichment at home.

Of special relevance here are the findings regarding autonomy and dependence. Initial interviews with mothers revealed strong needs for close ties with their children. When asked about children's behavior that pleased them most, relational behavior, such as being good to mother, was mentioned most frequently. Together with showing affection, being obedient, and getting along well with others, relational behavior accounted for almost 80% of desired behavior in children. In contrast, autonomy, while having a low priority among desired behaviors in children, loomed large among behaviors that angered mothers and accounted for more than half of the unacceptable behaviors. These findings are similar to those cited earlier in the discussion of independence-interdependence.

After the initial interviewing to obtain baseline data, some of the mothers participated in a training program for two years designed to provide them on the one hand with cognitive skills to teach their children and on the other hand with sensitization to the needs of the growing child. This extensive parent education intervention was carried out in terms of home instruction and supportive group discussions in the community. In these group discussions, the existing relatedness values and behaviors such as showing physical affection, being close, helping and supporting, and being good to and sensitive to the child were reinforced. However, new values were also introduced encouraging autonomy in the child, such as allowing the child to make decisions and to carry the responsibility for them, and to do things on his or her own. Care was taken to show that these new values of autonomy are not incompatible with harmonious close-knit human relatedness.

After the intervention, in the fourth year of the study, reassessments were done of mothers' child-rearing attitudes. It was found that mothers who participated in the parent education intervention valued autonomous behavior in their children more than nontrained mothers. Compared with the first-year baselines, the change in the experimental group was remarkable. Nevertheless, the great majority of mothers in both groups continued stressing affectionate and relational behavior in children as pleasing and otherwise demonstrated close-knit ties as reflected in their behaviors and values. Thus the trained mothers acquired a new positive orientation toward the child's autonomy while remaining as close to their children as the nontrained mothers. A synthesis of individualistic and relational values appears to have been achieved. Some of the other findings of the study have implications for individual autonomy and achievement also, such as higher aspirations and expectations of trained mothers regarding their children's school success and years of schooling, as well as their higher expectations of the child being able to succeed without asking for help from others.

Children's behaviors showed dramatic differences between the two groups, as well, especially with regard to superior cognitive skills and school performance of the children whose mothers participated in the home-based education. Findings specific to autonomy show that the children whose mothers were trained were, in fact, less dependent and less likely to ask for help. Thus as a result of the intervention, the mothers and the children changed toward more autonomous values and behaviors, respectively, while very much remaining in the family culture of relatedness.

This research provides us with an example of a new type of conceptualization and application. First of all, there is a recognition here of a different system of family values and dynamics—a diverse family culture. Second, no attempt is made to change this family culture to resemble the Western individualistic family. Rather a new model is developed to incorporate this diverse experience. Furthermore, an enrichment program is introduced working through the existing network of human relations and strengthening them for the eventual overall development of the child. In this way, the focus shifts from the individual to the interactions between the individual and his or her total environment, incorporating the total social context in a holistic approach.

Similarly, in the Thai study, new child-rearing information and behavior were introduced but in terms of integrating them into the existing child-rearing patterns rather than replacing those patterns. An empowerment model rather than a deficiency model was used in both studies in encouraging mothers to realize their own capacity and potential for promoting their children's development. Also, in both studies, familial and communal ties were utilized in terms of paraprofessional home visitors, group discussions, and local interactors/communicators to provide further support to the mothers.

CONCLUSION

This chapter has focused on the family in cross-cultural perspective and home-based intervention as an applied field of cross-cultural psychology. The existing evidence shows that independence values are prevalent in the Euro-American family interactions, whereas most non-Western family patterns are characterized more by interdependence.

With economic development, urbanization, and industrialization, material interdependencies decrease, but a corresponding reduction may not take place in the emotional realm. Even in the Western individualistic society, interdependent family relations are found to exist together with strong commitment to independence and self-sufficiency. These two opposing orientations were considered to derive from the two basic human needs for autonomy and dependence.

These considerations are not of theoretical importance alone, but they have direct relevance for applications. This is especially the case because often development plans are based on an implicit "model of man." This should not be an "exported model of man," rather, the human realities of the given situation should be recognized and accepted. The intervention must have ecological validity—it must make sense to the people involved. It needs to recognize different family patterns and needs to work through them while at the same time integrating desired behavioral change into the existing patterns. The two case studies of home-based education from Turkey and Thailand provide some examples of how this can be done. In such an approach, sensitivity to culture plays the key role. It is through this sensitivity that a new but culturally relevant and valid model of human-familial-societal development can be formulated.

Cross-cultural psychology can contribute to this cultural sensitivity. This is because cross-cultural comparisons draw our attention to how individual and family behavioral patterns are similar and how they are different across cultures. Cross-cultural psychology also strives to understand the underlying reasons for these similarities and differences. The better we understand how families function and how they change across cultures and through time, the better we can serve their needs. Applications regarding family welfare stand to gain by a cross-cultural conceptualization based on sound theory and research.

NOTES

1. This part is based on a chapter by the author titled "Family and Socialization in Cross-Cultural Perspective: A Model of Change" in *Nebraska Symposium on Motivation* (1989, Vol. 37).

2. The Value of Children Study was conducted in nine countries in the mid-1970s: Indonesia, Germany, Korea, the Philippines, Singapore, Taiwan, Thailand, Turkey, and the United States.

REFERENCES

Angyal, A. (1951). A theoretical model for personality studies. *Journal of Personality*, *20*, 131-142.

Bakan, D. (1966). *The duality of human existence*. Chicago: Rand McNally.

Bernstein, B. (1971). *Class, codes and control* (Vol. 1). London: Routledge & Kegan Paul.

Bernstein, B. (1975). *Class, codes and control* (Vol. 3). London: Routledge & Kegan Paul.

Berry, J. W. (1967). Independence and conformity in subsistence-level societies. *Journal of Personality and Social Psychology*, *7*, 415-418.

Brazelton, T. B., Tronick, E., Lechtig, A., Lasky, R., & Klein, R. (1977). The behavior of nutritionally-deprived Guatemalan neonates. *Developmental Medicine and Child Neurology*, *19*, 364.

Bronfenbrenner, U., & Weiss, H. B. (1983). Beyond policies without people: An ecological perspective on child and family policy. In E. F. Zigler, S. L. Kagan, & E. Klugman (Eds.), *Children, families and government: Perspectives on American social policy* (pp. 393-414). New York: Cambridge University Press.

Carvioto, J. (1981). *Nutrition, stimulation, mental development and learning*. W. O. Atwater Memorial Lecture, presented at the 12th International Congress of Nutrition, San Diego, CA.

Cashmore, J. A., & Goodnow, J. J. (1986). Influences on Australian parents' values: Ethnicity versus socioeconomic status. *Journal of Cross-Cultural Psychology*, *17*(4), 441-454.

Cohler, B. J., & Geyer, S. (1982). Psychological autonomy and interdependence within the family. In F. Walsh (Ed.), *Normal family processes* (pp. 196-227). New York: Guilford.

Dasen, P. (1988). Development psychologigue et activite's guotidiennes chez des enfants africains. *Enfance*, *41*, 3-24.

Ekstrand, L. H., & Ekstrand, G. (1987). Children's perceptions of norms and sanctions in two cultures. In Ç. Kâgitçibaşi (Ed.), *Growth and progress in cross-cultural psychology*. Lisse, Holland: Swets and Zeitlinger.

Erelcin, F. G. (1988). *Collectivistic norms in Turkey: Tendency to give and receive support*. Unpublished master's thesis, Bogazici University, Istanbul.

Fu, V. R., Hinkle, D. E., & Hanna, M. A. (1986). A three-generational study of the development of individual dependency and family interdependence. *Genetic, Social and General Psychology Monographs*, *112*(2), 153-171.

Furstenberg, F. F., Jr. (1966). Industrialization and the American family: A look backward. *American Sociological Review*, *31*, 326-337.

Inkeles, A. (1969). Making men modern: On the causes and consequences of individual change in six developing countries. *American Journal of Sociology*, *75*, 208-225.

Jolly, R. (1988). Deprivation in the child's environment: Seeking advantage in adversity. *Canadian Journal of Public Health Supplement*, *20*, 1-7.

Kagan, J. (1984). *Nature of the child*. New York: Basic Books.

Kâgitçibaşi, Ç. (1982a). Sex roles, value of children and fertility in Turkey. In Ç. Kâgitçibaşi (Ed.), *Sex roles, family and community in Turkey*. Bloomington: Indiana University Press.

Kâgitçibaşi, Ç. (1982b). Old-age security value of children and development. *Journal of Cross-Cultural Psychology*, *13*, 29-42.

Kâgitçibaşi, Ç. (1985). A model of family change through development: The Turkish family in comparative perspective. In I. R. Lagunes & Y. H. Poortinga (Eds.), *From a different perspective: Studies of behavior across cultures*. Lisse, Holland: Swets and Zeitlinger.

Kâgitçibaşi, Ç. (1987). Individual and group loyalties: Are they compatible? In Ç. Kâgitçibaşi (Ed.), *Growth and progress in cross-cultural psychology*. Lisse, Holland: Swets and Zeitlinger.

Kâgitçibaşi, Ç., Sunar, D., & Bekman, S. (1989). *Preschool education project*. Ottawa: IDRC Final Report.

Keniston, K. (1985). The myth of family independence. In J. M. Henslin (Ed.), *Marriage and family in a changing society* (2nd ed., pp. 27-33). New York: Free Press.

Kohn, M. L. (1969). *Class and conformity: A study of values*. Homewood, IL: Dorsey.

Kornadt, H. J. (1987). The aggression motive and personality development: Japan and Germany. In F. Halisch & J. Kuhl (Eds.), *Motivation, intention, and volition*. Berlin: Springer-Verlag.

Kotchabhakdi, N. J., Winichagoon, P., Smitasiri, S., Dhanamitta, S., & Valyasevi, A. (1987). *The integration of psycho-social components in nutrition education in Northeastern Thai villages* (Case study). Prepared for the Third Inter-Agency Meeting of the Consultative Group on Early Childhood Care and Development, Washington, DC.

Lambert, W. E. (1987). The fate of old-country values in a new land: A cross-national study of childrearing. *Canadian Psychology, 28*(1), 9-20.

Lantz, H. R., Keyes, J., & Schultz, M. (1975). The American family in the preindustrial period: From base lines in history to change. *American Sociological Review, 40*, 21-36.

Lesthaeghe, R. (1983). A century of demographic and cultural change in Western Europe: An exploration of underlying dimensions. *Population and Development Review, 9*(3), 411-437.

Lesthaeghe, R., & Surkyn, J. (1988). Cultural dynamics and economic theories of fertility change. *Population and Development Review, 14*(1), 1-47.

LeVine, R. A. (1974). Parental goals: A cross-cultural view. *Teachers College Record, 76*, 226-239.

Macfarlane, A. (1978). *The origins of English individualism*. New York: Oxford.

Mahler, M., Pine, F., & Bergman, A. (1975). *The psychological birth of the human infant*. New York: Basic Books.

McClelland, D. C., & Winter, D. G. (1969). *Motivating economic development*. New York: Free Press.

Minuchin, S. (1974). *Families and family therapy*. Cambridge, MA: Harvard University Press.

Myers, R. G., & Hertenberg, R. (1987). *The eleven who survive: Toward a re-examination of early childhood development program options and costs* (Report No. EDT69). Washington, DC: World Bank.

Neki, J. S. (1976). An examination of the cultural relativism of dependence as a dynamic of social and therapeutic relationships. *British Journal of Medical Psychology, 49*, 1-10.

Pettengill, S. M., & Rohner, R. P. (1985). Korean-American adolescents' perceptions of parental control, parental acceptance-rejection and parent-adolescent conflict. In I. R. Lagunes & Y. H. Poortinga (Eds.), *From a different perspective: Studies of behavior across cultures*. Lisse, Holland: Swets and Zeitlinger.

Rank, O. (1945). *Will therapy and truth and reality*. New York: Knopf.

Rohner, R. P., & Pettengill, S. A. (1985). Perceived parental acceptance-rejection and parental control among Korean adolescents. *Child Development, 56*, 524-528.

Saal, C. D. (1987). Alternative forms of living and housing. In L. Shamgar-Handelman & R. Palomba (Eds.), *Alternative patterns of family life in modern societies*. Rome: Collana Monografie.

Sinha, D. (1988). The family scenario in a developing country and its implications for mental health: The case of India. In P. R. Dasen, J. W. Berry, & N. Sartorius (Eds.), *Health and cross-cultural psychology: Toward applications*. Newbury Park, CA: Sage.

Sinha, D., & Kao, H. S. R. (1988). *Social values and development: Asian perspectives.* New Delhi: Sage.

Sinha, J. B. P. (1980). *The nurturant task leader.* New Delhi: Sage.

Sinha, J. B. P. (1985). Collectivism, social energy, and development in India. In I. R. Lagunes & Y. Poortinga (Eds.), *From a different perspective: Studies of behavior across cultures.* Lisse, The Netherlands: Swets and Zeitlinger.

Smilansky, M. (1979). *Priorities in education: Pre-school. Evidence and conclusions* (Working Paper No. 323). Washington, DC: World Bank.

Storer, D. (Ed.). (1985). *Ethnic family values in Australia.* Sydney: Prentice-Hall.

Thornton, A. (1984). Modernization and family change. In *Social change and family policies. Proceedings of the XXth International CFR Seminar.* Melbourne: Australian Institute of Family Studies.

Trommsdorf, G. (1985). Some comparative aspects of socialization in Japan and Germany. In I. R. Lagunes & Y. Poortinga (Eds.), *From a different perspective: Studies of behavior across cultures.* Lisse, The Netherlands: Swets and Zeitlinger.

Weil, S. (1987). Proximal households as alternatives to joint families in Israel. In L. Shamgar-Handelman & R. Palomba (Eds.), *Alternative patterns of family life in modern societies.* Rome: Collana Monografie.

Yang, C. (1988). Familism and development: An examination of the role of family in contemporary China mainland, Hong Kong, and Taiwan. In D. Sinha & H. S. R. Kao (Eds.), *Social values and development: Asian perspectives* (pp. 93-124). New Delhi: Sage.

Yang, K. S. (1986). Chinese personality and its change. In M. H. Bond (Ed.), *The psychology of the Chinese people.* New York: Oxford University Press.

7

INDIGENOUS PSYCHOLOGY
Science and Applications

UICHOL KIM

Wilhelm Wundt is recognized as the "father of modern psychology" (Boring, 1950). Psychology, as an "independent, experimental science," is said to have emerged when he established a psychological laboratory at Leipzig University in 1879. He was influential in introducing the experimental method as a tool for probing the human mind. He conducted systematic experiments to explore the content of human consciousness.

Wundt, however, recognized the limitations of the experimental method. He considered it to be appropriate for studying basic sensory processes and inappropriate for investigating psychological phenomena that are shaped by language and culture (Danziger, 1979). Wundt observed that thinking is heavily conditioned by language, custom, and myth. These areas are the primary concern for *Volkerpsychologie* (translated as "cultural psychology" or "ethnopsychology"; Danziger, 1979). He devoted the latter part of his life to analyzing sociocultural influences in human development. He produced a 10-volume publication of *Volkerpsychologie* (1910-1920). Wundt considered psychology to be a part of the *Geisteswissenschaften* (cultural science) tradition and not of the *Naturwissenschften* (natural science) tradition.

Indigenous psychologies represent the cultural science tradition emphasized by Wundt, whereas modern psychology represents the natural science tradition. Modern psychology adopted the experimental approach and emphasized the natural science tradition over the cultural science tradition (Danziger, 1979; Koch & Leary, 1985). Thus Wundt should not be considered as the "father of modern psychology" because he clearly articulated the limitations of the experimental method and the natural science approach.

The limitations of experimental psychology, and psychology as a branch of the natural sciences, are being pointed out by prominent psychologists (e.g., Cronbach, 1975; Gibson, 1985; Toulmin & Leary, 1985). These psychologists emphasize the need to reorient the discipline away from strict adherence to the natural science approach and to realign itself to the cultural science tradition.

Indigenous psychology is one such approach. It recognizes the fact that psychological phenomena are both meaning and context dependent. The goal of indigenous psychologies is to incorporate these factors into psychological research rather than destroying them. The second major difference lies with the way research is conducted. In scientific enterprise, there are three general aspects: description, explanation, and application. Each aspect contributes to the development of scientific knowledge. Experimental psychology has, however, largely bypassed perhaps the most important step: the descriptive phase. Indigenous psychologies, on the other hand, emphasize the need to provide a rich description of a psychological phenomenon as the first step in the scientific endeavor. Description involves recording one's observations. Specifically, it involves systematically organizing and classifying an often chaotic array of data. Francis Bacon emphasized that *systematic classification* of the facts is the first step in organizing and interpreting data (Kemble, 1966).

The second aspect of science involves explaining the observed regularities. Theories are developed to explain underlying regularity. From a particular theory, hypotheses and predictions are generated to test and verify its validity. The third aspect involves application. It involves applying scientific knowledge to find practical solutions to existing problems. The fields of engineering, agriculture, and medicine are a few examples of "applied sciences." Successful application rests largely upon the validity and relevance of the theory to a particular problem at hand. It also involves the appropriate translation of the existing theory to match the problem.

The Three Aspects of Science: An Example

The discovery of the laws of planetary motion can provide an excellent illustration of the three aspects of scientific discoveries. The discovery was a major breakthrough in the history of science, and Johannes Kepler (1571-1630) is credited with their discovery. Prior to Kepler's discovery of these laws, a rich source of data and explanations were available. Over 2,000 years of observations, especially chartings of the movement of the stars and planets, were available. These observations, however, were organized by the Ptolemaic view of the world, with the earth occupying the center of the universe and everything else revolving around it. Moreover, the observed regularity of the planetary motions was explained by the Christian worldview (i.e., the Divine Creation).

Nicolaus Copernicus (1473-1543), however, developed an alternative conception of the solar system, with the sun at the center and planets (including the earth) revolving around it. The new description simplified planetary motion and enabled a better organization of the data than the Ptolemaic theory did. As a result, a more accurate calendar could be developed if people adopted the Copernicus system. This new description was labeled as "heresy" because it challenged and contradicted the Christian worldview.

The third key figure in the discovery of the laws of planetary motion is Tycho Brahe (1546-1601). He devoted his life to systematically charting the locations of various planets and stars. This massive data set was then analyzed by Kepler. Using the Copernicus system, Kepler was able to organize the massive data set into three simple mathematical equations. With these three equations, he could accurately describe and predict planetary motion. He could not, however, explain why planets followed this regular pattern. Similarly, Galileo Galilei (1564-1642), through careful observation and experimentation, discovered that objects, regardless of their internal properties, accelerated in a constant motion. He, too, could not explain the observed regularity.

Sir Isaac Newton (1642-1727) was able to provide a coherent explanation for these observed regularities. The famous event, an apple falling on his head, led him to realize and formulate the Law of Gravitational Attraction. He was able to create a comprehensive theoretical framework that was capable of explaining not only the elliptical orbits of the planets but also the precession of the equinoxes, the behavior of falling bodies, and the oscillations of a pendulum (Kemble, 1966). These discoveries paved the way for advancements in both science and technology.

There are other scientific giants who have relied upon meticulous observation and descriptions that led to their momentous discoveries. Albert Einstein heavily relied upon the massive data set compiled by Rutherford and Bohr in formulating his theory of relativity. Observing and traveling in South America, especially in the Galapagos Islands, helped Charles Darwin to formulate his theory of evolution. In psychology, Sigmund Freud formulated his theory explaining the role of the unconscious by observing his patients in his clinic. Similarly, Jean Piaget formulated his developmental theory by observing and documenting the developmental progression of his children. Like other sciences, the first phase of research in indigenous psychology is description. It involves examining psychological phenomena in their natural environment using existing taxonomies. The second stage is explaining these observed regularities. The third stage may involve applying this knowledge to real-world problems. Beyond this orientation, there are specific qualities of indigenous psychologies that need to be articulated.

Indigenous Psychologies

Webster's Dictionary defines *indigenous* as

native: 1) not introduced directly or indirectly according to historical record or scientific analysis into a particular land or region or environment from the outside; 2) originating or developing or produced naturally in a particular land or region or environment; 3) of, relating to, or designed for natives.

The definition has three features: a) what it is (native); b) what it is not (transported or transplanted from another region); and c) what it is for (designed for natives).

Indigenous psychology can thus be defined as a psychological knowledge that is native, that is not transported from another region, and that is designed for its people. In other words, indigenous psychology is understanding rooted in a particular sociocultural context. It emphasizes the natural use of taxonomies. It examines a phenomenon in a particular sociocultural context and examines how this context affects, shapes, and guides psychological description, explanation, and application.

It is not a psychology of "exotic" people in faraway places. Indigenous understanding is needed for "developed" countries as well as "developing" and "underdeveloped" countries. Each culture needs to develop its own indigenous understanding of its own culture. Second, indigenous psychology does not assume cultural relativity, which emphasizes that each culture is unique and needs to be understood from its own framework, and comparisons with other cultures should not be made. Although the indigenous approach emphasizes the need to understand a culture from its own context, from its own perspective, and from the use of natural taxonomies, it emphasizes the need to search for psychological "universals." Whether or not we can compare results from various cultures to arrive at a universal understanding is a research question that cannot be decided at the outset. It is an issue that needs to be systematically investigated.

Third, it does not assume that one perspective is inherently superior over another. The assumption that one must have been born and raised in a particular culture to understand it is not always valid. It is true that such a person can develop a more accurate and in-depth understanding of his or her own culture. However, within a single culture, people may share common viewpoints and, consequently, view what is "cultural" to be "natural." In his chapter for this volume, Brislin suggests that certain issues are taken for granted and not debated or widely discussed. Such issues can indicate the *importance* of an issue in a culture. Someone with an external viewpoint can call attention to the possibility that what is accepted as "natural" is actually "cultural."

Even within a particular culture, there may not be a single, coherent standard of interpretation; a multitude of explanations can exist. More often than not, there are many different competing ways of organizing and interpreting the world. The debates and discussions on the merits of each approach can enrich a particular field. The merits of each explanation need to be verified by further analysis. Accepting one form of explanation over another often reflects an acceptance of a particular heuristic or convention rather than an "objective" viewpoint.

Fourth, acceptance of indigenous psychologies does not limit the use of a particular method. As Boulding (1980) points out, the goal of science is to find a match between a particular method for the investigation of a particular phenomenon. One cannot, from the outset, recommend either qualitative or quantitative methods. In general, a multiplicity of methods is strongly recommended to increase our confidence that a particular finding is valid and not an artifact of research methodology.

Fifth, indigenous psychology should not be equated with cultural anthropology. Cultural anthropology represents a particular perspective and methodology (such as cultural relativism and the use of ethnography). Although results from a particular society can be unique to that society, this conclusion cannot and need not be made at the outset. It is an empirical question that needs to be tested and validated. Ethnography can be useful in discovering regularities and in providing explanations of these findings. However, results can be method-bound. These results need to be verified by other methods and by other researchers. In cultural anthropology, this is usually not the case. A researcher rarely reexamines a finding of another anthropologist by going into the same field site and collecting additional data. (One notable exception is Freeman's, 1983, controversial reanalysis of Margaret Mead's work *Coming of Age in Samoa*, 1928.) As mentioned above, a multimethod approach can provide greater confidence that the results are reliable and valid. Finally, the focus of indigenous psychology, by definition, is on the psychological perspective, whereas cultural anthropologists focus on the cultural level.

Sixth, Enriquez (1979) distinguishes between indigenization from "within" and indigenization from "without." He describes indigenization from "without" as investigations of particular issues, concepts, and methods that are of interest to one particular culture (e.g., the United States) and are tested in another (e.g., the Philippines). There can be various attempts to modify the instrument to incorporate the local perspective. These modifications can range from simple translation to ensuring comparability and equivalence (i.e., the *derived etic* approach, see Berry, Poortinga, Segall, & Dasen, in press, for a detailed analysis). Although this approach attempts to incorporate and synthesize another culture's perspectives, they have, nevertheless, been preselected and they reflect the interest of the investigator. They may not reflect the interest of the people and the culture who are being investigated. Enriquez (1979) argues that such an approach is often a form of "colonization," although it is purported to be culturally sensitive.

Indigenization from "within" involves a study of issues and concepts that reflect the needs and aspirations of that culture. For example, issues such as illiteracy, poverty, national development, and rural psychology may be salient topics for India but not for industrialized nations (Sinha, 1986, and this volume). Boski (1986) notes that, in addition to indigenous issues and cultural values, *intellectual style* needs to be examined. Intellectual style often determines how one defines the situation, the method one adopts, and the interpretation one chooses. Indigenization from within is closer to the ideal scenario than indigenization from without. In reality, however, many societies do not have the resources to develop their own indigenous psychology. As a consequence, indigenization from without is still the dominant form of cross-cultural investigation.

In addition to the above-mentioned characteristics, there are two other aspects of indigenous psychology. First is the description and explanation of psychological phenomena rooted in their cultural context. The second aspect involves comparing results from one culture with another in search of "universal" generalizations. This second phase is labeled by Enriquez (1979) as the "cross-indigenous approach."

There is a worldwide call for indigenization, representing the "developed," "developing," and "underdeveloped" countries: in Canada (Berry, 1974), France (Moscovici, 1972), Germany (Graumann, 1972), Scandinavia (Smedslund, 1984), Hong Kong (Ho, 1982), China (Ching, 1984), Korea (Kwon, 1979), Japan (Azuma, 1984), the Philippines (Enriquez, 1979), Fiji (Samy, 1978), Turkey (Kâgitçibaşi, this volume), Zambia (Serpell, 1984), India (Sinha, 1986), and Mexico (Diaz-Guerrero, 1986). These scholars point out the limitations of general psychology and urge psychologists to develop their own indigenous psychologies.

Often, contributions from indigenous psychology will expand our conceptualizations of complex psychological concepts. For example, most definitions of *intelligence* in North America focus on cognitive abilities. In the West African community of Baoulé, Dasen (1984) has found that there is a characteristic shared between the U.S. and Baoulé cultures, that of viewing intelligence in terms of literacy, memory, and the ability to process information quickly. Dasen also found that, in addition to cognitive abilities, people in the Baoulé community emphasize "social intelligence" in children (the ability to get along with one another). In Baoulé, cognitive intelligence is not regarded as highly as "social intelligence" (such as serviceableness, responsibility, politeness, obedience). Older adults in Baoulé emphasize that the child's technical ability is useless unless it is applied for the good and well-being of the community. This research raises other empirical questions: Is there a concept of social intelligence in the United States? If so, what is its meaning and what is its relationship to cognitive intelligence? (See Lonner, this volume.) Thus a comparative study has increased our understanding of intelligence, and the discussion is further elaborated from a purely cognitive domain to include the social domain. Thus it has expanded our knowledge and understanding of intelligence as a whole.

In addition to culturally shared characteristics, Dasen (1984) found some unique features in Baoulé that are not found in the United States. One component of intelligence is "to be lucky, to bring good luck." This may reflect a spiritual domain that is neglected in the United States. It may, however, be found in other cultures where spirits are considered to be "real" and part of everyday life.

Extensive research carried out by different people in different parts of the world may lead to candidates for cultural universality. In many European languages, two pronouns (*Tu/Vous,* for example, in the French language) are used to distinguish underlying social relationships. In European languages (such as French, German, Italian, Spanish, and Yiddish), a person of superior standing uses the *Tu* form to address someone of lower standing. A person of lower standing uses the *Vous* form to address someone of higher standing. This reflects an unequal status differential between a dyad. Also, the *Tu* form is used between a dyad of intimate equals, whereas the *Vous* form is used between a dyad of strangers. This reflects social distance. Brown (1965) postulated the "invariant norm of address" to explain this observed regularity. The two underlying dimensions that regulate the kind of pronouns used are postulated to be status and solidarity.

This distinction—the differential use of pronouns—is found in many European languages, and it would constitute a culturally shared phenomenon. In English, however, such usage no longer exists (although, the *Thou/Thee* distinction was used in old English). Nevertheless, the two underlying dimensions are reflected in nominal forms of address, as seen in the use of titles such as *Mr., Dr., Professor* (constituting the formal form) and use of the first name or nickname (constituting the informal form).

In the Korean and Japanese languages, there are no pronomial equivalents to the *Tu/Vous* forms. However, the levels of formality are directly encoded in the verb endings. There are six identifiable levels of formality in the Korean language and four levels in the Japanese language (Martin, 1964). This situation represents a shared characteristic between these cultures that is different from the European form.

Although there are differences among these languages in the form of expression, there appear to be universal rules of address (Kroger, Woods, & Kim, 1984). In the analysis of Chinese, Greek, and Korean usage, Brown's (1965) invariant norm of address has been confirmed, and it can thus be considered as a candidate for a possible universal.

From the systematic analysis of indigenous psychologies (in this example, language use), it is possible to discover universal dimensions of human functioning. It is not an imposition of one's cultural value onto another (an *imposed etic* approach). The cross-indigenous approach can lead to the discovery of "true," empirically based universals. If a discovery is attained through the cross-indigenous approach, it can then be used to enrich the understanding of a particular culture. Moreover, not only is a universal dimension discovered, the range of understanding of the phenomenon is dramatically increased. Information is not lost but gained through a process of comparison. Thus the cross-indigenous approach can be viewed as an additive approach rather than as a subtractive approach.

THE INDIGENOUS APPROACH: TWO EXAMPLES

In the following section, education will be used to highlight the application of the indigenous approach. The first example focuses on the Hawaiian experience; the second example documents the Japanese experience.

Example One: The Hawaiian Experience

Culture is not a static entity but a fluid one. Fluidity ensures smooth transfer and transmission of cultural values, beliefs, and abilities to subsequent generations. *Fluidity* is also used to refer to the all encompassing and persistent forms of influence known as enculturation. *Enculturation* is learning without specific teaching. By an osmosislike process, children acquire the values, skills, and norms of a particular culture (Berry, Poortinga, Segall, & Dasen, in press; Brislin, this volume).

Often, an individual's hedonistic and selfish motives can be a source of conflict for a group. Hence there are deliberate attempts to shape, coax, and mold children's behavior to be socially acceptable and desirable. This is known as *socialization,* the explicit transmission of appropriate attitudes, beliefs, behaviors, and skills from one generation to another.

Socialization takes place in two forms, defined by context: socialization in the family and socialization in public institutions such as the school. Although the content and process of what is learned in each environment can vary, there is usually a close correspondence between the goal of socialization in the family and the goal in the school setting in any given culture. This close correspondence can be disrupted during the process of acculturation when one group dominates and imposes a different set of cultural values, norms, and skills over another (as experienced, for example, by native peoples in North America). In the school environment, certain people, such as Native American, Black American, and Hispanic American children, are often labeled as children at risk because they do not fully benefit from the learning experience, and they also often display "delinquent behaviors" that can disrupt classroom activities. For example, children of Hawaiian ancestry have the lowest level of academic achievement when compared with other ethnic groups and "mainstream" Americans (O'Donnell & Tharp, 1982). In the ordinary school setting, Hawaiian children are often described as lazy, disruptive, and unprepared in the language and cognitive skills necessary for progress in school. Often, these results are interpreted in a "cultural deficit model," where differences are seen as deficiencies.

Tharp and Gallimore (1979) have found that Hawaiian children do not do well in school because their home environments differ significantly from the school environment. Thus the differences in performance can be attributed to "cultural incompatibility" rather than to a "cultural deficit." In other words, values, norms, and skills propagated in the school environment are incompatible with the values, norms, and skills fostered in the home environment. This discrepancy is viewed as the cause of the poor performance and disruptive behavior of Hawaiian children in the school setting.

To empirically verify their contention, they initiated a systematic description of Hawaiian children in their home environments. In this context, they observe that, contrary to previous findings, children are highly responsible (participating in the life of the family, cooking, cleaning, and caring for their siblings) and need minimal adult supervision. An individual child takes initiative and performs tasks whenever he or she perceives a need to do so. Tharp and Gallimore (1979) note that, when work needs to be done in the family, siblings form a group and they are the unit that gets it done. They also notice that the school environment, in contrast, encourages individual initiative and responsibility and prevents collective activities. These findings support their explanation that poor performance and disruptive behavior in the classroom are due to the incompatibility of the school environment rather than to a "cultural deficit."

Taking this descriptive information, they created a new classroom environment that is compatible with the culture. The series of studies is called the Kamehameha Early Education Program (KEEP). In the newly formed classroom environment, collective initiatives and responsibilities are encouraged. The researchers made these observations:

> A teacher would come into a classroom and she gave no assignments and did not ask any children to join her. She merely allowed the children to observe the necessary work and allowed them to observe her in its performance. . . . Within a matter of days, a dependable group of about eight children appeared regularly each morning to participate in this morning work. Within a matter of weeks, the activity was so institutionalized that virtually every member of the class participated in some degree, on some days, as the spirit moved them. By the end of the school year, the academic tasks themselves were being organized by children; that is, they would look at the daily schedule of learning centers, and then they would count out appropriate work sheets, textbooks, and art supplies and distribute them around the room and into the storage boxes. (O'Donnell & Tharp, 1982, p. 302)

Observers were amazed at the pride exhibited by these children, and the sense of involvement and ownership they felt performing these tasks. With similar descriptive observations and interventions, they were able to significantly improve their sociolinguistic and cognitive skills comparable to the national average. Thus these children can no longer be viewed as children at risk. (Cushner, this volume, presents another perspective on this research.)

This program has shown consistently that, when the values, norms, and abilities of school environment are compatible with that of the home environment, children's performance improves. To put it in a broader context, we need to first appreciate children's existing skills, at both the individual and the cultural levels, and use those skills in achieving the desired goal. Researchers (Azuma, 1984; Berry, Poortinga, Segall, & Dasen, in press; Dasen, 1984) have found that children develop a set of values, norms, and skills that are emphasized and propagated by a particular culture and that are adaptive to a particular ecological context. However, when another culture imposes a different set of norms, individuals' previously learned responses can be adversely affected. In other words, Hawaiian children are not incompetent or disruptive by nature, but the imposed environment acts like a cultural straitjacket by blocking their "natural" way of functioning.

There is, however, an unfortunate side to the KEEP program. The positive effects of the program do not seem to last beyond the third year of primary school. When they enter the public school system after the third year, children's performance gradually declines and any gain they achieved is gradually lost. Once competent, confident children gradually begin to exhibit problem behaviors and become children at risk when they are put into an incompatible environment. These results replicate numerous other Head Start programs (early enrichment programs) that fail to produce a sustained short-term effect when the children are no longer in the program (see Sinha, this volume).

Kâgitçibaşi (this volume) has shown that improved confidence and competence can be maintained with an "appropriate" intervention. By understanding the collective nature of Turkish society, and by intervening at the family and the community levels (via mothers), she has shown that dramatic increases in the quality of life (in terms of excellent academic performance of the children, improved mother-child, father-child, and husband-wife relationships) can be permanent rather than temporary changes.

Example Two: The Japanese Experience

At the turn of the twentieth century, Asian Americans as a whole were viewed as "Yellow Perils" and labeled as "genetically inferior" (Kim, 1989). According to Vernon (1982), they were regarded as a "kind of inferior species, who could be used for unskilled labor and menial jobs, but could never be accepted as equals into the White community." They were subjected to great hardships, hostility, and discrimination. In 1924, the Oriental Exclusion Act forbade any Asian immigrants from entering the United States. This law was adopted due to fears that these "genetically inferior" individuals would pollute the genetic pool of the United States and lead to national degeneracy (Chorover, 1980).

Currently, however, that observed difference is reversed. Asian Americans are perceived and labeled as "model minorities." Their economic and educational achievements have been partly attributed to their "genetic superiority" (Vernon, 1982). They came to be regarded as better performers in the school than members of the White majority (Vernon, 1982). In addition to Japanese Americans, Japanese children in Japan show significantly higher performance in math and science abilities when compared with American children (Hess et al., 1986). Within a span of 50 years, how can a "genetically inferior" race suddenly become a "genetically superior" race?

To fully understand this issue, we must first develop a descriptive understanding of the Japanese culture. It has been systematically documented that Japanese students perform at significantly higher levels on tests of mathematics and science. These differences emerge at an early age. Stevenson and colleagues (1986) constructed mathematics tests to empirically verify this observed difference. By analyzing math textbooks from both countries, Japan and the United States, they were able to develop standardized math tests for grades one and five. They then proceeded to select comparable samples of children in both countries: 240 first graders and 240 fifth graders were chosen from each country. As expected, Japanese children scored significantly higher on these tests than American children at both the first and fifth grades. The difference between the two groups was greater in grade five than in grade one. They observed that, by the fifth grade, "the mean of the American classroom with the highest average level of performance lies below that of the worst performing fifth-grade classroom of Japanese children."

There are numerous possible explanations of why these differences are found. First, these findings can be attributed to the differences in the curriculum of each country. However, this is unlikely to be the case because the differences in performance appears at grade one. The children took the test in the first semester of the first grade when they had not been exposed to the curriculum for any significant duration. Even when the same content was introduced in the first grade, the Japanese students still performed at a higher level. The second possible reason is parents' educational status. It is possible that Japanese parents had higher educational achievement than American parents. The results, however, are in the opposite direction: The American parents had a higher educational level than the Japanese parents. The third possibility is that Japanese teachers may have had a higher educational level and greater experience than American teachers. This again was not the case. There are no differences between these two sets of teachers. The fourth possibility is that Japanese students are simply brighter than the American students. Overall, the results are in the opposite direction, with American children scoring higher on intelligence scales when compared with Japanese students.

Significant differences are observed, however, in the amount of time spent on mathematical tasks. Japanese students spend more time in school than American students, spend more time on mathematical tasks in school than American students, and spend more time doing their homework compared with American students. In addition to the sheer amount of time devoted to mathematical tasks, Japanese students are more likely to be engaged in groups, are more attentive, and engage in less inappropriate activities than American students.

Stevenson et al. (1986) conclude that parental contributions appear to be the significant reason that Japanese students outperform American students beyond the sheer amount of time and attention devoted to mathematical tasks. The socialization practices of the Japanese culture are seen as the key to understanding children's school performance. In other words, we need to understand the home environment to fully appreciate children's performance in the school environment.

The socialization practices of the Japanese culture have been systematically documented by several researchers (Azuma, 1984; Befu, 1986; Kojima, 1986; White & LeVine, 1986; Yamamura, 1986). The following summarizes key points in these articles. Azuma (1984) notes that, when a child is born into a family, a Japanese mother tries to minimize the distance between herself and the child and to gratify the child as much as possible. She remains close to the child to make the child feel secure, to make the boundary between her and her child minimal, and to try to meet all the needs of the child, even if that means a tremendous sacrifice on her own part. This type of socialization creates a bonding of interdependence (called *amae* in Japanese). The mother's devotion and indulgence evoke a strong sense of dependence in the child. At the same time, a child senses that it is through the mother that he or she obtains gratification, security, and love. The child gradually senses what pleases the mother and behaves accordingly. Doi (1986) notes that the concept of *amae* is the feeling of dependence coupled with the expectation of indulgence. A child may be demanding, even become tyrannical, but at the same time he or she remains sensitive to the caretaker's desires and feelings.

A child gradually learns of, and identifies with, the mother's values through an osmosislike process. By maintaining close physical and psychological contact, a child learns to identify with the mother and attempts to maintain the close link. The feeling of interdependence helps the child assimilate the mother's hopes and values, and it is through the *amae* relationship that a child learns to behave appropriately. The child attempts to please the mother by behaving in a manner consistent with the mother's desires. Identification with the mother's values and aspirations is essential in maintaining the close bond between them. The fear or punishment for the child is the perception of, or actual separation from, the mother. Thus the psychological and physical distance are often used to shape or correct a child's behavior. She establishes her control over the child through her devotion and indulgence.

As a Japanese child grows up, he or she is expected to transfer such identification and loyalty from his or her mother to other family members, to relatives, to other individuals such as teachers, and to larger social groups such as a company. The mother's job is to prepare her children for adult life and to provide a bridge between the home environment and external environments. She achieves this goal by gradually exposing her child to the culture's social values.

The concept of *sunao* is emphasized in socializing Japanese children. It is roughly translated as "compliance," "obedience," and "cooperation." It also carries a connotation of being open-minded, nonresistant, truthful, authentic in intent, and cooperative in spirit. This does not mean that a child must yield his or her personal autonomy for the sake of cooperation. In the Japanese context, cooperation does not necessarily suggest sacrificing one's wishes, as it may in the West. It implies that working together collectively and harmoniously is a way of expressing and enhancing oneself. In Japanese child development theory, children attempt to *align* the goals of self-fulfillment and the goals of social integration so that both can be met simultaneously.

Because the need for cooperation is paramount in Japan, *yutaka* (meaning "empathy," "receptiveness," or "open-heartedness") is highly valued. It connotes interpersonal sensitivity and anticipation of the needs of others. Although it appears to sound passive and feminine to Western ears, it implies hearty confidence, giving and receiving abundantly, and enjoying social relationships to the fullest. Thus *ningen-rashii* (meaning "humanlike"), which emphasizes the ability to maintain harmony in human relationships, is the most highly valued quality of a child.

Beyond the need to maintain harmonious interpersonal relationships, personal excellence is stressed. In the Japanese educational system, there is a fierce and competitive environment for achievement. Few students are able to attend prestigious universities. Graduation from these universities ensures economic stability and social status, and thus it is highly valued in Japan. The saying, "Pass with four, fail with five," is a common phrase among junior high schoolers in Japan. It means that if you sleep as much as five hours a night you are not studying hard enough. The striving effort is characterized by *gambaru* (persistence), *kuro* (suffering or hardship), *gaman* (endurance), *doryoku* (effort), and *isshokemmie* (utmost self-exertion). There is a strong positive value inherent in these Japanese words that English translations cannot adequately portray. This is why Japanese students are willing to spend more time in school and in doing their homework.

Lebra (1976), using a sentence-completion task, found that over 70% of Japanese respondents, both young and old, men and women, attribute success to diligence, effort, and endurance. Hess et al. (1986) found that, in Japan, poor performance in mathematics is attributed to a lack of effort. Similarly, Japanese children put greater weight on effort in achieving success in school when compared with American children. In contrast, American mothers were more likely to blame training at school if their children performed poorly. For Japanese children, competition is internally focused rather than outwardly directed. This focus on internal striving, rather than external competition, allows for social harmony to be maintained.

Excellence in performance is seen not only as evidence of individual ability but also as a way of cementing and contributing to the group. It provides evidence that a child has developed a moral character through perseverance and persistence. Similar to the Baoulé community, performance qualities are important, but they are only the visible demonstrations of the deeper capacity to be a good person. White and LeVine (1986) note that, in contrast, Americans tend to give priority to highly individualized skills and qualities, such as independence, and to see social abilities as more superficial, or as means rather than ends.

The typical climate of Japanese schools reaffirms the maternalistic protection and indulgence on the one hand, but also pressures the student to cooperate in a group. Because of the *amae* relationship that has been transferred to teachers, students attempt to please the teacher as much as possible. For this reason, Japanese students are more attentive and engage in less inappropriate activities than American students.

Thus, although Japanese classroom size is much larger when compared with American classroom size, Japanese teachers are more effective in disseminating knowledge.

White and LeVine note that, in Japan, there is greater congruence between socialization in the home environment and learning in the school environment than in the United States. This congruence minimizes conflict and contradiction in the development of children's character, ability, and values. They note:

> Clearly, Japanese goals for the child can more easily be achieved in the setting of the school than can ours. Our goals and ideologies are in conflict with the realities of children's development, regardless of cultural setting. Moreover, in the United States, the institution of the school has not provided an environment in which our ideologies of child development and actual qualities valued in the child can be inculcated. (White & LeVine, 1986, p. 61)

This close correspondence between home environment and external environment also applies to the work setting. Misumi (1985) notes that Japanese companies have been able to incorporate cultural features that have led to Japan's phenomenal economic growth and the high quality of Japanese products. They have found that those leaders and companies who emphasized both excellence in performance *and* interpersonal harmony were highly effective. These emphases correspond closely to their socialization experience and to their educational experience.

The relationship orientation is found not only in Japan but also in many other countries. Ho's (1982) analysis reveals that similar concepts are found in China and in the Philippines. Similar results are also found for Korea (Kim, 1988), Turkey (Kâgitçibaşi, this volume), and India (Sinha, 1986).

CONCLUSION

The goal of indigenous psychology is to identify knowledge as understood and experienced by people *within* a culture. Important steps in the indigenous psychology approach are the thorough description and explanation of psychological phenomena as they exist within their cultural context. The two examples presented here, what I have called for convenience "The Hawaiian experience" and "The Japanese experience," reveal that individuals and cultures are not haphazardly dealing with their physical and social environments. An individual is located in an extremely complex environment in terms of the variety of events and stimuli that impinge upon him or her. Possible responses to these events and situations can vary widely. The world from the individual's perspective, however, does not operate in a chaotic fashion but in a meaningful way, for most situations. Individuals systematically organize and interpret their world as a way of dealing with this complexity. Groups and cultures develop strategies to collectively represent and interpret their environment as a way of managing their affairs. These should be the fundamental units of analysis. They cannot and need not be destroyed during the research process. This is the "stuff" that makes human beings human.

REFERENCES

Azuma, H. (1984). Psychology in a non-Western country. *International Journal of Psychology, 19*, 145-155.

Befu, H. (1986). The social and cultural background of child development in Japan and in the United States. In H. Stevenson, H. Azuma, & K. Hakuta (Eds.), *Child development and education in Japan.* New York: Freeman.

Berry, J. W. (1974). Canadian psychology: Some social and applied emphasis. *Canadian Psychological Review, 19*, 93-104.

Berry, J. W., Poortinga, Y. H., Segall, M., & Dasen, P. (in press). *Cross-cultural psychology* (Vol. 2). New York: Cambridge University Press.

Boring, E. G. (1950). *A history of experimental psychology.* Englewood Cliffs, NJ: Prentice-Hall.

Boski, P. (1986). *Between the West and the East: Humanist values and concerns in Polish psychology.* Paper presented at the Eighth International Congress of Cross-Cultural Psychology, Istanbul, Turkey.

Boulding, K. (1980). Science: Our common heritage. *Science, 207*, 831-826.

Brown, R. (1965). *Social psychology.* New York: Free Press.

Ching, C. C. (1984). Psychology and the four modernizations in China. *International Journal of Psychology, 19*, 57-63.

Chorover, S. L. (1980). *From genesis to genocide: The meaning of human nature and power of behavioral control.* Cambridge: MIT Press.

Cronbach, L. J. (1975). The two disciplines of scientific psychology. *American Psychologist, 30*, 671-684.

Danziger, K. (1979). Social origins of modern psychology. In A. R. Buss (Ed.), *Psychology in social context.* New York: Irvington.

Dasen, P. (1984). The cross-cultural study of intelligence: Piaget and the Baoulé. *International Journal of Psychology, 19*, 407-434.

Diaz-Guerrero, R. (1986). *A Mexican ethnopsychology.* Paper presented at the Eighth International Congress of Cross-Cultural Psychology, Istanbul, Turkey.

Doi, T. (1986). *The anatomy of self: The individual versus society.* Tokyo: Kodansha International.

Enriquez, V. G. (1979). Toward cross-cultural knowledge through cross-indigenous methods and perspectives. *Philippine Journal of Psychology, 12*, 9-16.

Freeman, D. (1983). *Margaret Mead and Samoa: The making and unmaking of an anthropological myth*. Cambridge, MA: Harvard University Press.

Gibson, J. J. (1985). Conclusions from a century of research on sense perception. In S. Koch & D. E. Leary (Eds.), *A century of psychology as science*. New York: McGraw-Hill.

Graumann, C. F. (1972). The state of psychology. *International Journal of Psychology, 7*, 123-134.

Hess, R. et al. (1986). Family influences on school readiness and achievement in Japan and the United States: An overview of a longitudinal study. In H. Stevenson, H. Azuma, & K. Hakuta (Eds.), *Child development and education in Japan*. New York: Freeman.

Ho, D. Y. F. (1982). Asian concepts in behavioral science. *Psychologia, 25*, 228-235.

Kemble, E. C. (1966). *Physical science: Its structure and development*. Cambridge: MIT Press.

Kim, H. C. (1989). *Annotated bibliography of Asian-American experience*. Westport, CT: Greenwood.

Kim, U. (1988). *The parent-child relationship: The core of Korean collectivism*. Paper presented at the Ninth International Congress of Cross-Cultural Psychology, Newcastle, Australia.

Koch, S., & Leary, D. E. (1985). Introduction. In S. Koch & D. E. Leary (Eds.), *A century of psychology as science*. New York: McGraw-Hill.

Kojima, H. (1986). Child rearing concepts as a belief-value system of the society and the individual. In H. Stevenson, H. Azuma, & K. Hakuta (Eds.), *Child development and education in Japan*. New York: Freeman.

Kroger, R. O., Woods, L. A., & Kim, U. (1984). Are the rules of address universal? III: Comparison of Chinese, Greek and Korean usage. *Journal of Cross-Cultural Psychology, 15*, 273-284.

Kwon, T. H. (1979). Seminar on Koreanizing Western approaches to social science. *Korea Journal, 19*, 20-25.

Lebra, T. (1976). *The Japanese patterns of behavior*. Honolulu: University Press of Hawaii.

Martin, S. (1964). Speech levels in Japan and Korea. In D. Hymes (Ed.), *Language in culture and society*. New York: Harper & Row.

Mead, M. (1928). *Coming of age in Samoa*. New York: William Morrow.

Misumi, J. (1985). *The behavioral science of leadership*. Ann Arbor: University of Michigan Press.

Moscovici, S. (1972). Society and theory in social psychology. In J. Israel & H. Tajfel (Eds.), *The context of social psychology*. London: Academic Press.

O'Donnell, C. R., & Tharp, R. G. (1982). Community intervention and the use of multidisciplinary knowledge. In A. S. Bellack, M. Hersen, & A. E. Kazin (Eds.), *International handbook of behavior modification and therapy*. New York: Plenum.

Samy, J. (1978). Development and research for the Pacific, and a session on theory and methods. In A. Marmak & G. McCall (Eds.), *Paradise postponed: Essays on research and development in the South Pacific*. Rushcutters Bay, NSW: Pergamon.

Serpell, R. C. (1984). Commentary on the impact of psychology on Third World development. *International Journal of Psychology, 19*, 179-192.

Sinha, D. (1986). *Indigenization of psychology in India and its relevance*. Paper presented at the Eighth International Congress of Cross-Cultural Psychology, Istanbul, Turkey.

Smedslund, J. (1984). The invisible obvious: Culture in psychology. In K. M. J. Lagerspetz & P. Niemi (Eds.), *Psychology in the 1990's*. Amsterdam: North-Holland.

Stevenson, H. et al. (1986). Achievements in mathematics. In H. Stevenson, H. Azuma, & K. Hakuta (Eds.), *Child development and education in Japan*. New York: Freeman.

Tharp, R. G., & Gallimore, R. (1979). The ecology of program research and development: A model for evaluation succession. In L. Sechrest and associates (Eds.), *Evaluation studies review annual* (Vol 4). Beverly Hills, CA: Sage.

Toulmin, S., & Leary, D. E. (1985). The cult of empiricism in psychology and beyond. In S. Koch & D. E. Leary (Eds.), *A century of psychology as science.* New York: McGraw-Hill.

Vernon, P. E. (1982). *The abilities and achievements of Orientals in North America.* New York: Academic Press.

White, M. I., & LeVine, R. C. (1986). What is an Li Ko (good child)? In H. Stevenson, H. Azuma, & K. Hakuta (Eds.), *Child development and education in Japan.* New York: Freeman.

Yamamura, Y. (1986). The child in Japanese society. In H. Stevenson, H. Azuma, & K. Hakuta (Eds.), *Child development and education in Japan.* New York: Freeman.

8

INTERNATIONAL STUDENTS
Cross-Cultural Psychological
Perspectives

R. MICHAEL PAIGE

The purpose of this chapter is to examine a particular group, international students, and study the ways in which they exemplify many of the central issues in cross-cultural psychology. Today, international educational exchange—the movement of students and scholars across national boundaries—is a phenomenon in countries throughout the world. Upward of 1 million students annually are now studying in countries other than their own and the number is increasing. Few nations in the world are unaffected by the presence of international students in their own universities or the demand to study abroad on the part of their own students. The flow of students and scholars, along with the emerging global economy and growing interdependence among nations, is altering higher education as we know it. Once comparatively homogeneous student bodies are today becoming more culturally diverse. Faculties themselves are becoming ever more international in character. Curricula are being revised to include an international dimension. Our world in general and the educational world in particular are in a period of extraordinary change. The flow of international students is a very dynamic and important aspect of a world in transition.

The psychological status of international students—how they perceive and feel about themselves and how they are viewed by their hosts—is the central concern of this chapter. For students interested in cross-cultural psychology, international students provide examples of cross-cultural phenomena such as intercultural communication, cross-cultural adjustment (Berry, this volume), culture learning, and differing socialization histories. For practitioners in intercultural relations professions (e.g., international student advisers, cross-cultural counselors), international students represent a primary client group. The concept of "international student" itself will be discussed as well as the roles international students occupy in their host countries and the cross-cultural implications of their presence. The geographic focus of this chapter is the United States, the country with the world's largest international student population, but the issues are truly global in character and scope. For example, there are debates and controversies surrounding international students in both "receiver" and "sender" nations; these will be examined. There are major questions of concern to researchers and practitioners that cut across national boundaries; these too will be discussed. This chapter also has the goal of introducing international educational exchange, particularly at the tertiary education level, to students new to this field.

We shall see that international students occupy many roles in their host universities and societies. They are students and learners, teaching and research assistants, learning resources for domestic students, competitors for scarce resources, potential skilled workers and immigrants, consumers and economic contributors, the beneficiaries of specialized services, maintainers of enrollments for certain colleges and universities, cultural diplomats, friends at times and strangers at others. Some of these roles are contradictory. Some are viewed quite favorably and others are not. All of them create the mosaic that is the phenomenon of the international student presence abroad.

A vast literature now exists regarding international students. Two very helpful bibliographical reference works are Altbach, Kelly, and Lulat (1985), which lists 2,811 references from 1965 to 1984, and Altbach and Wang (1989), which adds 519 additional references covering the period from 1984 to early 1988.

WHAT IS AN *INTERNATIONAL STUDENT*? DEFINING THE TERM

For the purposes of this chapter, I will define *international students* as individuals who temporarily reside in a country other than their country of citizenship or permanent residence in order to participate in international educational exchange as students, teachers, and researchers. They are also distinguishable by virtue of being culturally different from their hosts.

This definition has three key emphases: the temporary status of the sojourners, the educational purpose of the sojourn, and the cultural backgrounds that distinguish international from host country students.

Later sections treat the important psychological implications of this conceptualization of the international student.

There are some problems with this definition that deserve mention. First, it excludes some groups such as refugees and immigrants. They are not included because they are no longer permanent residents or citizens of the countries they left, neither are they temporary sojourners in their new countries of residence. As Berry (this volume) suggests, their refugee or immigrant status alters their own psychological orientation to the new country as well as how they are received. Yet they are still culturally different in beliefs, values, and behaviors, and are thus similar to international students in that respect. Second, there has been much debate over what to call international students. Some argue that *foreign student* is preferred because it is less conceptually ambiguous (i.e., clearly differentiates domestic and nondomestic students) and more appropriate in a legal sense (e.g., the term used by many nations in immigration and other legal statutes). Others suggest that *foreign student* has a negative connotation and is too restrictive because it excludes domestic students who are studying abroad. In the United Kingdom and some other nations, *overseas student* is used. In general, I have elected to use *international student* in this chapter because of its more embracing nature. The exception is my reference to *foreign teaching and research assistants,* which is in common use in the United States. Let me add that my use of *international student* is not intended to deny the psychological fact that they are often seen as outsiders or "foreigners."

INTERNATIONAL STUDENT FLOWS

International Patterns

The past two decades have witnessed significant growth in the number of students pursuing academic programs in countries other than their own. International student flows across national boundaries increased from approximately 400,000 in 1970 to over 1 million in 1986, the most recent year for which worldwide statistics are available (UNESCO, 1988). As Sirowy and Inkeles (1985) point out, however, these student flows are uneven, being primarily from the developing to the developed nations. By 1986, approximately 75% of all international students were from the developing nations of Africa, Asia, Latin America, and the Middle East; in contrast, 75% of them were studying in Europe and North America (UNESCO, 1988). Clearly, the leading "receiver" nations are the industrialized countries, whereas the vast majority of the "sender" nations are in the developing world.

Among all receiver nations, the United States has the largest number of international students, hosting 356,187 international students, or 33% of the world's total, during the 1987-1988 academic year (Zikopoulos, 1987). According to UNESCO (1988), the United States in 1986 was followed by France (126,762), the Federal Republic of Germany (79,354), the Soviet Union (62,942), the United Kingdom (48,686), Italy (28,068), and Canada (27,210). Japan has emerged very recently as a major host nation, with 22,000 international students in 1988 and a projected 100,000 by the year 2000 (Soga, 1988). Several developing nations are listed by UNESCO among the top-50 receiver countries: Lebanon (25,515), Saudi Arabia (17,970), India (14,410), Syria (12,909), and Egypt (12,235).

What are the implications of these international student flows? First, in those countries where international students are most heavily concentrated, they have made their presence felt, affecting educational institutions and societies. One significant example is the emerging international debate about the economic costs and benefits of hosting international students. In the United States, there is considerable controversy over their impact on graduate-level education. Recognizing the significance of these student flows, both receiver and sender nations are beginning to formulate national policies regarding incoming and outbound students.

International Student Population in the United States

In 1987-1988, there were 356,187 international students in the United States, 6% of the total U.S. student population. (Note: This and other U.S. statistics presented in this section are taken from Zikopoulos, 1987.) The most rapid rate of growth occurred during the 1970s; in 1970-1971, international students numbered 144,708 and, by 1980-1981, this figure had increased dramatically to 311,882, leading some analysts at the time to project that there would be over 1 million international students in the United States by 1990 (Committee on Foreign Students and Institutional Policy, 1982). In fact, between 1980-1981 and 1987-1988, this population increased by only 44,305 to the 1987-1988 total.

Regions and countries of origin. The international student population in the United States is extremely heterogeneous. Zikopoulos (1987) reports that, in 1987-1988, there were students from 186 countries and other "places of origin." By region of origin, 48.8% were from Asia, 12.5% from Latin America, 12.2% from the Middle East, 10.3% from Europe, 9.1% from Africa, 4.7% from North America (Canada), and 1.2% from Oceania.

Noticeably, half of all international students in the United States today are from Asia and the number continues to grow (+5.8% from 1986-1987 to 1987-1988). China has experienced dramatic growth in the past five years and showed a striking 25.7% increase in the past year alone. However, the trend is downward for students from African nations (-9.9%) and the Middle East (-7.1%).

The 10 leading countries of origin in 1987-1988 were Taiwan (26,660), China (25,170), India (21,010), Korea (20,520), Malaysia (19,480), Japan (18,050), Canada (15,690), Hong Kong (10,650), Iran (10,420), and Indonesia (9,010). The most striking one-year increases were experienced by China (+25.7%), Japan (+19.8%), and India (+14.5%). The sharpest one-year declines were Iran (-14.8%) and Malaysia (-10%). The democracy movement in China (p. 174, this chapter) may have an impact on the number of students who travel abroad for study.

Academic fields of study. Since 1954-1955, the engineering fields have annually attracted the largest number of international students. In 1987-1988, 20.7% were enrolled in engineering, followed by 18.8% in business and management, 9.9% in mathematics and computer sciences, and 8.4% in the physical and life sciences. Conversely, over the past 35 years, there has been a steady decline in the number of international students enrolled in the humanities and the social sciences, from 30.8% of the total in 1954-1955 to only 12.3% in 1987-1988.

Additional demographic characteristics. First, undergraduate students slightly outnumber graduates, 49.6% compared with 43.8% in 1987-1988. Second, males significantly outnumber females. In 1987-1988, men accounted for 67.7% and women for 32.3% of the total. However, there has been a slow but steady increase in female enrollments since 1959-1960, when they represented only 21.7% of the international student population. Third, single students vastly outnumber married students, 79.8% to 20.2%, a statistic that has been relatively stable over the years. Finally, contrary to popular belief, most international students pay for their education with personal or family funds. Fully 75.6% receive their funds from home, compared with 24.4% who receive support from U.S. sources such as teaching and research assistantships or U.S. government sponsorship.

THE STATUS AND ROLES OF
INTERNATIONAL STUDENTS

The Legal Status of International Students

In most countries, international students have a special legal status generally codified in the host country's immigration laws. They are not citizens and do not have the same rights as citizens. In many countries, including the United States, there are employment restrictions or bans placed on international students. Under U.S. immigration law, "foreign" students are determined to be here for the primary purpose of obtaining an education. The student visa that permits them to enter the United States is explicitly for the purpose of academic study. They must always maintain full-time student status, and employment, when allowable, is usually limited to part-time work. In addition, tax laws in many countries apply differently to foreign nationals.

Although these regulations may be reasonable at first glance, they are undeniably discriminatory. In many receiver nations including the United States, international students pay a nonresident rate of tuition that can be twice as high as the cost to residents. Also, they do not have the same flexibility as host country students to drop in and out of school, reduce their course load, or work to help support themselves. This can cause great stress among those who find themselves having difficulties with their studies or are experiencing serious financial problems.

Second, international students in many if not most receiving countries do not have the same access to social welfare services as nationals. In the United States, it is a violation of the terms of the student visa to become "a ward of the state." Applying for a service or subsidy reserved for citizens (e.g., health care, food stamps) could endanger the applicant's visa status. Third, international students in some countries may not have the same protections under the law reserved for citizens and, even if they do, they do not always know how the legal system works, what those protections are, or how to gain access to legal assistance.

The Cultural Status of International Students

International students are culturally different from host nationals. They bring their cultural orientations with them: values, beliefs, patterns of behavior, ways of learning, and thinking (refer to the dimensions reviewed in the Triandis chapter of this volume). Some of these contrast sharply to those of the host culture and can cause serious communication and interaction problems between internationals and their hosts. Many features of the new culture are also subtle and difficult to recognize, leaving international students in a state of ambiguity and uncertainty. The sojourner's responses—frustration, anxiety, uncertainty, anger, extreme homesickness, depression—are popularly referred to by the term *culture shock* and in the theoretical literature as *cultural adjustment* and *culture learning*.

Adjusting to and learning about the culture. International students experience a process of cultural adjustment that at times is stressful and difficult to handle (Bennett, 1986; Grove & Torbiorn, 1986; Weaver, 1986). Cultures are exceedingly complex and learning about them can be fatiguing. According to Grove and Torbiorn (1986), the adjustment process is especially difficult for adults who are accustomed to functioning effectively in their own cultures. The new culture reduces their ability to function with the expected degree of proficiency and they begin to lose their self-esteem. Moreover, many international students, especially graduate students, experience a significant status reduction from professional person back to student. Their past accomplishments are not recognized, by and large, and they are in the uncomfortable position of being much lower in the status hierarchy. Researchers and practitioners have identified cultural adjustment as one of the major problems facing international students (Amoh, 1984; Thomas & Althen, 1989).

Adjusting to the academic environment. International students can be disoriented by the education system too. As Cushner (this volume) points out, the learning styles of the international students may not fit the new learning environment. Hoff (1979) coined the term "education shock" for the experience of encountering significant differences in the academic environment. In her study of two nationality groups studying in American universities, the respondents identified 56 classroom-generated differences, 16 of which were ongoing barriers to learning. Hamouda (1986) identified the following academic adjustment problems of international students: (a) adviser-related difficulties, (b) curriculum-program relevance, (c) discrimination, (d) instructor-related difficulties, and (e) university-system difficulties.

Psychological acculturation. International students experience the process of psychological acculturation and acculturative stress described by Berry in this volume. Pressure to conform to the values, norms, and patterns of behavior in the new culture is an issue facing every international student. Many want to participate in and learn as much as possible about the host culture, but they do not want to lose their sense of cultural identity. They are also concerned about becoming culturally marginal, that is, conversant in both cultures but not fully accepted by either. Marginalization becomes more severe when (a) there is pressure to conform to the new culture, (b) the new culture limits international students from full participation, (c) the students desire to become integrated into the new culture, (d) the students desire to maintain their own cultural identity, and (e) the student's own culture views returnees with suspicion.

Recently, a very insightful Chinese student told me that he was worried about being "Americanized" and then going home and having great difficulty fitting back in. To avoid this, he was consciously trying to resist adopting American ways. Yet he felt that his efforts were not proving entirely successful. As he put it, "Inevitably, I am going to be influenced by this culture, perhaps in ways that are not now clear to me. But the ways in which I have changed will be obvious to my professional associates, friends, and family."

In very personal terms, this Chinese student was posing the classical dilemma of becoming multicultural and marginal; sojourners are not fully integrated into the new culture, but neither do they feel completely accepted by the home culture (Adler, 1976). International students can adopt the strategy of maintaining a certain distance from the host culture, but they will learn less about it and have a less satisfying sojourn. Or they can participate actively and adapt well but then face a more difficult reentry adjustment process because they will have experienced greater personal change in beliefs, values, and behavioral norms. As we shall see later, one aspect of the reentry adjustment phenomenon is coming to grips with the personal changes that have occurred while abroad.

Practitioners should understand that some international students will strongly resist the pressures to conform to the host culture but will still need assistance adjusting to the new society and academic environment. Many universities have developed sophisticated cross-cultural orientation programs for international students (see Bhawuk, this volume, regarding cross-cultural orientation). On the matter of acculturation and acculturative stress, many advisers will encourage international students to seek a balance between participation in the new culture and the maintenance of their own cultural identities. Programs that provide international students with opportunities to serve as learning resources for domestic students have been successful in helping promote both the international students' integration into the academic community and their cultural self-esteem.

The Roles International Students Occupy and the Ways in Which They Are Perceived

The roles international students occupy and the ways they are perceived in their host countries vary greatly. They are, of course, students. But it is often perceived that they are here because of our superior education systems, advanced technologies, and developed economies. As Mestenhauser (1983) puts it, the prevailing viewpoint is they are here to learn from us. He hypothesizes that this perception has the psychological consequence of making us feel superior (especially to developing world students) and inhibits the degree to which we feel we can learn from them. In Morris's (1960) classic study, international students were found to be acutely sensitive to host country attitudes toward their nations. If they felt their countries were viewed negatively or as inferior, their attitude toward the United States would be negative and their adjustment to U.S. culture hampered. In addition, Mestenhauser (1983) asserts that international students are perceived as handicapped, that is, lacking adequate language ability, satisfactory academic preparation, sound analytical reasoning skills and academic writing skills, and familiarity about our education system and how it works. Psychologically, this again places us in the superior position but mitigates against our viewing international students as coequals.

Second, they compete for scarce resources (access to competitive academic programs, scholarships, assistantships) and thus are viewed as competitors. As the percentage of international students in graduate programs and holding teaching assistantships increases, this perception becomes stronger. From a psychological perspective, a negative reaction is predictable when the "outsider" begins to accumulate benefits that are limited. When foreign-trained medical doctors began to make major inroads into the American medical profession in the late 1960s and early 1970s, the U.S. Congress in 1976 passed PL 94-484 and PL 95-83 (Health Professions Educational Assistance Act), which placed severe restrictions on foreign medical graduates and virtually eliminated them as competitors for medical positions in the United States. That legislation still exists today.

Third, many international students serve as cultural resources who can enrich our students and our communities (Mestenhauser, 1976, 1983; Paige, 1983). The states of Oregon and Minnesota have programs that provide modest financial support to international students in return for their "international education" contributions to the community (e.g., making presentations to local schools and civic organizations). The Minnesota legislation, passed in 1976, explicitly recognized the contribution of international students to the state's "cultural mix." Generally, the cultural resource role is perceived very favorably and is one of the most important noneconomic benefits associated with international students. Fourth, they are economic resources who contribute to our economy. For some colleges and universities (especially the smaller ones), international students help maintain enrollments and are an important source of tuition revenue. For the local business community, international students are consumers, purchasing local goods and services. For purely economic reasons, international students are generally, although not always, perceived positively. Finally, international students occupy the role of the outsider. Although they may reside for long periods of time in the host country, they are still most likely to be viewed as "foreigners."

CRITICAL ISSUES REGARDING INTERNATIONAL STUDENTS

Foreign Teaching Assistants: Intercultural Contact and Conflict

In some countries, international students serve as teaching and research assistants. This is certainly true in the United States, where there is a long history of using graduate students to teach undergraduate courses and where there are not now enough qualified U.S. graduate students in many departments to fill these positions. However, there has been a significant amount of controversy surrounding foreign TAs. Critics have complained that foreign TAs lack the necessary English language skills and cannot communicate effectively with students, are taking jobs away from needy U.S. students, are unfamiliar with the testing and grading system, do not understand the norms and values of the new educational system, and lack strong teaching skills.

How dissatisfied are American students? Barber and Morgan (1988), reporting on their survey of graduate engineering program deans and faculty throughout the United States, found widespread dissatisfaction. Specifically, 74.1% of the respondents said foreign TAs had problems communicating with their students. Other problems included lack of understanding of U.S. undergraduate culture and unfamiliarity with academic norms.

The issue became volatile enough that, by 1988, 12 state legislatures had passed laws mandating U.S. higher education institutions to test TAs for English language ability (*Chronicle of Higher Education*, 1988). Although Brown and Fishman (1989) have raised serious questions regarding the legality of these English language requirements, the political pressure remains for universities to test for language competence.

What are the causes of the "foreign TA problem"? Bailey (1984) and Mestenhauser et al. (1980) have identified the following factors: a rapid and sizable increase in the number of foreign TAs during the 1970s and 1980s; ethnocentrism on the part of U.S. students; the attitude of consumerism among students; demands for quality education and accountability; the lack of adequate language and teaching skills; and inadequate understanding of the norms of the classroom environment among international students. I have hypothesized that an unequal status relationship existed that contributed to unfavorable American student attitudes toward foreign TAs. With the international student in the higher-status TA role, the American student was now in the unaccustomed lower-status position. Consequently, the American is now in the psychologically uncomfortable and unfamiliar role of being the status-inferior person (Paige, 1983). Several studies have made it clear that it is more than just a language problem. Brown (1988) studied the effects of country of origin, educational background, and native speaking background on students' attitudes toward nonnative instructors. Groups of American students were shown the same videotape of a foreign TA (who had been tested as being fluent in English and who spoke a mildly accented English) but told different things about the instructor's background. The results showed that U.S. students differentially evaluated the TA only on the basis of the written information provided. In effect, the more "foreign" the TA, the more negative the evaluations.

The foreign TA problem is significant to international educational exchange professionals because it is a potentially volatile and highly visible issue. When this becomes the dominant international student issue with its attendant negative publicity, public support for international education can be seriously eroded. Despite the actual causes of the host students' discontent, and there are many, blame is often placed on the international students themselves and the university administrators who hire them.

I believe educators need to alter the terms of this debate by focusing on the value of diversity and encouraging domestic students to view foreign TAs as resources for acquiring international and intercultural understanding as well as subject-matter-specific knowledge. It is also important for universities to offer training programs that can help orient foreign TAs to the new academic environment and, if necessary, help them improve their English. For a more detailed treatment of this topic, the reader is referred to Bailey, Pialorsi, and Zukowski-Faust (1984).

Economic Perceptions of International Students and International Education: Costs and Benefits

From a psychological perspective, I have argued that international students are perceived as outsiders. Consequently, they are not viewed as having the same claim host country citizens do to benefits that are highly valued but in limited supply such as scholarships and assistantships. Do international students gain "economic legitimacy" by paying more than domestic students for their education (as many do), helping colleges maintain enrollments, spending money on goods and services in their host communities, and upon their return home becoming consumers and importers of host country products? First, we must answer the question, "Do the costs of educating them outweigh the benefits?"

Costs and benefits to the receiving nations. There is an emerging literature on this issue (Dresch, 1987; Gale, 1988; Williams, 1981). Economic costs are generally measured in terms of (a) the full, non-subsidized cost of a student's education; (b) the cost of goods, services, and staff provided exclusively to international students (e.g., international student advisers, specialized international admissions officers); (c) scholarships and financial aid offered to international students (if any); and (d) the costs of recruiting international students. Blaugh (1981, p. 49) operationally defines benefits as (a) the market value of scientific research carried out by international students, (b) the contribution international students make to the nation's exports, (c) the contribution international students make to the nation's balance of payments, and (d) the contribution international students make to the demand for the nation's goods and services. Gale (1988) has defined "economic benefits" in terms of the impact international students make on the regional economy.

The results of empirical research studies have been contradictory. Blaugh (1981, p. 87), in his study of "overseas" students in the United Kingdom, concluded that "the net costs of overseas students exceed their economic benefits." However, several recently conducted U.S.

studies contradict Blaugh by showing that the positive economic impact on the educational institution and the regional economy far outweighed the costs (Blankenship, 1980; Rosenberg, 1987; University of Iowa, 1988; Wennergren & Juan, 1981). In addition, Dresch (1987) asserts that international students help maintain the productivity of graduate schools and, after graduating, serve as an increasingly important source of labor in the academic-scientific community. The weight of the evidence, at least in the United States, supports the view that international students make substantial economic contributions that outweigh the costs.

Are international students being perceived more favorably and gaining greater legitimacy to compete for scarce resources as a result of their economic contributions? Not entirely. Barber and Morgan (1988) suggest that there is widespread concern about our dependence on international graduate students, in spite of their economic contribution. In psychological terms, that very dependence can trigger resentment. The foreign TA controversy persists in spite of the empirical evidence that there are not enough qualified U.S. students in many departments to fill all of the available assistantship positions. Moreover, the results of these highly academic cost-benefit studies have not been well publicized. The public at large, and domestic students in particular, do not understand the full extent of the international students' economic contribution to the university or the community.

In my view, the economic argument of and by itself is not a sufficient rationale for educating international students. I believe universities must possess a philosophical commitment to international and intercultural learning as a core component of a university education, a commitment that can be implemented by a culturally diverse student body. This shifts the psychological ground to viewing international and domestic students of color as valuable resources within the university community.

Costs and benefits to sending nations. There is just as much controversy in sending nations about the value of dispatching students to other countries for their education. Proponents argue that study abroad helps the country develop badly needed, highly skilled human resources; in other words, an investment in overseas education is an investment in human capital. According to this theoretical position, students return home ready to contribute to national development efforts by serving as educators, high-level administrators, government officials, technical experts, and researchers. It is hypothesized that eventually these returnees help the sending country break the cycle of dependence on foreign education and foreign technology by providing those skills themselves. Fry (1984, p. 72) conducted an empirical study of the impact of study abroad on subsequent economic development in 84 developing nations and he found that "the global empirical data analyzed here indicate positive economic and political effects of study abroad over the long term."

There are risks to the sending nations. One is that the students may not return at all, preferring to remain in the host country (the "brain drain" problem). Another risk is that the returning students may attempt to force significant changes upon the home country's education and political systems. Hawkins (1984, p. 30), writing presciently about Chinese students returning to the People's Republic, observed that "there is an overt desire not only to transfer the techniques and technologies learned in the West but also to transform institutions and interpersonal relations in line with practices in the West and Japan." Although the evidence is unclear, many would argue that the Chinese prodemocracy movement of 1989 was encouraged, if not inspired, by students who had studied overseas.

Goodman (1984) argues that Western education creates psychological dependence. International students are socialized to believe in the superiority of Western forms of knowledge and the sanctity of educational institutions as the legitimizers of expertise in society. For example, physicians who are trained in Western-style medical schools replace traditional healers as the legitimate providers of health care. Goodman (1984, p. 18) concludes: "The current international institutionalization of education contributes to a dependence and lack of self-confidence in the developing world, and this will tend to inhibit the development of local theories of society and homegrown strategies for change." As an example of homegrown strategies, readers are referred to the chapter by Kâgitçibaşi and Kim (this volume).

Sending nations are also concerned about the relevance of overseas education for their students. Moock (1984) asserts that the knowledge and skills acquired abroad are often irrelevant to home country conditions; students are not properly prepared to utilize their newly acquired skills upon their return, and, therefore, cannot be expected to have much impact on improving local institutions. I have suggested that the question of relevance raises a serious challenge for educators in the industrialized receiver nations. University curricula are rarely concerned with Third World issues and international students are rarely provided with training in the appropriate transfer of technology (Paige, 1988).

Counseling International Students:
The Issue of Cultural Differences

The literature on cross-cultural counseling has been expanding in recent years and now includes valuable texts by Marsella and Pedersen (1980), Pedersen (1985), Pedersen, Draguns, Lonner, and Trimble (1976, 1981, 1989), and Sue (1981).

What are the central issues in the counseling of international students? Thomas and Althen (1989, pp. 9-13) have identified the following:

> The initial adjustment to the new culture . . ., academic difficulty stemming from the novelty of the academic system . . ., political, religious, and social conflicts that arise among their fellow nationals . . ., the impact of developments in their home countries—wars, radical changes in government, economic difficulties . . ., cross-cultural male-female relationships . . ., social isolation, depression, and paranoia . . ., financial difficulties . . ., anxiety brought on by fear of immigration authorities . . ., stressful relationships with particular Americans, especially advisers, roommates and landlords . . ., dealing with new-found freedom . . ., dealing with disappointed expectations . . ., dealing with death of family and friends at home . . ., anxieties about returning home.

The issues facing international students are varied and complex. The professional training of host country counselors rarely includes adequate preparation for serving culturally different clients. Moreover, international students are unlikely to share the counselor's conception of the counselor's role. Western counseling psychology focuses heavily on the counselor as a facilitator whose goal is to promote client self-reliance, independence, and personal responsibility. Many international students come from "collectivist cultures," where the focus is on the community and where codependence replaces independence as the norm (Triandis, this volume; Triandis, Brislin, & Hui, 1988). Not only are these students more likely to become dependent on and seek more direction from the counselor, they may avoid or reject counselors who insist that they behave more independently. In a broader sense, the beliefs international students have regarding physical and mental health, the causes and consequences of disease, and appropriate health care providers may be substantially at odds with those of the host culture (for more on this topic, the reader is referred to Ilola, this volume).

What are the implications for international student advisers and counselors? In my view, the professional training and ongoing professional development of counselors must include a strong cross-cultural counseling component. More specifically, Thomas and Althen (1989) propose that counselors should learn to modify their communication style, modify their counseling strategies to be more consistent with client needs and expectations, explain the adjustment process to their clients, deal with the depression syndrome associated with adjustment stress, and acknowledge cultural differences. For more on this topic, the reader is also referred to Draguns (this volume).

International Students in U.S. Graduate Education

Today, some U.S. graduate programs are dependent upon international students for their very existence. This is most noticeable in graduate engineering programs, where they constitute 50% or more of the total student population. As Barber and Morgan (1988) discovered in their survey of 651 departmental chairpersons and 943 faculty in U.S. engineering schools, the large percentage of international students has raised some concerns. Their inquiry focused on five provocative questions concerning the impact of international students: (1) Are U.S. students being displaced by internationals in graduate engineering programs? (2) Is the process and content of engineering education changing to meet the needs of international students? (3) Are international students affecting the quality of engineering education and research? (4) Are international students inhibiting the ability of faculty to conduct research considered sensitive to national security? (5) Are changes occurring in the composition of faculty?

Regarding the access question, respondents reported that there is a shortage of U.S. citizen applications and that international students are not displacing U.S. students. Indeed, just the opposite appears to be the case, that is, they are helping maintain graduate student enrollments. Although the majority of respondents would prefer to admit more U.S. students, those students are not there in adequate supply. On the second question, there is little evidence that engineering education has changed to meet the needs of international graduate students. For example, only 10.3% of the faculty used relevant teaching examples and only 20.6% reported utilizing international students as resources in classroom discussions.

Questions regarding the impact of international students on quality produced a mixed response. Although they were seen to be quite satisfactory as students, there were negative consequences in two areas: the impact on instruction as a result of using foreign TAs and the impact on research from using foreign research assistants. Foreign TAs were not perceived to be as effective as U.S. TAs. Foreign research assistants were perceived to be too theoretical and not practical enough in orientation. In addition, U.S. faculty reported having to spend more time and effort teaching international students compared with U.S. students. Interestingly, on many of these issues, foreign-born faculty respondents held more favorable attitudes than U.S. faculty toward international graduate engineering students. On the matter of national security, few of the faculty reported problems (e.g., international students being barred from research projects) that inhibited their ability to pursue their research ideas. Finally, the character of U.S. engineering faculties is changing. Today, 30.6% of faculty are foreign-born. We can expect to continue to recruit faculty from international Ph.D. recipients, and quite likely the percentage of foreign-born faculty will increase.

What do the authors conclude? First, due to the inadequate supply of U.S. students, graduate engineering education is dependent upon international students. It is thus vulnerable to shifts in demand and worldwide changes in the patterns of student flows. Similarly, U.S. academia and to a lesser extent U.S. industry have become dependent on foreign-born, U.S.-educated scientists and engineers. If international graduate engineering students ceased coming, there would be a negative impact on higher education (a shortage of qualified TAs) and industry (where foreign-born people now constitute 3.5% of all professional employees). The authors conclude it is not in the national interest to become excessively dependent on international students, especially if America's research agenda shifts more toward national defense and commercial applications of findings.

From a psychological perspective, I believe there is an uneasiness about our dependence on international students in engineering. We can hypothesize that this relates to the distrust of the outsider and to our discomfort about being dependent on foreigners for maintaining enrollments and quality programs. Unfortunately, the findings provide little evidence to suggest that international students are being utilized in a positive sense to promote the internationalization of graduate engineering education.

International Students as Learning Resources:
Implications for Domestic Students and
for Internationalizing the Curriculum

"Internationalizing the curriculum" is a popular phrase today in education circles. Greater attention is being placed on providing students at all levels with international knowledge and skills. Many are referring to this as the global education movement. Lamy (1987, p. 6) identifies four intellectual goals of global education: (a) knowledge acquisition from a multiple perspective, meaning, "substantive and verifiable information . . . selected to represent the variety of cultural, ideological, historical, and gender perspectives present in our world"; (b) the exploration of worldviews, that is, "a careful review of the values, assumptions, priorities and policy orientations which are used to interpret both public and private issues"; (c) skills for understanding, that is, skills that enable students to critically analyze and evaluate information; and (d) strategies for participation and involvement, so that students can connect global issues and local concerns.

Can international students contribute to these global education efforts? Mestenhauser (1976, 1983; Mestenhauser, Marty, & Steglitz, 1988) believes they can. He suggests they can assist domestic students in the learning of foreign languages and learning about Third World development issues, economic interdependence, the international transfers of technology, gender roles across cultures, international inequalities, global poverty, the problems of nation-building confronting the comparatively newer nation-states, and a host of other global issues. It has been shown that international students can also help U.S. students acquire new skills in cross-cultural communication, interdisciplinary thinking and problem solving, and the interviewing of native informants (Paige, 1983, 1988). For example, I have taken international students to communities throughout the state of Minnesota to discuss their cultures, their countries, and global issues with K-12 teachers and students. The evaluations have been highly favorable (Paige, 1983). Mestenhauser (1976) has effectively utilized international students as teachers in a wide range of university-level courses.

Internationalizing the curriculum of any course or discipline is a matter of both content and process. International students can introduce innovative content by presenting new, alternative perspectives on the issues under consideration. The can make presentations about their own countries. They also introduce writings by home country authors. For U.S. students preparing to go abroad, international students from those destinations can be excellent resources. They can help the prospective sojourners begin to familiarize themselves with the country and its culture as well as answer specific questions the students might have. They can realistically discuss the issue of cultural adjustment for they themselves have already gone through it. And they can motivate and encourage U.S. students about the upcoming adventure in learning. Moreover, through their interactions with domestic students, international students themselves gain new insights into the host culture and reevaluate the stereotypes they brought with them initially. Kâgitçibaşi (1978), one of the contributors to this volume, found in an earlier study that Turkish students who spent a year in the United States showed a significant increase in world-mindedness and a corresponding decrease in authoritarianism.

The Emerging Cultural Diversity Agenda and the Involvement of International Students

In many nations, ethnic, racial, and other forms of diversity is a fact of life. So, unfortunately, is racism and conflict among groups. In the past few years, the United States has witnessed ugly incidents of racism on college campuses directed against domestic minority students (Steele, 1989). Many U.S. colleges and universities have responded by promoting the positive value of cultural diversity and by offering programs designed to increase tolerance and respect across cultures. These efforts are relatively new and, in the main, have been designed to reduce conflict between domestic majority and minority students.

International students are also in the minority and are vulnerable to attack from prejudiced, ultranationalistic, and ethnocentric students. For example, the period of the Iranian hostage crisis was a very difficult time for Iranian (and other) international students in the United States. Psychologically, all Iranians were lumped together and viewed by some Americans as the enemy. The intriguing question here is how we might relate multicultural issues, by which I mean the improvement of domestic interracial relations, with international issues, in this quite specific context, meaning better relations between domestic and international students. Cross (1989) suggests that international and domestic minority students can learn a great deal from each other. By way of example, international students can acquire important perspectives about racism and poverty in America, as well as about the ways in which the United States has responded, from domestic students of color. Domestic minority students can explore the problems of diversity in the context of national development from Third World students. Both groups can enhance their intercultural communication skills.

For practitioners, the emerging cultural diversity agenda includes the central objective of reducing prejudice and racism. My view is that programs pertaining to cultural diversity should promote both multicultural and international learning for all students, a more favorable climate for both cross-national and interracial relations on campus, and specialized opportunities for domestic students of color and international students to learn from each other.

International Women and Families: The Dilemmas of Value Conflict and Cultural Adjustment

Many international women (and some men) accompany their spouses to the new country and find that they are faced with many challenges. If they bring their children, they may be the primary caretaker. They may also need to work in order to assist the family financially. And they have to deal with their own and the family's social and cultural adjustment. The student spouse has a well-defined academic purpose for being in the new country and a support structure consisting of other students and university resources into which to fit. Generally, however, the "accompanying" spouse and other family members lack a clear support structure and can feel quite isolated. In addition, international women from more traditional societies often occupy roles that are sharply differentiated from those of men and they often experience serious cultural value conflicts when exposed to life in the industrial societies. Advisers frequently encounter female clients who accompanied their husbands primarily for the purpose of looking after the needs of the home, the children, and the husband. However, as they become aware of the educational opportunities that are readily available to them, they often wish to take advantage of them and come to resent being constrained by the responsibility of managing the household. This problem is compounded when they are strongly encouraged to pursue their goals by their host country friends. To pursue their goals, however, may put them at odds with their own cultures. Domestic strife is not uncommon among married international students, and many attribute the cause to the changing views international women come to have regarding their own needs and goals. Practitioners need to be aware of the special needs of families and help create support systems such as special orientation programs, access to advising services, opportunities to socialize and feel integrated into the university community, and so forth.

Reentry: The Final Dilemma

Eventually, international students must confront the prospect of returning home and this often causes great anxiety. The literature suggests that "reentry shock" is as powerful as culture shock and that there are many issues associated with reintegrating oneself back into the home society (Goodwin & Nacht, 1986; Hood & Schieffer, 1984; Martin, 1984).

What are the dominant concerns? First, they are very concerned about finding employment congruent with their aspirations and consistent with their education and training. They are also worried about how they are going to infuse the skills and knowledge they acquired abroad into the workplace in the home culture milieu. Can the technology they learned be transferred back home? Will books and equipment be available to allow them to continue doing the kind of research and scholarship they did abroad? Will they fit culturally into the workplace? Will they be accepted by their peers (especially those who didn't study overseas)? Will they, in turn, be able to respect their colleagues, especially those who have not studied abroad or attained the same advanced level of education? Second, there is great concern about fitting back into the home culture. Will it be the same? Will things have changed at home? Will they have changed so much that they won't be comfortable? Third, they worry about family life and the many obligations that they temporarily left behind. Fourth, they worry about the degree to which the different values, habits, customs, and patterns of behavior that they acquired abroad will have actually become preferred values and behaviors. Fifth, they worry about losing the skills they acquired.

There are also reentry issues facing spouses, particularly international women, and families. For example, parents worry about their children having become too assimilated and facing difficulties fitting in back home. International women who have taken advantage of new learning opportunities abroad wonder if they will be able to utilize their skills and knowledge in new ways at home. In summary, there are numerous issues facing the returnees, and practitioners should be prepared to help them explore these issues. Some universities are offering reentry programs, workshops, and courses for students about to depart for their home countries.

CONCLUSION

As we have seen, the issues associated with international students are numerous and complex. At the national level, their presence has prompted government officials and educators in the receiver nations to question their impact on national security, academic quality and curricula, and the economy. The sender nations are equally concerned about the long-term impact of having so many of their most talented youth studying abroad. Although they may return home and provide badly needed skills for national development purposes, they may also be a source of destabilization. At the individual level, international students experience profound psychological changes during their sojourn abroad and after they return home. They also have an important impact on host country nationals who come in contact with them. The nature of cross-cultural relations between international students and host country nationals, whether these are positive or negative, is strongly influenced by how host country institutions and individuals perceive international students.

I will conclude with the observation that one of the best ways to have access to cross-cultural learning and cross-cultural research is through extensive interactions with international students. Their presence provides an extraordinary learning opportunity that is all too often neglected. Through our mutual interactions, we can acquire new perspectives on our societies, learn about other nations and cultures, acquire intercultural communication skills, gain a more global understanding of the knowledge being produced in the academic disciplines, and more effectively prepare ourselves for future careers with multicultural and international dimensions. The opportunity for personal and professional growth is profound.

The psychological barriers to learning across cultures are formidable. International students are outsiders who challenge our beliefs and ways of doing things. They compete with us not only in the international marketplace but ever more frequently for scarce and desirable resources in our own countries. They may express points of view and represent economic or political systems that are unpopular. To the degree that they resist the pressures to conform or assimilate, they can make us feel uncomfortable. The challenge for practitioners is to design learning environments that help surmount these barriers and thus encourage the unique opportunities for learning across cultures that are possible.

REFERENCES

Adler, P. S. (1976). Beyond cultural identity: Reflections on cultural and multicultural man. In L. A. Samovar & R. E. Porter (Eds.), *Intercultural communication: A reader* (pp. 362-378). Belmont, CA: Wadsworth.

Altbach, P. G., Kelly, D. H., & Lulat, G. M. (Eds.). (1985). *Research on foreign students and international study: An overview and bibliography.* New York: Praeger.

Altbach, P. G., & Wang, J. (1989). *Foreign students and international study: Bibliography and analysis, 1984-1988.* Washington, DC: National Association for Foreign Student Affairs.

Amoh, K. O. (1984). *Newly arrived foreign students at a U.S. university: Their adjustment difficulties and coping strategies.* Unpublished doctoral dissertation, University of Minnesota.

Bailey, K. M. (1984). The foreign TA problem. In K. M. Bailey, F. Pialorsi, & J. Zukowski-Faust (Eds.), *Foreign teaching assistants in U.S. universities* (pp. 3-15). Washington, DC: National Association for Foreign Student Affairs.

Bailey, K. M., Pialorsi, F., & Zukowski-Faust, J. (Eds.). (1984). *Foreign teaching assistants in U.S. universities.* Washington, DC: National Association for Foreign Student Affairs.

Barber, E. G., & Morgan, R. P. (1988). *Boon or bane: Foreign graduate students in U.S. engineering programs.* New York: Institute of International Education.

Bennett, M. J. (1986). Towards ethnorelativism: A developmental model of intercultural sensitivity. In R. M. Paige (Ed.), *Cross-cultural orientation: New conceptualizations and applications* (pp. 27-69). Lanham, MD: University Press of America.

Blankenship, E. S. (1980). *International education in Florida community colleges: An analysis.* Unpublished doctoral dissertation, University of Florida.

Blaugh, M. (1981). The economic costs and benefits of overseas students. In P. Williams (Ed.), *Overseas student question: Studies for a policy* (pp. 47-90). London: Heinemann.

Brown, K. A. (1988). *Effects of perceived country of origin, educational status, and native speakerness on American college student attitudes toward non-native instructors.* Unpublished doctoral dissertation, University of Minnesota.

Brown, K., & Fishman, P. (1989). *Language proficiency legislation and the international teaching assistant.* Paper presented at the annual conference of the National Association for Foreign Student Affairs, Minneapolis.

Chronicle of Higher Education. (1988, September 1). U.S. role call: Tests of competence in English language for teaching assistants. *Chronicle of Higher Education Almanac,* p. 18.

Committee on Foreign Students and Institutional Policy. (1982). *Foreign students and institutional policy: Toward an agenda for action.* Washington, DC: American Council on Education.

Cross, D. (1989). *The integration of multicultural and international programs.* Presentation to the Consultants Group of the National Association for Foreign Student Affairs, Minneapolis.

Dresch, S. P. (1987). *The economics of foreign students.* New York: Institute of International Education.

Fry, G. W. (1984). The economic and political impact of study abroad. *Comparative Education Review, 28*(2), 203-220.

Gale, J. R. (1988). *Foreign students in a regional economy: A method of analysis and an application* (IIE Research Report No. 17). New York: Institute of International Education.

Goodman, N. (1984). The institutionalization of overseas education. In E. Barber, P. Altback, & R. Myers (Eds.), *Bridges to knowledge: Foreign students in comparative perspective* (pp. 7-18). Chicago: University of Chicago Press.

Goodwin, C. D., & Nacht, M. (1986). *Decline and renewal: Causes and cures of decay among foreign-trained intellectuals and professionals in the Third World.* New York: Institute of International Education.

Grove, C. L., & Torbiorn, I. (1986). A new conceptualization of intercultural adjustment and the goals of learning. In R. M. Paige (Ed.), *Cross-cultural orientation: New conceptualizations and applications* (pp. 71-109). Lanham, MD: University Press of America.

Hamouda, R. A. I. (1986). *A case study of academic and sociocultural adjustment problems of graduate international students: Recommendations for curricular development.* Unpublished doctoral dissertation, University of Pittsburgh.

Hawkins, J. N. (1984). Education exchanges and the transformation of higher education in the People's Republic of China. In E. Barber, P. Altback, & R. Myers (Eds.), *Bridges to knowledge: Foreign students in comparative perspective* (pp. 19-31). Chicago: University of Chicago Press.

Hoff, B. L. R. (1979). *Classroom-generated barriers to learning: International students in American higher education.* Unpublished doctoral dissertation, U.S. International University.

Hood, M. A. G., & Schieffer, K. (Eds.). (1984). *Professional integration: A guide for students from the developing world.* Washington, DC: National Association for Foreign Student Affairs.

Kâgitçibaşi, Ç. (1978). Cross-national encounters: Turkish students in the United States. *International Journal of Intercultual Relations, 2,* 141-159.

Lamy, S. L. (1987). *The definition of a discipline: The objects and methods of analysis in global education.* New York: Global Perspectives in Education.

Marsella, A. J., & Pedersen, P. B. (Eds.). (1980). *Cross-cultural counseling and psychotherapy.* New York: Pergamon.

Martin, J. N. (1984). Intercultural reentry: Conceptualization and directions for future research. *International Journal of Intercultural Relations, 8,* 1-22.

Mestenhauser, J. A. (1976). *Learning with foreign students.* Minneapolis: University of Minnesota, International Student Advisor's Office.

Mestenhauser, J. A. (1983). Learning from sojourners. In D. Landis & R. W. Brislin (Eds.), *Handbook of intercultural training* (Vol. 2, pp. 153-185). New York: Pergamon.

Mestenhauser, J. A. et al. (1980). *Report of a special course for foreign student teaching assistants to improve their classroom effectiveness.* Minneapolis: International Student Advisor's Office.

Mestenhauser, J. A., Marty, G., & Steglitz, E. (Eds.). (1988). *Culture, learning and the disciplines: Theory and practice in cross-cultural orientation.* Washington, DC: National Association for Foreign Student Affairs.

Moock, J. L. (1984). Overseas training and national development objectives in Sub-Saharan Africa. *Comparative Education Review, 28*(2), 221-240.

Morris, R. (1960). *The two-way mirror: National status in foreign students' adjustment.* Minneapolis: University of Minnesota Press.

Paige, R. M. (1983). Cultures and contact: On intercultural relations among American and foreign students in the United States university context. In D. Landis & R. W. Brislin (Eds.), *Handbook of intercultural training* (Vol. 3, pp. 102-129). New York: Pergamon.

Paige, R. M. (1988). International development education. In J. M. Reid (Ed.), *Building the professional dimension of educational exchange* (pp. 87-103). Washington, DC: National Association for Foreign Student Affairs.

Pedersen, P. (Ed.). (1985). *Handbook of cross-cultural counseling and therapy.* Westport, CT: Greenwood.

Pedersen, P., Draguns, J., Lonner, W., & Trimble, J. (Eds.). (1976). *Counseling across cultures.* Honolulu: University of Hawaii Press.

Pedersen, P., Draguns, J., Lonner, W., & Trimble, J. (Eds.). (1981). *Counseling across cultures* (2nd ed.). Honolulu: University of Hawaii Press.

Pedersen, P., Draguns, J., Lonner, W., & Trimble, J. (Eds.). (1989). *Counseling across cultures* (3rd ed.). Honolulu: University of Hawaii Press.

Rosenberg, L. J. (1987). *The whole is greater than the sum of its parts: A study of international involvement at the University of Massachusetts/Amherst.* Amherst: University of Massachusetts.

Sirowy, L., & Inkeles, A. (1985). University-level student exchanges: The U.S. role in global perspective. In E. G. Barber (Ed.), *Foreign student flows* (pp. 29-85). New York: Institute of International Education.

Soga, N. (1988). Higher education for foreign students. In *From the world to Japan, from Japan to the world: Searching for Japan's future role in international education* (pp. 7-19). Tokyo: Japan Association for Foreign Student Affairs.

Steele, S. (1989). The recoloring of campus life. *Harper's Magazine, 278*(2), 47-55.

Sue, D. W. (1981). *Counseling the culturally different: Theory and practice.* New York: John Wiley.

Thomas, K., & Althen, G. (1989). Counseling foreign students. In P. Pedersen, J. Draguns, W. Lonner, & J. Trimble (Eds.), *Counseling across cultures* (3rd ed., pp. 205-241). Honolulu: University of Hawaii Press.

Triandis, H. C., Brislin, R., & Hui, C. H. (1988). Cross-cultural training across the individualism-collectivism divide. *International Journal of Intercultural Relations, 12,* 269-289.

UNESCO. (1988). *Statistical yearbook.* Paris: Author.

University of Iowa. (1988). Foreign students contribute $14 million to area economy. In *International highlights* (pp. 1-3). Iowa City: University of Iowa, Office of International Education and Services.

Weaver, G. R. (1986). Understanding and coping with cross-cultural adjustment stress. In R. M. Paige (Ed.), *Cross-cultural orientation: New conceptualizations and applications* (pp. 111-145). Lanham, MD: University Press of America.

Wennergren, E. B., & Juan, M. L. Del Rosario. (1981). *The economic importance of international assistance activities at Utah State University.* Logan, UT: Economics Research Center.

Williams, P. (1981). *The overseas student question: Studies for a policy.* London: Heinemann.

Zikopoulos, M. (1987). *Open doors: 1987-1988 report on international educational exchange.* New York: Institute of International Education.

9

WORK ATTITUDES, LEADERSHIP STYLES, AND MANAGERIAL BEHAVIORS IN DIFFERENT CULTURES

C. HARRY HUI

The proliferation of multinational corporations and joint business ventures during the last two decades has greatly stimulated cross-cultural research in job-related behaviors (Bass, 1981; Redding & Wong, 1986; Ronen, 1986). The present chapter summarizes what we know in three of these areas, namely, work attitudes, leadership styles, and managerial behaviors. Wherever appropriate, I shall relate them to the concept of individualism-collectivism, which is fast becoming a unifying theme for many cross-cultural investigations (Triandis, this volume).

JOB SATISFACTION

Definition and Components of *Job Satisfaction*

Job satisfaction refers to an employee's emotional and affective responses toward his or her job. Just as a job has many facets, job satisfaction can have several components too. A widely used instrument for the measurement of the construct assumes the presence of five independent components, namely, satisfaction with work itself, supervision, pay, promotion, and coworkers (Smith, Kendall, & Hulin, 1969).

Cross-Cultural Comparisons

Some researchers have observed that individuals from different cultures have fairly dissimilar levels of job satisfaction. For example, Francophones in Canada are more satisfied than Anglophones with their

AUTHOR'S NOTE: The preparation of this chapter was supported, in part, by a grant from the Committee of Research and Conference Grants, University of Hong Kong. Miss Veronica Leung assisted in various stages of this project. My gratitude also goes to Geoffrey Blowers, Sing Lau, and Nirmala Rao, who made helpful comments on an earlier draft.

jobs (Jain, Normand, & Kanungo, 1979; Kanungo, Gorn, & Dauderis, 1976). Polling done in over 10 countries (de Boer, 1978) found that Sweden had the largest proportion of workers who reported satisfaction (63%), followed by the United Kingdom (54%), Brazil (53%), and Switzerland (50%). Japan had the smallest proportion of satisfied workers (20%). Other researchers (Azumi & McMillan, 1976; Lincoln and Kalleberg, 1985) have also found that Japanese employees have lower general job satisfaction when compared with Americans.

More recently, Griffeth and Hom (1987) analyzed survey data of managers of a U.S. corporation in 15 Western countries, with a view to grouping these countries according to their similarity in several aspects of job satisfaction. They found three country clusters. One cluster comprised Latin countries (Spain, Belgium, Italy, Portugal, and Greece). The other was made up of two English-speaking nations (England and Canada) and Holland. The third included Norway, Sweden, Finland, Denmark, Germany, Austria, and Switzerland. In comparison with the other two clusters, the Latin cluster had lower satisfaction with coworkers, pay, supervision, and promotion. The Anglo cluster had the highest satisfaction with promotion and work load. The Nordic and Central European countries were most satisfied overall.

Differences were also reported in studies that involved ethnic minorities in the United States. Moch (1980) found that Mexican Americans were more satisfied than Whites, who were, in turn, more satisfied than Blacks. Along the same lines, O'Reilly and Roberts (1973) found a higher degree of satisfaction among White employees than their non-White counterparts of comparable educational and occupational level. They traced the higher satisfaction of Whites to basic discrepancies in frames of reference and comparison used by the samples. More specifically, Blacks may have been concerned with extrinsic job factors (e.g., coworkers), and Whites may have been concerned with both extrinsic and intrinsic (i.e., the work itself) factors. However, when Jones, James, Bruni, and Sells (1977) compared Whites and Blacks on naval ships, they found that Black sailors were more satisfied than their counterparts. They noted that "such differences appeared to reflect lower needs reported by Black sailors" (Jones et al., 1977, p. 15). Gavin and Ewen (1974) likewise reported that Black employees tended to be more satisfied than Whites with "job and company," "pay and working conditions," "advancement," and "cooperation among coworkers and supervisors." They attributed such differences to reference groups or prior negative personal experiences in work settings.

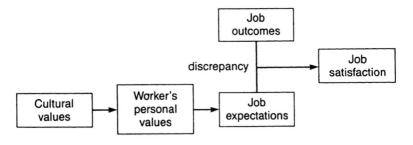

Figure 9.1. A Simplified Discrepancy Model of Job Satisfaction

Admittedly, these explanations are often post hoc and sometimes contradictory. They do nevertheless demonstrate the complex relationship among antecedents of job satisfaction. Of these, the fit between outcomes of the job and one's many needs may be particularly relevant for a fuller understanding of cross-cultural differences. Thus Locke (1976, p. 1328) was correct in his observation that job satisfaction "results from the attainment of values which are compatible with one's needs." Writers in industrial psychology have been quite explicit about the role of compatibility in job satisfaction. Their conceptualization can be summarized and extended in a heuristic model (Figure 9.1) to depict two relationships.

First, job (dis)satisfaction results from perceived discrepancies between actual outcomes of the job and one's own expectations. In other words, either unrealistically high expectations or perceived deficient outcomes, or both, can lead to low job satisfaction. Hence, other things being equal, workers of a technologically backward or economically impoverished country will be more dissatisfied. Workers with very high expectations will also report low job satisfaction. India and the Philippines are probably examples of the former, whereas Japan and France are examples of the latter (de Boer, 1978). Along the same line, Cole (1979) argued that the strong commitment and motivation of Japanese workers heightens their expectations and subsequently leads to dissatisfaction.

Second, a person's expectations from a job are determined by the personal goals (e.g., material enjoyment, prestige, and social harmony) and the cultural values in which the person has been socialized. Many of these are related, at least partially, to work. The next subsection is, therefore, devoted to a brief review of work values.

Cross-Cultural Studies on Work Values

Universality. There is a certain degree of universality in work values, particularly within some occupational groups and organizational positions. Slocum and Strawser (1972) found that both Black and non-Black certified public accountants rated self-actualization needs and autonomy needs as the most important. Both groups rated esteem needs as the least important. In another study, a comparison was done among part-time MBA students from the United States, Australia, Canada, and Singapore on their ranking of 10 work rewards (Popp, Davis, & Herbert, 1986). Again, the respondents all ranked growth, achievement, and responsibility the highest, and recognition, security, and pay the lowest. In their study of supervisors and managers in the United States, Colombia, Peru, and Chile, Peters and Lippitt (1978) also found that supervisors and managers in the four countries had similar work values, although good pay (among others such as opportunity for self-development and improvement, and feeling that the job is important) was named as an important motivator.

Cultural uniqueness. Against the backdrop of similarities, cultural uniqueness has been described. Nevis (1983), for instance, drastically revised Maslow's need hierarchy on the basis of his experience in Mainland China. On the new hierarchy, the most basic needs are belonging (social) needs. These needs are to be satisfied first, before physiological needs, safety needs, and needs for self-actualization, respectively, become dominant. The socialist orientation of the model is also reflected in the conceptualization of self-actualization in terms of service to one's nation and community. Although it is unclear whether the hierarchy depicts an ideal or the reality, it suffices to state that this contending view has considerable implications for managerial philosophies and practices, which will inevitably be different from those developed in the West.

Other studies have found Anglophones and Francophones fairly different in work values, although both considered "interesting nature of work" as the most important job outcome (Jain et al., 1979; Kanungo et al., 1976). Anglophone employees placed greater values on autonomy and achievement in work (both being intrinsic rewards) than Francophone employees. On the contrary, Francophone employees in both studies were more concerned about job security, promotion opportunities, and fringe benefits (all being extrinsic rewards).

The most frequently cited comparative study on work values to date was carried out by Hofstede (1980) in national branches and subsidiaries of a multinational corporation. In the study, employees from over 40 countries rated the importance of several work goals. Cross-national differences were found on importance ratings of work goals such as "having challenging work to do," "having a good working relationship with one's manager," and "having an opportunity for high earnings." We shall describe Hofstede's conceptualization in greater detail shortly.

In another systematic study (MOW International Research Team, 1987), "work centrality" was found to differ across eight countries (Belgium, Germany, Britain, Israel, Japan, the Netherlands, the United States, and Yugoslavia). Japan was the highest on this construct, which was defined as "the degree of general importance that working has in the life of an individual at any given point in time" (MOW International Research Team, 1987, p. 81) irrespective of the purpose and goals of working.[1] Britain, Germany, and the Netherlands were the lowest. Supplementary data revealed that the Japanese worked 48.9 hours per week and Germans worked 9 hours per week less.

Misumi (1988) attributed the high work centrality score of the Japanese to the long-held belief that working makes one's life worth living. The Japanese view their workplace as not only a place to work but also a place where various sports, cultural, and communal activities occur. Thus working and leisure are not separated. However, Misumi (1988) also cautioned that work centrality was declining among Japanese who were born after World War II.

The prevailing "work ethic" varies across countries. Researchers of the MOW project distinguished between two societal norms. One norm focuses on rights and the other on duties connected to working. The "entitlement norm" stresses that "all members of society are entitled to meaningful and interesting work, proper training to obtain and continue in such work, and the right to participate in work/method decisions" (Misumi, 1988, p. 94). The "obligation norm," on the other hand, stresses that "everyone has a duty to contribute to society by working, a duty to save for their own future, and the duty to value one's work, whatever its nature" (p. 94). It was found that both norms were equally endorsed in Japan, Britain, Yugoslavia, and Israel. In the Netherlands, West Germany, and Belgium, "entitlement" was endorsed more often than "obligation." The opposite was true for the United States. People also differ in their views about the economic function of work.[2] The Dutch ranked the economic aspects lower on importance than did their counterparts in Germany, Britain, and Belgium.

Explanations. Religion is one cultural hypothesis advanced to account for work value differences, primarily those observed within the Western world. The reformist Luther believed that the best way to serve God was to diligently perform one's duty through work. Calvin, another theologian, believed that work was intrinsically good. Some writers (e.g., Kanungo et al., 1976) have postulated that the Protestant work ethic in societies influenced by Christianity has resulted in a strong emphasis on achievement. This position, which can be traced back to Max Weber (1930/1976), has provided a framework for studying Anglo-French differences. Its applicability in the present inquiry is, however, questionable. One problem, among others, is that the hypothesis fails to account for the high work centrality in some Oriental nations such as Japan.

Another explanation for cultural differences in work attitudes is cultural collectivism, which is most often cited in comparative studies of Oriental-traditional-developing countries with Western-modern-developed countries. This construct has been used for understanding cultural differences in various other areas (see the chapters by Triandis, Leung, and Kâgitçibaşi in this volume). The following subsection will provide a brief account of what we currently know about the concept.

Individualism-Collectivism

Hofstede's conceptualization. Although many social scientists have written about this construct, Hofstede (1980) was the first to study it empirically. Using a statistical procedure called factor analysis, Hofstede distilled his multinational data on work values and extracted a factor that he labeled individualism. He also described societal norms underlying this concept:

- people to care for self and immediate family
- "I" consciousness
- self-orientation
- identity based in the individual
- emotional independence of individual from organizations or institutions
- emphasis on individual initiative and achievement
- right to a private life and opinion
- autonomy, variety, pleasure, individual financial security
- decisions to be made individually
- universal application of value standards

Hofstede's work, and in particular his theoretical thinking, are cited extensively in managerial and cross-cultural psychology publications, despite some limitations in data analysis and interpretation.[3] One reason that Hofstede's conceptualization is so well received lies in its agreement with a widely endorsed idea: Orientals such as the Chinese and the Japanese are collectivist, other centered, and are willing and ready to sacrifice their own interests for the well-being of collectives such as the nation or society at large. On the contrary, Westerners, and Americans in particular, are individualist, self-centered, hedonistic, and perhaps narcissistic to some extent.

The literature is not lacking in writings that explicitly or implicitly support this view. The assumption that the Chinese put group goals ahead of individual needs has been held by some researchers. For instance, according to Nevis (1983), workers in Mainland China declared that serving the country's needs for the Four Modernizations was of utmost importance, whereas being personally promoted up the organizational ladder and becoming an expert in a field were relatively unimportant. Presumably, unlike their American counterparts, Chinese workers looked down upon work motivations incongruent with national goals. According to Hofstede (1980), people in Japan and Taiwan derive satisfaction from being in a job that is well recognized. In individualist societies like the United States and Great Britain, individual success, individual responsibility, individual merit, individual achievement, self-actualization, and self-respect are stressed.

An alternative view: Target-specific collectivism. Although Hofstede's conceptualization of individualism-collectivism provides us with a simple way of classifying cultures, it basically assumes that collectivists treat most people alike. Taking a different position, Hui (1988; Hui & Triandis, 1985) argued that collectivism is target specific. Individuals feel solidarity with some people but not others. They distribute their time and psychic energy among various recipients in predictable ways. When a bigger portion of resources are allocated to one particular group of individuals, the other groups receive less attention and concern. Hence, what is of real significance is not whether an individual is concerned with others (is or is not a collectivist?), but the way the psychological involvement is distributed (is a collectivist with whom?).

In general, one's concern and psychological involvement with other people increases as a function of kinship, acquaintanceship, friendship, and geographical proximity. They decline as the identity of the target person or target group being dealt with changes from being a close next of kin to a fellow countryman to a national of a country at war with one's own.

There are individual and cultural differences in the slope of the decline, however. Socialization in some cultures may foster a sharper distinction between "in-groups" and "out-groups" (and enemy groups) than others. Cultures may also differ in their locus of concern. Based on previous findings, we may thus postulate that many Japanese men are most psychologically involved with their organizations and the workplace. Chinese who still hold on to traditional folk values are concerned with their own needs as well as the needs of their immediate families. All of these psychological involvements are at the expense of other people whom the individual does not know or those the individual believes are not compatible with attaining his or her goals.

Perceived Values of Work Outcomes

I have suggested that workers from different parts of the world have their own reasons for working as well as their own circles of target persons and groups to be concerned about. Depending on a persons' level of concern with specific people and groups, very diverse values may be ascribed to a work outcome. As an illustration, frequent out-of-town business trips can be highly valued by people who enjoy making friends and acquaintances from various places and by those who do not have a family. The outcome may not be equally valued (or may even be construed negatively) by family-oriented executives who want to keep their weekends and weeknights exclusively for their spouses and children. Likewise, people may assign the same value to an item for rather different reasons. For example, Japanese employees consider it important for their company to have a gymnasium on company premises, because this will open up more opportunities for them to interact with colleagues and to remain "in the company" after work. American employees welcome the addition of a gymnasium because their children can use the facilities during weekends.

On the basis of the above discussion, we can draw attention to findings such as that Japanese managers were the highest in rating the importance of "personal assertiveness-control" when compared with American, Australian, Indian, and Korean managers (England & Koike, 1970). In Japan, toughness is strongly emphasized not because it will bring personal success but because it is seen to be instrumental in bringing about desirable outcomes such as a sense of accomplishment for one's own company, with which a person is very psychologically involved.

Summary

In the above paragraphs, I have postulated how cultural values influence personal work values, which may, in turn, determine job satisfaction. Conclusive data bearing on the relationships among cultural values, work values, and job attitudes are, however, still lacking. It is hoped that this heuristic model will be useful in guiding future research. In the following sections, we shall shift our focus to the impact of culture on managerial behaviors.

LEADERSHIP STYLES

During the past 50 years or so, a multitude of answers have been provided by social scientists to the question: "What makes a good manager/leader?" These can be summarized under three headings: those adopting personalistic approaches (which usually contrast relatively stable personal characteristics of effective leaders to those of less effective leaders), behavioral approaches (which examine observable behavioral patterns), and contingency approaches (which focus on interaction effects between the leader and the environment). Studies based on personalistic approaches have provided conflicting results (see Stogdill, 1974). They are, therefore, not covered in this review. Instead, I shall devote the following paragraphs to one behavioral approach that has received much international attention. Readers interested in the contingency approach should refer to Tannenbaum's (1980) chapter in the *Handbook of Cross-Cultural Psychology*.

The behavioral approach I shall describe in the following categorizes leader behaviors along two unrelated dimensions. The two dimensions were identified by researchers at the Ohio State University and the University of Michigan independently. One dimension is called "person orientation" (or consideration). A leader with person-oriented behaviors is friendly, supportive, concerned with subordinates' welfare, and nonpunitive. This leader also consults with subordinates, delegates responsibility and authority to them, establishes two-way communication, and represents their interests. The other dimension is "production orientation" (or initiating structure), which consists of planning, goal setting, giving explicit instructions, solving problems, coordinating subordinates' activities, evaluating subordinates, and emphasizing production. There is evidence that subordinates are more satisfied with a high-consideration superior and more productive under a superior who is high on initiating structure. However, data from Western studies suggest that the most desirable leader is someone high on both dimensions (e.g., Tjosvold, 1984).

Research in the East is even more clear-cut on the importance of being both person oriented and production oriented. Sinha did a series of research studies on leadership in India and concluded that the most effective leader is a "nurturant task leader," who is "active, strong, dominating, firm, independent, alert, encouraging and extraverted. He is strict and can get work done . . ., is democratic, respected, satisfying, secure and skillful" (Sinha, 1980, pp. 193-194). In short, in India, the most effective leader exhibits both person-oriented behaviors and production-oriented behaviors.

A program of field and laboratory studies conducted in Japan by Misumi (1985) and his colleagues has led to similar conclusions. Misumi's PM concept is somewhat analogous to the two dimensions described above. He called actions that seek to solve problems or motivate achievement of group goals "P leadership." "M leadership," on the other hand, consists of actions

> oriented toward promoting and reinforcing the tendency toward self-preservation [of the group] . . ., directed toward dispelling excessive tensions that arise in interpersonal relations within a group or organization, promoting the resolution of conflict and strife, giving encouragement and support, providing an opportunity for minority opinions to be expressed, inspiring personal need fulfillment and promoting an acceptance of interdependence among group members. (Misumi, 1985, p. 11)

On the basis of subordinates' rating on the two dimensions, Misumi categorized leaders/supervisors into one of four types, PM, Pm, pM, and pm. As can be expected, there are variations in leadership behaviors among the four groups. Moreover, the PM leader, that is, the person who both prompts group achievement and maintains group solidarity, is consistently found to be the most effective.

Research with Chinese people supplies further converging findings. Cheng and Yang (1977) studied over 200 Taiwan workers and reported that their job satisfaction was positively related to both consideration and initiating structure. In Mainland China, there are now some studies that adopted the two-dimensional behavioral approach (see Ling, 1989). In keeping with the Chinese emphasis on leaders' morality, a third dimension, "moral character," has been included in the theorizing. It is possible that, as with samples from other geographical locations, all three dimensions are linked with leadership effectiveness, although empirical verification has not been reported.

Why is the most effective leader usually a person high on both maintenance and initiating structure (that is, a nurturant task leader in Sinha's terminology or PM leader in Misumi's)? We can perhaps speculate on a few reasons that are of particular significance to Oriental cultures. First, this type of leader gives the subordinates a feeling that they belong to his or her in-group. The same feeling may also emerge within the leader him- or herself, after acting benevolently toward subordinates. The resultant sense of solidarity fosters team spirit, mutual understanding, and cooperation on the one hand and discourages disputes and sabotage on the other. In short, a nurturant leader can realize all the potential strengths of a closely knit in-group. Second, high productivity in terms of goal accomplishment, which is more likely under a leader high on initiating structure than someone low on it, is perceived to be beneficial to the entire group. This production-oriented leader is moreover seen as instrumental to the subordinates' providing for people (e.g., family members) about whom they are very much concerned. Yet another reason lies in the collectivists' special psychological needs. Hui and Villareal (1989) found that their needs for nurturance and affiliation are higher when compared with individualists. Within a work group, these needs are more likely satisfied by a nurturant leader than by somebody who is less people oriented. A nurturant leader, therefore, receives a warmer welcome.

MANAGERIAL BEHAVIORS

Although current research indicates few differences among cultures in their preference for leadership styles, actual managerial behaviors vary a great deal. A quarter of a century ago, Haire, Ghiselli, and Porter (1966) surveyed 3,500 managers in 14 countries around the globe. They found that approximately 28% of the variance in managerial attitudes could be accounted for by nationality alone. The researchers were also able to group the countries, on the basis of the managers' responses, into four clusters: Nordic-European, Latin-European, Anglo-American, and developing countries. Over the years, many researchers have similarly assumed that cultural values have a substantial bearing on styles of management and supervision. Again, cross-national differences on individualism-collectivism have received the most attention.

Individualism-Collectivism and the Chinese Familism

As mentioned in the preceding section, individualism-collectivism cannot be meaningfully discussed without considering the target persons or groups to whom it is directed. In some cultures, people nurture their relationships with certain close target groups, even at a cost to other groups. In other cultures, members maintain a fair number of ties with target groups that may appear remote. In some respects, many Chinese are like the first type, structuring their lives around their families and relatives. Such familism obviously has an impact on organizational and managerial behaviors.

The term *Chinese familism* refers to two fundamental characteristics of Chinese culture. The first is paternalism: The father is at the center of authority in a family. In all important issues, he legitimately holds the decision-making power. The second is a tendency to categorize individuals into either an in-group or out-group, the membership in which forms the basis of much social interaction.

Family members usually belong to the in-group. Within the in-group, the parent-child tie constitutes the nucleus. Less central but adjacent to this core union are relationships within the nuclear family, the extended family, and then other people associated through marriage or adoption. Moving further away from the center, one finds distant relatives, kinsfolk, covillagers, and so forth, who may or may not be in-group members. Ordinary friends and acquaintances, as well as strangers and competitors, are usually in the out-group.[4] These individuals receive only a minimal amount of concern. This notion of in-group complements the conceptualization of individualism-collectivism put forward earlier.

Along similar lines, Hwang (1987) described three types of relationships among the Chinese. The first consists of "expressive" or "affective" ties and is marked by a steady and long-lasting social relationship, almost always among family members. The relationship is maintained for the sake of satisfying needs for nurturance, love, security, and belongingness. The second type consists of "mixed" ties with acquaintances outside the family. There is an affective component, but its size varies considerably from one relationship to another. The third type of relationship is "instrumental" ties with people with whom one has no expectation of long-term relationship but who can sometimes be used as means toward an end (e.g., working with an agricultural agent to learn about fertilizer). Expressive ties are clearly more frequent within in-groups, whereas instrumental ties are common between a person and someone in the out-group.

There are considerable differences in behaviors between cultures that emphasize in-group/out-group distinctions (such as the Chinese) and those that do not. Triandis (in press, manuscript p. 42) postulated that

> there is more self-disclosure, attraction, perceived similarity, display of nonverbal affiliative expressiveness, shared networks, and attributional confidence in ingroup relationships than in outgroup relationships in collectivist than in individualist cultures. . . . When interacting with ingroup members, collectivists [the Chinese familists, in the present case] tend to be very cooperative and helpful, while when interacting with strangers [i.e., outgroup members] they tend to be competitive and not helpful. The ingroup-stranger contrast is of much less importance for individualists who behave more or less equally well toward both ingroup and strangers.

We shall see shortly that many of the above descriptions are true of managerial behaviors in Chinese family businesses.

Managerial Behaviors in Chinese Family Businesses

Like many Western family businesses in their formative years, Chinese family businesses are usually small, most hiring fewer than 300 employees. Both management and ownership are often under the same person. This person runs the business with a circle of close family members, while a substantial number of key positions are filled by relatives and close friends. Several features associated with a sharp in-group/out-group distinction can be observed in this kind of enterprise:

(1) Identity and impact. In a Western culture, people's identity is closely linked to what they have accomplished. In a culture where the in-group/out-group distinction is emphasized, however, identity is established on the basis of people to whom one is related. Likewise, status in a Chinese organization is more determined by whether one belongs to the boss's in-group than by whether one has been a hardworking and able employee. In such an organization, views and opinions on organizational matters have a greater impact when expressed by in-group members, or someone close to the in-group, than when expressed by others. For example, in Hong Kong, many senior managers of spinning mills owned by refugees from Shanghai (a large industrial city in China) are Shanghainese speakers (Wong, 1988). Fellow regionals have a better chance of gaining entry into the owners' in-group.

(2) Theory X versus Theory Y. McGregor (1960) distinguished between two philosophical positions underlying managerial behaviors. The first position, which he called Theory X, assumes that most workers are not ambitious, have little desire for responsibility, and prefer to be directed or even coerced to achieve organizational objectives. The other position, called Theory Y, assumes that people are self-directed and creative at work if properly motivated.

As we can see, Chinese superiors assume out-group members to be lazy and unreliable, just as X-theorists would think of their workers. A carrot-and-stick management style is typical. The same managers would, however, appear more friendly with their subordinates in the in-group. This allows them to form a more positive impression about their subordinates. Theory Y aptly summarizes the treatment of subordinates within the in-group.

Therefore, there is a dynamic alternation between the two "theories" as a manager deals with different subordinates. Characterizing superiors as either "Theory X" or "Theory Y" is deficient, for neither set of assumptions is complete in accounting for their day-to-day activity.

(3) Differential treatment. As suggested in the preceding paragraph, the manager-owner treats employees already initiated into the in-group differently from employees in the out-group. They are more likely to exchange favors with and be more accommodating toward in-group subordinates. Moreover, because these subordinates are assumed to be willing to remain in the in-group relationship, and hence maintain employment in the company for an extended period of time, they are often given easier access to resources and promotion opportunities than other employees. On the contrary, a manager's treatment of employees in the out-group is characterized by domineering control behaviors and careful scrutiny. Formal rules and contracts are used as the basis of disciplining "ordinary" subordinates. There is still an exchange of favors, but delays in reciprocation are less tolerable.

(4) Mistrust. One eye-catching phenomenon in many Chinese family-owned companies is the lack of trust (Negandhi, 1973). This lack of interpersonal trust within a business organization can again be traced to the way Chinese define an in-group.

Trust generally develops from authenticity in self-presentation as well as from accuracy of social perception and attribution. Naturally, there would be a greater degree of authenticity and accurate perception between good friends than between acquaintances and in an in-group relationship than between two persons who consider each other out-group members.

Unfortunately, as stated earlier, the management and a sizable portion of the employees in a Chinese firm customarily regard each other as out-group members. Within a sociocultural milieu that emphasizes the distinction between "we" and "they," a superior and a subordinate in an interaction would be very reluctant to divulge privileged information and to engage in self-disclosure. Worse still, they are likely to use cues about the other person's "out-groupness" as an aid in their attempt to interpret ambiguous behaviors and information gathered from other sources. It is not surprising that this does not often result in favorable attributions and impressions and further confirms the perceiver's prior categorization of the target person in the out-group. This reciprocal defense cycle found in most low-trust organizations perpetuates the defensive behavior of the management. Some Chinese business people resort to nepotism because, as in-group members, their relatives are seen as more trustworthy than others.

(5) Autocratic management. When the entrepreneurs and superiors do not have a reasonable level of trust in their subordinates, an autocratic style of management is almost inevitable. Problems and difficulties faced by the organization are usually treated as secret (Cheng, 1988). They are kept within the "inner circle" and not shared with employees. The sole responsibilities of most employees (out-group members) are to complete the assigned tasks, without knowing too much about the problems and objectives. Seldom do bosses solicit or accept subordinates' opinions in their decision-making process (see Strauss, 1977). Upward influence is usually discouraged. Participative decision making is rare.

(6) Power distance. According to Hofstede (1980, p. 99), "the power distance between a boss B and a subordinate S in a hierarchy is the difference between the extent to which B can determine the behavior of S and the extent to which S can determine the behavior of B." Data collected by Hofstede showed that employees in the Philippines, Singapore, Hong Kong, Thailand, Taiwan, and various Latin American countries are on the high side of the scale. In line with this observation, power has been found to be highly centralized in Chinese organizations (Bond & Hwang, 1986; Redding & Casey, 1976; Redding & Wong, 1986). The bosses are "stern father figures," to command respect and fear as well as to guarantee loyalty from their subordinates. Delegation of authority is synonymous with giving away control and influence in the company's affairs to "someone from outside," which is unthinkable to many Chinese business people.

To strengthen their position of authority, Chinese bosses are usually boastful about their own achievements while slighting contributions of their subordinates. Attributing subordinates' outstanding performance to external factors is common. This feature distinguishes Chinese organizations from the Japanese, wherein bosses express appreciation of their subordinates' performance, recognize their dependence upon them, and, therefore, strive to develop a cordial relationship with them (Silin, 1976). In return, Japanese employees have a high sense of belonging to the organization.

(7) Interdepartmental rivalry. Mistrust occurring on a more macro, organizational level within a business organization has adverse effects on interdepartmental cooperation. Negandhi (1973) reported that, in day-to-day operations, supervisors and managers in Taiwan businesses were department oriented, whereas their counterparts in American firms in Taiwan looked at things from the perspective of the organization. Members of departments in a Chinese business are more concerned with their own department's goals than with the organization's goals. In some cases, individual members may not even have any knowledge of the organization as a whole. The smooth running of one's own department (or assembly line) rather than attainment of organizational goals becomes the primary or major objective. The loyalty is to a small department rather than to the bigger organization. The department may effectively become an in-group and the rest of the organization the out-group.

Will Chinese Businesses Thrive?

Having considered these characteristics of Chinese managerial behaviors, we may be tempted to think that, while Western businesses will continue to flourish, many Chinese businesses will very soon collapse. However, we must be wary of two traps. The first is a misconception that behaviors such as differential treatment, mistrust, autocratic management, and interdepartmental rivalry are absent from Western organizations. The second is an oversight of those sociocultural factors that may work to the advantage of Chinese family businesses.

The first misconception can be easily eliminated after a close look into the literature on organizational behaviors in the West. In fact, many of the features described under the preceding subsection can also be found in other places of the world. Interdepartmental rivalry, for example, is not new to American corporations like Sears and IBM or to the American military services.

Neither is differential treatment absent from Western organizations. According to vertical dyad linkage theory (Dansereau, Graen, & Haga,

1975), which has been developed in the United States explicitly around the theme of differential treatment, there are two types of subordinates. The first type consists of those subordinates believed by their manager to be trustworthy and competent, whereas the second type consists of those believed to be average or below average on these desirable characteristics. Whether one belongs to the first or second type determines the kind of supervisory behaviors one will receive. The manager does not have an "average leadership style," for the subordinates are not all alike from the manager's perspective. Thus this tendency to treat subordinates differentially is already present among Western managers. However, its extensive propagation is only possible in Chinese soil, where familistic collectivism is one of the guiding values.

Furthermore, we do not have to reason that, because the Chinese are collectivists, they will necessarily be autocratic, mistrustful, and nepotistic. These features may be not only the result but also the antecedents of the organizational members' collectivist outlook. Organizational development involving changes to these features may to some extent alter people's level of individualism or collectivism. We can foster coworker collectivism and team spirit within an organization through consultative management and the implementation of an egalitarian reward system. Profit-sharing, widely practiced in many Western companies, is also effective in instilling a sense of company collectivism. Organizational changes like these give employees an expectation that their own effort is related to the outcomes of their efforts. To a certain extent, the company and the individual employee can then appear as one entity.

Let us now take a look at the other trap. Admittedly, some of the aforementioned managerial behaviors are dysfunctional. A general neglect of management development further aggravates the situation. These problems, coupled with the failure to promptly implement remedial action, have led to financial difficulties and even to bankruptcies. In Hong Kong, a lot of small and medium-sized Chinese firms that existed 10 years ago are not doing business today (Sit & Wong, 1988).

However, let us not forget that in the United States there are the Fords, Kennedys, and Rockefellers in which we can observe many of the same Chinese managerial behaviors. For instance, a large proportion of shares are usually retained by family members when these family businesses go public. Self-perpetuation and self-preservation of profits are major motivations in maintaining power and control, irrespective of culture. At times, certain so-called dysfunctional managerial practices can result in high profitability, be it East or West. In fact, given the present political and cultural milieu, it is only natural that Chinese business people behave as they do.

Moreover, during the past few decades, there have been social, economic, and political situations highly favorable to the growth of Chinese businesses. At a more micro level, personal characteristics and sociocultural beliefs among some Chinese business people also contribute to the growth of their enterprises. Sit and Wong (1988, p. 116) provide the following description of Chinese business people in Hong Kong:

> The small industrialists . . . extol conservative values of hard work and dependability. They are apparently strongly imbued with the work ethic, and they are stability-oriented. . . . When they are asked about the ideal qualities essential for industrial success, 43% of them emphasize diligence and self-exertion and about 20% uphold the virtue of responsibility.

Komin (1988) reported that Chinese in Thailand ranked "ambitious and hardworking" thirteenth among a list of 23 values, whereas the Thais ranked it the lowest in importance.

This view is in line with the post-Confucian hypothesis advanced by scholars such as Kahn (1979). According to this hypothesis, major economic takeoffs in several Asian countries are due to the Confucian ethic. This ethic encompasses "sobriety, a high value on education, a desire for accomplishment in various skills, . . . and seriousness about tasks, job, family, and obligations" (Kahn 1979, p. 121) as well as an emphasis on complementarity of relations and a sense of hierarchy. These often have the effect of controlling tendencies toward anarchy within organizations.

In addition to the Confucian ethic, Chinese business people have the ability to respond quickly to and capitalize on changing market opportunities (Sit & Wong, 1988). They are innovative and have insightful perspectives for the future. This entrepreneurial sense particular to people under the influence of Confucianism might further neutralize any negative consequences of the managerial behaviors mentioned above.

Finally, the social milieu of Chinese society actually reinforces much of the above managerial behaviors, such as autocratic decision making. The same familistic concern that prompts managers to keep all major decisions to themselves and the in-group members also operates within the subordinates of the out-group. Most of these subordinates do not see the company as theirs. These people, having little concern for the overall well-being of the company they are working in, may not be impressed with an invitation from the management to make contributions (which eventually may not be used) for some higher-level decisions. They may find the demand excessive and wasteful of their time. Familistic employees would rather have a boss who makes all the decisions but pays them on time so they can feed their families.

There are, in fact, other places in the world where a participative leader is not welcome. Bass (1968, cited by Ronen, 1986) found that only 22.2% of Greek subordinates (who were family collectivist) were satisfied with decision-making meetings with participative superiors, as compared with 62.5% of Dutch-Flemish and 45.8% of Anglo-American subordinates who felt the same way. The situation in India is very similar (see Padaki, 1989). Very often, a participative superior is seen as indecisive and, therefore, not worthy of respect. Admittedly, this general attitude toward participative decision making is present among workers in Western organizations as well. But it is more typical where familism is emphasized.

CONCLUSION

In the first major section of this chapter, I described how job satisfaction varies across cultures. A heuristic model was used to organize the rather diverse empirical findings. It was argued that job satisfaction was a result of the discrepancy between actual job outcomes and subjective job expectations. Job expectations were, in turn, determined by work values, which were affected by predominant cultural values.

The second part of this chapter shows that countries are not too dissimilar in their most effective leadership style. The final part contains a discussion on Chinese managerial behaviors, with an acknowledgment that the behaviors and styles concerned may to some extent be present in non-Chinese businesses. Nevertheless, both parts demonstrate that choice of leadership and management styles is affected and sustained by the cultural environment.

The cultural environment is a primary agent for the formation of managers' own values and beliefs, which, in turn, influence their choice of management styles. Depending partly on the employees' expectations (which, again, may be under the influence of culture), the choice may result in job satisfaction or dissatisfaction. Hence we can appreciate the role of cultural values as an overarching concept related to such variables as attitudes, preferences, and expectations of organizational members, superiors and subordinates alike.

In various places in this chapter, I have used one cultural value, individualism-collectivism, and have integrated it with research findings. There are two reasons for doing so. First of all, in models describing processes that involve macroscopic variables such as culture and individual variables such as job satisfaction, meaning of work, and managerial behaviors, a link depicting the relationship between the societal and the individual levels is highly desirable. Individualism-collectivism appears to provide the needed link. Second, although it is easy and convenient to fall into a comfortable mind-set of an East-West dichotomy, it must be remembered that a categorization of cultures or countries merely by geographical location is not a sufficiently informative grouping for cross-cultural comparative purposes. Fortunately, our present knowledge about individualism-collectivism has advanced beyond the stage of simplistically labeling the Western world as individualist and the Oriental collectivist. Collectivism is target specific. In fact, the differentiation of targets of prospective concern into in-group and out-group cuts across organizations and cultures, although it is more apparent in some than in others. Thus the construct of target-specific individualism-collectivism holds good promise in facilitating more in-depth understanding of both intercultural and intracultural variations of organizational behaviors.

NOTES

1. There were two ways to measure work centrality. First, respondents assigned a total of 100 points to indicate how important five areas (leisure, community, work, religion, and family) were in their lives. Second, they answered the question: "How important and significant is working in your total life?" on a seven-point scale.

2. In the MOW project, the researchers made a distinction among four dimensions of work goals. They were the expressive dimension (interesting work, match between job and personal qualities, a lot of variety, autonomy), the economic dimension (good pay, promotion, job security), the comfort dimension (good physical conditions, convenient working hours), and the learning/improvement opportunity dimension. Common across the eight countries studied is the high importance rankings assigned to the expressive dimension. The comfort and the learning/improvement opportunity dimensions were not accorded much importance in any country. Cross-national differences are concentrated on the importance of the economic aspects.

3. The individualism factor was loaded on rated importance of personal time, freedom, and challenging work, and unimportance of using one's skills, good physical working conditions, and training opportunities. One conceptual problem is that these work goal items do not have a readily appreciable connection with the construct. It takes much

imagination before one can agree, for example, that a collectivist (more than an individualist) would consider training opportunities important to his or her job.

4. A clear demarcation between in-group members and out-group members must be contingent upon the situation and type of transaction. For the present discussion, however, a crude classification may suffice.

REFERENCES

Azumi, K., & McMillan, C. J. (1976). Worker sentiment in the Japanese factory: Its organizational determinants. In L. Austin (Ed.), *Japan: The paradox of progress* (pp. 215-229). New Haven, CT: Yale University Press.

Bass, B. M. (1968). *A preliminary report on manifest preferences in six cultures for participative management* (Technical Report 21). Rochester: University of Rochester, Management Research Center.

Bass, B. M. (1981). Leadership in different cultures. In B. M. Bass (Ed.), *Stogdill's handbook of leadership* (pp. 522-549). New York: Free Press.

Bond, M. H., & Hwang, K. K. (1986). The social psychology of Chinese people. In M. H. Bond (Ed.), *The psychology of the Chinese people* (pp. 213-266). Hong Kong: Oxford University Press.

Cheng, B. S. (1988). *Familism and leadership behavior: An analysis of private enterprises in Taiwan.* Paper presented at the Symposium on Chinese Psychology, University of Hong Kong (in Chinese).

Cheng, B. S., & Yang, K. S. (1977). Supervisory behavior, skill level, and interpersonal dominance as determinants of job satisfaction. *Bulletin of the Institute of Ethnology, 44*, 13-45 (in Chinese).

Cole, R. E. (1979). *Work, mobility, and participation.* Berkeley: University of California.

Dansereau, F., Jr., Graen, G., & Haga, W. J. (1975). A vertical dyad linkage approach to leadership within formal organizations: A longitudinal investigation of the role making process. *Organizational Behavior and Human Performance, 13*, 46-78.

de Boer, C. (1978). The polls: Attitudes toward work. *Public Opinion Quarterly, 42*, 414-423.

England, G. W., & Koike, R. (1970). Personal value systems of Japanese managers. *Journal of Cross-Cultural Psychology, 1*, 21-40.

Gavin, J. F., & Ewen, R. B. (1974). Racial differences in job attitudes and performance: Some theoretical considerations and empirical findings. *Personnel Psychology, 27*, 455-464.

Griffeth, R. W., & Hom, P. W. (1987). Some multivariate comparisons of multinational managers. *Multivariate Behavioral Research, 22*, 173-191.

Haire, M., Ghiselli, E. E., & Porter, L. W. (1966). *Managerial thinking: An international study.* New York: John Wiley.

Hofstede, G. (1980). *Culture's consequences: International differences in work-related values.* Beverly Hills, CA: Sage.

Hui, C. H. (1988). Measurement of individualism-collectivism. *Journal of Research in Personality, 22*, 17-36.

Hui, C. H., & Triandis, H. C. (1985). Individualism-collectivism: A study of cross-cultural researchers. *Journal of Cross-Cultural Psychology, 17*, 225-248.

Hui, C. H., & Villareal, M. J. (1989). Individualism-collectivism and psychological needs: Their relationships in two cultures. *Journal of Cross-Cultural Psychology, 20*, 310-323.

Hwang, K.-K. (1987). Face and favor: The Chinese power game. *American Journal of Sociology, 92,* 944-974.

Jain, H. C., Normand, J., & Kanungo, R. N. (1979). Job motivation of Canadian Anglophone and Francophone hospital employees. *Canadian Journal of Behavioural Science, 11*(2), 160-163.

Jones, A. P., James, L. R., Bruni, J. R., & Sells, S. B. (1977). Black-White differences in work environment perceptions and job satisfaction and its correlates. *Personnel Psychology, 30,* 5-16.

Kahn, H. (1979). *World economic development: 1979 and beyond.* Boulder, CO: Westview.

Kanungo, R. N., Gorn, G. J., & Dauderis, H. J. (1976). Motivational orientation of Canadian Anglophone and Francophone managers. *Canadian Journal of Behavioural Science, 8*(2), 107-121.

Komin, S. (1988). *Culture and work values in Thai organizations.* Paper presented at the International Symposium, "Social Values and Effective Organizations," Taipei, Taiwan.

Lincoln, J. R., & Kalleberg, A. L. (1985). Work organization and workforce commitment: A study of plants and employees in the U.S. and Japan. *American Sociological Review, 50,* 738-760.

Ling, W.-Q. (1989). Pattern of leadership behavior assessment in China. *Psychologia, 32,* 129-134.

Locke, E. A. (1976). The nature and causes of job satisfaction. In M. D. Dunnette (Ed.), *Handbook of industrial and organizational psychology* (pp. 1297-1349). Chicago: Rand McNally.

McGregor, D. (1960). *The human side of enterprise.* New York: McGraw-Hill.

Misumi, J. (1985). *The behavioral science of leadership: An interdisciplinary Japanese research program.* Ann Arbor: University of Michigan.

Misumi, J. (1988). *The meaning of work (MOW) for the Japanese and action research on small group activities in Japanese industrial organizations.* Paper presented at the International Symposium, "Social Values and Effective Organizations," Taipei, Taiwan.

Moch, M. K. (1980). Racial differences in job satisfaction: Testing four common expianations. *Journal of Applied Psychology, 65*(3), 299-306.

MOW International Research Team. (1987). *The meaning of working.* London: Academic Press.

Negandhi, A. R. (1973). *Management and economic development: The case of Taiwan.* The Hague, The Netherlands: Martinus Nijhoff.

Nevis, E. C. (1983). Cultural assumptions and productivity: The United States and China. *Sloan Management Review, 24,* 17-29.

O'Reilly, C. A., & Roberts, K. H. (1973). Job satisfaction among Whites and non-Whites: A cross-cultural approach. *Journal of Applied Psychology, 57,* 295-299.

Padaki, R. (1989). Job attitudes. In J. Pandey (Ed.), *Psychology in India: The state-of-the-art: Vol. 3. Organizational behavior and mental health* (pp. 19-95). New Delhi: Sage.

Peters, E. B., & Lippitt, G. L. (1978). The use of instruments in international training. *Journal of European International Training, 2*(7), 24-25.

Popp, G. E., Davis, H. J., & Herbert, T. T. (1986). An international study of intrinsic motivation composition. *Management International Review, 26,* 28-35.

Redding, S. G., & Casey, T. W. (1976). Managerial beliefs among Asian managers. In R. L. Taylor, M. J. O'Connell, R. A. Zawacki, & D. D. Warwick (Eds.), *Proceedings of the Academy of Management 36th Annual Meeting* (pp. 351-366). Mississippi State, MS: Academy of Management.

Redding, G., & Wong, G. Y. Y. (1986). The psychology of Chinese organizational behaviour. In M. H. Bond (Ed.), *The psychology of the Chinese people* (pp. 267-295). Hong Kong: Oxford University Press.

Ronen, S. (1986). *Comparative and multinational management.* New York: John Wiley.

Silin, R. H. (1976). *Leadership and values: The organization of large-scale Taiwan enterprises.* Cambridge, MA: Harvard University Press.

Sinha, J. B. P. (1980). *The nurturant task leader: A model of effective executive.* New Delhi: Concept.

Sit, V. F. S., & Wong, S. L. (1988). *Changes in the industrial structure and role of small and medium industries in Asian countries: The case of Hong Kong.* Tokyo: Institute of Developing Economics.

Slocum, J. W., Jr., & Strawser, R. H. (1972). Racial differences in job attitudes. *Journal of Applied Psychology, 56,* 28-32.

Smith, P. C., Kendall, L. M., & Hulin, C. L. (1969). *The measurement of satisfaction in work and retirement.* Chicago: Rand McNally.

Stogdill, R. M. (1974). *Handbook of leadership: A survey of theory and research.* New York: Free Press.

Strauss, G. (1977). Managerial practices. In J. R. Hackman & J. L. Suttle (Eds.), *Improving life at work* (pp. 297-363). Santa Monica, CA: Goodyear.

Tannenbaum, A. S. (1980). Organizational psychology. In H. C. Triandis & R. W. Brislin (Eds.), *Handbook of cross-cultural psychology* (Vol. 5, pp. 281-334). Boston: Allyn & Bacon.

Tjosvold, D. (1984). Effects of leader warmth and directiveness on subordinate performance on a subsequent task. *Journal of Applied Psychology, 69,* 422-427.

Triandis, H. C. (in press). Cross-cultural industrial and organizational psychology. In M. D. Dunnette (Ed.), *Handbook of industrial and organizational psychology* (pp. 1297-1349). Chicago: Rand McNally.

Weber, M. (1976). *The Protestant ethic and the spirit of capitalism.* London: Allen & Unwin. (Original work published 1930)

Wong, S.-L. (1988). *Emigrant entrepreneurs: Shanghai industrialists in Hong Kong.* Hong Kong: Oxford University Press.

Yang, K. S., & Cheng, B. S. (1988). *Traditional values, individual modernity, and organizational behavior: An empirical micro-level verification of the neo-Confucianism hypothesis.* Paper presented at the International Conference of Chinese Management, Hong Kong (in Chinese).

10

DISPUTE PROCESSING
A Cross-Cultural Analysis

KWOK LEUNG
PEI-GUAN WU

Conflict and disputes are common events in everyday life and have captured the interest of researchers in a variety of disciplines. In the study of conflict, a new dimension has gradually emerged, namely, the cross-cultural dimension. The reason for this recent development is simple—the world is getting smaller and smaller for a number of reasons. First, because of migration patterns in the last several decades, more and more countries are becoming multicultural. For instance, the United States has moved away from an insistence upon a melting pot culture. Canada has openly endorsed multiculturalism. Australia has publicly announced the death of the White Australia policy. In short, cultural homogeneity is quickly disappearing on the surface of the Earth.

Second, globalization has become the name of the game in business. For instance, major multinational companies such as Mobil Oil and IBM are active in more than 50 countries (Kim, 1983). Multinational operations bring people of different cultures together. In a firm that we recently visited in Hong Kong, there were eight nationalities among its staff of 50. Third, global crises often bring different nations together. For instance, the recent problem of the ozone layer brought many nations together to work out a solution. International talks concerning arms reduction, peace treaties, and trade arrangements appear in newspapers almost every day.

Given that cross-cultural interactions are burgeoning, there has never been such a sore need for knowledge about dispute processing in different societies to cope with disputes at the cultural interfaces. The present chapter attempts to provide a succinct, up-to-date summary of what we currently know about cultural differences in dispute processing.

THE DEFINITION OF CONFLICT

Schmidt and Kochan (1972) have provided a very useful conceptual framework for understanding the process of conflict. They proposed two prerequisites for conflict to occur, namely, perceived goal incompatibility and perceived opportunity for interference or blocking. Goal incompatibility refers to a zero-sum relationship between the goals of the two parties concerned. "Zero-sum" refers to the total benefits of the two parties. If one wins a benefit (+1) and the other loses (−1), the sum is zero. For instance, if two job applicants are competing for a job, their goals are incompatible because only one applicant can get it. Interference or blocking refers to an intended activity that is perceived as detrimental to the attainment of a goal. For instance, if a man wants to sleep (the goal) and there is a constant loud noise from next door that keeps him awake, the noise will be perceived as an interference provided it is seen as an intended act.

Cross-Cultural Analysis of Goal Incompatibility

In a cross-cultural analysis of dispute processing, it is useful to make a distinction between subjective and objective dimensions of these two prerequisites. The zero-sum relationship between two goals in a state of objective goal incompatibility can be verified objectively. For instance, the competition for promotion between two employees involves objective goal incompatibility. On the other hand, the zero-sum relationship in a state of subjective goal incompatibility is mainly based on the interpretations that people make. There is no necessary correspondence between the perceived goal incompatibility and the physical state of things. For instance, two children who are competing for their parents' attention may experience strong subjective goal incompatibility, but both in reality may be able to obtain their desired levels of attention simultaneously.

Objective goal incompatibility should not be influenced much by culture. For instance, when two employees are competing for promotion, both should experience goal incompatibility regardless of their cultural backgrounds. On the other hand, culture can have very drastic effects on subjective goal incompatibility. What is regarded as compatible in one culture may be regarded as incompatible in another. A good example is workers' attitude toward automation and robotization in the United States and Japan (Alston, 1985). In the United States, workers resist automation because it is seen as a threat to their job security and their bargaining power with management. In other words, automation and worker well-being are seen as incompatible. On the other hand, Japanese workers welcome automation and robotization. They see it as a way to get rid of unpleasant and dangerous jobs and to increase bonuses. Thus automation is actually seen as conducive to their well-being.

The above analysis suggests that subjective goal incompatibility is sometimes culture specific and varies according to the dominant norms and values of the cultures. A thorough understanding of the "subjective culture" of a society, which includes such things as values, norms, and beliefs, is useful for identifying the effects of culture on subjective goal incompatibility (see Triandis, 1972, for an elaboration of the meaning of *subjective culture*).

Cross-Cultural Analysis of Blocking Behavior

As in goal incompatibility, blocking behavior can be classified as objective or subjective. In objective blocking behavior, the interference is related to some physically defined damages and obstructions. For instance, if a student constantly makes noise during a lesson, this action is a blocking behavior because it distracts the teacher from teaching and other students from listening. On the other hand, in subjective blocking behavior, the interference is related to psychological damages and obstructions and cannot be physically defined. For instance, the rejection of a proposal made by a subordinate may be seen by the subordinate as an interference with his or her goal to perform well in the company.

As in goal incompatibility, culture's effects on blocking behavior are mostly in the subjective domain. The subjective culture will affect the interpretation of a behavior as being beneficial, neutral, or harmful. Thus what is perceived as an interference in one culture may be seen as a benign action in another. A number of organizational examples can be cited to illustrate this point. For instance, whereas business contracts are valued by American business people as a sign of commitment, they are seen by Japanese as a sign of distrust (Sullivan, Peterson, Kameda, & Shimada, 1981). Insistence on signing a contract in an initial stage of business negotiation may be seen by Japanese business people as a lack of commitment to the collaboration.

American negotiators are usually argumentative but impersonal. Opposing someone's proposal usually does not generate substantial animosity between the parties involved. On the other hand, Malays see a much stronger association between a person and his or her position on an issue. Rejection of a position is often seen as rejection of the person and can often create significant interpersonal tension (Renwick, 1985). Williams, Whyte, and Green (1966) found that perceived closeness of supervision and satisfaction with the boss was positively correlated in Peru and negatively correlated in America. Obviously, close supervision is probably seen by American workers as inappropriate and undesirable, whereas close supervision in Peru may be seen as a sign of concern and strong leadership.

To conclude, subjective goal incompatibility and subjective blocking behavior are likely to be influenced by culture. To understand why conflict occurs in one society but not in another under similar situations, it is necessary to examine the subjective culture of the cultural groups concerned. Dominant values, norms, and beliefs of the cultural groups need to be determined and their relationship with subjective goal incompatibility and subjective blocking behavior mapped out. For instance, we should know that *amae* is an important value in Japan. *Amae* denotes the mutual dependence on each other's goodwill and kindness (Alston, 1985), and knowing this we can easily understand why Japanese business people see contracts as a sign of distrust. Contracts are necessary only when both parties are trying to maximize their own interest without considering the interest of the other party. Thus the requirement of a typical American contract that specifies courses of actions and contingency plans constitutes a challenge to one's integrity and sense of honor. On the other hand, if we know that interpersonal relationships are characterized by informal contracts rather than *amae* in the United States, we would not be surprised when Americans view business contracts as a sign of commitment.

CULTURE AND INTENSITY OF CONFLICT

One factor that affects the intensity of a conflict is the value placed on a goal. If a goal is highly valued and is incompatible with the goal of another person, the intensity of the resulting conflict will obviously be high. For instance, people would not get into a major confrontation for 10 dollars but would take a case to court if a million dollars were involved.

In many comparative studies on American and Japanese management practices, it was found that Japanese companies tend to take a long-term perspective on business development, whereas American companies are much more focused on short-term issues. Thus American companies usually value immediate profits whereas Japanese companies are more concerned with market shares. Pascale and Athos (1981) cited Matsushita (which sold its products under the brand names National, Panasonic, Quasar, and Technics) as a prime example of this business approach. As soon as the products of Matsushita generated cost savings through high production volumes, the company would reduce their prices in order to drive competitors away and capture a larger share of the market. Thus in Japanese-U.S. joint ventures, one frequent difficulty is that the two partners cannot agree on the priority of their goals. Conflict arises because the Japanese want deeper market penetration at the cost of a slow return on their investment whereas their American partners put fast profits above other considerations (e.g., Peterson & Shimada, 1978).

In 1977, the government of India demanded that Coca-Cola turn over its ownership and technology to Indian investors. The Coca-Cola Export Company Corporation, which supplied Coke concentrate to Indian bottlers, agreed to reduce its equity to 40%, but insisted that it should retain manufacturing control to protect its secret beverage formula, which was seen as something that could not be compromised. But the Indian government insisted that it should acquire the majority ownership as well as the manufacturing know-how of Coca-Cola in India. Both parties insisted on their position, and Coca-Cola withdrew from India in 1977 (for details, see Gladwin & Walter, 1980, pp. 280-282). This final example illustrates dramatically how culture affects goal priority. For the Indian government, their tough stance was motivated by an ideological desire to downplay the role of foreign firms in the Indian economy. They regarded the majority control of a company as only symbolic, and they would not meet their objective if they could not have control over the manufacturing process. If the Indian government valued economic pragmatism more than nationalistic ideology, the conflict would have ended once Coca-Cola was willing to give up its majority ownership.

The above analysis suggests that conflict intensity may vary as a function of culture because the value attached to a goal is influenced by subjective culture. What is perceived as a major conflict in one culture may be quite minor in another.

MODES OF CONFLICT RESOLUTION

There are a number of commonly used methods for handling a dispute, and different names have been used to describe them. Two basic categories can be distinguished, namely, violent versus nonviolent (Mack & Snyder, 1973). Violent modes include wars, armed suppression, riots, armed rebellions, and strikes at the group level, and threats, coercion, and physical assaults at the interpersonal level. It is beyond the scope of this chapter to cover the violent dimensions of conflict processing, but interested readers may be referred to Goldstein and Segall (1983). In the nonviolent mode of conflict processing, several methods can be identified.

In *negotiation,* the two parties or their representatives try to work out a solution that is acceptable to both parties without the help of a third party. A variety of tactics are frequently observed in negotiations, such as persuasion, threats, and other forms of coercion, bluffing, reward, exchange, and concessions. Although these tactics are primarily based on a zero-sum, win/lose mentality, some authors have also advocated win-win or problem-solving approaches. These procedures involve the acceptance of the rights and interests of both parties and a search for common grounds and solutions that will maximize the benefits of both parties.

In *adjudication* or *arbitration,* a third party acts as a decision maker for the two disputing parties, with or without their consent. This adjudicator is vested with the legitimate power and authority to intervene in the dispute, to render a decision about the dispute, and to enforce compliance with the decision. A typical procedure in adjudication involves a presentation by the disputants or their representatives to the third party. The two disputants may interrogate each other or be interrogated by the third party or his or her representatives. The third party will then make a decision based on the information that he or she has collected about the case and on some predetermined criteria, such as legislation and precedents.

It is quite obvious that adjudication constitutes the basic procedure used in a court of law. Two major forms of adjudicatory procedures can be distinguished. Lind and Tyler (1988) gave a succinct description of these two procedures by comparing the French criminal trial, which adopts *inquisitorial adjudication,* and the American criminal trial, which adopts *adversary adjudication.*

In the American trial, most of the evidence is produced through the questioning of witnesses by the attorneys for the prosecution and defense.

Each attorney asks questions designed to elicit information favorable to the side of the case he or she represents. The judge is largely passive, ruling on objections when the attorneys raise them but participating only infrequently in the questioning of witnesses. Each attorney is given extensive opportunities to present arguments favorable to his or her side of the case. When both sides have concluded their presentations, the judge or jury renders a verdict. In a French trial, most of the evidence is available to the judge or judges at the beginning of the trial, having been discovered by an investigating judge and included in a *dossier* that seeks to present all information relevant to the case. In a French trial witnesses are questioned almost exclusively by the judge. In the French trial, it is up to the judge, not to the attorneys for the sides, to decide when enough evidence has been heard. (Lind & Tyler, 1988, p. 17)

In essence, the responsibility for the development of issues and the presentation of arguments at trial is assigned to the disputants in adversary adjudication, whereas the decision maker assumes control over the development of issues and evidence in inquisitorial adjudication.

In *mediation,* an agreed-upon third party tries to facilitate the process for the two disputing parties to arrive at a mutually acceptable solution. The third party has no authority to force the parties to accept his or her suggestions or decisions, but, once the parties agree on a solution, the agreement is usually binding through formal control (e.g., a legal contract) or informal control (e.g., public opinion).

There are a number of characteristics common to successful mediators. Kochan (1980) suggested that acceptability to both parties is important. Witty (1980) concluded that, across a wide variety of cultures, mediators are usually respected and senior members of the community.

According to Folberg and Taylor, mediation tries to achieve the following objectives:

Reduce the obstacles to communication between participants.

Maximize the exploration of alternatives.

Address the needs of everyone involved.

Provide a model for future conflict resolution. (Folberg & Taylor, 1984, p. 9)

Mediators may use a number of tactics to facilitate the emergence of a mutually acceptable solution. For instance, Kochan (1980) has provided a description of the behavior of a mediator in the whole process of mediation. The mediator usually assumes a passive, listening role in the beginning of the mediation process, with the aim of getting an accurate diagnosis of the dispute and the obstacles involved. With a reasonable understanding of the relative priorities and bottom-line positions of the parties, the mediator then tries to set up a framework and a procedure for the exchange of proposals and counterproposals between the two parties. Finally, the mediator may try to close the gap between the two parties by pushing them to make concessions.

Finally, two different types can be distinguished in *yielding,* in which one party stops dealing with the dispute. In *lumping,* one party does not press his or her claim or complaint, but at the same time does not admit to any fault for the dispute (e.g., Felstiner, 1974). In *avoiding,* one party withdraws from the situation and tries not to have contact with the other party (e.g., Hirschman, 1970). A major difference between lumping and avoidance is that, in lumping, the relationship between the parties continues, whereas, in avoidance, the relationship is restricted or even broken. There are a number of factors that encourage lumping and avoidance, such as the triviality of the issues involved or the difference in the relative power of the two disputing parties.

CULTURE AND PREFERRED MODE OF CONFLICT RESOLUTION

The four major types of conflict resolution procedures can probably be found in all cultures in the world (Gulliver, 1979). A question of significant theoretical and practical importance can be raised: Does the relative preference for these procedures vary across different cultures and why? Extensive research has been undertaken to seek an answer to this question in anthropology, psychology, legal studies, communication, and international management. The following provides an integrated description of the work conducted in these areas.

Social Structure and Procedural Preference

The anthropologist Gluckman (1954) is probably the first who provided an extensive account of how the structure of social relationships influences the procedure adopted for dispute processing. He makes a distinction between two types of social relationships. A *simplex* relationship is confined to a single interest, and a good example would be that between a doctor and a patient. A *multiplex* relationship, on the other hand, serves many interests. Gluckman gave an example from

Barotse society, where the "headman" was related to his villagers by political as well as kinship bonds. Because of the significant interdependence involved in a multiplex relationship, continuation of the relationship is very important to the well-being of the participants. Thus multiplex relationships demand conflict resolution procedures that allow compromises so that the relationship can continue smoothly. Nader and Todd (1978, p. 13) summarized Gluckman's model as follows:

> Disputants in multiplex or continuing relationships will rely on negotiation or mediation in settlement attempts which will lead to compromise outcomes.

Disputants in simplex relationships will rely on adjudication or arbitration in settlement attempts which will lead to win-or-lose outcomes.

A corollary is that negotiation and mediation will be more prevalent in societies where multiplex relationships dominate, whereas adjudication and arbitration will be more prevalent in societies where simplex relationships dominate.

Gluckman's (1954) model has received extensive support in the anthropological literature. For instance, in Rock Island, a fishing community of 314 persons located off the Atlantic coast of an industrialized Western nation, the relationships among the local residents fit nicely into Gluckman's multiplex category (Yngvesson, 1978). Everyone is related to everyone else in the community in a number of ways (e.g., ties based on kinship, friendship, and coworkership). As predicted, negotiation and yielding were reported as principal modes of conflict processing in the community. As examples of yielding, a car mechanic who persuaded female teenagers to participate in nude swimming became the object of gossip and indirect criticism but was never confronted about his misconduct. A woman was confronted with evidence about her shoplifting behavior, but no legal action was taken against her. Both incidences indicate the preference for yielding as a response to the conflict. On the other hand, Yngvesson (1978) also found that the fishermen were not at all reluctant to take *outsiders* to court for adjudicated settlements, a pattern also consistent with Gluckman's model.

Another example can be found in a Turkish village, where neighbors were likely to be tied through kinship and usually cooperated in food preparation, child care, and cultivation. Again, these villagers were involved in a multiplex relationship with each other. Consistent with the Gluckman model, villagers preferred informal negotiation for settling disputes because the outcomes were more flexible and mutually satisfactory. They turned to the village council and the village *muhtar* (headman) for arbitrated outcomes as a last resort.

Finally, the United States is seen by many as a ligitious society. Tanaka (1976) reported that there were eighteen lawyers per 10,000 people in the United States, and the corresponding figures were four for West Germany, two for France, and one for Japan. This strong preference for adjudication in the United States can be explained by the predominance of simplex relationships in U.S. society (e.g., Alston, 1985; Lasch, 1979).

Mediation in a Modern Era

This review may give readers an impression that negotiation and mediation are more popular in cultures where the means of subsistence is traditional, such as agricultural or fishing, whereas adjudication is more popular in industrialized societies. However, Felstiner (1974) argued that, even in what he called technologically complex, rich societies, institutionalized adjudication may still be problematic because the rules involved will be complex and quite different from everyday norms. A glance at the codes of law will quickly confirm this view. Thus specialists must be hired by the litigants to represent their cases. This is why most people find institutionalized adjudication inconvenient, slow, time-consuming, expensive, and ineffective. For instance, in America, there is a growing concern about the ineffectiveness of the American legal system in addressing the needs and grievances of people involved in conflict (e.g., Galanter, 1974) and a mounting need to search for alternative forms of institutionalized dispute processing (e.g., Burger, 1982).

Felstiner (1974) argued that institutionalized mediation is not likely to be successful in technologically complex, rich societies. In such societies, role differentiation is intense, and people's experience with mediation skills is usually quite limited. Thus very few people are qualified to be mediators because they are unlikely to have experience common to a large number of potential disputing parties. Without such experience, it is difficult for mediators to guide the disputants to a compromised solution because of their lack of an intimate and detailed knowledge of the perspectives of the disputants.

Recent work has suggested, however, that shared experience is only one factor that determines the success of mediation (e.g., Folberg & Taylor, 1984; Witty, 1980). Community mediation programs have actually been on the rise in the United States, a highly industrialized nation (Kressel & Pruitt, 1985).

Witty (1980) has argued that, if certain conditions exist, mediation will be effective regardless of the extent of industrialization and urbanization of the community. She summarized these conditions as follows:

1. Some degree of on-going personal interaction exists between disputants.

2. Both parties are willing to settle in a private forum.

3. Both parties are willing to express personal wants and needs.

4. A shared cultural or community identity exists.

5. A willingness or necessity to continue in a relationship with the other disputing party exists.

6. Both parties believe in the relative egalitarian relationships within the context of the disputes.

7. Intangible social resources such as status, honor, prestige, and personal satisfaction are equal to or more important than tangible resources such as money, property, or land.

8. Reaching an agreement is more important than determining absolute right or wrong.

9. People are more likely to adhere to agreements they understand and have an integral part in making than to agreements that are externally imposed. (Witty, 1980, p. 10)

Witty (1980) has studied an urban mediation program in the United States in which mediators are recruited from the local community and intensively trained to handle cases of both a civil and a criminal nature. These mediators are long-time residents of the community and this feature enhances their ability to develop trust, rapport, and credibility with the disputants. Most of the cases handled involved interpersonal disputes between people with ongoing relationships. Thus most of the preconditions for mediation were fulfilled, and the program was indeed very successful. Witty (1980) reported a success rate of about 75%, leading her to conclude that, even in urban settings, the preconditions for mediation may still exist.

Roehl and Cook (1985) also came to a similar conclusion in their extensive review of neighborhood justice centers in the United States in which mediation is employed as the principal mode of dispute processing. Neighborhood justice centers are staffed by trained volunteers who assist people in settling disputes away from the time-consuming, expensive, and stressful formal legal system. Roehl and Cook concluded that these mediation programs are more efficient in settling disputes than court adjudication, they produce settlements that are long-lasting, and they result in high satisfaction levels in the participants.

It is interesting to note that Witty (1980) based her conclusion on a comparison of mediation in Lebanon and in urban America. She suggested that, despite the many differences in the two societies, the Lebanese experience in mediation has direct implications for legal reform in the United States. On the other hand, Merry (1982), another anthropologist, pointed out that mediation is bound to be less successful in an urban society than in a traditional society because community leaders in a traditional society are more respected and are vested with more informal power. Other critics of community mediation programs have argued that these programs suffer from underutilization because they are not known to the majority of citizens. Another problem is that these programs may lead to violation of citizen rights. Some participants, especially the poor and the uneducated, may be misled or forced to accept settlements that are to their disadvantage (for a review of these criticisms, see Roehl & Cook, 1985).

It is thus clear that, to be effective, mediation in an urban setting cannot just copy the practices that have worked well for centuries in traditional societies. However, comparative studies of mediation in urban and in traditional societies, such as the study by Witty (1980), are useful for identifying elements that need to be modified to make mediation work in a modern environment.

International Law and the Japanese Style of Dispute Resolution

As much as domestic adjudicatory systems are under criticism, the effectiveness of international courts, which are also based on an adjudicatory model, has also been seriously questioned (Okuwaki, 1985). The major problem is that the enforcement of law requires a centralized power, whereas in the international scene, power is highly decentralized and uncoordinated. Given this inherent difficulty in international adjudication, some recent developments that are quite foreign to traditional Western legal thinking have been attempted. For instance, the International Court of Justice now obliges the disputing states to undertake further negotiation to resolve their dispute. Another example is that many international treaties now include a provision for the contracting parties to negotiate between themselves when disputes arise from the interpretation and application of these treaties. A Japanese legal scholar,

Okuwaki (1985), has suggested that international law has much to learn from the Japanese style of conflict resolution, which is oriented toward the avoidance of a zero-sum relationship between the disputing parties. He has proposed a "law as implicit mediator" model, which emphasizes the guiding function of law in attaining a compromise without the use of coercion. Although the details of his model are probably debatable, the interesting point to note here is that international law, which is dominated by Western adjudicatory thinking, may benefit substantially from the input of other forms of judicial thinking.

A Cross-Cultural Analysis of Adjudicatory Procedures

Systematic psychological research on the relationship between cultural values and procedural preference began in the 1970s (for a review, see Leung, 1988). The surge of interest in this area was actually a natural consequence of the pioneering work of Thibaut and Walker (1975) on procedural justice.

Thibaut and Walker (1975, 1978) and their associates compared the preference for two adjudicatory models and found a consistent preference for adversary adjudication over inquisitorial adjudication in the United States (see the description of these two models above). They argued that adversary procedures differ from inquisitorial procedures in that the former grant the disputants *process control* during the hearing of the dispute. The perceived fairness and preference effects favoring adversary procedures can be explained by a pervasive preference among those who are subject to any formal procedure to have a "voice" in the decision-making process. Subsequently, studies have shown similar preferences for procedures that allow those affected to have a voice or process control in a number of nonlegal settings (see Lind & Tyler, 1988, for a review).

Lind, Erickson, Friedland, and Dickenberger (1978) argued that the American preference for adversary adjudication may be produced by the endorsement of such a procedure in the American legal system. To evaluate this possibility, Lind, Erickson, Friedland, and Dickenberger conducted a study in the United States and England, where adversary adjudication is used, and in France and West Germany, where inquisitorial adjudication is used. The results supported the position of Thibaut and Walker and showed that adversary adjudication was preferred in all four nations. National endorsement of the two procedures had little effect on people's procedural preference.

Cultural Collectivism and Procedural Preference

Advances in research on dimensions of culture have helped clarify the relationship between cultural values and procedural preference. Recent work has shown that individualism-collectivism is a major dimension of culture and is related to a wide range of social behaviors (for a review, see Triandis, this volume). Briefly put, *individualism* refers to the tendency to be more concerned about the consequences of one's behavior on one's own needs, interests, and goals, whereas *collectivism* refers to the tendency to be more concerned about the consequences of one's behavior on in-group members and to be more willing to sacrifice personal interests for the attainment of collective interests.

Leung and Lind (1986) have argued that the preference for adversary adjudication was established only in individualist cultures (the United States, England, France, and West Germany) but was never tested in collectivist societies, and that some evidence exists that may challenge the universal preference for adversary adjudication. For instance, Tanabe (1963) observed that, although Japan has adopted an adversary legal system, litigants still rely on the judge to provide the facts of the case and ultimate justice. Tanabe has noted that an integration of the adversary and the inquisitorial system has been under way in Japan. In this new approach, the judge may clarify the case to ensure that its development is proper and fair. The litigants and their lawyers, however, still have the right to develop the case in any way they want. Additional evidence is found in a survey of district court judges, county attorneys, and public defenders in Tokyo and Minnesota by Benjamin (1975). Benjamin found that the Americans were more likely to respond positively to statements that endorsed what we would term "litigant process control," whereas the Japanese were more likely to endorse more statements in line with "judge process control." Finally, Leung and Lind (1986) found that, whereas American college students preferred adversary adjudication over inquisitorial adjudication, Chinese college students showed no difference in their preference for these two procedures. In sum, it is quite clear that the preference for adversary adjudication is more prominent in individualist societies.

Cultural Collectivism and Other Modes of Conflict Resolution

Cultural collectivism is also related to the preference for other methods of conflict resolution. For instance, Sullivan et al. (1981)

found that Japanese managers perceived the level of trust to be higher when an American partner requested a mutual conferral to resolve disputes rather than binding arbitration. Cushman and King (1985) argued that Americans prefer competition in handling a conflict, whereas Japanese and Yugoslavians prefer collaboration or compromise. Note that Yugoslavia is also characterized by Hofstede (1980) as a collectivist culture.

It is also well known that mediation plays a prominent role in dispute processing in Chinese societies (e.g., Doo, 1973). Convincing proof of this pattern was provided by Leung (1987), who compared the procedural preference of Chinese college students and citizens in Hong Kong with that of their American counterparts. As expected, Chinese respondents showed a stronger preference for negotiation and mediation, and a weaker preference for adjudicatory procedures, than did American respondents.

One characteristic of collectivism is a heightened distinction between in-groups and out-groups (see Hui, this volume). For instance, in Greece, the in-group (family and friends) is a source of protection and social insurance. In contrast, Greeks are more suspicious of and competitive with out-group members (e.g., strangers; Triandis, 1972). Leung (1988) tested how this feature of collectivism may affect conflict avoidance. He found that the Chinese were more likely to sue a stranger, and less likely to sue a friend, than were Americans. This pattern supports the argument that collectivists' choice of conflict resolution procedure is affected by the group membership of the other disputing party.

Other Cultural Dimensions

Leung, Bond, Carment, Krishnan, and Liebrand (in press) have examined the impact of cultural femininity on procedural preference. According to Hofstede (1980), in "feminine" cultures, interpersonal cooperation, a friendly atmosphere, and sympathy for the weak are more emphasized, whereas, in "masculine" cultures, achievement, recognition, and challenge are more emphasized (see Hui, this volume). Cultures high in femininity include Sweden, Norway, and the Netherlands, and cultures high in masculinity include Japan, Canada, Austria, and Venezuela. With Dutch subjects representing the feminine, and Canadian subjects representing the masculine, Leung, Bond, Carment, Krishnan, and Liebrand (in press) predicted and in general confirmed that Dutch subjects preferred harmony-enhancing procedures—such as mediation and negotiation—more, and confrontational procedures—such as threats and accusations—less.

Integrating Anthropology and Cross-Cultural Psychology

It is obvious that anthropologists focus on social structure as an explanatory tool for procedural preference, whereas cross-cultural psychologists focus on values and cognitions. This difference affects their choice of data sites, so that anthropologists mainly study traditional societies, whereas cross-cultural psychologists tend to compare industrialized societies. A tentative conclusion may be drawn at this point. If societies are very different in social structure and organization, the functionalist/structuralist position adopted by anthropologists seems to be very useful in explaining the cross-cultural differences observed in procedural preferences. On the other hand, in industrialized nations, where social structure and social organization are more similar, values and cognitions become more powerful explanatory tools. In the anthropological work of Witty (1980) discussed earlier, where mediation in Lebanon and American was compared, both structural characteristics of a social situation (e.g., ongoing relationships) and psychological mechanisms (e.g., personal needs) were included in her theory of mediation. This integration provides a useful empirical avenue for integrating these two close but distinct disciplines.

CROSS-CULTURAL DIFFERENCES IN NEGOTIATION BEHAVIOR

As the opportunities for cross-cultural negotiation become more prevalent, the research on cross-cultural differences in negotiation behavior is also on the rise (for a review, see Adler, 1986). Recent work has also uncovered significant cross-cultural differences in a number of negotiation behaviors.

Persuasion Styles

Glenn, Witmeyer, and Stevenson (1977) have discussed three major persuasion styles—rational, affective, and ideological (see also Glenn, 1981; Triandis, 1983)—and have argued that North Americans adopt the rational approach to negotiation. Facts and logic play a dominant role in the negotiation process. Arabs, on the other hand, use the affective approach to negotiation, where arguments are often based on feelings. Finally, the Russian style of persuasion is axiomatic, where ideological concerns form the basis of their arguments.

Using a simulation of labor-management negotiations, Porat (1970) reported cultural differences in *negotiation flexibility,* defined as the extent to which planned strategies are changed along the way of negotiation. Negotiators from Spain turned out to be the most flexible, followed in descending order by those from the United Kingdom, Switzerland, Denmark, and Sweden.

Confrontation

Some cultures prefer direct objections, heated debates, and confrontation in the negotiation process, such as France (e.g., Campbell, Graham, Jolbert, & Meissner, 1988), Brazil (e.g., Graham, 1985), and the United States (e.g., Moran, 1985). Druckman, Benton, Ali, and Bagur (1976) found that Indians were even more competitive in bargaining than Americans. On the other hand, other cultures prefer a more subtle way of bargaining, where balance and restraint are important. For instance, the Japanese are well known for their polite manners, ambiguous objections, and hidden emotions at the bargaining table (e.g., Graham & Sano, 1984). Similar patterns are also found in Malay negotiators (e.g., Renwick, 1985).

Some cultural groups see negotiation as what happens around the negotiation table and do not attempt to establish a social relationship with the other side. For instance, Schmidt (1979) suggested that Germans tend to keep a distance from their opponents because they feel that a personal relationship may hinder their performance in the negotiation. Similarly, American negotiators usually do not attempt to establish a close relationship with their opponents (e.g., Graham, 1981). On the other hand, in some cultures, negotiators spend a great deal of time getting to know each other and establishing a personal relationship before and during the negotiation. Examples are Japan (e.g., Graham, 1981; Moran, 1985) and Malaysia (Renwick, 1985). These cultural groups also take a long-term perspective on negotiation in which the long-term relationship is more important than maximizing immediate profit. For instance, in Japan, buyers and sellers are in a vertical, hierarchical relationship, where buyers usually can get what they request (Graham & Sano, 1984). On the other hand, buyers also have the obligation to protect the interests and well-being of sellers. For instance, in a simulation of a buyer/seller negotiation where the buyers had a structural advantage over the sellers, Harnett and Cummings (1980) found that American and European (from Belgium, Finland, France, and Spain) buyers were better at using their bargaining strength to obtain a larger profit, whereas Japanese and Thai buyers were more willing to settle on an egalitarian division of profit with the sellers.

Initial Positions

Culture plays a significant role in influencing the initial offers made by negotiators. A number of cultural groups are found to assume a very extreme position in their initial offer, such as Russians (Glenn et al., 1977; Ikle, 1964), Arabs (Glenn et al., 1977), the Chinese (Pye, 1982), and the Japanese (Graham & Andrews, 1987). On the other hand, American negotiators tend to make moderate initial offers.

Concession Patterns

Some cultures are more reluctant to make concessions, such as Russians (Glenn et al., 1977). Russians tend to view opponents' concessions as weakness and thus seldom reciprocate. In contrast, other cultural groups are more likely to make concessions and to reciprocate opponents' concessions, such as North Americans and Arabs (Glenn et al., 1977) and Malays (Renwick, 1985). In an experiment using prisoner's dilemma games, Maxwell and Schmitt (1975) found that Norwegians were even more willing to reciprocate. They were more likely than Americans to respond to a cooperative choice with a cooperative choice.

Nonverbal Behavior

Given that cultures differ substantially in the meaning and occurrence of different types of nonverbal behaviors (e.g., LaFrance & Mayo, 1978), it is not surprising that nonverbal behavior in negotiation varies as a function of culture. For instance, in a experimental simulation of negotiation behavior, Graham (1985) identified a number of differences among Japanese, American, and Brazilian negotiators. Japanese negotiators used silence most, followed by Americans, and then Brazilians. On the other hand, Japanese exhibited the least amount of facial gazing, and Brazilians exhibited the largest amount. Brazilians also exhibited a larger amount of touching and conversational overlaps than did Japanese and Americans.

Need for Training in Cross-Cultural Negotiation

The above review makes it clear that there are significant and extensive cultural differences in negotiation behavior. Negotiating for dispute settlement is already no easy task (recall protracted labor-management disputes that are frequently reported in newspapers). With the addition of cultural barriers, cross-cultural negotiation may seem next to impossible. Obviously, negotiators who are unfamiliar with these barriers are likely to leave the bargaining table confused, frustrated, and even upset, and unnecessary delays, deadlocks, and escalation of the conflict will follow. For instance, White (1977) has discussed the major misperceptions that were partly responsible for the escalation of the Arab-Israeli conflict. Negotiators must, therefore, be adequately prepared and trained for cross-cultural negotiation. See Bhawuk (this volume) for discussions of various training methods.

CONCLUSIONS

Why do we want to study dispute processing cross-culturally? From a theoretical point of view, cross-cultural research can test the generality of our theories and extend the range of the phenomena that we study. From a practical point of view, cross-cultural research can bring about at least two major benefits. First, countries that are undergoing legal reforms can learn from each other's experience. For instance, if the United States is trying to institute more neighborhood-based mediation programs, it is useful to consult the experience of cultures that have practiced mediation for a long time. In a similar vein, if a culture does not have a well-established tradition of adjudication, it would be useful to consult the United States for its experience in adversary adjudication.

Second, cross-cultural research on dispute processing will yield knowledge useful to the resolution of disputes involving different cultural groups, such as in trade negotiations and arms reduction talks. On a micro level, this knowledge can be used to design training programs to reduce the impact of such negotiation barriers as biased perception, stereotypes, prejudice, misattribution, misunderstanding, and communication breakdown (for examples of training programs, see

Brislin, Cushner, Cherrie, & Yong, 1986; and for barriers to cross-cultural interaction, see Brislin, 1981). For instance, an interesting case of how White divorce mediators can sidestep cultural barriers to help Black couples to settle divorce disputes is provided by Donohue (1985). On a macro level, this knowledge can be used to guide multinational corporations, ethnic leaders, and national governments to formulate policies and strategies that are effective in intercultural and international negotiations (Wells, 1977).

Despite the importance of knowledge about dispute processing in different cultures, many authors have pointed out that the information available is surprisingly small compared with the scope and breadth of the questions that have been raised (e.g., Gulliver, 1979; Harnett & Cummings, 1980). This chapter has summarized some major findings in the area, and we hope it will stimulate more research on this important topic in different parts of the world.

REFERENCES

Adler, N. J. (1986). *International dimensions of organizational behavior.* Boston: Kent.

Alston, J. P. (1985). *The American samurai: Blending American and Japanese managerial practice.* Berlin: Walter de Gruyter.

Benjamin, R. W. (1975). Images of conflict resolution and social control: American and Japanese attitudes to the adversary system. *Journal of Conflict Resolution, 19,* 123-137.

Brislin, R. W. (1981). *Cross-cultural encounters: Face-to-face interaction.* New York: Pergamon.

Brislin, R. W., Cushner, K., Cherrie, C., & Yong, M. (1986). *Intercultural interactions: A practical guide.* Beverly Hills, CA: Sage.

Burger, W. (1982). Isn't there a better way? *American Bar Association Journal, 68,* 274-277.

Campbell, N. C. G., Graham, J. L., Jolbert, A., & Meissner, H. G. (1988). Marketing negotiations in France, Germany, the United Kingdom, and the United States. *Journal of Marketing, 52,* 49-62.

Cushman, D. P., & King, S. S. (1985). National and organizational cultures in conflict resolution: Japan, the United States and Yugoslavia. In W. B. Gudykunst, L. P. Stewart, & S. Ting-Toomey (Eds.), *Communication, culture, and organizational processes* (pp. 114-133). Beverly Hills, CA: Sage.

Donohue, W. A. (1985). Ethnicity and mediation. In W. B. Gudykunst, L. P. Stewart, & S. Ting-Toomey (Eds.), *Communication, culture, and organizational process* (pp. 134-154). Beverly Hills, CA: Sage.

Doo, L. (1973). Dispute settlement in Chinese-American communities. *American Journal of Comparative Law, 21,* 627-663.

Druckman, D., Benton, A. A., Ali, F., & Bagur, J. S. (1976). Cultural differences in bargaining behavior. *Journal of Conflict Resolution, 20,* 413-449.

Felstiner, W. L. F. (1974). Influences of social organization on dispute processing. *Law and Society Review, 9,* 63-94.

Folberg, J., & Taylor, A. (1984). *Mediation: A comprehensive guide to resolving conflicts without litigation.* San Francisco: Jossey-Bass.

Galanter, M. (1974). Why the "haves come out ahead": Speculation on the limits of legal change. *Law and Society Review, 9,* 95-160.

Gladwin, T. N., & Walter, I. (1980). *Multinationals under fire: Lessons in the management of conflict.* New York: John Wiley.

Glenn, E. (1981). *Man and mankind: Conflict and communication between cultures.* Norwood, NJ: Ablex.

Glenn, E. S., Witmeyer, D., & Stevenson, K. A. (1977). Cultural styles of persuasion. *International Journal of Intercultural Relations, 1,* 52-66.

Gluckman, M. (1954). *The judicial process among the Barotse of Northern Rhodesia.* Manchester: University Press for the Rhodes-Livingstone Institute.

Goldstein, A. P., & Segall, M. (1983). *Global perspective on aggression.* New York: Pergamon.

Graham, J. L. (1981). A hidden cause of America's trade deficit with Japan. *Columbia Journal of World Business, 16,* 5-13.

Graham, J. L. (1985). The influence of culture on business negotiations. *Journal of International Business Studies, 16,* 81-96.

Graham, J. L., & Andrews, J. D. (1987). A holistic analysis of Japanese and American business negotiations. *Journal of Business Communication, 24,* 63-77.

Graham, J. L., & Sano, Y. (1984). *Smart bargaining: Doing business with the Japanese.* Cambridge, MA: Ballinger.

Gulliver, P. H. (1979). *Disputes and negotiations: A cross-cultural perspective.* New York: Academic Press.

Harnett, D. L., & Cummings, L. L. (1980). *Bargaining behavior: An international study.* Houston: Dame.

Hirschman, A. (1970). *Exit, voice, and loyalty: Responses to decline in firms, organizations and states.* Cambridge, MA: Harvard University Press.

Hofstede, G. (1980). *Culture's consequences: International differences in work-related values.* Beverly Hills, CA: Sage.

Ikle, F. C. (1964). *How nations negotiate.* New York: Harper & Row.

Kim, S. H. (1983). *International business finance.* Richmond, VA: Dame.

Kochan, T. A. (1980). *Collective bargaining and industrial relations.* Homewood, IL: Irwin.

Kressel, K., & Pruitt, D. (1985). Themes in the mediation of social conflict. *Journal of Social Issues, 41,* 179-198.

LaFrance, M., & Mayo, C. (1978). Cultural aspects of nonverbal communication: A review essay. *International Journal of Intercultural Relations, 2,* 71-89.

Lasch, C. (1979). *The culture of narcissism.* New York: Norton.

Leung, K. (1987). Some determinants of reactions to procedural models for conflict resolution: A cross-national study. *Journal of Personality and Social Psychology, 53,* 898-908.

Leung, K. (1988). Some determinants of conflict avoidance. *Journal of Cross-Cultural Psychology, 19,* 125-136.

Leung, K., Bond, M. H., Carment, D. W., Krishnan, L., & Liebrand, W. B. G. (in press). *Effects of cultural femininity on preference for methods of conflict processing: A cross-cultural study.* Manuscript submitted for publication.

Leung, K., & Lind, E. A. (1986). Procedure and culture: Effects of culture, gender, and investigator status on procedural preferences. *Journal of Personality and Social Psychology, 50,* 1134-1140.

Lind, E. A., Erickson, B. E., Friedland, N., & Dickenberger, M. (1978). Reactions to procedural models for adjudicative conflict resolution. *Journal of Conflict Resolution, 22,* 318-341.

Lind, E. A., & Tyler, T. R. (1988). *The social psychology of procedural justice.* New York: Plenum.

Mack, R. W., & Snyder, R. C. (1973). An analysis of social conflict: Toward an overview and synthesis. In F. Jandt (Ed.), *Conflict resolution through communication.* New York: Harper & Row.

Maxwell, G., & Schmitt, D. R. (1975). *Cooperation: An experimental analysis.* New York: Academic Press.

Merry, S. (1982). Defining "success" in the neighborhood justice movement. In R. Tomasic & M. Feeley (Eds.), *Neighborhood justice: Assessment of an emerging idea* (pp. 172-192). New York: Longman.

Moran, R. T. (1985). *Getting your yen's worth: How to negotiate with Japanese, Inc.* Houston: Gulf.

Nader, L., & Todd, H. F. (1978). *The disputing process: Law in ten societies.* New York: Columbia University Press.

Okuwaki, N. K. (1985). International conflict and peace: Legal perspective. In Y. S. Cho (Ed.), *Conflict and harmony in modern society* (pp. 297-314). Korea: Keimyung University Press.

Pascale, R. T., & Athos, A. G. (1981). *The art of Japanese management: Applications for American executives.* New York: Warner.

Peterson, R. B., & Shimada, J. Y. (1978). Sources of management problems in Japanese-American joint ventures. *Academy of Management Review, 3,* 796-804.

Porat, A. M. (1970). Cross-cultural differences in resolving union-management conflict through negotiations. *Journal of Applied Psychology, 54,* 441-451.

Pye, L. (1982). *Chinese commercial negotiating style.* Cambridge, MA: Oelgeschlager, Gunn & Hain.

Renwick, G. (1985). *Malays and Americans: Definite differences, unique opportunities.* Yarmouth, ME: Intercultural Press.

Roehl, J. A., & Cook, R. F. (1985). Issues in mediation: Rhetoric and reality revisited. *Journal of Social Issues, 41,* 161-178.

Schmidt, K. D. (1979). *Doing business in France, Germany, and the United Kingdom* (pamphlets). Menlo Park, CA: SRI International, Business Intelligence Program.

Schmidt, S. M., & Kochan, T. A. (1972). Conflict: Toward conceptual clarity. *Administrative Science Quarterly, 17,* 359-370.

Sullivan, J., Peterson, R. B., Kameda, N., & Shimada, J. (1981). The relationship between conflict resolution approaches and trust: A cross cultural study. *Academy of Management Journal, 24,* 803-815.

Tanabe, K. (1963). The process of litigation: An experiment with the adversary system. In A. T. von Mehren (Ed.), *Law in Japan: The legal order in a changing society* (pp. 73-110). Cambridge, MA: Harvard University Press.

Tanaka, H. (1976). *The Japanese legal system.* Tokyo: University of Tokyo Press.

Thibaut, J., & Walker, L. (1975). *Procedural justice: A psychological analysis.* Hillsdale, NJ: Lawrence Erlbaum.

Thibaut, J., & Walker, L. (1978). A theory of procedure. *California Law Review, 66,* 541-566.

Triandis, H. C. (1972). *The analysis of subjective culture.* New York: John Wiley.

Triandis, H. C. (1983). Dimensions of cultural variations as parameters of organizational theories. *International Studies of Management and Organization, 12,* 139-169.

Wells, L. T. (1977, January-February). Negotiation with Third World governments. *Harvard Business Review,* pp. 72-80.

White, R. K. (1977). Misperception in the Arab-Israeli conflict. *Journal of Social Issues, 33,* 190-221.

Williams, L. K., Whyte, W. F., & Green, C. S. (1966). Do cultural differences affect workers' attitudes? *Industrial Relations, 5,* 105-117.

Witty, C. J. (1980). *Mediation and society: Conflict management in Lebanon.* New York: Academic Press.

Yngvesson, B. (1978). The Atlantic fishermen. In L. Nader & H. F. Todd, Jr. (Eds.), *The disputing process: Law in ten societies* (pp. 59-85). New York: Columbia University Press.

11

PSYCHOLOGY OF ACCULTURATION
Understanding Individuals
Moving Between Cultures

JOHN W. BERRY

In cross-cultural psychology, there is interest in two broad domains: the comparative examination of psychological similarities and differences across broad ranges of cultures, and the psychological adaptations made by individuals when they move between cultures. The former is the preeminent line of inquiry in cross-cultural psychology, which attempts to link variations in individual behavior to cultural and ecological contexts by way of general enculturation and specific socialization; the latter is a relatively new area, which seeks to understand continuities and changes in individual behavior that are related to the experience of two cultures through the process of acculturation. It is with this latter domain that we are concerned in this chapter.

Psychological studies of acculturation are particularly relevant at the current time and in a variety of cultures. International migration, major refugee upheavals, and the painful process of decolonization have all increased intercultural contact, as have tourism and telecommunication. Previously culturally isolated and homogeneous peoples now rub shoulders on a daily basis with persons, ideas, and products from scattered parts of the globe, setting afoot a process of cultural and psychological adaptation to their new circumstances. How individuals negotiate their course through this process of acculturation is the focus of this chapter. We begin by outlining the process at both the cultural and the psychological levels, then turn to a consideration of variations in acculturating groups and strategies, and finally review a number of specific phenomena, including acculturation attitudes and the stresses associated with the process.

Within anthropology, the first major studies of acculturation were in the 1930s. The two classic definitions of *acculturation* are contained in related publications:

> Acculturation comprehends those phenomena which result when groups of individuals having different cultures come into continuous first-hand contact, with subsequent changes in the original culture patterns of either or both groups ... under this definition acculturation is to be distinguished

232

from culture change, of which it is but one aspect, and assimilation, which is at times a phase of acculturation. (Redfield, Linton, & Herskovits, 1936, pp. 149-152)

In another formulation, *acculturation* was defined as

culture change that is initiated by the conjunction of two or more autonomous cultural systems. Acculturative change may be the consequence of direct cultural transmission; it may be derived from noncultural causes, such as ecological or demographic modification induced by an impinging culture; it may be delayed, as with internal adjustments following upon the acceptance of alien traits or patterns; or it may be a reactive adaptation of traditional modes of life. (Social Science Research Council, 1954, p. 974)

It is useful to provide a concrete example of acculturation, employing the case of native peoples in the Western Hemisphere. In the sixteenth and seventeenth centuries, European and native peoples came into direct contact, leading to changes in both groups: Initially, Europeans learned more from native peoples (e.g., clothing, transportation and hunting techniques), but the tide soon turned and native peoples began to take on many features of European life, especially those cultural characteristics brought by colonial governments, missionaries, and teachers. As this process continued, the relative power (political, military, population) of the two groups gradually favored the Europeans, leading to significant changes in native life. However, native influence on the emerging European-based societies continued and can be seen in a large range of cultural phenomena, including language, political organization, and food. We can thus observe continuing and mutual influences as well as changes triggered in each society by the initial contact.

Acculturation Framework

The definitions presented above draw our attention to some of the key issues to be discussed in this chapter. First of all, there is a distinction between two levels: the *population* level (ecological, cultural, social, and institutional) and the *individual* level (the behaviors and traits of persons). Although this distinction has not usually been made by workers in anthropology, it has become of major importance for studies of individual acculturation. Graves (1967) has coined the term *psychological acculturation* to refer to the changes that an individual experiences as a result of being in contact with other cultures and as a result of participating in the process of acculturation that one's cultural or ethnic group is undergoing. The distinction between *acculturation* and *psychological acculturation* is important for two reasons. One is that the phenomena are different at the two levels, as we shall see later in the chapter. For example, at the population level, changes in social structure, economic base, and political organization frequently occur, whereas at the individual level, the changes are in such phenomena as behavior, identity, values, and attitudes.

A second reason for distinguishing between the two levels is that not every acculturating individual participates in the collective changes that are under way in one's group to the same extent or in the same way. Thus if we want to eventually understand the relationships between culture contact and psychological outcomes for individuals, we will need to assess (using separate measures) changes at the population level, and participation in these changes by individuals, and then relate both of these measures to the psychological consequences for the individual.

This discussion of the need for two levels brings us to the second major distinction, that between the antecedents to change and the consequents of change. Generally speaking, the flow of events is from antecedents to consequences, and the goal is to understand the population- and individual-level consequences in relation to the antecedents. Reverse influences can and do occur, but our focus in this chapter is on the eventual psychological outcomes.

A third distinction is between external and internal sources of change. As noted in the definitions quoted at the outset, change can come about through events that impinge on a group or an individual from outside the culture. Both diffusion and acculturation are examples of this source of change and include such phenomena as the introduction of single items such as the plow, writing, and firearms (all examples of diffusion) and of whole institutions such as education, colonial government, and industrialization (all examples of acculturation). Internal sources of change are those that do not come from outside contact and include phenomena such as invention, discovery, and innovation (ongoing dynamics at the population level) and insight, creativity, and drive (at the individual level).

A fourth consideration is that of the *processes* involved in change. The term *culture change* refers to the process that results in population-level changes that are due to dynamic internal phenomena such as innovation, discovery, or major ecological disaster. The term *acculturation* refers to the process that results in population-level changes that are due to contact with other cultures. Finally, the term *psychological acculturation* refers to the process by which individuals change, both by being influenced by contact with another culture and by being participants in the general acculturative changes under way in their own culture. This process necessarily involves some degree of input from, and continuity with, an individual's traditional psychological characteristics.

Although many disciplines have been working for a long time at the population level (including anthropology, international development studies, rural sociology, economics, and political science), the task has fallen mainly to cross-cultural psychology to study the individual level and its relationships with the population level.

To illustrate these distinctions, we may consider two concrete cases of individuals experiencing psychological change as a result of their membership in a changing cultural group. Although there are many categories of such individuals, we may take first the case of an immigrant moving to set up a new life in another country. This would be an example of acculturation, because external culture contact is involved, followed by both the cultural and the individual changes. First, the decision to emigrate is often based upon some prior contact, knowledge, and influence. Here the notions of "push" and "pull" factors may be useful. "Push" factors are those that have negative valence in one's own society, leading to a decision to migrate in order to *avoid* some aversive situation (e.g., poverty, civil strife, persecution). "Pull" factors are those that have positive valence in the new society, leading to a decision to migrate in order to *obtain* some more attractive situation (e.g., economic gains, peace, personal freedoms). Perhaps other individuals, even members of one's own family, have already settled in the new country, and this has led to some changes in one's home culture, such as the foreign language being taught in the schools, new industries being established, and the presence of mass media showing the way of life in the new country. On immigration to the new country, there can be some dramatic and sometimes overwhelming contact experiences followed by psychological reactions. Differences in climate, language, work habits, religion, and dress, for example, can all challenge the immigrant, and some response is required. These cultural differences may be accepted, interpreted, or denied, and the individual may ride with them or be run over by them.

For a second example, we may take the case of a person whose country and culture have been colonized. In this case, there is no choice made to enter into culture contact, because dominant cultures have a history of entering, uninvited, into many parts of the world, especially in Africa, Asia, and the Americas. Precontact experiences and positive motivation to acculturate are, therefore, lacking. However, once the process has started, individuals and communities may vary greatly in how they deal with the acculturative influences. Some may turn their backs, others may embrace, and yet others may selectively engage the new, while merging it with the old. Many options are possible (as we shall see later in this chapter), but in all cases the intercultural contact and the individual psychological response will be related to each other. It is the task of cross-cultural psychology to examine these relationships, to understand them, and finally to attempt to find systematic features in order to produce some generalizations about the processes involved in psychological responses to culture contact and change.

Acculturation Process

From the definitions of acculturation presented earlier, we may identify some key elements that are usually studied in cross-cultural psychology. First, there needs to be *contact* or interaction between cultures that is continuous and firsthand; this rules out short-term, accidental contact, and it rules out diffusion of single cultural practices over long distances. Second, the result is some *change* in the cultural or psychological phenomena among the people in contact, usually continuing for generations down the line. Third, taking these first two aspects together, we can distinguish between a *process* and a *state*: There is activity during and after contact that is dynamic, and there is a result of the process that may be relatively stable. This outcome may include not only changes in existing phenomena but also in some novel phenomena that are generated by the process of cultural interaction. For example, during the process of acculturation, individuals and groups are faced with many choices (about how to live, what to eat, what language to speak) and much day-to-day variability can be observed in the choices made. Later on, however, a fairly stable pattern of behavior may be exhibited as people settle into a preferred way of living in the acculturative arena.

Considering these distinctions as part of a general system of acculturation, the framework in Figure 11.1 can be proposed (see Berry, Trimble, & Olmeda, 1986). It depicts two cultures (A and B) in contact. In principle, each could influence the other equally (in a form of symbiosis), but, in practice, one tends to dominate the other; in this framework, the "dominant group" (or "donor") is Culture A and the "acculturating group" (or "receptor") is Culture B. For completeness,

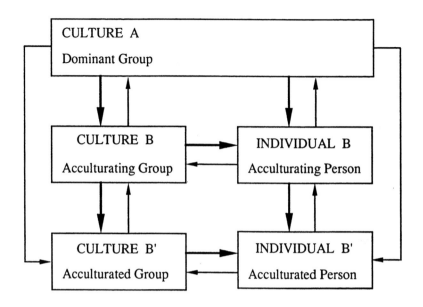

Figure 11.1. Framework for Identifying Variables and Relationships in Acculturation Research
SOURCE: From Berry, Trimble, and Olmeda (1986).

mutual influence is depicted by the two arrows between Cultures A and B, as is the influence of Culture A directly on individuals in Culture B. However, the consequences for culture group A are not represented and for the balance of this chapter we will focus on a single culture (B), the one receiving the greater influence. This is not to say that changes in the dominant culture are uninteresting or unimportant: Acculturation often brings about population expansion, greater cultural diversification, attitudinal reaction (prejudice and discrimination), and policy development (for example, in the areas of immigration, cultural pluralism, bilingualism, and schooling). Moreover, there may also be a substantial need for an organized and rational response by government in such areas as training for improved intercultural relations (see the chapter by Bhawuk, this volume) and a more ready attitude to modify existing institutions such as schools, hospitals, and broadcasting.

One result of the contact and influence is that aspects of group B become transformed so that cultural features of the acculturated group (B[1]) are not identical to those in the original group at the time of first contact. Of course, if contact is still maintained, further influence from Culture A is experienced. A parallel phenomenon is that individuals in group B undergo psychological changes (as a result of both influences from their own group and from group A), and, again, if there is continuing contact, further psychological changes may take place.

What are the characteristics of the dominant group that are important to examine? The essential ones are the following: *Purpose*: Why is the contact taking place? What are its goals? Clearly, acculturation phenomena will vary according to whether the purpose is colonization, enslavement, trade, military control, evangelization, education, and so on. *Length*: For how long has the contact been taking place, and does it occur daily, seasonally, or annually? *Permanence*: Is the dominant group here to stay? Have they settled in, or is it a passing venture? *Population size*: How many are there? Do they form a majority, or are there only a few? *Policy*: What are the policies being exercised toward acculturating groups? Is it assimilation, eventual extermination, indirect rule, ghettoization, dispersion, or the like? *Cultural qualities*: Are there cultural qualities possessed by the dominant group that can meet specific needs or improve the quality of life of the acculturating group? Potentially desirable cultural traits such as medicines, guns, and traps (for hunter populations) and seeds, plows, and irrigation techniques (for agricultural populations) will obviously lead to acculturative changes more than will unwanted or nonfunctional culture traits. This list serves as an example of the kinds of cultural variables that may contribute to the ways in which acculturation takes place. Without some indication of the nature of these variables, no account of acculturation would be complete.

A parallel account is needed of the characteristics of Culture B. It includes the following: *Purpose*: Is the group in contact voluntarily (e.g., immigrants) or under duress (e.g., native peoples)? *Location*: Is the group in its traditional location, with its land and other resources available, or are they displaced to some new environment (e.g., a reservation, a refugee camp)? *Length and permanence*: These variables are much the same as for the description of Culture A. In particular, the phase of acculturation needs to be specified: Has contact only begun? Have acculturative pressures been building up? Has a conflict or crisis appeared? *Population size*: How many are there? Are they a majority or minority? Is the population vital (sustaining or increasing in number) or declining? *Policy*: To what extent does the group have an organized response to acculturation? If there is a policy orientation, is it one of resistance or exclusion (get rid of acculturative influence), of inclusion (accepting the influence), or of control (selective inclusion according to some scale of acceptability)? *Cultural qualities*: Are there certain aspects of the traditional culture that affect the acculturation process?

For example, hunter/gatherers are susceptible to habitat destruction due to war, forest reduction, or mineral exploration, whereas agricultural peoples may be dispossessed of their land by permanent settlers from Culture A who want to build cities. More complex societies may be better able to organize politically and militarily than less complex societies to alter the course of acculturation, whereas nomads may be in a position to disperse to avoid major acculturative influences.

In addition to these specific characteristics that may be discerned in particular groups, it is also important to consider how the cultural-level phenomena listed above for Culture B are distributed across individuals in the group: Do they vary according to the person's age, sex, family position, personal abilities, and the like? As noted earlier, the crucial point is that not every person in the acculturating group will necessarily enter into the acculturation process in the same way or to the same degree. Hence assessment of the individual experience of acculturation is an important aspect of the study of psychological acculturation.

At this point, we turn our attention to the changes that have actually taken place (Culture B^1) as a result of the acculturation process (recognizing, of course, that in many cases the acculturative influences continue to affect the group). These general consequences of acculturation have received considerable attention in the literature (see Berry, 1980, for a review of some general trends) and include such global descriptors as Westernization, modernization, industrialization, Americanization, and so on. Some specific phenomena are these: *Political*: Have there been changes in political characteristics as a result of acculturation? For example, has independence been lost? Have previously unrelated (even warring) groups been placed within a common framework? Have new authority systems (e.g., chiefs, mayors, religious leaders, governors) been added? Have people with regional similarities been categorized as "tribes" or "provinces"? *Economic*: Has the subsistence base been changed, or the distribution of wealth been altered? For example, have hunter/gatherers been converted into herders or farmers, and others into industrial or wage workers? Have previous concentrations of wealth in certain families or regions been eliminated, or, conversely, has a new wealthy class emerged from a previously uniform system? Have new economic activities been introduced such as mining, forestry, game management, tourism, manufacturing? *Demographic*: Has there been a change in the population size, its urban/rural distribution, its age or sex profile, or in regional dispersion? *Cultural*: To what extent are there new languages, religions, modes of dress, schooling, transportation, housing, and forms of social organization and social relations in the acculturated group? How do these relate to the previous norm? Do they conflict with them, partially displace them, or merge (as in some forms of Creole or of African Christian churches)? All of these, and possibly many more depending on one's particular research location, are important markers of the extent to which acculturation has taken place in the group.

As we have noted previously, there are very likely to be individual differences in the psychological characteristics that a person brings to the acculturation process; and not every person will necessarily participate to the same extent in the process. Taken together, this means that we need to shift our focus away from general characterizations of acculturation phenomena to a concern for variation among individuals in the group undergoing acculturation.

We also need to be aware that individual acculturation (as well as group-level phenomena) do not cohere as a nice neat package. Not only will groups and individuals vary in their participation and response to acculturative influences, some domains of culture and behavior may become altered without comparable changes in other domains. For example, attitudes toward the value of traditional technology may change without a parallel change in beliefs and behaviors associated with it. That is, the process of acculturation is an uneven one and does not affect all cultural and psychological phenomena in a uniform manner.

The Selection of Variables for Research

The central issue here is the extent to which a particular individual has engaged in the acculturation process. Numerous indicators may be sought and from a variety of sources (the individual, an informant, or by direct observation).

We approach the topic in two ways: First, we list (and briefly comment on) many of the variables that appear in the literature, and, second, we present illustrative measures to show how the variables have actually been employed in fieldwork. The list includes the following: *Education*: How far has an individual gone in the formal schooling that has been introduced from outside? If there is only one single indicator of individual contact and participation that can be assessed, previous research suggests that this is likely to be the most fruitful one (see the chapter by Cushner, this volume). *Wage employment*: To what extent have the individuals entered the work force for wages as opposed to remaining with traditional economic activity? *Urbanization*: In predominantly rural societies, to what extent have individuals migrated to, and lived in, a new urban agglomeration? To what extent have they traveled to or visited these urban areas? *Media*: To what extent do individuals listen to radio, watch television, and read newspapers and magazines that introduce them to Culture A? *Political participation*: To what extent do individuals involve themselves in the new political structures, including voting, running for office or volunteering for boards, and so on? *Religion*: Have individuals changed their religion to one introduced by Culture A, and to what extent do they practice it? *Language*: What is the extent of knowledge and use of the language(s) introduced by Culture A? *Daily practices*: To what extent is there a change in personal dress, housing and furniture styles, food habits, and so on? *Social relations*: To what extent do the individuals relate to (marry, play with, work with, reside with) those of Culture A as opposed to those of their own group?

These numerous variables are likely to be interrelated; thus we find in the literature attempts to develop scales or indices of contact and participation that sum across these various experiences. Two examples of these follow:

An Index of Contact (de Lacey, 1970) was developed as a general contact index for Australian Aboriginal children with Euro-Australian society. It contains two sections: exposure variables (which include some cultural-level as well as individual-level variables) and adaptation variables. Exposure was assessed by the proportion of the population that is Euro-Australian, visits to Euro-Australian houses, shopping experiences of children, travel to Euro-Australian centers, use of English, and access to mass media and to Euro-Australian artifacts. Adaptation was assessed by ratings of persistence of Aboriginal culture, use of Euro-Australian games and hobbies, use of Euro-Australian food, the home physical environment (Euro-Australian versus Aboriginal), and community organization (primarily tribal versus virtually Euro-Australian). Total scores were then calculated for each child. This index illustrates how acculturation may be assessed at the individual level, but, of course, the actual items will vary depending on the population and research goals.

Another contact scale (Berry, van de Koppel, et al. 1986) was developed for use in Central Africa with Biaka Pygmy and Bangandu Villagers. It consists of eight variables: number of local languages spoken; knowledge of French; knowledge of Sango (the national lingua franca); ownership (with items for knives, pottery, ornaments, outside goods); employment and technology (scaled from traditional hunter or farmer through to wage earner); religion (animism through to Islam); adoption of clothing (in European style) and travel (to towns and cities).

All these variable were positively and (in most cases) significantly correlated, and they were used to create a single, standardized index for each person.

An Ownership Index was developed (by Berry & Annis, 1974) for use among the James Bay Cree. The items in the scale were ownership of radio, outboard motor, snowmobile, clothes washer, freezer, bank account, and life insurance. The intention is to obtain objective evidence of the extent to which an individual has "bought into" Euro-Canadian society. Once again, this is illustrative of how to assess one aspect of acculturation rather than suggesting a standard instrument that can be used in all field settings.

It should be emphasized that these scales and indices are not universally valid, ready-made, or standard instruments that can be taken "as is" for use in any field setting. Some variables are clearly more relevant to Pygmies than to a community of Italian Americans (e.g., adoption of clothing), whereas others may be more relevant to an ethnic group undergoing acculturation (such as the language spoken in the family) than to a linguistically homogeneous community in Central Africa.

Acculturating Groups

Although many of the generalities found in the literature about the effects of acculturation have been based on a single type of group, it is clear that there are numerous types, and adaptations may vary depending upon this factor. In the review by Berry et al. (1987), five different groups were identified, including immigrants, refugees, native peoples, ethnic groups, and sojourners (see Figure 11.2). This classification into five kinds of groups represents a view from Canada, where, in principle, all people are thought to be attached in some way to a particular heritage culture. The generic term *ethnic group* is most frequently used to refer to people who identify with, and exhibit, a common heritage in the second or subsequent generation after immigration. By convention, the term *native peoples* is used to refer to those Indigenous or Aboriginal groups that were resident prior to European colonization and who remain as nations (in the cultural sense) within the larger society. *Immigrants* and *refugees* are both first-generation arrivals into the population by way of migration from some other part of the world, whereas *sojourners* are temporary immigrants who reside for a specific purpose and time period, and who intend to return eventually to their country of origin.

VOLUNTARINESS OF CONTACT

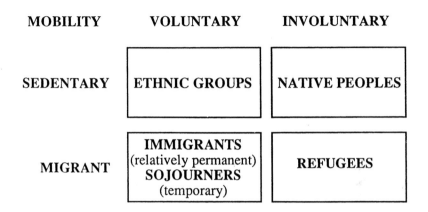

MOBILITY	VOLUNTARY	INVOLUNTARY
SEDENTARY	ETHNIC GROUPS	NATIVE PEOPLES
MIGRANT	IMMIGRANTS (relatively permanent) SOJOURNERS (temporary)	REFUGEES

Figure 11.2. Varieties of Acculturating Groups
SOURCE: From Berry, Kim, Minde, and Mok (1987).

In other countries, the classification of groups may take different forms, based upon different histories and ideologies. However, this classification derives also from three distinctions that have import for psychological acculturation. There are variations in the degree of voluntariness, movement, and permanence of contact, all factors that might affect the health of members of the group. Those who are voluntarily involved in the acculturation process (e.g., immigrants) may experience less difficulty than those with little choice in the matter (e.g., refugees and native peoples), because their initial attitudes toward contact and change may be more positive. Further, those only temporarily in contact and who are without permanent social supports (e.g., sojourners) may experience more health problems than those more permanently settled and established (e.g., ethnic groups).

Acculturation Attitudes

The goals of acculturation are not necessarily toward modernity or any other single alternative. Moreover, the goal as articulated by Culture A in their policy statements may not be the preferred course among the leaders or individuals in Culture B. In Australia (Sommerlad & Berry, 1970), an attempt was made to discover what the attitudes of

Aborigines were to their future in Australia; the Commonwealth government proposed assimilation, but others were not so sure. Since then the argument has been made (Berry, 1980) that acculturation can be viewed as a multilinear phenomenon, as a set of alternatives, rather than as a single dimension ending in assimilation or absorption into a "modern" society.

The ways in which an individual (or a group) of Culture B wishes to relate to Culture A have been termed *acculturation attitudes* (see Berry, Kim, Power, Young, & Bujaki, 1989, for a review of the reliability, validity, and correlates of these attitudes). In a sense, they are conceptually the result of an interaction between ideas deriving from the modernity literature and the intergroup relations literature. In the former, the central issue is the degree to which one wishes to remain culturally as one has been (e.g., in terms of identity, language, way of life) as opposed to giving it all up to become part of a larger society. In the latter, the central issue is the extent one wishes to have day-to-day interactions with those of other groups in society, as opposed to turning away from other groups, and relating only to those of one's own group. A third issue is that of which group has the political power to choose the responses to the first two issues. In some societies, the dominant group virtually dictates the ways in which the nondominant groups may act, whereas in other societies, nondominant groups are largely free to select their own course (Berry, 1974).

When the first two issues are posed simultaneously, a conceptual framework (Figure 11.3) is generated that posits four varieties of acculturation. It is, of course, recognized that each issue can be responded to on an attitudinal dimension, but, for purposes of conceptual presentation, a dichotomous response ("yes" or "no") is shown. When an individual in Culture B does not wish to maintain his or her identity (and so on) and seeks daily interaction with Culture A, then the assimilation (a) path or mode is defined. When this course is freely chosen by the acculturating group, we have the "melting pot"; but when it is forced by the dominant group, we may call it a "pressure cooker." In contrast, (b) when there is a value placed on holding onto one's original culture, and at the same time a wish to avoid interaction with others, then the separation alternative is defined. If, however, such cultural distinctiveness is required by the dominant society, and the nondominant group is kept at a distance from them, then we have the classic situation of segregation. When there is an interest both in maintaining one's original culture and in daily interactions with others (c) integration is the option; here, there is some degree of cultural integrity maintained, while moving to participate as an integral part of

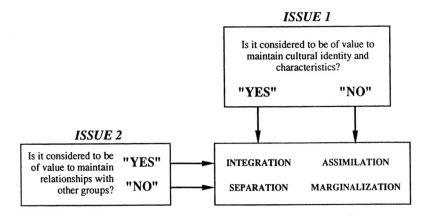

Figure 11.3. Four Varieties of Acculturation, Based on Orientations to Two Basic Issues
SOURCE: From Berry and Kim (1988).

the larger social network. Such a course is possible only where the dominant society is open and accepting of the wishes of the various acculturating groups. It should be noted that the term *integration* as used here is clearly distinct from the term *assimilation* (although the two sometimes appear in the literature as synonyms); cultural maintenance is sought in the former case, but there is little or no interest in such continuity in the latter. It should also be noted that acculturation may be "uneven" across domains of behavior and social life; for example, one may seek economic assimilation (in work), linguistic integration (by way of bilingualism), and marital separation (by endogamy).

Finally (d), when there is little interest in cultural maintenance, or in relations with other groups, the option of marginalization is defined. When this situation of being out of touch with either culture is the result of actions by the dominant society (for example, by forced cultural loss, along with forced exclusion), the concepts of "deculturation" or "ethnocide" have sometimes been employed. However, the classic concept of marginalization (Stonequist, 1935) now appears to be used generically to refer to this situation of being on the margin of two cultures, being accepted or supported by neither one.

To exemplify these four acculturation strategies, we may consider a hypothetical family that has migrated from Italy to Canada. The father may lean toward integration in terms of job prospects, wanting to get involved in the economics and politics of his new society, and learning English and French, in order to obtain the benefits that motivated his migration in the first place. At the same time, he may be a leader in the Italian-Canadian Community Association, spending much of his leisure and recreational time in social interaction with other Italian-Canadians. Hence he has a preference for integration when his leisure time activities are considered. In contrast, the mother may hold completely to Italian language use and social interactions, feeling that she is unable to get involved in the work or cultural activities of the host society. She employs the separation strategy, having virtually all her personal, social, and cultural life within the Italian world. In further contrast, the teenage daughter is annoyed by hearing the Italian language in the home, by having only Italian food served by her mother, and by being required to spend most of her leisure time with her extended Italian family. Instead, she much prefers the assimilation option: to speak English, participate in her school activities, and generally be with her Canadian age mates. Finally, the son does not want particularly to recognize or accept his Italian heritage ("What use is it here in my new country?") but is rejected by his schoolmates because he speaks with an Italian accent and often shows no interest in local concerns such as hockey. He feels trapped between his two possible identity groups, neither accepting nor being accepted by them. As a result, he retreats into the social and behavioral sink of marginalization, experiencing social and academic difficulties and eventually coming into conflict with his parents.

Acculturative Stress

One of the most obvious and frequently reported consequences of acculturation is that of societal disintegration and personal crisis. The old social order and cultural norms often disappear, and individuals may be lost in the change. At the group level, previous patterns of authority, of civility, and of welfare no longer operate, and, at the individual level, hostility, uncertainty, identity confusion, and depression may set in. Taken together, these changes constitute the negative side of acculturation, changes that are frequently, but not inevitably, present. The opposite, that of successful *adaptation,* may also take place; as we shall see, the outcome appears to vary as a function of a number of variables.

The concept of *acculturative stress* (Berry & Annis, 1974) refers to one kind of stress, that in which the stressors are identified as having their source in the process of acculturation. In addition, there is often a particular set of stress behaviors that occur during acculturation, such as lowered mental health status (especially confusion, anxiety, depression), feelings of marginality and alienation, heightened psychosomatic symptom level, and identity confusion. Acculturative stress is thus a phenomenon that may underlie a reduction in the health status of individuals (including physical, psychological, and social aspects). To qualify as *acculturative* stress, these changes should be related in a systematic way to known features of the acculturation process as experienced by the individual.

In a recent review and integration of the literature, Berry and Kim (1988) attempted to identify the cultural and psychological factors that govern the relationship between acculturation and mental health. It was concluded that, clearly, mental health problems often do arise during acculturation. However, these problems are not inevitable and seem to depend on a variety of group and individual characteristics that enter into the acculturation process. That is, acculturation sometimes enhances one's life chances and mental health and sometimes virtually destroys one's ability to carry on. The eventual outcome for any particular individual is affected by other variables that govern the relationship between acculturation and stress.

This conception is illustrated in Figure 11.4. On the left of the figure, *acculturation* occurs in a particular situation (e.g., migrant community or native settlement), and individuals participate in and experience these changes to varying degrees. Thus the individual acculturation experience may vary from a great deal to rather little. In the middle, *stressors* may result from this varying experience of acculturation; for some people, acculturative changes may all be in the form of stressors, whereas for others, they may be benign or even seen as opportunities. On the right, varying levels of *acculturative stress* may become manifest as a result of acculturation experience and stressors.

The first crucial point to note is that relationships among these three concepts (indicated by the solid horizontal arrows) are probabilistic rather than deterministic. The relationships all depend upon a number of moderating factors (indicated in the lower box), including the nature of the larger society, the type of acculturating group, the mode of acculturation being experienced, and a number of demographic, social, and psychological characteristics (including coping abilities) of the group and individual members. That is, each of these factors can influence the degree and direction of the relationships between the three variables at the top of Figure 11.4. This influence is indicated by the broken vertical arrows drawn between this set of moderating factors and the horizontal arrows.

Results of studies of acculturative stress have varied widely in the level of difficulties found in acculturating groups. Early views were that

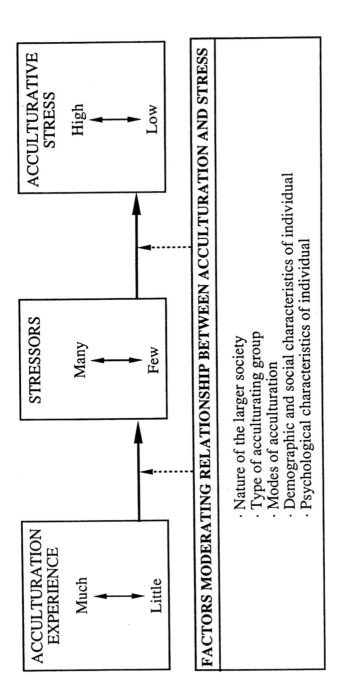

Figure 11.4. Relationships Between Acculturation and Stress, as Modified by Other Factors

SOURCE: From Berry, Kim, Minde, and Mok (1987).

culture contact and change inevitably led to stress. However, current views are that stress is linked to acculturation in a probabilistic way, and the level of stress experienced will depend on a number of factors.

There is evidence (Berry & Kim, 1988) that mode of acculturation is one important factor: Those who feel marginalized tend to be highly stressed, and those who maintain a separation goal are also stressed; in contrast those who pursue integration are minimally stressed, with assimilation leading to intermediate levels.

Another factor is the way in which the host society exerts its acculturative influences. One important distinction is the degree of pluralism extant (Murphy, 1965). Culturally plural societies, in contrast to culturally monistic ones, are likely to be characterized by two important factors. One is the availability of a network of social and cultural groups that may provide support for those entering into the experience of acculturation (i.e., provide a protective cocoon), and the other is a greater tolerance for or acceptance of cultural diversity (termed *multicultural ideology* by Berry, Kalin, & Taylor, 1977). Related to this general tolerance for ethnic diversity (which is usually found in plural societies) is the pattern of specific ethnic and racial attitudes in the larger society: Some acculturating groups may be more accepted and placed higher in the prestige hierarchy, whereas others may occupy the lower ranks in the societies' prejudice system. These latter people are likely to be the targets of abuse and discrimination, leading to a weaker self-concept and lower mental health status. Taken together, one might reasonably expect the stress of persons experiencing acculturation in plural societies to be less than those in monistic societies that pursue a forced inclusion or assimilationist ideology.

A related factor, paradoxically, is the existence of policies that are designed to *exclude* acculturating groups from full participation in the larger society. To the extent that acculturating people wish to participate in the desirable features of the larger society (such as adequate housing, medical care, political rights), the denial of these may be cause for increased levels of acculturative stress.

There are also many social and cultural qualities of the acculturating group that may affect the degree to which acculturative stress is experienced by its members. The list of possible factors identified in the literature is extremely long, thus we only attempt to provide a selective overview here. It is useful to distinguish between original (precontact) cultural characteristics and those that evolve during the process of acculturation. However, some factors involve the interaction of variables from these two sets (pre- and postcontact).

One basic cultural factor that appears in the literature is the traditional settlement pattern of the group: Nomadic peoples, who are usually hunters, gatherers, or pastoralists, may suffer more negative consequences of acculturation than peoples who were sedentary prior to contact. A complex of factors have been suggested to account for this proposal: Nomadic peoples are used to relatively large territories, small population densities, and unstructured sociopolitical systems. During acculturation, sedentarization into relatively dense communities with new authority systems is typically required, and this induces relatively greater tension among nomadic peoples than among others.

Status is also a factor even when one's origin is in a relatively stratified society. For example, one's "entry status" into the larger society is often lower than one's "departure status" from the home society. This relative loss of status may result in stress and poor mental health. For example, physicians who immigrate to a new country very often have to start (and sometimes have to remain) working as nurses or in paramedical roles. One's status mobility in the larger society, whether to regain one's original status or just to keep up with other groups, may also be a factor. In addition, some specific features of status (such as education and employment) provide one with resources to deal with the larger society, and these likely affect one's ability to function effectively in the new circumstances.

Some standard indicators, such as the age and gender group one belongs to, may also play a role: Relatively older persons, and often females, have frequently been noted to experience more stress, as have those who are without a partner (unmarried, either because of loss or unavailability). Perhaps the most comprehensive variable in the literature is that of social supports. This refers to the presence of social and cultural institutions for the support of the acculturating individual. Included here are such factors as ethnic associations (national or local), residential enclaves ("ghetto"), extended families (including endogamy), availability of one's original group (for return visits), and more formal institutions such as agencies and clinics devoted to providing support.

A final set of social variables refers to the acceptance or prestige of one's group in the acculturation setting. Some groups are more acceptable on grounds of ethnicity, race, or religion than others. Those less acceptable run into barriers (prejudice, discrimination, exclusion) that may lead to marginalization of the group and that are likely to induce greater stress. The point here is that, even in plural societies (those societies that may be generally more tolerant of differences), there

are still relative degrees of social acceptability of the various acculturating groups.

Beyond these social factors, numerous psychological variables may
play a role in the mental health status of persons experiencing acculturation. Here again, a distinction is useful between those characteristics
that were present prior to contact and those that developed during
acculturation. In the precontact set of variables are included certain
experiences that may predispose one to function more effectively under
acculturative pressures. These are prior knowledge of the new language
and culture, prior intercultural encounters of any kind, motives for the
contact (voluntary versus involuntary contact), and attitudes toward
acculturation (positive or negative). Other prior attributes that have
been suggested in the literature are one's level of education and employment, values, self-esteem, identity confusion, rigidity/flexibility,
and cognitive style.

Contact experiences may also account for variations in acculturative
stress. Whether one has a lot of contacts with the larger society (or few
of them), whether they are pleasant (or unpleasant), whether they meet
the current needs of the individual (or not), and in particular whether
the first encounters are viewed positively (or not) may set the stage for
all subsequent ones and affect mental health.

Among factors that appear during acculturation are attitudes toward
the various modes of acculturation. As noted in the previous section,
individuals within a group do vary in their preference for assimilating,
integrating, or rejecting. These variations, along with experiences of
marginalization, are known to affect one's mental health status (Berry,
Kim, Minde, & Mok, 1987). Another variable, the sense of cognitive
control that an individual has over the acculturation process, also seems
to play a role. Those who perceive that the changes are opportunities
that they can manage may have better mental health than those who feel
overwhelmed by them. In essence, then, the attitudinal and cognitive
perspectives suggest that it is not the acculturative changes themselves
that are important but how one sees them and what one makes of them
(Brislin, Cushner, Cherrie, & Yong, 1986).

Finally, a recurring idea is that the congruity between expectations
and actualities will affect mental health. Individuals for whom there is
a discrepancy, such that they aspire to or expect more than they actually
obtain during acculturation, may have greater acculturative stress than
those who achieve some reasonable match between them. That is, prior
expectations and goals (and whether they can be met) appear to be major
predictors of how individuals and groups will fare during the course of
acculturation. Recent work (reviewed in Beiser et al., 1988) indicates

that a desire to participate in the larger society, or a desire for cultural maintenance, if thwarted, can lead to a serious decline in the mental health status of acculturating individuals. Policies or attitudes in the larger society that are discriminatory (not permitting participation and leading to marginalization or segregation) or assimilationist (leading to enforced cultural loss) are all predictors of psychological problems. In my view, acculturative stress is always a possible concomitant of acculturation, but its probability of occurrence can be much reduced if both participation in the larger society and maintenance of one's heritage culture are welcomed by policy and practice in the larger acculturative arena.

CONCLUSION

Applications of findings reported in this chapter, especially if done with continuing evaluation and validation, should go a long way to helping the millions of individuals who find themselves in a situation of culture contact and change. Refugees, immigrants, and guest workers can all be provided with information, counseling, and other forms of psychological assistance based on these data. Receiving countries can also develop policies and programs based on these findings, and public education of the host population may also be attempted. Enough information is now available about the process of acculturation, and about factors affecting various psychological outcomes, that there could, with better programs, be a significant reduction in problems experienced by acculturating peoples. However, with the possibility that there will be increasing numbers of refugees in the world, and perhaps increasing numbers of temporary migrants (out-migration, followed by return-migration), the problem potential is not likely to diminish. Hence the findings reported in this chapter, and the basic principles they point to, urgently require interpretation and transfer to those responsible for managing acculturation, in both the donor and the receiving countries.

REFERENCES

Beiser, M., Barwick, C., Berry, J. W., et al. (1988). *After the door has been opened: Mental health issues affecting immigrants and refugees in Canada*. Ottawa: Ministries of Multiculturalism, and Health and Welfare.

Berry, J. W. (1974). Psychological aspects of cultural pluralism: Unity and identity reconsidered. In R. Brislin (Ed.), *Topics in culture learning* (Vol. 2, pp. 17-22). Honolulu, HI: East-West Center.

Berry, J. W. (1980). Social and cultural change. In H. C. Triandis & R. Brislin (Eds.), *Handbook of cross-cultural psychology: Vol. 5. Social psychology.* Boston: Allyn & Bacon.

Berry, J. W., & Annis, R. C. (1974). Acculturative stress: The role of ecology, culture and differentiation. *Journal of Cross-Cultural Psychology, 5,* 382-406.

Berry, J. W., Kalin, R., & Taylor, D. M. (1977). *Multiculturalism and ethnic attitudes in Canada.* Ottawa: Supply and Services.

Berry, J. W., & Kim, U. (1988). Acculturation and mental health. In P. Dasen, J. W. Berry, & N. Sartorius (Eds.), *Health and cross-cultural psychology* (pp. 207-236). London: Sage.

Berry, J. W., Kim, U., Minde, T., & Mok, D. (1987). Comparative studies of acculturative stress. *International Migration Review, 21,* 491-511.

Berry, J. W., Kim, U., Power, S., Young, M., & Bujaki, M. (1989). Acculturation attitudes in plural societies. *Applied Psychology, 38,* 185-206.

Berry, J. W., Trimble, J., & Olmeda, E. (1986). The assessment of acculturation. In W. J. Lonner & J. W. Berry (Eds.), *Field methods in cross-cultural research.* London: Sage.

Berry, J. W., van de Koppel, J. M. H., Sénéchal, C., Annis, R. C., Bahuchet, S., Cavalli-Sforza, L. L., & Witkin, H. A. (1986). *On the edge of the forest: Cultural adaptation and cognitive development in Central Africa.* Lisse, The Netherlands: Swets and Zeitlinger.

Berry, J. W., Wintrob, R. M., Sindell, P. S., & Mawhinney, T. A. (1982). Psychological adaptation to culture change among the James Bay Cree. *Naturaliste Canadien, 109,* 965-975.

Brislin, R., Cushner, K., Cherrie, C., & Yong, M. (1986). *Intercultural interactions: A practical guide.* Newbury Park, CA: Sage.

de Lacey, P. R. (1970). An index of contact. *Australian Journal of Social Issues, 5,* 219-223.

Graves, T. D. (1967). Psychological acculturation in a tri-ethnic community. *Southwestern Journal of Anthropology, 23,* 337-350.

Murphy, H. M. B. (1965). Migration and the major mental disorders. In M. B. Kantor (Ed.), *Mobility and mental health.* Springfield, IL: Charles C Thomas.

Redfield, R., Linton, R., & Herskovits, M. J. (1936). Memorandum on the study of acculturation. *American Anthropologist, 38,* 149-152.

Social Science Research Council. (1954). Acculturation: An exploratory formulation. *American Anthropologist, 56,* 973-1002.

Sommerlad, E. A., & Berry, J. W. (1970). The role of ethnic identification in distinguishing between attitudes towards assimilation and integration of a minority racial group. *Human Relations, 23,* 23-29.

Stonequist, E. V. (1935). The problem of the marginal man. *American Journal of Sociology, 41,* 1-12.

12

THE ENVIRONMENT, CULTURE, AND BEHAVIOR

JANAK PANDEY

In the last two decades, people from different parts of the world have focused their attention on issues concerning the environment, especially its degradation, exploitation, and management. Some recent disastrous events, for example, at Bhopal (India), Chernobyl (the Soviet Union), Three Mile Island (the United States), and their dangerous effects on people and their environments indicate that environmental problems are far from being solved. In recent years, many ecologically minded national and international groups around the world have formulated action plans for changing laws, changing people's attitudes concerning ecological balance, and implementing their concerns with safeguards for the environment. In spite of these efforts, problems of air and water pollution, overpopulation, acid rain, toxic and nuclear waste, noise, the depletion of natural resources, and so forth are increasing. Many disciplines have responded to environmental issues, leading to the creation of new fields of scientific study, such as environmental psychology. The objective of these new fields has been primarily to understand the relations between people and their physical environments.

Environmental psychology has expanded enormously in terms of the publication of textbooks, monographs, advances, handbooks (e.g., Altman & Wohlwill, 1977; Baum, Singer, & Valins, 1978; Bell, Fischer, & Loomis, 1978; Stokols & Altman, 1987), review chapters (Russell & Ward, 1982; Stokols, 1978), and the establishment of new journals (e.g., *Environment and Behavior* in 1969). During the same period, the last two decades, cross-cultural psychology has emerged as a major development with its emphasis on the role of cultural and subcultural variables in the understanding of behavior. The work of cultural anthropologists and cultural geographers suggests obvious linkages across behavior, culture, and the physical environment. However, due to the very gradual recognition of cultural variables in psychology, the scientific study of behavior, culture, and physical environment has with few exceptions been neglected (Altman & Chemers, 1980a, 1980b).

The physical environment influences people and their cultures and, in turn, is influenced by them. Altman and Chemers (1980a, p. 1) suggest that people, cultures, and physical environments form a social "system." These parts of the system work together in an integrated way. We may take houses as an example. Houses created by people in different parts of the world differ a great deal in design, materials used, neighborhoods, and ecological context. For example, homes in the Middle East have high ceilings to minimize the effects of oppressive heat, but, in Alaska, Eskimo igloos are designed to conserve heat to provide protection from freezing temperatures and wind. Although modern architectural science has had a tremendous impact on house building, some cultural considerations may be found to influence the design of houses. In India, houses are frequently oriented toward sacred directions, ignoring the topographical suitability of the land. The quality and design of the houses depend on the economic prosperity of a society and its individuals. The physical environment and culture affect each other reciprocally. The understanding of relationships among the members (people, culture, environments) of this trio has applied value for architects and designers, planners, policymakers, and all those who influence environments.

CONCEPTUALIZING ENVIRONMENT, CULTURE, AND BEHAVIOR

Herskovits (1948), an anthropologist, defined *culture* simply as "the man-made part of the human environment." This definition, according to Triandis (1980, p. 2), includes "both physical objects (roads, buildings, and tools that constitute *physical culture*), and subjective responses to what is man-made (myths, roles, values, and attitudes), which constitute *subjective culture*." Subjective responses, however, may also be toward the natural environment (mountains, rivers, deserts, and so on). This definition of culture and its physical and subjective dimensions reveals a very close relationship with the environment. White (1949) emphasizes symbolic behavior, especially language, that helps in the transmission of wisdom concerning skills for coping with the environment. Culture appears in people's perceptions, beliefs, values, norms, customs, and behaviors as well as in objects and the physical environment. Home designs, layouts of villages, communities, and cities, public buildings and places reflect the values and beliefs of a culture. The concept of culture indicates ways of behaving and relating to the environment. It is important to understand how different aspects of culture affect and are affected by the physical environment.

The effect of environment on behavior was well recognized by Kurt Lewin (1951, p. 25), who stated "that behavior (B) is a function of the person (P) and the environment (E), B = (P, E)." In his formula, he considered person and environment as interdependent variables. Lewin's assertion regarding the relationship between person and environment is widely accepted. Sinha has argued that, despite acceptance of the role of environment in behavior, the discipline of psychology has given relatively more importance to individual variables than to the environment. Various psychological processes such as perceptions, cognitions, attitudes, beliefs, and abilities, both physical and mental, are affected by environmental influences. Recognizing the importance of environmental variables, Sinha (1981, p. 27) comments: "The nature of environment provides the necessary inputs, stimulation, and experiential base for the development of perceptual skills of various kinds." In addition, overt behaviors that help to achieve privacy and to control territories, migrations, use of land, and so forth act in relation to the environment.

Human geographers argue that, because all food, clothing, shelter, and other material things that surround people are derived from things produced by the earth, it becomes important to examine people's natural surroundings, called "the human habitat." The characteristics of various habitats result from the interplay of earth's surface features, water, vegetation, and soil. People's experience in making a living from earth resources has differed in various geographical areas of the world, leading to changes in habitats and culture. Therefore, some human geographers, cultural anthropologists, cross-cultural psychologists, and others have advocated comparative study. We may identify three major domains of environments:

(1) natural environments (geographical features, landscapes, wilderness, disasters, pollution, energy sources, flora and fauna, and so on);

(2) built environment (buildings, architectures, roads, cities, communities, farms, technology, and so on); and

(3) social environment (territory, crowding, space, and so on).

This chapter discusses the nature and dimensions of these three domains. The major objective of the chapter is to bring a cross-cultural perspective to understanding how different societies relate to their physical environments. Quite frequently, cross-cultural analysis is rewarding in and of itself. Our knowledge of other cultures helps our understanding of our own culture (see the chapter by Brislin, this volume).

NATURAL ENVIRONMENT

The ability of human beings to adapt, individually and socially, to naturally or artificially occurring conditions of their environment is striking. Some geographers and historians have tried to account for the rise and fall of civilizations on the basis of the strategies used to adapt to environmental conditions. For example, Toynbee (1962) suggested that the environment (topography, climate, vegetation, water, and so on) presents a challenge to its inhabitants. Responses of the inhabitants to their environment may be adaptive, maladaptive, or creative. Rural people in India and some other regions of the world burn dried animal dung for heating and cooking in the absence of an adequate supply of firewood. This response could be first considered adaptive and creative, but in the long run such a practice destroys the environment because the dung is no longer available for use as a fertilizer. There is a very delicate relationship between people and their natural environment.

Whiting (1964), in his study of the role of the environment in the development of culture and individual personality, found that in tropical climates diets are mostly based on fruits and roots, leading to low consumption of protein. To compensate for protein deficiency, children depend on mother's milk, and, therefore, weaning in such regions takes place quite late. Children, because of long periods of breast-feeding, develop very strong bonds to their mothers. Whiting has tried to show causal influences of climate on culture and personality development. Some others, like Barry, Bacon, and Child (1957), have argued that the relationships of culture and personality to the environment are mostly bidirectional and interdependent. They argue that nonnomadic agricultural cultures seem to emphasize dependence, responsibility, and obedience in child-rearing practices. Hunter/gatherer cultures, on the other hand, emphasize independence and innovation. People who are stationed at one place in an organized community, rural or urban, require structured organization, and, therefore, they require obedience and compliance. On the other hand, hunter/gatherers inculcate independence and resourcefulness in their children, so that children can face unpredictable environmental demands. It seems that an environment provides fertile soil for the development of a culture and an individual that can best survive in that particular environment.

In the process of adaptation to the environment, equilibrium is achieved through the dual processes of adaptation (changes in people and culture) and adjustment (changes in the environment). It is important to mention that, in many cases, this equilibrium is threatened

when we fail to take a long-term perspective on the aftereffects of
changes in the environment in which we live. For example, uncontrolled
use of various kinds of pesticides may provide the short-term advantage
of increased production of a crop, but it may produce long-term negative effects such as loss of lives of birds and the introduction of new
diseases in man, animals, and plants. It may lead to long-term deleteri-
ous effects on the ecological balance between humans and environment.
The killing of frogs in the paddy fields of Kerala, India, for export to
earn money and to meet Western demands for a food delicacy creates
an imbalance in the ecology of the paddy fields, leading to an increase
in the population of insects (no longer eaten by frogs) that destroy the
crops.

Naturalistic Study in Behavior Settings

Barker and his associates (Barker & Wright, 1950, 1955/1971)
founded a research program in the late 1940s with emphasis on the
environment more than on individual persons. Barker (1978) recognized the importance of studying behavior in its environmental context
and focused on "behavioral settings." Behavior settings, according to
Barker, are small-scale systems that include people and inanimate
objects. Wicker (1987, p. 614) noted that, "within the temporal and
spatial boundaries of the system, the various components interact in an
orderly, established fashion to carry out the setting's essential functions." Barker and his associates have conducted research on behavior
settings in schools, churches, a national park, and in offices (Barker,
1978). The most extensive research was conducted in the U.S. Midwest at the Psychological Field Station in Oskaloosa, Kansas, followed
by parallel research in Leyburn, North Yorkshire, England. Barker's
(1978) findings are very interesting and useful for understanding behavior in different environmental contexts that also vary in terms of
culture. For example, Barker (1978) found place-specificity as a fundamental fact of behavior. In Oskaloosa, Barker and his associates identified 884 places in the public areas of the town with distinctive patterns
of behavior in each area. Russell and Ward (1982, p. 652) have also
noted that, "as people move from one place to another, their behavior
changes accordingly." Although cross-cultural psychologists have not
used implications of Barker's method of behavioral settings, apparently
his assertions and findings have implications in understanding differences and similarities in behaviors due to cultural variations. Recently,
Barker (1987, p. 1420) has written: "The place specificity of behavior

in Oskaloosa was impressive. The differential distinctiveness of the behavior of second graders in music class, playground, and cafeteria was so obvious that we considered using a sample of such geographical areas as sites for observing child behavior in the town."

Barker (1978) has taxonomized various behavior settings along different dimensions. He has identified as one dimension the number of performers required to operate properly in the behavior setting. In any behavioral setting, an optimal number of people can best function efficiently and achieve their goals. According to Barker, when there are fewer than the optimal number of people in the setting, it is called *undermanned*. While extending this concept, Wicker (1973) has also recognized the *overmanning* of behavioral settings. According to Wicker, when the number of performers is greater than the optimal number of the behavior setting's capacity, it is *overmanned*. Undermanning and overmanning are threats to the balanced functioning of the system, but in different ways. In the undermanning context, the performers have to work more and in diverse settings, but, in the overmanning situation, more and more people are to be accommodated in a lesser number of jobs. An overmanned setting may even change its goals and functions to accommodate people by providing new jobs. The application of this concept is significant for crowding research. These concepts could be extended to understand the way businesses and organizations are managed in more crowded and less crowded societies. For example, in India and other densely populated countries, one can easily find more than the optimal number of people employed to do jobs in offices and industries. Sometimes, one can find that overmanning in a setting is very high and leads to inefficiency and low productivity. Overmanning probably causes and aggravates diffusion of responsibility among the performers. Undermanning in less populous societies has probably led to more innovative technologies to help a lesser number of performers than the optimum level manage the diverse jobs in offices and industries. I will not examine Barker's complex theory of behavioral ecology in detail here. However, his innovative methods of studying behavior in natural contexts, and concepts such as behavioral setting and manning, have important implications for understanding the realities of varied environments.

Extreme and Unusual Environmental Settings

Environments may be identified on the basis of dimensions of unusualness and extremeness. The extreme dimension involves dangers and discomfort. The unusualness dimension, however, indicates the novelty aspect of the environment. Scholars have provided various categorization systems of such environments (Suedfeld, 1987). Here I will identify some extreme and unusual environments as examples and describe briefly some salient features of each.

Polar and circumpolar environments. The terrain of such environments is dangerous with rapidly rising fogs and ice breakups. People in these environments have to adapt to periods of prolonged darkness and light and face dangers of working on snow and ice. Skin disorders, retinal damage, disrupted sleep and activity rhythms, loss of sense of time, nutritional problems, and so forth are found among the inhabitants. Physiological adaptation is relevant, but more important is cultural adaptation. In the subarctic regions of North America and Europe, cold has not been found by some researchers to be a significant stressor for Algonquian Indian groups and others who live there (Steegman, 1983) given their adaptive efforts over centuries.

Hot climates. Hot climates may be further classified as (a) hot-dry and (b) hot-humid. The desert environment is hot-dry and changes from daytime heat to nighttime mild temperatures. Adaptation is required to the changing temperature as well as to the scarcity of food and water (Hanna & Brown, 1983). Excessive sweating may lead to dehydration and salt deficiency. Heatstroke and heat exhaustion are common. However, in the hot-humid environments, due to jungles and cloud cover, solar radiation is less of a problem than in hot-dry desert areas. One can find cultural differences in hot-dry and hot-humid environments. For example, in hot-dry zones, people (Arabs) use more clothing than the people (Singapore, Malaysia) of hot-humid areas. Some personal habits of people related to use of water are quite different in these environments, which are alike on the temperature dimension but different in dryness and humidity.

Natural high-altitude environments. High-altitude environments require physiological adaptation in the form of increased efficiency of oxygen flow. Those who move to high mountains require acclimatization without which one may develop altitude sickness at 3,000 meters or higher. Such sickness includes breathlessness, headache, insomnia, vomiting, and loss of appetite. Indigenous mountaineers may show a larger chest capacity, which is not found to be inherited. Among soldiers operating in cold high-altitude environments, feelings of loneliness, homesickness, depression, anxiety, boredom, and decreased interpersonal communications are found (Sharma, Vaskaran, & Malhotra, 1976).

Comparative studies. Among the emotional reactions in extreme and unusual environments, fear, anxiety, aggression, boredom, and transcendental (religious) experiences are frequently mentioned (Suedfeld, 1987). It has been argued that aggression is triggered or facilitated by ambient heat. Boyanowsky, Calvert, Young, and Brideau (1981-1982) have documented evidence to show that "long hot summers" are associated with urban riots.

A series of studies conducted by Robert Baron and his associates (Baron, 1972; Baron & Bell, 1975, 1976) lead to the conclusion that there is a critical range of uncomfortably warm ambient temperatures that facilitate aggressive behavior in humans. Extremely high temperatures, probably because of the debilitating effects of the heat, reduce aggression. Extremely cold temperatures, probably due to reduced arousal, decrease aggressive behavior. Moderately warm and cold temperatures, however, facilitate aggression (Bell & Baron, 1977).

There have been some attempts to determine the relationship between occurrence of illness (such as minor respiratory infections, intestinal infections) and seasonal changes in weather conditions (Hope-Simpson, 1958). High and low temperatures in combination with humidity have been found to have an adverse effect on cardiovascular systems, including coronary heart disease and anginal symptoms (see the glossary in Ilola, this volume). Individuals with heart diseases are extremely sensitive to high temperatures and particularly to moist heat. Thus it may be concluded that atmospheric conditions of temperature, humidity, sunshine, wind, rainfall, and so on influence human performance and well-being.

Environmental Disaster and Catastrophe

Daily newspapers occasionally report abnormally intense natural disasters with accounts of loss of human lives and property taking place somewhere in the world. Some frequently occurring natural disasters are earthquakes, volcanic eruptions, monsoons, floods, tornadoes, hurricanes, storms, and lightning. In recent years, man-made nuclear (Chernobyl, in the Soviet Union) and other industrial (Bhopal, India) disasters have been experienced. It is obvious that, although disaster is primarily a physical event, it has serious psychological, sociological, and economic consequences. The study of psychological consequences of disasters is particularly difficult to conduct because unpredictable events in nature can be studied only after they have occurred. Because disasters create devastation and highly chaotic conditions, the choice of measurements and samples are restricted. Despite these problems, some studies have been done regarding the impact of disasters. Sometimes, adequate warning of storms, floods, and excessive monsoons are provided, but more often people receive no such warnings. Therefore, we view natural disasters as unpredictable and uncontrollable phenomena. The destructive power of natural disasters, which sometimes last only a few seconds (like earthquakes), is enormous, and natural disasters are unique as stressors.

Technological and industrial catastrophes are the result of breakdowns in our person-built environment. Technological catastrophes may not be as abrupt as natural disasters. Human negligence, failure in planning and design, inadequate safety measures, along with a host of other factors, cause such accidents. Industrial catastrophes and stress caused by them threaten victims' feelings of perceived control and confidence (Baum, Fleming, & Davidson, 1983). Industrial catastrophes may cause long-term physical and mental consequences. For example, in the case of the Bhopal accident of December 1984, a large number of people are still receiving medical and psychological aid.

The effects of disasters are varied. Researchers report a stunned and numb response to the immediate impact of disasters (Crashaw, 1963; Lifton & Olson, 1976; Quarantelli, 1985). Quarantelli and Dynes (1972) have noted that panic is typically rare among survivors, with most people acting calmly and rationally. One may question, however, the generality of such findings across situations and in varied cultural groups. For example, in the 1930s and in the 1950s, some classic studies on catastrophic situations were conducted in India (Prasad, 1935; Sinha, 1952). Prasad (1935), in his study of the Great Indian Earthquake of 1934, found a feeling of emotional instability and uncertainty affecting the cognitive processes of individuals. Sinha (1952) studied the impact of the worst landslide of 1950, which took place in Darjeeling, a beautiful 7,000-foot-high hill resort in the Himalayas. Sinha (1952, p. 200) described the disaster as follows:

> The loss of life and damage to property were heavy and extensive. Hundreds of breaches occurred on the Darjeeling Siliguri road, the only motorable approach from the plains. In the town itself houses collapsed and victims lay buried under the debris. For over two days, rain poured incessantly down the hill slopes which continued to loosen and slide. Collapsed houses and landslides lay across the roads, and mud flowed everywhere. The water supply to the town was breached. The supply of electricity failed. Over a hundred and fifty persons lost their lives in the district, about thirty of them in the town itself. Over a hundred were

injured. More than two hundred houses were damaged, and over 2000 people were rendered homeless. Refugees poured into the town from the outlying districts with tales of woe and misery.

While the disaster was still in progress, Sinha was able to collect data on "the processes of perception and recall, and on the spread of rumors in a catastrophic situation" about damage, rainfall, and the earthquake. Sinha supplemented the data with newspaper reports. He found that rumors were mostly explanatory in nature. People tried to understand conflicting reports and make predictions about events. Sinha has argued that distortions in perception and reporting were primarily due to anxiety produced by the feeling of insecurity in the situation.

Much recent work has concentrated upon psychiatric interviews of victims of disasters. Investigators have identified anxiety, depression, and other stress-related disturbances among the victims of floods, hurricanes, and other natural disasters (Logue, Hansen, & Struening, 1979; Taylor & Quarantelli, 1976). These studies report that there are individual differences in the intensity and duration of psychological symptoms following a disaster. Some of these individual differences have been accounted for by differences in the extent of the loss experienced.

Although it is not possible to make completely accurate predictions, with the help of modern technologies, many nations of the world have developed disaster warning systems. Mass communication systems like radio and television are used to inform people regarding possible disasters such as tornadoes, floods, excessive rain, earthquakes, and the like to help the people cope with the unusual events efficiently and safely. Fritz (1968) found that people often fail to respond to warnings, even though it would be in their own self-interests to do so. Some other investigators report that residents of hazardous environments adapt to environmental danger by making attributions to fate, luck, chance, and God (see the chapter by Sinha, this volume) and attempt to deny the existence of hazards altogether (Burton & Kates, 1964). Thus the findings suggest that there is a need to develop strategies so that people hear and respond to warnings in disaster areas.

BUILT ENVIRONMENT

The *built environment* refers to what people create in the form of homes, hospitals, schools, communities, cities, roads, parks, and other modifications of the natural environment. It seems that humans are by nature builders. We are continuously in the process of planning, designing, and constructing private and public buildings and other facilities. The built environment, once created, constantly influences our interpersonal relationships. Our experiences of the built environment help us to reshape and construct our future environment.

The built environment is greatly influenced by natural environmental factors such as climate, landscape, available resources, and culture. For example, Rapoport (1969) has related home and community design to cultural factors. For example, in the Dogon and Bambara communities (Niger, Africa), people build villages in pairs to represent heaven and earth. They believe that the world is created spirally, and, therefore, agricultural fields are arranged in spirals. Rapoport (1969) has mentioned that, in some Baltic countries, villages are designed in a manner to relate to heavenly bodies like the path of the sun. The streets in the village run north-south, and doors and facades of the houses face east-west to receive preferred sun positions during the day. Some cultures emphasize privacy, and, therefore, homes are often surrounded by walls (Iran, India, Japan). In several African communities too, people build walls around their houses or clusters of houses to maintain privacy and territoriality.

The growth and demand for space is a major force in the development and preservation of the environment. Unfortunately, because of unabated population growth, particularly in India and other developing countries, usable land has shrunk significantly in size and proportion (Pandey & Nagar, 1987). With the exception of only a small percentage of affluent people, a larger percentage of the population in developing countries are facing greater problems of housing due to overcongestion in cities and, in some countries, even in villages. The growth of slums in the developing countries is primarily the result of excessive population growth and poverty. Although the built environment is influenced by cultural characteristics, variables like available space, density of population, economic resources, building materials, and so forth determine the design and construction of houses, public facilities (parks, schools, hospitals, roads), villages, and cities.

In his chapter on residential environments, Tognoli (1987) identified some salient sociocultural functions of the home. First, the home is the central place of human existence and provides a sense of rootedness and attachment. Second, the home includes aspects of heritage and connections with one's origin. Third, the home provides privacy, security, and ownership. Fourth, an individual develops self-identification of belonging and a feeling of control. Individuals decorate their homes according to their personalities and cultures. Fifth, home provides a context for social and family relations. Sixth, home is conceptualized as a sociocultural unit (Rapoport, 1969). According to Rapoport, any conceptualization of home is highly culture-bound. House-settlement complexes must be examined in relation to activities that occur there, and these activities have some commonality and differences across cultures. Altman and Chemers (1980a, 1980b) consider home as the outcome of the "interplay" of environmental and cultural factors. Tognoli (1987) suggests that physical factors such as climate and house construction materials and techniques are less important than primary sociocultural factors such as style of life, social structure and hierarchy, ways of fulfilling basic needs, family structure, position of women and men, privacy, territoriality, social relations, and so forth.

The term *housing* is a pluralistic concept and it has been used in the context of neighborhoods. The residents of a neighborhood value compatibility for their social adjustment. For example, in India's traditional villages, one may find houses built together among people of similar caste and/or among people who have similar professions. The hierarchy of castes is also easily observable in the segregation of houses of different castes. The design and size of homes differ in the same culture due to professional differences and structure of the families. For example, a farmer's house in a village will be different from the house of a carpenter or a barber. Housing is linked with race and class issues in the United States and in many other developed countries. Although, in the United States, segregation and discrimination have been found in housing, some scholars have noted that residents of a desegregated community managed to maintain a stable neighborhood when residents were of an equal social status (Heuman, 1979).

SOCIAL ENVIRONMENTS

Our reactions and adjustments in various environments are most severely and most often affected by the other people who surround us. Our use of personal space, decisions about territories, sense of privacy, and reactions to crowding are determined by the people with whom we interact in various physical environments. Privacy, personal space, territoriality, and crowding are environmental issues, but they are highly social and cultural in nature.

With the pioneering work of Hall (1966) and Sommer (1969) on personal space and the equally compelling and popular work of Ardrey (1966) on territoriality, the initial understanding of how animals as well as human beings use and react to physical space in the actual or implied presence of others began to show signs of theoretical development. From then onward, scholars have made significant headway in theorizing and empirically demonstrating how people in a densely populated environment tend to regulate their spatial needs and thus reduce the discrepancy between desired and attained levels of privacy so as to overcome mismatches between their needs and environmental demands. For instance, it is often noticed that, in a crowded rural Indian home, some inhabitants tend to sleep outdoors in summer, partly to attain desired privacy. They also tend to adjust their timing with other residents (sleeping, eating, staying at home) as a way to reduce the adverse effects of crowding-related annoyance. The objective here is not to review all the interrelated studies on personal space, territorial behavior, privacy regulation, and crowding but just to highlight some studies to support a coherent theme regarding the impact of physical environment on social behaviors in varied cultural contexts.

Proxemics

The term *proxemics* was first used in a cross-cultural context by an anthropologist, Edward Hall (1966). The use of this term largely centered on the characterization of interpersonal distance in various cultural groups. However, the concept has become broadened: It incorporates the role of various spatial factors and is used as a determinant as well as a consequent of social behavior.

With some exceptions (Altman, 1975), most scholars have attempted to use the concepts of crowding, personal space, privacy, and territoriality interchangeably and have tried to unite them in a single broad theoretical framework of proxemics. Crowding-related effects are often explained by scholars in terms of personal space violation (Worchel & Teddlie, 1976), and privacy regulations, in terms of territorial behavior. Irwin Altman (1975) emphasized the importance of privacy and viewed it as a dialectic process in his theory of the environment-behavior interface. Utilizing a transactional perspective, Altman and his colleagues have identified several important characteristic features of this concept (Altman & Chemers, 1980a, 1980b). They conceived privacy as a dynamic interplay between the opposing forces of openness and closedness. Irrespective of the cultural setting, people have a general tendency to open or close the level of social interaction and thus regulate their social contact with others. We can see this in our own lives. Sometimes we want solitude, and thus we make ourselves unavailable even to our friends by closing curtains and doors. At other times, we make ourselves open to visual surveillance and social interaction. In addition, openness and closedness vary over time and across situations and are viewed as boundary-control processes.

To achieve privacy and to regulate the quality of social interaction, a series of behavioral mechanisms are used: verbal, paraverbal, and nonverbal behaviors. Another distinctive feature of privacy is selective control. This suggests that we all seek optimum privacy, and any deflection from an optimal degree of openness of the self to others is perceived by the individual as mentally harmful and socially undesirable. It seems plausible to expect that culturally universal processes to manage desired privacy are operative across different cultures (Lonner, 1980). However, specific behavioral mechanisms used to regulate privacy might differ across diverse cultures because of different norms, sanctioned behavioral patterns, and cultural styles. In the Muslim culture, young women cover their faces with veils while going out, and, in North Indian traditional societies, curtains are used to keep women circulating in the house from being noticed by visitors.

Crowding

The unabated increase in the population of the world and issues related to population growth are receiving a great deal of attention by behavioral scientists, demographers, policymakers, and concerned lay people. An initial study carried out by Calhoun (1962) on overpopulation among rodents (to be described below) did not attract a lot of immediate research attention. However, since the 1970s, a great deal of work has been done on crowding and spatial behavior, and some elaborate reviews (Baum & Paulus 1987; Paulus & Nagar, in press; Sundstromm, 1978) are available.

The term *crowding* has been operationalized in a variety of ways depending upon the nature of the study to be carried out. In the laboratory setting, crowding is generally equated with density. Various forms of density can be manipulated, such as (a) spatial density and (b) social density that reduces interpersonal distance, to bring about crowding-related effects. This objective indicator of crowding resulting from density manipulation has been used across different cultures (Griffitt & Veitch, 1971; Jain, 1987; Paulus, Annis, Seta, Schkade, & Matthews, 1976). Stokols (1972) made an important distinction between density and crowding. He considers density in terms of a physical parameter of population concentration. Density in physical terms can be measured in terms of number of people in a limited space, in terms of number of people per square acre, or by census data. Stokols (1972) pointed out that density can be an important antecedent condition of crowding; it is not at all a sufficient condition. Crowding, a subjective feeling, is often experienced when density causes stress and discomfort. Another way of distinguishing density from crowding is to imagine two people in a small room with 10 others. One person may feel "crowded," the second quite comfortable, even though the objective density is the same.

The most dramatic results on crowding were found in early studies on animals. Calhoun (1962) created a rat colony. He left the animals free to breed, providing them with adequate resources. Unrestricted breeding led to extremely high density, and normal maternal behavior deteriorated and evidence of higher mortality was observed, eventually leading to a behavioral sink. Similar evidence of crowding-related pathological disturbances was obtained by Christian (1963). The enlarged adrenal glands in crowded animals were found to be a result of stress. Despite a great deal of consistency in results obtained with animals, the generalizability of these results for human populations have been questioned by scholars (Freedman, 1979). However, animal studies on crowding do provide a stimulus for conducting research on human populations.

Another phase of crowding research was correlational in nature and was done mostly by sociologists with human subjects. These studies attempted to focus on relationships between urban density and various measures of pathology. The early study of Schmitt (1966) reported evidence of a positive relationship between density and a number of pathologies such as death rate, incidence of tuberculosis, venereal disease, juvenile delinquency, and admissions to mental hospitals. The Chicago study of Galle, Gove, and McPherson (1972) also reported similar results. Outside the United States, Booth and Welch (1974) conducted a multinational study and gathered data in 65 different countries. Their results provide direct evidence of relationships between density and life expectancy, mortality, and homicide. The correlational results reported by Pandey and Nagar (1988) provide evidence that rural students were more affected by home crowding relative to their urban counterparts. Additional findings suggest that the buffering effect of interpersonal relationships is a potent way to ameliorate density-induced pathological effects. A supportive interpersonal climate and an effective coordination of various day-to-day activities by residents may help ameliorate the negative effects of crowding. Even a casual observer can find this coping strategy among the people of crowded homes in big cities of the world.

The role of cultural coping mechanisms in response to density and crowding has been noted by many scholars (Altman & Chemers, 1980a, 1980b; Michelson, 1970; Rapoport, 1980). For instance, Rogler (1967) investigated squatter families in Colombia and Peru. These communities evolved their own methods of privacy regulation to overcome the ill effects of density. For instance, strong reactions to intrusion, the seclusion of children, and the rejection of newcomers were the methods for coping employed by these communities. The same theme emerges in analyses of crowding in Mexican slums, where people did not visit one another's home. People's need to be with others was satisfied through day-to-day proximity. The same people's efforts to obtain privacy were assisted through the avoidance of home visits.

Earlier studies dealing with residential crowding used limited dimensions of perceived crowding. Thus in a recent study, an attempt was made to incorporate the broad underlying dimensions of perceived crowding and to construct and ascertain the predictive validity of the crowding experience scale (Nagar & Paulus, 1988). A factor analysis of the 27 items of the crowding experience scale indicated evidence of four distinct components: spaciousness, positive or supportive relationships, negative or disruptive relationships, and uncontrolled disturbances. Interestingly, these components were found to be uniquely associated with various other outcome measures: symptomatology, well-being, individual home ratings, and neighborhood evaluation. The uncontrolled disturbance factor uniquely predicted problematic symptomatology, while the most potent predictors of well-being were space satisfaction and absence of negative relationships. For the rating of the individual home, space satisfaction was the only key predictor, and, finally, neighborhood evaluation was predicted uniquely by interpersonal positive relationships. The perceived crowding measures were found to play an important mediating role between objective density and outcome measures. Furthermore, even after controlling for demographic characteristics, housing type, and type of residents, then entering the objective density measures first in the regression equation, the components of perceived crowding emerged as potent predictors of various outcome measures. Thus this study seems to suggest that the scope of the perceived crowding components extends far beyond the simple density measures, and they provides a better index of crowding. This study was stimulated in part by the research on perceived crowding in India (Pandey & Nagar, 1988).

In some U.S. studies, sufficient empirical evidence exists regarding the mitigating role of controllability over the environment such that negative effects of crowding stress are lessened (Rodin, 1976). In a recent study, Ruback and Pandey (1988) examined the effects of perceived environmental control for married couples in an Indian urban population. Their results indicate some striking similarities across two diverse cultural groups (in the United States and India). Individuals experiencing low levels of perceived control reported high mental distress, more physical symptoms, and more upset by environmental stressors such as crowding and noise relative to the subjects who were high on perceived control.

An interesting examination of the effects of dormitory architecture and crowding on social behavior was carried out by Baum and Valins (1977). Despite the fact that all residents occupied space of equal square footage, their reactions were markedly different in different styles of dormitories. Imagine two dormitories, one with a few long corridors and the other with a larger number of short corridors. Residents of long-corridor dormitories felt more helpless and acted more competitively than did short-corridor residents. The long-corridor residents were more likely to encounter unwanted social intrusion than their short-corridor counterparts. Similar results were obtained by Paulus (1987) among prison inmates living in different dormitory-style accommodations. Returning to studies of the university environment, the forced occupancy of tripled students in double-loaded corridor dormitory rooms also led to crowding-related stress effects (Baum & Valins, 1977). It seems that tripled students perceived goal blockage as a result of resource scarcity, and their grades suffered. Male students did not show a tendency of coalition formation but tended to pursue their goals in alternative settings other than their dormitory rooms (e.g., study in the university library).

Field studies conducted in various residential and dormitory environments provide a generally consistent picture: Density in a real-world situation can have some ill effects in different cultural contexts. In a recent review, Paulus and Nagar (in press) have delineated certain salient facilitative/inhibiting environmental conditions that may block optimal human functioning and create stress-related reactions. However, various behavioral mechanisms seem to mediate between crowding and ill effects. People of various cultural groups adopt different coping styles to reduce the misfit between environment and human behavior. Various psychological factors such as control, tolerance, and available coping resources, as well as certain personality dispositions, may mediate the adverseness of physical environmental stressors on human health and well-being. This seems amply documented in various cultural groups (Baum & Paulus, 1987; Jain, 1987).

Yet another phase of crowding research has been conducted in laboratory settings with humans. In a typical study, students are asked to perform various cognitive tasks and their social behavior, mood state, and performance are examined when they work in crowded settings. Most sessions last for less than one hour. Most studies conducted in the United States, Europe, and India have provided a fairly consistent picture regarding debilitated performance on cognitively complex tasks, disruptions of normal social behavior, and negative mood states (Jain, 1987; Nagar & Pandey, 1987; Paulus et al., 1976). In a recent study conducted in India by Nagar and Paulus (1988), an attempt was made to determine cross-situational effects. An examination was made to measure the impact of previous residential crowding experiences on reactivity to the environmental stressors of noise and crowding. Their results indicated a tendency of tolerance development in those students who had reported high crowding experiences in the residential environment. The high experience-of-crowding subjects not only performed better on cognitively complex tasks, but they also exhibited more positive mood states in conditions of high density relative to their low experience-of-crowding counterparts. No effect on simple task performance was found as a result of density increase. The Indian studies (Jain, 1987) seem to suggest that people living in the most crowded countries develop heightened tolerance as a way of reducing density-induced annoyance.

In conclusion, studies conducted in different cultures do provide some consistent trends. People in all parts of the world seem to suffer from crowding-related pathological effects and perform poorly on complex tasks. However, a certain level of adaptation, tolerance, and coping seems to mitigate the harmful effects of crowding stress in various cultural groups.

ENVIRONMENTAL ATTITUDES AND SOCIAL POLICY

In recent years, at both the national and the international levels, various governmental and voluntary organizations have shown concern and have launched programs for the improvement of environmental quality (Stokols & Altman, 1987). To maintain the earth as a habitable planet, environmental challenges and dangers must be thwarted. This section briefly presents various aspects of planning and actions related to our environment.

The most important question for this chapter concerns the applicability of perception and attitudes in solving environmental problems. Although social psychological research often documents a weak relationship between attitudes and behavior, some studies concerned with the environment have shown a strong relationship (e.g., Heberlein & Black, 1976; Weigal & Newman, 1976). Under certain conditions, attitudes influence behavior and behavior influences attitudes. Sometimes we have conflicting attitudes, and the attitudes differ in degree of importance in certain situations. For example, people may not like the taste of spinach, but they might eat it because they think that it is good for their health. If they eat spinach because it is good for their health, they may eventually start liking its taste. Heberlein and Black's (1976) research has demonstrated that attitudes predict proenvironmental behavior, if both are assessed at a similar level of specificity. They tried to predict the use of lead-free gasoline. The lead in gasoline is an air pollutant. In 1973, the use of lead-free gasoline was mostly voluntary in the United States. In increasing order of specificity, the following four levels of attitudes were measured: (a) general attitude about proenvironmental behaviors, (b) beliefs about air pollution, (c) beliefs about lead-free gasoline, and (d) one's personal obligation to use lead-free gasoline. It was found that, as the level of attitude became more specific, the relationship between behavior and attitude became stronger. The obligation to use lead-free gasoline was highly correlated with actual use. The findings of the study strongly suggest that, to induce proenvironmental behavior, it would probably be more effective to strengthen the feeling of personal obligations to perform specific behaviors than to try to change general attitudes. In other research, Weigal and Newman (1976), however, found that a general attitude may not help in predicting specific behaviors, but a general attitude was a good predictor of overall proenvironmental behaviors. They have reported that people with proenvironmental attitudes participated in more projects to improve the environment relative to those who were less proenvironmental.

With the growth of population, people have started to realize the serious consequences of their unrestricted behavior toward the environment. There is a need to understand culturally determined attitudes related to the environment in order to develop general proenvironmental attitudes as well as specific proenvironmental attitudes among people so that their antienvironmental general as well as specific behaviors are changed.

Energy and Resource Conservation

In the last two decades, the study of energy production, energy use, and energy conservation have attracted the attention of social scientists. The energy crisis is, however, just one consequence of the reality that the earth's other natural resources are also limited. Supplies of some natural resources are rapidly nearing exhaustion (Ehrlich, Ehrlich, & Holdern, 1977). There is an imbalance in consumption of the produced raw materials among the nations of the world. For example, according to some statistics, the United States uses about one-third of the world's population of raw materials (Ehrlich et al., 1977). Most of the used metals are discarded rather than recycled into new products (Hays, 1978). In wastefully depleting our natural resources, we are also degrading our environment. For example, use of firewood for cooking purposes in many developing countries has led to indiscriminate cutting of trees in rural areas and has created a serious ecological imbalance. Oskamp (1984) has argued that the use of energy is central to environmental issues. Escalating fuel prices, problems related to nuclear power plants and nuclear waste disposal, use of trees as firewood for cooking and heating, and so forth have influenced both poor and rich nations of the world.

Because there are behavioral aspects to all these problems, and the issues involved are not limited to geographical boundaries of nations, cross-cultural psychology has a role in solving these problems. To save energy, studies have been done and efforts have been made in a variety of locales in the world, but rarely have cross-cultural studies been conducted on such issues with comparable questions using similar methods. In brief, however, behavioral research suggests that simple presentation of information and persuasion are not very effective in making people's behavior proenvironmental unless combined with behavioral consequences, such as reinforcement and feedback (Oskamp, 1984). Relationships between attitudes and behavior become stronger particularly when people publicly commit themselves to their attitudes (Kiesler, 1971). Pallak and Cummings (1976) applied commitment theory to conservation of residential energy consumption in the United States. They have reported that, relative to private commitment, public commitment resulted in lower natural gas consumption.

CONCLUDING COMMENTS

It seems that unrestrained individual use of finite resources and our callous actions toward the environment will lead to depletion of these resources and make our environment dangerous for us. This chapter presents arguments that problems related to water and air quality, littering, energy and resources, population, and so forth could be solved to a great extent by developing proenvironmental attitudes and norms. The indigenous (see Kim, this volume) and culture-based approach would be more acceptable and suitable in solving such problems. To a great extent, the environmental problems mentioned in this chapter can be considered as "tragedies of the commons" (Hardin, 1968). The social situations that motivate people to pursue their individual self-interest rather than to consider and act in the long-term common interest are "social traps" (Platt, 1973). We need to reverse such motivations and protect our environments by involving small, local, face-to-face groups whose members must learn to manage our limited scarce resources for the common good.

REFERENCES

Altman, I. (1975). *The environment and social behavior.* Monterey, CA: Brooks/Cole.

Altman, I., & Chemers, M. M. (1980a). *Culture and environment.* Monterey, CA: Brooks/Cole.

Altman, I., & Chemers, M. M. (1980b). Cultural aspects of environment-behavior relationships. In H. C. Triandis & R. W. Brislin (Eds.), *Handbook of cross-cultural psychology* (Vol. 5, pp. 355-393). Boston: Allyn & Bacon.

Altman, I., & Wohlwill, J. (Eds.). (1977). *Human behavior and environment: Advances in theory and research.* New York: Plenum.

Ardrey, T. (1966). *The territorial imperative.* New York: Athaneum.

Barker, R. G. (Ed.). (1978). *Habits, environments, and human behavior: Studies in ecological psychology and eco-behavioral science from the Midwest Psychological Field Station, 1947-1972.* San Francisco: Jossey-Bass.

Barker, R. G. (1987). Prospecting in environmental psychology. In D. Stokols & I. Altman (Eds.), *Handbook of environmental psychology* (Vol. 2, pp. 1413-1432). New York: John Wiley.

Barker, R. G., & Wright, H. F. (1950). *Methods in psychological ecology: A progress report.* Topeka, KS: Ray's Printing Service.

Barker, R. G., & Wright, H. F. (1971). *Midwest and its children: The psychological ecology of an American town.* Hamden, CT: Archen. (Original work published 1955)

Baron, R. A. (1972). Aggression as a function of ambient temperature and prior anger arousal. *Journal of Personality and Social Psychology, 21,* 183-189.

Baron, R. A., & Bell, P. A. (1975). Aggression and heat: Mediating effects of prior provocation and exposure to an aggressive model. *Journal of Personality and Social Psychology, 31,* 825-832.

Baron, R. A., & Bell, P. A. (1976). Aggression and heat: The influence of ambient temperature, negative affect and a cooling drink on physical aggression. *Journal of Personality and Social Psychology, 33,* 245-255.

Barry, H., Bacon, M., & Child, I. (1957). A cross-cultural survey of some sex differences in socialization. *Journal of Abnormal Psychology, 55,* 327-332.

Baum, A., Fleming, R., & Davidson, L. M. (1983). Natural disaster and technological catastrophe. *Environment and Behavior, 15,* 333-354.

Baum, A., & Paulus, P. B. (1987). Crowding. In D. Stokols & I. Altman (Eds.), *Handbook of environmental psychology* (Vol. 1, pp. 533-570). New York: John Wiley.

Baum, A., Singer, J. E., & Valins, S. (Eds.). (1978). *Advances in environmental psychology.* Hillsdale, NJ: Lawrence Erlbaum.

Baum, A., & Valins, S. (1977). *Architecture and social behavior: Psychological studies in social density.* Hillsdale, NJ: Lawrence Erlbaum.

Bell, P. A., & Baron, R. A. (1977). Aggression and ambient temperature: The facilitating and inhibiting effects of hot and cold environments. *Bulletin of the Psychonomic Society, 9,* 443-445.

Bell, P. A., Fischer, J. D., & Loomis, R. H. (1978). *Environmental psychology.* Philadelphia: W. B. Saunders.

Booth, A., & Welch, S. (1974). *Crowding and urban crime rates.* Paper presented at the annual meeting of the Midwest Sociological Association, Omaha, NE.

Boyanowsky, E. O., Calvert, J., Young, J., & Brideau, L. (1981-1982). Toward a thermo-regulatory model of violence. *Journal of Environment Systems, 11,* 81-87.

Burton, I., & Kates, R. W. (1964). The perception of natural hazards in resource management. *Natural Resources Journal, 3,* 412-441.

Calhoun, J. B. (1962). Population density and social pathology. *Scientific American, 206,* 139-148.

Christian, J. J. (1963). The pathology of over population. *Military Medicine, 128,* 571-603.

Crashaw, R. (1963). Reactions to a disaster. *Archives of General Psychiatry, 9,* 157-162.

Ehrlich, P. R., Ehrlich, A. H., & Holdern, J. P. (1977). *Ecoscience: Population, resources, environment.* San Francisco: Freeman.

Freedman, J. L. (1979). Reconciling apparent differences between the responses of humans and other animals to crowding. *Psychological Review, 86,* 80-85.

Fritz, C. E. (1968). Disaster. In D. Sills (Ed.), *International encyclopedia of the social sciences* (Vol. 4, pp. 202-207). New York: Macmillan.

Galle, O., Gove, W., & McPherson, J. (1972). Population density and pathology: What are the relationships for man? *Science, 176,* 23-30.

Griffitt, W., & Veitch, R. (1971). Hot and crowded: Influences of population density and temperature on interpersonal affective behavior. *Journal of Personality and Social Psychology, 17,* 92-98.

Hall, E. T. (1966). *The hidden dimension.* New York: Doubleday.

Hanna, J. M., & Brown, D. E. (1983). Human heat tolerance: An anthropological perspective. *Annual Review of Anthropology, 12,* 259-284.

Hardin, G. (1968). The tragedy of the commons. *Science, 162,* 1243-1248.

Hays, D. (1978). *Repairs, reuse, recycling: First steps toward a sustainable society* (Worldwatch Paper 23). Washington, DC: Worldwatch Institute.

Heberlein, T. A., & Black, J. S. (1976). Attitudinal specificity and the prediction of behavior in a field setting. *Journal of Personality and Social Psychology, 33,* 474-479.

Herskovits, M. J. (1948). *Man and his works.* New York: Knopf.

Heuman, L. F. (1979). Racial integration in residential neighborhoods: Towards more precise measures and analysis. *Evaluation Quarterly, 3*(1), 59-79.

Hope-Simpson, R. E. (1958). The epidemiology and non-infectious diseases. *Royal Society of Health Journal, 78.*

Jain, U. (1987). *The psychological consequences of crowding*. New Delhi: Sage.

Kiesler, C. A. (1971). *The psychology of commitment: Experiments linking behavior to belief*. New York: Academic Press.

Lewin, K. (1951). *Field theory in social science*. New York: Harper & Row.

Lifton, R. J., & Olson, E. (1976). The human meaning of total disaster: The Buffalo Creek experience. *Psychiatry, 39*, 1-18.

Logue, J. N., Hansen, F., & Struening, E. (1979). Emotional and physical distress following Hurricane Agnes in the Wyoming Valley of Pennsylvania. *Public Health Reports, 94*, 495-502.

Lonner, W. J. (1980). The search for psychological universals. In H. C. Triandis & W. W. Lambert (Eds.), *Handbook of cross-cultural psychology* (Vol. 1, pp. 143-204). Boston: Allyn & Bacon.

Michelson, W. (1970). *Man and his urban environment: A sociological approach*. Reading, MA: Addison-Wesley.

Nagar, D., & Pandey, J. (1987). Affect and performance on cognitive task as a function of crowding and noise. *Journal of Applied Social Psychology, 17*, 147-157.

Nagar, D., & Paulus, P. B. (1988). *Residential crowding experience scale: Assessment and validation*. Unpublished manuscript, University of Texas at Arlington.

Oskamp, S. (1984). *Applied social psychology*. Englewood Cliffs, NJ: Prentice-Hall.

Pallak, M. S., & Cummings, W. (1976). Commitment and voluntary energy conservation. *Personality and Social Psychology Bulletin, 2*, 27-30.

Pandey, J. (1978). Effects of crowding on human social behavior. *Journal of Social and Economic Studies, 6*, 85-95.

Pandey, J., & Nagar, D. (1987). Experiences of indwelling and outdwelling crowding and social psychological consequences. *Social Science International, 3*, 1-9.

Pandey, J., & Nagar, D. (1988). *Residential crowding in India: Its social psychological consequences*. Paper presented at the 24th International Congress of Psychology, Sydney, Australia.

Paulus, P. B. (1987). *Prison crowding: A psychological perspective*. New York: Springer-Verlag.

Paulus, P. B., Annis, A., Seta, J., Schkade, J., & Matthews, R. W. (1976). Density does affect task performance. *Journal of Personality and Social Psychology, 34*, 248-253.

Paulus, P. B., & Nagar, D. (1987). Environmental influences on social interaction and group development. In C. Hendrick (Ed.), *Review of personality and social psychology* (Vol. 9, pp. 68-90). Beverly Hills, CA: Sage.

Paulus, P. B., & Nagar, D. (in press). Environmental influences on groups. In P. B. Paulus (Ed.), *Psychology of group influence*. Hillsdale, NJ: Lawrence Erlbaum.

Platt, J. (1973). Social traps. *American Psychologist, 28*, 241-251.

Prasad, J. (1935). The psychology of rumour: A study relating to the Great Indian Earthquake of 1934. *British Journal of Psychology, 26*, 1-15.

Quarantelli, E. L. (1985). What is a disaster? The need for clarification in definition and conceptualization in research. In B. J. Sowder (Ed.), *Disaster and mental health: Selected contemporary perspectives* (DHHS Publication No. [ADM] 85-1421). Washington, DC: Department of Health and Human Services.

Quarantelli, E. L., & Dynes, R. R. (1972). When disaster strikes. *Psychology Today, 5*(9), 66-70.

Rapoport, A. (1969). *House form and culture*. Englewood Cliffs, NJ: Prentice-Hall.

Rapoport, A. (1980). Cross-cultural aspects of environmental design. In I. Altman, A. Rapoport, & J. F. Wohlwill (Eds.), *Environment and culture*. New York: Plenum.

Rodin, J. (1976). Crowding, perceived choice and response to controllable and uncontrollable outcomes. *Journal of Experimental Social Psychology, 12*, 564-578.

Rogler, L. H. (1967). Slum neighborhood in Latin America. *Journal of Inter-American Studies, 9*, 507-528.

Ruback, R. B., & Pandey, J. (1988). *Crowding and perceived control in India.* Unpublished manuscript, Allahabad University, Allahabad.

Russell, J. A., & Ward, L. M. (1982). Environmental psychology. *Annual Review of Psychology, 33,* 651-688.

Schmitt, R. C. (1966). Density, health, and social disorganization. *American Institute of Planners Journal, 32,* 38-40.

Sharma, V. M., Vaskaran, A. S., & Malhotra, M. S. (1976). Social compatibility under prolonged isolation and high altitude. *Indian Journal of Applied Psychology, 13,* 11-15.

Sinha, D. (1952). Behavior in a catastrophic situation: A psychological study of reports and rumours. *British Journal of Psychology, 43,* 200-209.

Sinha, D. (1981). Towards an ecological framework of deprivation. In D. Sinha, R. C. Tripathi, & G. Misra (Eds.), *Deprivation: Its social roots and psychological consequences.* New Delhi: Concept.

Sommer, R. (1969). *Personal space.* Englewood Cliffs, NJ: Prentice-Hall.

Steegman, A. T. (Ed.). (1983). *Boreal forest adaptations.* New York: Plenum.

Stokols, D. (1972). On the distinction between density and crowding: Some implications for future research. *Psychological Review, 79,* 275-278.

Stokols, D. (1978). Environmental psychology. *Annual Review of Psychology, 29,* 253-295.

Stokols, D., & Altman, I. (Eds.). (1987). *Handbook of environmental psychology* (Vols. 1, 2). New York: John Wiley.

Suedfeld, P. (1987). Extreme and unusual environments. In D. Stokols & I. Altman (Eds.), *Handbook of environmental psychology* (Vol. 1, pp. 863-887). New York: John Wiley.

Sundstromm, E. (1978). Crowding as a sequential process: Review of research on the effects of population density on humans. In A. Baum & Y. M. Epstein (Eds.), *Human response to crowding.* Hillsdale, NJ: Lawrence Erlbaum.

Taylor, V., & Quarantelli, E. (1976). *Some needed cross-cultural studies of disaster behavior.* Columbus, OH: Disaster Research Center.

Tognoli, J. (1987). Residential environments. In D. Stokols & I. Altman (Eds.), *Handbook of environmental psychology* (Vol. 2, pp. 655-690). New York: John Wiley.

Toynbee, A. (1962). *The study of history.* New York: Oxford University Press.

Triandis, H. C. (1980). Introduction. In H. C. Triandis & W. W. Lambert (Eds.), *Handbook of cross-cultural psychology* (Vol. 1, pp. 1-14). Boston: Allyn & Bacon.

Weigal, R. H., & Newman, L. S. (1976). Increasing altitude-behavior correspondence by broadening the scope of the behavioral measures. *Journal of Personality and Social Psychology, 33,* 193-802.

White, L. (1949). *The science of culture.* New York: Grove.

Whiting, J. W. M. (1964). Effects of climate on certain cultural processes. In W. H. Goodenough (Ed.), *Explorations in cultural anthropology.* New York: McGraw-Hill.

Wicker, A. W. (1973). Undermanning theory and research: Implications for the study of psychological and behavioral effects of excess human population. *Representative Research in Social Psychology, 4,* 185-206.

Wicker, A. W. (1987). Behavior settings reconsidered: Temporal stages, resources, internal dynamics, context. In D. Stokols & I. Altman (Eds.), *Handbook of environmental psychology* (Vol. 1, pp. 613-656). New York: John Wiley.

Worchel, S., & Teddlie, C. (1976). The experience of crowding: A two factor theory. *Journal of Personality and Social Psychology, 34,* 30-40.

13

CULTURE AND HEALTH

LISA MARIE ILOLA

This book has been divided into separate chapters to focus the task of each writer. The contents of each are related to each other through the cross-cultural perspective running through them. Draguns's chapter discusses mental health. This chapter focuses on physical health. The division is artificial because physical health is the product of complex biopsychosocial interactions. In the context of cross-cultural studies of health, it is clear that health is not unidimensional. In this chapter, the relationship between culture and health is highlighted among other equally important factors that affect health status. Cross-cultural psychology has provided useful concepts that apply to the biological sciences; acculturation helps explain shifts in disease profiles among migrant groups, for example (see Berry, this volume). The first part of this chapter deals with medical geography and cross-national studies of the epidemiology of health and disease. The aspects of epidemiology of particular concern here are those related to values and behaviors embedded in culture. The second part deals with variations in the perception and treatment of disease in relation to health care institutions. The interactions to be discussed are admittedly complex. That is because health itself is complex and, as Triandis (1975) has suggested, cross-cultural sophistication requires increased cognitive complexity.

EPIDEMIOLOGY AND MEDICAL GEOGRAPHY

A young physician wondered whether the health problems he would see during his residency in a rural area in Tennessee would differ greatly from those he had seen in the metropolitan university medical center where he had been trained. Not long after arriving in the small community, he encountered some diseases of which he had never heard in medical school. His patients gravely reported to him conditions such as "very close veins," "sick-as-hell anemia," and an ominous sounding "Smiling Mighty Jesus" (spinal meningitis; J. Bondranko, personal communication, January 4, 1988). Discernment of variation in the patterns of the health status of defined populations is the first step toward better understanding health. The next step is to unravel the intertwined genetic, environmental, and cultural factors accounting for those variations.

Some of these variations can be traced to geographic features such as latitude, rainfall, waterways, average temperature, and country boundaries, as in the case of malaria. Other patterns can be traced to socioeconomic factors, as with malnutrition. That genetic factors account for some differences in health status among certain populations is well documented (e.g., sickle-cell anemia among Blacks) and is not discussed at length here.

In its most simple form, medical geography examines relationships between disease and the environment. Morbidity, mortality, debility, and other data about indicators of health are mapped at various levels of scale. At the micro level, data may be collected through various ethnographic field methods, household surveys, or clinic records in a Peruvian village, for example. At the macro level, data reported in the *World Health Statistics Annual* can be used to construct global maps of health. The "whodunit" and "why" are then deduced from these data. Geographic patterns of illness and health and their associations are studied using simple descriptive methods as well as complex inferential statistical procedures such as multivariate modeling techniques that take into account cultural values and beliefs as well as political, economic, and institutional factors. Cartography and epidemiology have been used to produce the *Atlas of Cancer Mortality for U.S. Counties: 1950-1969,* for example, among numerous other publications in the field of medical geography.

When epidemiology is used to infer the relationships between culture and health status, inferences are also made about the etiology and epidemiology of morbidity and mortality in general. These inferences are typically based on correlational studies of indices of health, usually vital statistics. Experimental research is still needed to confirm the inferences about culture-related etiology and epidemiology of morbidity and mortality (and, deductively, of health). But it is not as easy to manipulate cultural variables as, say, the number of pellets of food given to a pigeon. Ethnic groups who have migrated are a natural "experiment" and provide important information about cultural factors that affect health. Some of these studies will be cited later. First, however, we need to consider some basic problems in cross-cultural epidemiology (see Poortinga & Malpass, 1986, for more on drawing inferences from cross-cultural data).

Although it is health status that is of interest in epidemiological research, a reverse logic of sorts is used when morbidity and mortality are used as the sole indicators of health. Additional problems are caused by worldwide differences in the nomenclature and classification of diseases as well as inconsistencies in the monitoring and reporting of morbidity and mortality. Both of these problems are being addressed by recent efforts coordinated by the World Health Organization (WHO). Consistencies in the collection, coding, monitoring, and reporting procedures of different countries are increasing as a function of a number of WHO publications: *International Classification of Procedures in Medicine* (Volume 1, 1976), *International Classification of Disease* (ninth revised edition, 1977), *International Classification of Procedures in Medicine* (Volume 2, 1978), *International Classification of Impairments, Disabilities, and Handicaps: A Manual of Classification Relating to the Consequences of Disease* (1980), and *International Nomenclature of Diseases: Infectious Diseases* (Volume 2, 1985).

The increasing use of these publications will make cross-national comparisons more informative and contribute to a clearer understanding of culture and health. In 1986, a total of 146 WHO member states submitted reports on the monitoring and evaluation of their national health strategies to WHO (WHO, 1988).

Another important development is the articulation of a comprehensive definition of *health*. WHO has defined *health* as a complete state of physical, mental, and social well-being and not just the absence of infirmity or disease. In 1977, WHO launched a primary health care campaign, "Health for All by the Year 2000" (HFA2000). Twelve indicators of health were specified when the "Global Strategy for HFA2000" was developed in 1981. These indicators, grouped under four areas, can be summarized as follows (WHO, 1987, pp. vi-viii):

(1) *Health policy indicators are the number of countries in which*
   (a) Health for All has received endorsement at the highest official level;
   (b) mechanisms for involving people in implementation of HFA have been formed and are functioning; and
   (c) at least 5% of the gross national product (GNP) is spent on health.
(2) *Social and economic indicators are that*
   (d) a reasonable percentage of the national health expenditure is devoted to local health care;
   (e) resources are equitably distributed; and
   (f) the developing countries with well-defined strategies for HFA2000 that spent at least 5% of the GNP on health care are also receiving support from more affluent countries.
(3) *Indicators of provision of health care are that*
   (g) primary health care is available to the whole population with at least the following: safe water within a 15-minute walking distance, basic

immunizations, local health care with at least 20 essential drugs, and maternal and infant care (for infants up to the age of 1).

(4) *Indicators of health status are that*

    (h) the nutritional status of children is adequate with at least 90% of newborn birth weights greater than or equal to 2,500 grams and at least 90% of children are at weight-for-age;

    (i) infant mortality is less than 50/1,000 live births;

    (j) life expectancy at birth is greater than 60 years;

    (k) adult literacy for both sexes is greater than 70%; and

    (l) GNP per head is greater than U.S. $500.

The collection of accurate vital statistics (data about births, deaths, health, disease) is an essential part of monitoring and evaluating progress toward national and worldwide HFA2000 objectives. Even in the light of less-than-ideal standards for data collection and reporting, it is very clear that chronic diseases (e.g., heart disease, cancer) and accidents account for the greatest morbidity and mortality in industrialized countries. And, although incidence is worldwide, infectious and parasitic diseases are most prevalent in Africa, Asia, and Latin America.

Onchocerciasis (river blindness), for example, has been a major public health problem throughout Western Africa, with high infection rates in endemic pockets in savanna and river basin areas (e.g., the Volta river basin area). Onchocerciasis is also an obstacle to socioeconomic development in fertile river valleys because of the seriousness of infection. The parasitic worm (Onchocerca Volvulus) that causes onchocerciasis is transmitted through the bite of an infected female blackfly (primarily Simulium Damnosum). Adult worms live and breed in their human hosts 11-16 years, causing humans to become a long-term parasite reservoir. These breeding worm bundles contain thousands of microfilariae and cause skin lesions, subcutaneous nodules and cysts, and, more seriously, eye lesions. It is estimated that, in 1974, 1-1.5 million people were infected. Of that number, 35,000 were blinded by eye lesions and at least as many had their vision severely impaired. Because there is no viable treatment or medication for onchocerciasis, prevention is crucial.

This pattern changed dramatically as a result of the WHO-coordinated Onchocerciasis Control Program. After 12 years of larviciding the river rapids where the blackfly breeds, and other vector control activities, more than a 95% drop in the intensity and severity of disease was obtained (as measured by Community Microfilarial Load, see Figure 13.1; WHO, 1987). The prevalence of the most serious of physical symptoms, ocular lesions and blindness, had already fallen by

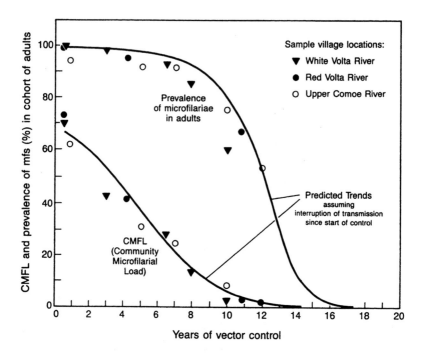

Figure 13.1. Observed and Expected Epidemiological Trends in the Central Onchoceriasis Control Program Area

NOTE: Results for three hyperendemic villages with very high intensity of infection before the start of control.

50% after 10 years of control. Present projections are that, after 15 years of control, the human reservoir of infection will also be eliminated.

Many other infectious and communicable diseases have been controlled through medical and environmental interventions such as immunizations, vaccines, larvicides, pesticides, mosquito netting, sanitation, and the proper disposal of human wastes. Although not true for onchocerciasis, many diseases can also be treated and cured. The American Public Health Association (APHA) has identified four basic approaches for the control of communicable diseases: (a) prevention and treatment, (b) sanitation, (c) proper nutrition, and (d) research (see APHA, 1985, for disease-specific detection, treatment, and control measures). But we have also experienced failures after initial successes; malaria control in Sri Lanka and UNICEF's child survival efforts in Bangladesh both failed because human factors that are involved in the transmission and maintenance of these problems were not taken into account (Harkness, Wyon, & Super, 1988). For both malaria control and child survival, effective intervention must also involve health education that results in needed behavioral changes. In this volume, Sinha and Kâgitçibaşi (the Thai study, in particular) demonstrate the importance of cultural and behavioral changes if long-term solutions to malnutrition and child welfare are to be achieved.

Human factors, especially behavioral, are even more important in the etiology of noncommunicable or chronic disease. There is no vaccination for cancer or stroke. There is no drug that will cure liver disease, dental caries, or heart disease. The epidemiologies of these diseases are related to life-style: dietary habits, physical activity, alcohol and tobacco use, and other factors that together form clear risk profiles.

BIOLOGICAL AND BEHAVIORAL FACTORS IN HEALTH AND DISEASE

An example of genetic factors interacting with behavioral ones to produce disease states can be found in the Framingham Heart Study. This study compared coronary heart disease (CHD) in middle-aged men in Framingham (Massachusetts), Honolulu (a sample of Japanese-Americans), and Puerto Rico, and found that the U.S. White population had twice the CHD death rate of Puerto Ricans and four times that of Honolulu Japanese (Gordon, Garcia-Palmieri, Kagan, Kannel, & Schiffman, 1974). Certain features of CHD epidemiology were constant across ethnic groups while a few varied. In all three populations, serum cholesterol and blood pressure were related to CHD incidence. Cigarette smoking was also related to CHD in the first two sites, but not in Puerto Rico. Another difference was that, for the U.S. White population, relative weight was less of a risk factor than for the other two populations.

This study highlights both genetic (ethnicity) and behavioral factors working together in the etiology of disease. Unfortunately, it does not elucidate the nature of that interaction. Little can be done to control etiologic environmental factors like radiation from lava, or genetic factors, except through genetic counseling perhaps. And nothing can be done about age, ethnicity, or gender. Much can be done to modify human behavior, however, and for this reason it is particularly important to understand behavioral components of health and disease. Studies of migrant ethnic groups are helpful here because the genetic pool as represented by ethnicity is held constant while exogenous factors change. The Ni-Hon-San Study (Nipon-Honolulu-San Francisco), part of the Honolulu Heart Study, is a good example. It is an ongoing prospective study of about 12,000 Japanese men in Hiroshima and Nagasaki (Japan), Honolulu, and San Francisco (146 studies, 1966-1989). When the study began in 1964, Japan had one of the lowest rates of CHD worldwide and the United States had one of the highest. Conversely, Japan had one of the highest rates of cerebrovascular disease (CBVD, or stroke) worldwide, and stroke remained the leading cause of death in Japan for years until it was surpassed by cancer in 1981.

The concept of acculturation (see Berry, this volume) is very useful in understanding why the Japanese in Japan had the lowest rates of CHD, with intermediate rates in Hawaii, and the highest rates among those who migrated to California. The process of acculturation involves physical (e.g., new house or city), biological (e.g., dietary patterns), cultural (e.g., linguistic, religious), and psychological changes. As the Japanese migrated and underwent acculturation, their serum cholesterols, glucose levels, uric acid levels, relative weight (eight kilograms difference between Japan and California), and blood pressures all increased. Dietary patterns also changed. Although total calories were only slightly lower in Japan, average dietary fat intake was 40% that of the Hawaii and California cohort. Fish, complex carbohydrates (vegetables, fruits, unrefined grains), and soybean curd (tofu) were replaced by greater consumption of bread, pork items (ham, bacon, and sausage), and high-fat foods (butter, margarine, and cheese). Spam, eggs, and rice for breakfast, and sandwiches and hamburgers, replaced more traditional food items. The greater dietary intake of saturated fat, animal protein, and dietary cholesterol was accompanied by consistent and positive relationships with higher serum cholesterol levels.

Some indices of cultural assimilation (e.g., number of years lived in Japan, frequency of speaking Japanese and reading Japanese newspapers, ethnicity of coworkers) were also found to correlate with CHD and the risk factors of CHD. The more traditional Japanese men had lower serum cholesterol and uric acid, smoked fewer cigarettes, were less obese, and were more physically active than the more Westernized men (Kagan, Marmot, & Kato, 1980; Kato, Tillotson, Nichaman, Rhoads, & Hamilton, 1973; Lichton, Bullard, & Sherrell, 1983; Reed et al., 1982; Tillotson et al., 1973).

Although the associations of risk factors with CHD tend to be stronger in the Hawaii cohort than in Japan, these differences were not statistically significant. This suggests that, although there may be cultural variations in disease etiology, key risk factors can also be identified. Systolic blood pressure was the greatest and most consistent CHD risk factor. Other risk factors include age, serum cholesterol, cigarette smoking, and serum glucose. Alcohol consumption and physical activity were negatively correlated with CHD, suggesting that they protect the individual against developing CHD (Yano et al., 1988).

Pace of Life, CHD, and Stroke

Brislin (1980) notes that cross-cultural studies are essential in research that involves environmental factors because the combination of etic plus emic aspects of a phenomenon, in this case CHD, is needed for the development of a more complete understanding of it. "Problems" or deviant cases that arise when trying to test the robustness of a risk factor cross-culturally can provide insights into the epidemiology of a disease that might not have been gained from monocultural research. To examine the role of stress in CHD etiology, Levine and Bartlett (1984) correlated CHD with pace of life and punctuality in Japan, Taiwan, Indonesia, Italy, England, and the United States. Of that sample, England had the greatest number of deaths from CHD per 100,000 (317) followed by the United States (295), Italy (152), and Japan (40). Mortality data were not available for Taiwan and Indonesia.

They chose pace of walking, accuracy of clocks, and pace of working as measures of pace of life. All three were highly correlated with each other and with degree of economic development and city size. But pace of life, using these measures, did not correlate with CHD as was expected. Japan had the fastest pace of life using these measures, but it had the lowest incidence of death from CHD. This contradicted the hypothesis that a faster pace of life would be related to CHD. Some reasons that a strong correlation between stress and CHD was not found were that there may be cultural variations in the construct of psychological stress; cultural mediating factors of stress (e.g., more social support in collectivistic cultures; see Triandis, this volume); cultural variations in the epidemiology of a chronic disease; and the overriding importance of hypertension, smoking, diet, obesity, and a sedentary life-style in CHD etiology. Perhaps the most important oversight in this study is that Japan has had one of the highest mortalities for stroke reported worldwide. Clinical records and autopsy findings have demonstrated that stroke is associated with CHD risk factors, that is, hypertension, high serum cholesterol, severe atherosclerosis of the coronary arteries and aorta, and diabetes. Cigarette smokers had two to three times the risk of stroke, and stopping smoking reduced the risk by more than half. The most notable difference between CHD and stroke risk profiles is that, whereas alcohol consumption is negatively correlated with CHD (i.e., has a protective effect), it is positively related to hemorrhagic stroke. Light drinkers have more than twice the risk, and moderate to heavy drinkers have a three- to fourfold increased risk for stroke compared with nondrinkers. As with CHD, the presence of multiple factors magnified the risk of stroke. Another indication of the similarity between CHD and stroke etiology is that autopsies of Japanese men in Hawaii revealed evidence of prior strokes (cerebral infarcts) in 58% of CHD cases (Abbott, Donahue, MacMahon, Reed, & Yano, 1987; Abbott, Yin, Reed, & Yano, 1986; Donahue, Abbott, Reed, Yano, 1986; Stemmermann et al., 1984).

CHD incidence increased in Japanese males as they migrated, whereas their incidence of stroke decreased to less than one-third that of the cohort in Japan. Stroke death rates for Japanese American men dropped to figures equivalent for U.S. White men of the same age as early as 1960, and were significantly lower than the Japan cohort in older age groups. This indicates that, in a Western environment, the risk factors change and take effect more quickly for stroke than for CHD. One hypothesis is that the protein- and/or fat-poor diets of postwar Japan coupled with the greater alcohol intake by Japanese men are involved in the epidemiology of stroke in Japan. Among all cohorts, hypertension has been found to be the single most important risk factor, although alcohol consumption, smoking, age, and diabetes are also important independent risk factors (Kagan, Popper, Rhoads, & Yano, 1985). Even though the Honolulu Heart Study has provided important information about cultural factors related to CHD and stroke epidemiology, it must be remembered that members of the study sample all belong to the Japanese ethnic group, and so questions regarding the role of genetic factors remain.

Cross-national studies can elucidate health factors associated with culture by adding to information on risk factors tied to genetics and ethnicity. Miller (1982) reviewed over 70 national and international studies of gastrointestinal cancer. Group comparisons show that Blacks in the United States have higher rates than Whites for cancer of the esophagus, stomach, liver, and pancreas. Esophageal, liver, colon, and pancreatic cancer in males are higher in urban areas. Members of two religious groups with similar dietary practices, Seventh-Day Adventists and Mormons, both have a low risk of colorectal cancer. Both descriptive and analytical studies show that total fat and animal protein intake (especially for beef) and deficiency of dietary fiber correlate with colon cancer incidence and mortality. Correlational studies can be misleading, however, when studying diseases that take a long time to develop.

As Miller points out, current dietary or other factors are usually correlated with current information on incidence and mortality, whereas dietary and other information of 20-30 years ago might be more appropriate for correlational studies of gastric cancer. When the latent period of disease etiology is long, as with colon cancer, other methods have to be used to understand it.

The Life-Style of an Ethnically Diverse Group

Prospective and cross-cultural studies of ethnically diverse groups of people who have a long history of certain health behaviors can help overcome problems due to interactions with time or ethnicity. Seventh-Day Adventists, members of an evangelical Protestant denomination, meet these criteria, and the Adventist Health Study (157 studies, 1954-1988) has helped to identify both cancer and cardiovascular risk factors. Numerous studies from different countries have shown that Seventh-Day Adventists (SDAs) live longer and are healthier than their countrymen. Their dietary practices are based on biblical principles, and the nurturing of physical, mental, and spiritual health are an important part of their values. A well-balanced diet with generous consumption of unrefined foods, grains, vegetable protein, fruits, and vegetables is advocated. In a survey of 40,000 SDAs in the United States, one-half were nonvegetarian (with restricted meat consumption, such as no pork), one-fourth were lifetime lacto-ovo vegetarians, and one-fourth adopted the vegetarian diet at some time in their lives. About 84% drank less than one cup of coffee per day, 99% were nonsmokers, and 90% were nondrinkers (Phillips, Kuzma, Beeson, & Lotz, 1980). These practices are institutionally and socially supported, and it is highly unlikely that meat (certainly not pork), alcohol, coffee, or tea would be served at a church-operated hospital or university cafeteria or at the church potluck that follows many worship services.

Because smoking is the primary etiology of most lung cancer, the low incidence of lung cancer among SDAs is obviously attributable to the virtual absence of smoking. But an even lower incidence of lung cancer is found among nonsmoking SDAs when compared with nonsmoking non-SDAs. This suggests that there are factors in addition to smoking involved in the etiology of lung cancer (Phillips et al., 1980).

Not only do SDAs in the United States have a lower risk of lung cancer, they also have less cancer of any type: breast cancer, pancreas cancer, and colorectal cancer. CHD stroke and other circulatory disease incidence are also significantly lower than in comparable cohorts.

Moreover, lower incidence rates are accompanied by higher survival rates for cancer. These lower risks should not only be viewed as the result of what SDAs do not do, such as smoke or consume much alcohol or animal protein. Better health is also the product what *replaces* risk-related behaviors. As seen in the Ni-Hon-San Study, lower levels of animal protein consumption are contrasted to higher levels of vegetable protein consumption (e.g., vegetable protein products, beans, lentils, peas). In the case of fatal pancreatic cancer, for example, increasing consumption of vegetable protein and dried fruits are all associated with significant protective relationships to risk (Mills, Beeson, Abbey, Fraser, & Phillips, 1988). Health consciousness also affects behavior after disease develops, and lower breast cancer death rates among SDA women as compared with the general population are in part due to better survival patterns due to a shorter interval between onset of symptoms and subsequent diagnosis and treatment. These women are more likely to react quickly and obtain needed health care once their health is endangered (Zollinger, Phillips, & Kuzma, 1984).

SDAs in Australia have a lower prevalence of risk factors associated with cardiovascular and respiratory diseases in general. They have lower levels of systolic and diastolic blood pressures, plasma cholesterol, plasma urate concentrations, and incidence of obesity, and higher lung ventilator capacity (Simons, Gibson, Jones, & Bain, 1979; Webster & Rawson, 1979). A 10-year study of mortality patterns of SDAs in the Netherlands found that they had significantly lower standardized mortality ratios for total mortality, cancer, and cardiovascular diseases compared with the total Dutch population (Berkel & deWaard, 1983). The Tromsø Heart Study found that Norwegian SDA coronary risk factor patterns were similar to that of SDAs in other parts of the world, and, compared with non-SDAs, they had lower serum cholesterol (men and women) and blood pressure levels (women) (Fønnebø, 1985).

Degree of adherence to the SDA life-style represents a dose-response relationship. An increasing gradient of risk is associated with decreasing adherence to the SDA life-style. Again, the concept of acculturation is useful in understanding the finding that SDAs who are more similar to non-SDAs also have comparable risks for disease. In Norway, SDAs who were religiously inactive were found to have risk factor patterns similar to non-SDA Norwegians (Fønnebø, 1985). In the United States, SDAs whose adherence to the SDA life-style is poor in general have a risk of disease slightly less than or statistically equal to the risk of nonsmoking non-SDAs (Phillips et al., 1980). These findings are not surprising as the presence of multiple factors has already been shown to magnify the risk of other chronic diseases. The converse is also true.

Health programs that succeed in reducing the number of risk factors in a population also succeed in reducing morbidity and mortality, as will be discussed later.

PSYCHOLOGICAL FACTORS IN
CHRONIC DISEASE ETIOLOGY

According to chapter divisions in this book, this section of this chapter might more appropriately belong in Draguns's chapter on mental health. Psychological factors have emerged as such an important factor to consider in chronic diseases, however, that the link between psychological and physiological interactions in disease epidemiology will be examined briefly. Levy (1988) reviewed 10 psychobiological studies linking behavior to vulnerability to and mortality of cancer. A sense of well-being and happiness predicted reduced cancer incidence and mortality from hormonally dependent tumors for women (the Alameda County Study). Perceptions of inadequate social support, helplessness, and inadequate expression of negative emotions were associated with progression of cancer and death.

It appears that severe and chronic stressors (e.g., depression, marital discord, caring for family members with Alzheimer's disease, and bereavement) can decrease cellular immunity and increase one's vulnerability to disease. Unlike rats, humans do not appear to adapt to chronic stress (Glaser & Glaser-Kiecolt, 1988; Glaser-Kiecolt & Glaser, 1988). Rubinow and associates (1988) found that Acquired Human Immunodeficiency Syndrome (AIDS) victims, compared with matched homosexual males without AIDS, had more histories of depression. Other suppressors of cellular immune response include cocaine and marijuana (THC). It is possible that the recreational use of these substances makes users more vulnerable to cancer and AIDS and to other diseases in which a compromised immune system is part of the disease epidemiology (Friedman et al., 1988; Klein, Newton, & Friedman, 1988).

Social support and the withdrawal of social support has emerged as a factor in a number of studies. In a 21-country study of values and disease, Bond (n.d.) controlled for GNP (because a country's economic state obviously plays a crucial role in the health status of its citizens) and found social support to be related to health. He found "integration" (a factor very similar to collectivism) to be a protective factor in morbidity (e.g., malignant neoplasms) in general. This confirmed the hypothesis that a cohesive and harmonious in-group is a prophylactic for disease when controlling for the effects of GNP (Triandis, Bontempo, Villareal, Asai, & Lucca, 1988). Psychoimmunological studies have also found associations between feelings of distress and increased risk of clinical and subclinical infection; and, on the positive side, a lowered risk associated with social support and "hardiness" (a sense of control, commitment, and challenge; Temoshok, 1988). Cohen (1988) contrasts the process of social withdrawal that characterizes both patients suffering a terminal disease and victims of voodoo death. In both, the withdrawal of social support is accompanied by feelings of separation, loss, depression, and hopelessness. He maintains that these are significant factors in the progression of both cancer and AIDS, and they are comparable to the psychological process involved in other sudden deaths such as voodoo death or Hmong Sudden Death Syndrome. He advocates a biopsychosocial rather than a biomedical perspective for research on diseases like AIDS and advocates the "biology of hope." He cites research that demonstrates the healing effects of hope, humor, a sense of mastery over the illness, self-esteem, community support, meditation, prayer, relaxation, and mental imagery. Of course, social support has its negative side as well. Belonging to a group results in responsibilities to the group: personal, temporal, and financial.

The discovery of etiological psychological variables among one population and the international incidence of any disease is not enough to understand its epidemiology fully. Many issues in cross-cultural psychological testing need to be considered (see Lonner, this volume). Research has yet to be done to find out if the psychological variables identified in the United States are etiologically involved in disease epidemiology cross-culturally.

HEALTH EDUCATION AND
THE NORTH KARELIA PROJECT

It has already been shown that the presence of multiple factors magnifies the risk for disease, both communicable and chronic. We will also see that health programs that succeed in reducing the number of risk factors in a population succeed in reducing morbidity and mortality. A good example is that of Finland, and the Karelia area in eastern Finland, in particular. It has had one of the highest mortality rates due to cardiovascular diseases (CVD) in the world for many years. In 1972, the North Karelia Project, in conjunction with the Ministry of Health, began systematically to treat hypertension and, through community-based prevention programs, to reduce the presence of risk factors already discussed: serum cholesterol, blood pressure, smoking, and consumption of animal fat (including butter and cream). These efforts paid excellent dividends. From 1972 to 1984, mortality from stroke, from ischaemic heart disease, and from all CVD declined more steeply in Karelia than in the rest of Finland, even though it remains higher than in the United States or in other Western European countries (Nissinen, Tuomilehto, & Puska, 1989; Tuomilehto et al., 1986; Tuomilehto, Piha, Nissinen, Geboers, & Puska, 1989).

In the United States, the individual bears the load of responsibility for health status and care. Personal financial considerations account for the great disparity in even basic health services received by Americans. Health education efforts rely heavily on appeals to the individual to take responsibility for personal health, to jog three times a week, to stop smoking, or to perform a monthly breast exam. A cultural variable that should not be overlooked in accounting for the success of the North Karelia Project is that of individual versus institutional roles in health maintenance and care. Like many other countries in Europe, health care in Finland is socialized, and government intervention is responsible for the national availability and provision of high-quality and low-cost health services. Whereas some Americans indignantly decry legislative efforts to make helmet-wearing for motorcyclists compulsory, Finns unprotestingly comply with national legislation and both motorcyclists and moped drivers wear helmets. Both driver and rear seat passengers wear seat belts, young children are secured in car child seats, and all vehicles are driven with their headlights on both day and night in nonmunicipal areas (it increases the visibility of oncoming traffic). Tobacco products cannot be advertised in the media or on billboards and heavy luxury taxes drive up the price of cigarettes. Smoking cessation and other health education programs are delivered by the Ministry of Health on the state-controlled television channels. The alcohol industry, Alko, is a state-owned and operated monopoly. Beer only, not wine and other spirits, may be bought in grocery stores, and Alko has its own shops with regulated hours. There is less drunk driving than in the United States because of the strict penalties for driving while intoxicated (penalties such as three months in jail, fines, and forfeiting one's driver's license for a period of time). It is clear that health education efforts will be more successful in a culture such as Finland, where institutional intervention and support is viewed as positive and not a violation of individual rights or responsibilities.

Health status is the product of biological causes. It is also directly related to health care and the institutionalization of health care in the form of legislation, hospitals, health education, health personnel education, and research. There are many other examples that illustrate this. Although clearly written in a journalistic manner and less empirical than might be hoped, Payer (1988), for example, makes an engaging argument that differences in national values account for some important differences in perceptions of disease and medical practices in four countries with comparable life expectancies: France, West Germany, Great Britain, and the United States.

English values, she notes, encompass empiricism, self-control ("keeping a stiff upper lip"), and frugality. English physicians are more skeptical about their power to heal and are sensitive to the importance of providing comfort and relief from pain. Death is not something to be delayed at any cost. The emphasis is on the quality, not the length, of life. Because greater emphasis is placed on the side effects of drugs and treatments (including negative psychosocial ones), fewer drugs, except tranquilizers and pain reducers, are prescribed overall. As a result, randomized, controlled trials (RCT) with no-treatment controls are more common than in the United States. This is consonant with English empiricism, coupled with their doubts about the value of medical intervention. Fewer routine exams and tests (e.g., blood pressure measurements, x-rays) and fewer diagnoses are made than in the other three countries. There is also less surgery. English surgeons do, proportionately, only one-sixth the number of coronary bypass surgeries done in the United States and treat breast cancer with tylectomies (lumpectomies). These are cheaper and easier to perform than mastectomies. In comparison with France, West Germany, and the United States, Great Britain also places more emphasis on geriatrics, including geriatric psychiatry, to make the life of senior citizens more comfortable although not necessarily longer.

PERCEPTION AND TREATMENT OF DISEASE: WHEN EAST MEETS WEST

Variations in the perception and treatment of disease are often due to very fundamental differences in cultural assumptions. Records of ancient cultures and anthropological studies of non-Western groups document that many of these cultures have a more integrated perception of determinants of health than that presently held in Western nations. As a consequence, their explanation of health, illness, and death is more integrated and multidimensional. In a study of beliefs about patient suffering, nurses from six cultures rated the physical pain and psychological distress of descriptions of patients with cardiovascular disease, cancer, infection, trauma, and psychiatric conditions (Davitz, Sameshima, & Davitz, 1976). Contrary to Western stereotypes about the stoicism of Asians, the nurses from Japan, Korea, Thailand, and Taiwan all believed patients suffered higher degrees of physical pain than did American or Puerto Rican nurses. Japanese and Korean nurses also rated patients as suffering more psychological distress, although Thai and Taiwanese nurses rated less psychological distress than did American and Puerto Rican nurses. Clearly, physical distress does not necessarily accompany psychological distress or vice versa. Puerto Rican nurses inferred relatively low physical pain but high psychological distress for the same patients.

Differences in the perception of illness and the expression of it through illness behavior are also found among patients. For example, the somatic expression of psychological distress appears to be more common for Asians than for Westerners and has been reported to be one of the most important clinical problems in Southeast Asian immigrants and refugees when it occurs within the context of Western medicine. *Somatization* has been operationally defined as the reporting of physical symptoms for which a clinical investigation reveals no detectable organic etiology, or as physical symptoms as a function of an underlying psychiatric disorder. In a rigorously conducted two-month study of immigrants and refugees in the United States from China, the Philippines, Vietnam, and Laos (Lowland and Mien), over one-third of patients' problems were diagnosed as somatization (Lin, Carter, & Kleinman, 1985). These patients were more costly in physicians' time and lab investigations, and, when the diagnoses of somatization were finally made, the next problem was the selection of appropriate treatment.

Illness behavior is understood and treated more readily in its cultural context. Tobin and Friedman (1983) describe a case study of a Hmong refugee, Vang Xiong, that illustrates this. Vang had an acute mental health crisis, or what the Hmong call a "spirit problem," shortly after arriving in the United States. During successive nights, Vang dreamed that first a cat, then a large black dog, and then a white-skinned female spirit (called a *Chia*) pinned him to the bed and almost crushed the breath out of him. Vang was afraid to return home and contacted a Hmong resettlement worker for help.

It was thought that Vang had survived an attack of "nightmare death" or "Hmong Sudden Death Syndrome," an inexplicable cause of death most frequent among the Hmong but also occurring among other Laotians, Kampucheans, and Vietnamese, according to Centers for Disease Control statistics. Victims (usually young/middle-aged males) die in their sleep. Subsequent autopsies yield no evidence of tissue damage or other biological or pathological etiology. The etiology is believed to be the somatization of psychological distress, and Vang's psychological profile was not good. He had trauma reactions associated with combat fatigue (he had become a soldier at 15); survivor guilt; disorientation, anxiety, and culture-shock associated with the refugee experience; and a premorbid personality (unresolved psychological guilt because engagement in combat prevented him from observing the prescribed mourning rituals when his parents died).

It was felt that, even with a bilingual translator, Western psychotherapy would not help due to the complexity, acuteness, and potential dangerousness of Vang's case. A 50-year-old woman respected in the Hmong community as a shaman was called instead. The shaman came to the home, used her powers to divine that it was indeed a spirit problem, and then performed some ceremonies (e.g., having Vang crawl through a hoop and between two outspread knife blades "so the spirits would have difficulty following"). What might have taken months or even years of conventional psychotherapy for Vang's cure was accomplished in a manner culturally understood by Vang and his family within a matter of a few hours. It may be that, in the future, under extreme duress, Vang's physical, emotional, and psychological resources will become depleted again and the shaman will have to return to perform the same or a similar service. This does not invalidate the efficacy of the treatment and healing experienced in this incident any more than we would call a second organ transplant years later a failure.

Many Western health professionals, however, are uneasy about nontraditional health care practices. The evolution of the medical system and their own socialization within that system have contributed to that uneasiness. The observation has been made that the concept of a medical system is

> based on a single, historically recent system: a bureaucratically ordered set of schools, hospitals, clinics, professional associations, companies and regulatory agencies that train practitioners and maintain facilities to

conduct biomedical research, to prevent or cure illness and to care for or rehabilitate the chronically ill. From this perspective other forms of health care are outside the medical system and they are usually ignored. When they are not ignored they are derogated as curiosities, or as fringe medicine, quackery and superstition. (Leslie, 1980, p. 191)

Leslie takes a world perspective that defines *disease* as both biological and social (perceptual) realities and advocates a pluralistic structure of medical care large enough for alternative therapists. Certainly, studies of refugees and immigrants from Southeast Asia and Indochina underscore the value of utilizing traditional healers in addition to educating Western health professionals about these groups' cultural perspectives, health beliefs, and sick roles (see Van Deusen, 1982, for an extensive review). A medical system that excludes and is intolerant of nontraditional health care practices also excludes some of those who need help the most.

That health services are an important part of the health status of any population is very clear. Availability and accessibility (including cultural and financial accessibility) and the training of health personnel are only part of the institution of health care. There is also the issue of home health care: measures taken before institutionalized health care is even sought. Both of these are issues of such magnitude that they deserve entire chapters to cover relevant issues adequately. A few guidelines to providers of primary health care will complete this section on health care and services.

PROVIDERS OF PRIMARY HEALTH CARE AND CROSS-CULTURAL PSYCHOLOGY

The cross-cultural etics that are helpful to providers of primary health care sound platitudinous but perhaps could be summarized as the Golden Rule: to do unto others as one would like to have done to oneself. This means culturally appropriate "doing" by seeing the world from the other's perspective—culturally, politically, and economically. It is essential to have a firm grounding in the emics of the cultural group one is working with to do this successfully. The contributions of social and medical anthropologists are invaluable here. Sinha (1988) provides a review of the changes in the Indian family that have affected human development and mental health status during the past 40 years or so. The changes that he identifies apply to developing countries in general, such as changes in the status, role, and employment of women and consequent child-rearing practices. Knowledge of how these affect human development is important to any health care provider.

Various handbooks for mental health workers are available. McDermott, Tseng, and Maretzki (1980) provide an overview of 11 cultural groups that live in Hawaii, and Pedersen, Draguns, Lonner, and Trimble (1981) provide an overview of core issues in cross-cultural counseling in general. The Native Hawaiian Health Research Consortium (1985a, 1985b) provides a model of culture-specific health program planning for Native Hawaiians. It outlines a health program that combines the incidence and epidemiology of Native Hawaiian morbidity and mortality with knowledge gleaned from medical and cultural anthropology. Read (1966) outlined the culture, health patterns, and some of the traditional systems of care for sickness among various groups in tropical rural areas of developing countries, and she presents examples from Africa. Pulsford and Cawte (1972) did the same for Melanesia, with a particular focus on Papua New Guinea. These are but a few of the many resources available for primary health care providers. The remainder of this chapter summarizes some reasonable generalizations that can be made about the individual's role in his or her own health.

ETICS OF HEALTH

Some key factors that appear to be correlated with health cross-culturally are a psychological sense of well-being, consumption of a balanced diet low in animal fat and high in fiber, lack of chronic stressors, clean air (free from environmental pollution, including tobacco smoke), adequate physical exercise, avoidance of toxic chemicals and drugs (in the environment or recreationally used), and restriction of exposure to causes of disease through behavioral and medical means (e.g., vaccines). Social support is another important correlate of health that has emerged as a factor in the epidemiologies of cancer and AIDS (Levy, 1988), and it has been considered a factor contributing to the health of Adventists (Webster & Rawson, 1979). The other half of prevention is health care. Here, prompt and appropriate health care and services are important.

The importance of cultural factors when considering determinants of health should be clear. Culture provides a context within which perceptions of health and treatment of illness occur. Cultural variables are also involved in the actual biological processes of health and illness. Cross-national and cross-cultural research have helped untangle interactions between biological, psychological, cultural, and social factors. We can anticipate further illumination from such research.

GLOSSARY

This glossary defines some of the most important terms used in this chapter. In each case, the meaning given corresponds to the usage in the text. More detailed definitions may be obtained by consulting a medical dictionary.

Atherosclerosis. This type of arteriosclerosis is a degenerative disease of the arteries and a type of CVD disease. The deposition of fatty substances in and fibrosis of the inner layer of the arteries and blood vessels result in the narrowing, hardening, and loss of elasticity of vessel passages, obstructing blood flow and contributing to hypertension (high blood pressure).

Cancer. A malignant neoplasm is a new growth of tissue of potentially unlimited growth that expands locally by invasion and systemically by metastasis (the transmission of cancerous cells from an original site through the blood of lymphatic pathways to another part of the body with the development of a similar lesion in the new location); disease marked by such growths. A cancerous or malignant tumor serves no physiological function and, when untreated, tends to infiltrate, metastasize, and terminate fatally. Cancer etiology is a combination of carcinogenic and predisposing factors, such as chronic lung irritation by tobacco smoke plus heredity and age.

CBVD. Cerebrovascular diseases (CBVD) relate to or involve the cerebrum and the blood vessels that supply it; for example, one of several types of stroke. This is a type of CVD.

CHD. Coronary heart disease (CHD), coronary artery disease, or coronary disease is a condition (such as sclerosis or thrombosis) that reduces the blood flow through the coronary arteries to the heart muscle. This is a type of CVD.

Chronic diseases. Diseases that involve degeneration of the body or any of its functions as opposed to acute onset and self-limiting conditions such as mumps. Associated with predisposing behavioral and clinical risk factors; see CVD, cancer.

Communicable or infectious diseases. Diseases that, under natural conditions, can be transmitted between humans (e.g., AIDS) or between humans and animals (zoonotic diseases such as brucellosis, rabies).

CVD. Cardiovascular disease (CVD) is a general term that describes a number of diseases that relate to or involve the heart and blood vessels, such as atherosclerosis, coronary heart disease, and cerebrovascular diseases (CBVD). CVD etiology is a combination of arteriosclerotic and other predisposing factors, such as elevated serum cholesterol, hypertension, smoking, heredity, and age.

Epidemiology. A branch of medical science that deals with the incidence, distribution, and control of disease in a population. Also, the sum of the factors controlling the presence or absence of a disease or the ecology of a disease or pathogen.

Etiology. All of the causes of a disease or abnormal condition. The branch of medical science concerned with the causes and origins of diseases.

Morbidity. The relative incidence or state of disease.

Mortality. The number of deaths in a given time or place or the proportion of deaths in a population.

Prospective study. A study concerned with or relating to the future that may track cohorts during a period of years or decades, such as the Honolulu Heart Study and the Adventist Health Study.

Serum cholesterol. This is cholesterol in the blood (as opposed to dietary cholesterol, such as eggs). Consumption of dietary cholesterol and saturated fats, which the body synthesizes into cholesterol, can elevate serum cholesterol. Some cholesterol is essential to physiological processes, but elevated levels of serum cholesterol have been implicated as a risk factor in arteriosclerosis and CVD.

REFERENCES

Abbott, R. D., Donahue, R. P., MacMahon, S. W., Reed, D. M., & Yano, K. (1987). Diabetes and the risk of stroke: The Honolulu Heart Program. *Journal of the American Medical Association, 257*(7), 949-952.

Abbott, R. D., Yin, Y., Reed, D. M., & Yano, K. (1986). Risk of stroke in male cigarette smokers. *New England Journal of Medicine, 315,* 717-720.

American Public Health Association. (1985). *Control of communicable disease in man* (14th ed.). Washington, DC: Author.

Berkel, J., & deWaard, F. (1983). Mortality pattern and life expectancy of Seventh-Day Adventists in the Netherlands. *International Journal of Epidemiology, 12*(4), 455-458.

Bond, M. H. (n.d.). *Chinese values and health: A cultural-level examination.* Unpublished manuscript, Chinese University, Shatin, NT, Hong Kong.

Brislin, R. W. (1980). Cross-cultural research methods: Strategies, problems, applications. In I. Altman, A. Rapoport, & J. F. Wohlwill (Eds.), *Human behavior and environment* (Vol. 4). New York: Plenum.

Cohen, S. I. (1988). Voodoo death, the stress response, and AIDS. In T. P. Bridge & A. F. Mirsky (Eds.), *Psychological, neuropsychiatric, and substance abuse aspects of AIDS: Advances in biochemical psychopharmacology* (Vol. 44, pp. 95-109). New York: Raven.

Davitz, L. J., Sameshima, Y., & Davitz, J. (1976). Suffering as viewed in six different cultures. *American Journal of Nursing, 76*(8), 1296-1297.

Donahue, R. P., Abbott, R. D., Reed, D. M., & Yano, K. (1986). Alcohol and hemorrhagic stroke: The Honolulu Heart Program. *Journal of the American Medical Association, 255*(17), 2311-2314.

Fønnebø, V. (1985). The Tromsø Heart Study: Coronary risk factors in Seventh-Day Adventists. *American Journal of Epidemiology, 122*(5), 789-793.

Friedman, H., Klein, T., Specter, S., Pross, S., Newton, C., Blanchard, D. K., & Widen, R. (1988). Drugs of abuse and virus susceptibility. In T. P. Bridge & A. F. Mirsky (Eds.), *Psychological, neuropsychiatric, and substance abuse aspects of AIDS: Advances in biochemical psychopharmacology* (Vol. 44, pp. 125-137). New York: Raven.

Glaser, R., & Glaser-Kiecolt, J. (1988). Stress-associated immune suppression and acquired immune deficiency syndrome (AIDS). In T. P. Bridge & A. F. Mirsky (Eds.), *Psychological, neuropsychiatric, and substance abuse aspects of AIDS: Advances in biochemical psychopharmacology* (Vol. 44, pp. 203-215). New York: Raven.

Glaser-Kiecolt, J., & Glaser, R. (1988). Major life changes, chronic stress, and immunity. In T. P. Bridge & A. F. Mirsky (Eds.), *Psychological, neuropsychiatric, and substance abuse aspects of AIDS: Advances in biochemical psychopharmacology* (Vol. 44, pp. 217-224). New York: Raven.

Gordon, T., Garcia-Palmieri, M. R., Kagan, A., Kannel, W. B., & Schiffman, J. (1974). Differences in coronary heart disease in Framingham, Honolulu and Puerto Rico. *Journal of Chronic Disease, 27,* 329-344.

Harkness, S., Wyon, J. B., & Super, C. M. (1988). The relevance of behavioral sciences to disease prevention and control in developing countries. In P. R. Dasen, J. W. Berry, & N. Sartorius (Eds.), *Health and cross-cultural psychology: Toward applications* (pp. 241-255). Newbury Park, CA: Sage.

Kagan, A., Marmot, M. B., & Kato, H. (1980). The Ni-Hon-San study of cardiovascular disease epidemiology. In H. Kesteloot & J. V. Joossens (Eds.), *Epidemiology of arterial blood pressure* (pp. 423-436). The Hague, The Netherlands: Martinus Nijhoff.

Kagan, A., Popper, J. S., Rhoads, G. G., & Yano, K. (1985). Dietary and other risk factors for stroke in Hawaiian Japanese men. *Stroke, 16*(3), 390-396.

Kato, H., Tillotson, J. Nichaman, M. Z., Rhoads, G. G., & Hamilton, H. B. (1973). Epidemiological studies of coronary heart disease and stroke in Japanese men living in Japan, Hawaii and California. *American Journal of Epidemiology, 97*(6), 372-384.

Klein, T. W., Newton, C. A., & Friedman, H. (1988). Suppression of human and mouse lymphocyte proliferation by cocaine. In T. P. Bridge & A. F. Mirsky (Eds.), *Psychological, neuro-psychiatric, and substance abuse aspects of AIDS: Advances in biochemical psychopharmacology* (Vol. 44, pp. 225-239). New York: Raven.

Leslie, C. (1980). Medical pluralism in world perspective. *Social Science and Medicine, 14B,* 191-195.

Levine, R. V., & Bartlett, K. (1984). Pace of life, punctuality, and coronary heart disease in six countries. *Journal of Cross-Cultural Psychology, 15*(2), 233-255.

Levy, S. M. (1988). Behavioral risk factors and host vulnerability. In T. P. Bridge & A. F. Mirsky (Eds.), *Psychological, neuropsychiatric, and substance abuse aspects of AIDS: Advances in biochemical psychopharmacology* (Vol. 44, pp. 225-239). New York: Raven.

Lichton, I. J., Bullard, L. R., & Sherrell, B. U. (1983). A conspectus of research on nutritional status in Hawaii and Western Samoa—1960-1980 with references to diseases in which diet has been implicated. *World Review of Nutrition and Dietetics, 41,* 40-75.

Lin, E. H. B., Carter, W. B., & Kleinman, A. M. (1985). An exploration of somatization among Asian refugees and immigrants in primary care. *American Journal of Public Health, 75*(9), 1080-1084.

McDermott, J. F., Jr., Tseng, W., & Maretzki, T. W. (Eds.). (1980). *People and cultures of Hawaii: A psychocultural profile.* Honolulu: University Press of Hawaii.

Miller, A. B. (1982). Risk factors from geographic epidemiology for gastrointestinal cancer. *Cancer, 50,* 2533-2540.

Mills, P. K., Beeson, W. L., Abbey, D. E., Fraser, G. E., & Phillips, R. L. (1988). Dietary habits and past medical history as related to fatal pancreas cancer risk among Adventists. *Cancer, 61,* 2578-2585.

The Native Hawaiian Health Research Consortium. (1985a, December). *E Ola Mau: The Native Hawaiian health needs study: Nutrition/dental task force report.* Honolulu, HI: Alu Like, Inc.

The Native Hawaiian Health Research Consortium. (1985b, December). *E Ola Mau: The Native Hawaiian health needs study: A preliminary plan for improving native Hawaiian health through health promotion, disease prevention, and health protection.* Honolulu, HI: Alu Like, Inc.

Nissinen, A., Tuomilehto, J., & Puska, P. (1989). From pilot project to national implementation: Experiences from the North Karelia Project. *Scandinavian Journal of Primary Health Care, 1*(Suppl.), 49-56. (From Medline, 1989, Quarter 2, Abstract No. 89145762)

Payer, L. (1988). *Medicine and culture: Varieties of treatment in the United States, England, West Germany, and France.* New York: Henry Holt.

Pedersen, P. P., Draguns, J. G., Lonner, W. J., & Trimble, J. E. (1981). *Counseling across cultures.* Honolulu: University Press of Hawaii.

Phillips, R. L., Kuzma, J. W., Beeson, W. L., & Lotz, T. (1980). Influence of selection versus lifestyle on risk of fatal cancer and cardiovascular disease among Seventh-Day Adventists. *American Journal of Epidemiology, 112*(2), 296-314.

Poortinga, Y. H., & Malpass, R. S. (1986). Making inferences from cross-cultural data. In W. J. Lonner & J. W. Berry (Eds.), *Field methods in cross-cultural research* (pp. 17-46). Beverly Hills, CA: Sage.

Pulsford, R. L., & Cawte, J. (1972). *Health in a developing country: Principles of medical anthropology in Melanesia.* Brisbane: Jacaranda.

Read, M. (1966). *Culture, health, and disease.* London: Tavistock.

Reed, D., McGee, D., Cohen, J., Yano, K., Syme, S. L., & Feinleib, M. (1982). Acculturation and coronary heart disease among Japanese men in Hawaii. *American Journal of Epidemiology, 115*(6), 894-905.

Rubinow, D. R., Joffe, R. T., Brouwers, P., Squillace, K., Lane, H. C., & Mirsky, A. F. (1988). Neuropsychiatric impairment in patients with AIDS. In T. P. Bridge & A. F. Mirsky (Eds.), *Psychological, neuropsychiatric, and substance abuse aspects of AIDS: Advances in biochemical psychopharmacology* (Vol. 44, pp. 225-239). New York: Raven.

Simons, L. Gibson, J., Jones, A., & Bain, D. (1979). Health status of Seventh-Day Adventists. *Medical Journal of Australia, 2,* 148.

Sinha, D. (1988). The family scenario in a developing country and its implications for mental health: The case of India. In P. R. Dasen, J. W. Berry, & N. Sartorius (Eds.), *Health and cross-cultural psychology: Toward applications* (pp. 48-70). Newbury Park, CA: Sage.

Stemmermann, G. N., Hayashi, T., Resch, J. A., Chung, C. S., Reed, D. M., & Rhoads, G. G. (1984). Risk factors related to ischemic and hemorrhagic cerebrovascular disease at autopsy: The Honolulu Heart Study. *Stroke, 15*(1), 23-28.

Temoshok, L. (1988). Psychoimmunology and AIDS. In T. P. Bridge & A. F. Mirsky (Eds.), *Psychological, neuropsychiatric, and substance abuse aspects of AIDS: Advances in biochemical psychopharmacology* (Vol. 44, pp. 241-247). New York: Raven.

Tillotson, J. L., Kato, H., Nichaman, M. Z., Miller, D. C., Gay, M. L., Johnson, K. G., & Rhoads, G. G. (1973). Epidemiology of coronary heart disease and stroke in Japanese men living in Japan, Hawaii, and California: Methodology for comparison of diet. *American Journal of Clinical Nutrition, 26*, 177-184.

Tobin, J. J., & Friedman, J. (1983). Spirits, shamans and nightmare death. *American Journal of Orthopsychiatry, 53*(3), 439-448.

Triandis, H. C. (1975). Culture training, cognitive complexity and interpersonal attitudes. In R. W. Brislin, S. Bochner, & W. J. Lonner (Eds.), *Cross-cultural perspectives on learning* (pp. 39-77). New York: John Wiley.

Triandis, H. C., Bontempo, R., Villareal, M. J., Asai, M., & Lucca, N. (1988). Individualism and collectivism: Cross-cultural perspectives on self-ingroup relationships. *Journal of Personality and Social Psychology, 54*, 323-338.

Tuomilehto, J., Geboers, J., Salonen, J. T., Nissinen, A., Kuulasmaa, K., & Puska, P. (1986). Decline in cardiovascular mortality in North Karelia and other parts of Finland. *British Medical Journal, 293*(6554), 1068-1071. (From Medline, 1986, R89, Abstract No. 87027384)

Tuomilehto, J., Piha, T., Nissinen, A., Geboers, J., & Puska, P. (1989). Trends in stroke mortality and in antihypertensive treatment in Finland from 1972 to 1984 with special reference to North Karelia. *Journal of Human Hypertension, 1*(3), 201-208. (From Medline, 1989, Quarter 2, Abstract No. 89145762)

Van Deusen, J. M. (1982). Health/mental health studies of Indochinese refugees: A critical overview. *Medical Anthropology, 6*(4), 231-247.

Webster, I. W., & Rawson, G. K. (1979). Health status of Seventh-Day Adventists. *Medical Journal of Australia, 1*, 417-420.

World Health Organization. (1987). *World health statistics annual.* Geneva: Author.

World Health Organization. (1988). *The work of WHO 1986-1987: Biennial report of the Director-General to the World Health Assembly.* Geneva: Author.

Yano, K., MacLean, C. J., Reed, D. M., Shimizu, Y., Sasaki, H., Kodama, K., Kato, H., & Kagan, A. (1988). A comparison of the 12-year mortality and predictive factors of coronary heart disease among Japanese men in Japan and Hawaii. *American Journal of Epidemiology, 127*(3), 476-487.

Zollinger, T. W., Phillips, R. L., & Kuzma, J. W. (1984). Breast cancer survival rates among Seventh-Day Adventists and non-Seventh-Day Adventists. *American Journal of Epidemiology, 119*(4), 503-509.

14

APPLICATIONS OF CROSS-CULTURAL PSYCHOLOGY IN THE FIELD OF MENTAL HEALTH

JURIS G. DRAGUNS

The objective of this chapter is to identify those findings of cross-cultural psychology that are of potential relevance for working clinicians, that is, professionals in psychology, psychiatry, and several related fields, and to introduce a number of key ideas to students who may enter these professions. They are, actually or potentially, the people "on the firing line," whose work brings them into intensive contact with distress and disability, the two DSM-IIIR criteria of mental disorder (American Psychiatric Association, 1987). The training and experience of these professionals are expected to equip them with techniques for alleviating the suffering of their patients or clients and to improve or restore their patients' and clients' competence in facing the challenges of their daily lives. The activities in which mental health professionals engage include assessment and diagnosis, intervention in the form of behavior modification and psychotherapy, and extension of the impact of their operations through consultation with community agents, family members, and other professionals. This chapter attempts to bring to bear insights and conclusions based on cross-cultural psychological research on these practical areas of activity.

The field of application to which this chapter pertains is vast and the potentially relevant results of basic research are highly heterogeneous. As in other topical areas, the term *culture* is employed in this chapter in two interrelated senses. On the one hand, it pertains to the characteristics of diverse peoples scattered around the globe. On the other hand, it refers to social variations among the various components of contemporary pluralistic American society and other similarly heterogeneous nations. Cultural diversity then can be observed and studied close at hand, indeed, often around the block. Most clinical professionals are primarily concerned with *culture* in the second sense of the term, that is, as it is represented in the composition of their clientele. They may only be peripherally interested, if at all, in the manifestations of disturbance in peoples far removed from them both geographically and culturally. Yet, as I hope to be able to demonstrate, the intertwining of culture and psychopathology holds practical and relevant implications regardless of the site of its occurrence. How culture and abnormal behavior interrelate is more than an object of idle curiosity. As we observe and record the variations in manifestations of psychopathology in different cultural milieus, these variations are not a mere collection of curiosities or a psychiatric zoo. Rather, relationships of clinical interest can be observed both in the microcosm of several interacting cultures sharing their physical habitat and in the macrocosm of cultural groups separated geographically and unrelated historically.

The meaning of research should be delimited for the purposes of this chapter. *Research,* in current usage, refers to observations and findings based on systematic, usually quantified, operations and characterized by objectivity, explicit statistical designs and detailed advance planning of observational and data processing activities. The difficulties in abiding by this set of criteria for the topic of this chapter are twofold. First, research approximating such standards has simply not been extended to many topics of central interest to the working clinician. I am just not aware, for instance, of any psychotherapy outcome research in which culture or ethnicity has been included as an independent variable. On the other hand, such research as exists on abnormal behavior and culture has been carried out mainly for the sake of extending knowledge. Thus little thought to the application of these findings has been given. The challenge is to extract practical or applicable features from these arrays of findings. Unfortunately, the yield of such practice-oriented suggestions may be meager.

To increase its scope, I intend to extend the chapter in two directions. For one, I have chosen to assimilate into the concept of research the results of naturalistic observations of clinically relevant behavior in culturally distinctive settings by anthropologists, psychiatrists, and others. Virtually the entire literature on the activities of shamans or native healers rests on the foundation of naturalistic reports. Second, a limited number of findings from general cross-cultural psychology will also be included, in addition to the results directly pertinent to clinical psychology. This extension is not without dangers in that it invariably involves inference bordering on speculation. This danger, however, will be reduced by specific indications, wherever they may be appropriate, of the tentative or unconfirmed nature of such inferences. The suggestion to the working clinicians is this: Apply these tentative principles in your work with your clients on the case level and monitor the impact of such application.

CONSTANCY AND VARIATION IN THE MANIFESTATION OF THE PSYCHOLOGICAL DISORDER SCHIZOPHRENIA

A series of international studies sponsored by the World Health Organization (Sartorius, Jablensky, Korten, & Ernberg, 1986; World Health Organization, 1973, 1979) have succeeded in demonstrating the existence of a number of characteristic symptoms of schizophrenia at nine culturally very different locations. In the first study in this series (World Health Organization, 1973), a set of nine such symptoms were identified: restricted affect, poor insight, thinking aloud, poor rapport, incoherent speech, unrealistic information, and widespread, bizarre, and/or nihilistic (i.e., pertaining to nothingness) delusions (Carpenter, Strauss, & Bartko, 1973). The international research team also identified three symptoms that were atypical for schizophrenia. These were waking early, depressed facial features, and expression of elation. The nine countries included in this investigation were carefully chosen to represent a maximum of possible contrasts in political systems, degree of economic development, cultural tradition, and location. In alphabetical order, the nations included were China (Taiwan), Colombia, Czechoslovakia, Denmark, India, Nigeria, the Soviet Union, the United Kingdom, and the United States.

In the more recent phases of this research (World Health Organization, 1979), the existence of this core syndrome was confirmed and its presence at all of the nine research locations was extensively corroborated. These reports, however, also brought into focus a number of significant differences in the course of this disorder at the several research centers. Moreover, a number of unexpected interactions between culture and the other relevant prognostic indicators were identified.

Let me briefly focus on two such findings. Upon follow-up, the prognosis of schizophrenia was found to differ in a somewhat counterintuitive manner: Patients in the poorer and less developed countries recovered more rapidly and in higher proportions than their counterparts in such prosperous and economically developed nations as the United States, the United Kingdom, and Denmark. Cooper and Sartorius (1977) tried to explain this unexpected result. They concluded post hoc that schizophrenia, with its bizarre and autistic features, fits especially poorly into the modern style of life of industrialized countries, organized into nuclear family units and governed by the clock, the machine, and now increasingly by the computer. This characterization stands in contrast to the traditional preindustrial social order in which the extended family was the typical unit. Under such circumstances, a modest slot could be found for the partially disabled schizophrenic family members, and the standards of acceptability for their behavior were liberal. Cooper and Sartorius speculated that such a situation is more likely to occur in developing than in the developed countries.

Modernization then may be a mixed blessing as far as the prognosis of schizophrenics and other chronic patients are concerned. Torrey (1980) greatly extended Cooper and Sartorius's thesis. In the process, he revived the old and controversial idea that schizophrenia and the advent of modern, technologically developed, and complex culture are connected. On the basis of the available historical evidence, he contends that the earliest clinical descriptions of schizophrenia are only 400 years old. Moreover, he maintains, on the basis of the available historical data, that the incidence of schizophrenia in Europe and North America rose dramatically in the nineteenth century, that is, during a rapid period of industrialization and modernization. His argument is further supported by the absence of observed cases of schizophrenia, or its low rate of occurrence in small, traditional, and non-Western cultures. Torrey does not claim that schizophrenia is unique to the modern West, but he asserts that a strong relationship exists between worldwide modernization and the increase in rates of schizophrenia to their current, reasonably constant level in the developed and industrialized countries of the world.

Even though the World Health Organization's research on schizophrenia was a unique and impressive undertaking, with large numbers of subjects, carefully standardized measures, and intensive and sophisticated analyses, it should be kept in mind that its widely publicized conclusions about the better prognosis of schizophrenia in the Third World rest on only three developing countries. Do India, Nigeria, and Colombia adequately represent this major proportion of humanity? It is possible to remain skeptical, pending further extension of these findings.

The other finding of the World Health Organization's follow-up investigation is equally surprising. It is well established in the economically prosperous and advanced West that higher occupational and educational status is positively related to favorable prognosis in schizophrenia as well as in other disorders. The results of the World Health Organization research run counter to this trend. Again, in both India and Nigeria, high occupational and educational indicators were predictive of poor prognosis for schizophrenia. They may represent the incompatibility of high social status in these two Third World locations with "fitting in" at a reduced level of functioning, as Cooper and Sartorius emphasized in their explanation. The alternative interpretation is that only extremely disturbed persons of formerly high status would be found in the public psychiatric hospitals of the Third World. Such individuals would have poor prognosis not because of their high status but because of the seriousness and intensity of their disturbance. It may be worth recalling that the earlier review of the relationship of social status and psychiatric disorder by Dohrenwend and Dohrenwend (1969) did not establish such a reversal of the worldwide trend whereby poor and disadvantaged people were selectively susceptible to serious psychological disturbance. It is true that the Dohrenwends based their conclusions primarily on epidemiological data from Western and other developed countries, such as Japan. However, some non-Western data from developing nations were included in their survey.

The most recent report of the World Health Organization's series of projects (Sartorius et al., 1986) was based on the intensive study of 1,300 schizophrenics in Colombia, Denmark, Great Britain, India, Japan, and two U.S. research centers located in Rochester, New York, and in Honolulu, Hawaii, respectively. The results of this phase of research further highlighted both the constancy and the variability of schizophrenia across cultures. The existence of the core syndrome was, once again, replicated at all sites of the study, but there was a much higher proportion of undifferentiated and catatonic schizophrenia reported in the developing countries. These may well be short-term states with a relatively benign prognosis, by comparison with the paranoid and related manifestations prevalent among schizophrenics in developed countries of the East and West.

As such, the findings from the series of World Health Organization projects join a multitude of reports in the literature on cultural variations in symptoms of schizophrenia. Mutism and immobility as well as regressive, childish behavior, the hallmarks of catatonic and disorganized or hebephrenic schizophrenia, have by this time become rare in the West; they continue to be prominent in many locations of the developing world. Major variations in schizophrenic symptomatology have been reported that point to more crystallized, specific, cognitive symptoms in the Western World and more global confusional states in various non-Western locations (Draguns, 1980, in press; Murphy, 1982). Leff (1981) has introduced the concept of emotional differentiation in order to make sense of these cultural differences. According to him, diffuse emotional expression in which anger, depression, and anxiety are confounded prevails in traditional cultures. To quote Leff's (1981, p. 72) own words:

Emotions are important in determining the choice of action in relationships, there is also a restriction on the possibility of consciously experiencing a variety of emotions. In traditional societies, where relationships are more or less stereotyped, emotions remain unexplored and undifferentiated. As a society moves from the traditional to the modern roles on the features enumerated above, individuals become more important than the roles they perform, freedom of action in relationships increases, and a variety of emotions begins to be explored in the context of relationships with others. The unique qualities of the individual become prized and introspection consequently flourishes.

The effect of these profound changes in emotional expression is to shift them from the somatic to the psychological mode and to increase differentiation between emotions.

There remains the question of the antecedents of schizophrenia from the cross-cultural perspective. As is well known, there has been a shift in the prevailing professional opinion about the origins of schizophrenia in recent years. No longer is there a consensus that schizophrenia is a response to pathogenic socialization in the family. The focus has shifted to its likely biological sources and courses. Nonetheless, the social roots of schizophrenia, within and outside the family, remain worthwhile and promising objects of exploration, and it is unlikely that the early environment of schizophrenics is irrelevant to their subsequent adaptation.

In the cross-cultural arena, there have been studies of such early influences, which Sanua (1980) has thoroughly reviewed. He concluded that it is premature to dismiss family influences as irrelevant to the development of schizophrenia in adults and children. Ammar and Ledjri (1972), in Tunisia, and Erichsen (1973), in Germany, focused on the role of the remote, authoritarian, and cold father in the development of schizophrenia in their offspring. These findings were based on intensive clinical observations rather than on systematic cross-cultural comparison with the use of comparable objective measures. Therefore, they constitute the point of departure, but not the end of the trail, for cross-cultural research in this area. Unanswered questions remain: Is the father's pathogenic influence rooted in his authority and power in historically authoritarian, patriarchal, and masculine cultures? Is it inherent in the behavior of the parent or in the eye of the psychiatric observer? Sanua's conceptualization, however, remains family centered, although he does not restrict himself to the limited number of supposedly pathogenic intrafamily interactions that loom large in the Western clinical literature.

Murphy (1982) broke new ground in this area by extending his sights beyond the family. According to Murphy, schizophrenia is fostered by an individual's confrontation with ambiguous, conflicting, or otherwise complex information. Such confrontation, he contends, is more likely to occur in some cultures than in others. Specifically, he concentrated his sights upon two examples: Western Ireland and the Karst region of Croatia in the Northwestern portion of Yugoslavia. Both of these locations are known for a high incidence of schizophrenia and a high rate of emigration. In Murphy's view, these two phenomena are connected, and the "missing link" between them is the prominence of mutually contradictory or at least confusing messages to which members of these cultures are typically exposed. In Murphy's (1982, p. 70) words, "a great many individuals must from childhood have been struggling with the almost impossible task of retaining the mother culture and the family attachments, while striving for material advantages comparable to those obtainable overseas." The author of these ideas is, however, the first to admit that such ideas must remain merely conjecture until ways are found for testing them.

What is the import of all of these findings for the practicing mental health professional or for a student in these fields? I would contend that the available research data emphasize the occurrence of schizophrenia in a wide variety of very different cultures around the world.

The worldwide distribution of schizophrenia and the demonstration of its common core in nine very different cultural settings strongly point to the deep roots of this condition regardless of the milieu in which it occurs. These findings are difficult to reconcile with the formulations of such radical theorists as Szasz and Laing, who see in schizophrenia the result of role-playing and personal choice or regard it as an expression of social and political rebellion against intolerable hypocrisy in the families of the schizophrenics and in the general culture. Although these notions are not widely accepted in the clinical community, the cross-cultural data make them less plausible, even though they do not refute them. Second, the cross-cultural data point to the significant if limited social plasticity of schizophrenia. Around its presumably humanly universal core, it does vary with cultural factors in its manifestation, course, and outcome. Such variation as has been uncovered does not represent the final word on the subject. Nonetheless, the available data suggest the nature of social milieus to which schizophrenics can more easily or successfully adjust while avoiding social withdrawal and distortion of reality.

Murphy (1982) has extended his revised double-bind hypothesis to highlight the importance of "simplicity" and clarity in planning rehabilitation for schizophrenics. Schizophrenic patients are easily confused by complex, contradictory, and ambiguous rules of living. They retreat from situations in which such rules are formulated and applied to their socially unshared and arbitrary personal world. Conversely, clarity, explicitness, sincerity, and simplicity of such rules makes their retreat into the subjective reality of their own creation less likely. Finally, Murphy's extended hypothesis on unresolved contradictions among widely held social values and goals, reproduced above, deserves to be more widely disseminated among working clinicians. Even though it is admittedly based on very limited data, its merit is to invite clinicians to extend their sights beyond the family in order to identify social influences that may not cause schizophrenia but foster it or make its occurrence less likely. On the most general plane, the available findings should help the practitioner to acquire a more balanced view of schizophrenia beyond the two extremes of viewing it as a disorder unrelated to social factors or, conversely, determined entirely by them.

AFFECTIVE DISORDERS, MAINLY DEPRESSION

In the case of depression, the point of departure is another international study sponsored by the World Health Organization. More recently initiated and somewhat more modest in scope, it also points to a common foundation of depressive experience in very different cultural settings. The two available reports on this project (Jablensky, Sartorius, Gulbinat, & Ernberg, 1981; World Health Organization, 1983) have identified these common elements in four different countries: Iran, Japan, Canada, and Switzerland. The common elements are sad affect, loss of enjoyment, anxiety, tension, lack of energy, loss of interest, inability to concentrate, and ideas of insufficiency, inadequacy, and worthlessness. These results, based on coordinated operations and equivalent symptom scales, are generally compatible with the findings of an earlier and preliminary mail survey of practicing psychiatrists in over 30 countries in all parts of the world by Murphy, Wittkower, and Chance (1967). These investigators found that the more cross-culturally constant manifestations of depression included loss of sexual interest, loss of appetite, weight reduction, fatigue, and self-accusatory ideas. Murphy, Wittkower, and Chance, however, failed to come up with as clear-cut a pattern of universals. Thus they reported that, in nine countries, all of them non-Western, the above array of symptoms was not present. Instead, the mode of expression of depression in those locations tended to be through agitation, ideas of influence, and partial mutism.

These findings join a large number of descriptive reports, at various degrees of thoroughness and objectivity, of non-Western settings: Africa south of the Sahara, the Middle East, South and East Asia, and the islands of the Pacific. The reviews by Marsella (1980) and Marsella, Sartorius, Jablensky, and Fenton (1985) document two phases in the description of depressive manifestations outside the Euro-American region. Initially, blanket and extreme statements were made to the effect that depression is unknown in Africa south of the Sahara, and similar assertions were made about other regions. The more recent and empirically and methodologically more solid reports back away from the older absolutist conclusions. Rather, two general trends have been identified by the reviewers of the evidence. First, rates of depression are probably substantially lower in Africa and the various regions of Asia than they are in the countries of Western Europe and North America. Qualifiers must, however, be inserted into this statement because of the major methodological difficulties in comparing the incidence of depression across cultures. These complications are especially prominent in deciding where to draw the line, on a cross-culturally constant basis, on the periphery of depression. What are the minimal necessary manifestations of depression for it to be diagnosed, in hospital or community settings, anywhere in the world? This question has proved to be more difficult to answer in the case of depression than in the case of schizophrenia.

Second, on closer analysis, the earlier statements on the alleged absence of depression in such places as Western Africa, India, or Thailand have been decisively refuted. Careful standardized observations and sensitive clinical exploration have revealed that depression is indeed present in all of these places but is differently and in some cases less directly and obtrusively expressed. Rates of reported depression rise with Westernization and, in fact, there may be prestige attached in the formerly colonial countries of Africa and perhaps elsewhere to patients reporting depressive experiences and to professionals noting them (see Prince, 1968). For better or worse, a positive value is attached by many mental health professionals to internalizing psychological disturbance rather than expressing it externally, through overt action. Apparently, this evaluation has spread to a lot of people around the world, including potential or actual patients, some of whom may selectively perceive and communicate their depressive experiences.

Over and above this contemporary trend, affecting the most modernized segments of the African population, depression in the various non-Western settings tends to be differently expressed and may easily escape detection by a person from an alien culture. This difference above all is inherent in the prominence of the vegetative symptoms of depression, as exemplified by the loss of appetite, insomnia, inability to experience sexual pleasure and to enjoy formerly pleasurable activities, and constant lassitude or fatigue, in the absence of any prior expenditure of physical or mental effort. Conversely, what is absent or at least not prominent in depression in West Africa and, possibly, other non-Western cultures is the experience of guilt, especially in its most direct and extreme forms (Diop, 1967). Even when it occurs, it is either isolated or projected in the form of self-accusatory ideas. These findings potentially provide an important corrective to Western-based ideas about the basic nature of depression. In the several psychodynamic formulations going back to Freud's own writings on melancholia, the experience of unrealistic and exaggerated guilt was considered a cornerstone.

Modern data from around the world cast doubt on the central role of guilt in depressive experience and shift the focus to its psychophysiological substrate, which may be more directly influenced by norepinephrine depletion and other likely biological processes in major depression. Another aspect of the accumulated observations from other cultures brings to the fore the cross-cultural plasticity of depressive experience, especially in relation to using bodily distress as an avenue for its expression. Kleinman's (1982) research in Mainland China demonstrates that somatization served as a typical channel of expression and as a basic component of depressive experience. *Somatization* refers to the reporting of psychological problems in terms of bodily symptoms such as headaches, back problems, and stomach ailments. For instance, the Chinese rarely complain, especially to medical and mental health professionals, of feeling sad or depressed. Rather, they refer in these communications to the body as the medium of their distress. In China, as well as in many other cultures, somatization serves as the channel of communication for the experience of helplessness and even despair, as a culturally sanctioned and generally understood cry for help. (See Ilola, this volume, for a discussion of somatization.)

Somatization, however, is also used by many Western patients or clients (see Kirmayer, 1984) even though it is not highly valued within the mental health community or among the sophisticated and well-informed segments of the American population. Rather, it is associated in this country with patients possessing a limited level of education, low occupational status, and little readiness to engage in psychological self-exploration. Such patients remain on the fringes of the therapy-oriented portions of the mental health establishment while they are only marginally and grudgingly accepted by the biomedical professional community.

Antecedents

The antecedents of depression in the lifetime experience of individuals have received relatively little study even in the Euro-American cultural milieu. It is, therefore, not surprising that this work has been very sparingly extended to other cultures. Recent work by Perris, Maj, Perris, and Eisemann (1985) in Sweden has identified the socialization pattern of loveless control (retrospectively reported by children about their parents) as a cross-culturally constant factor in the early experience of depressives. So far, this research has been conducted in several countries of Western Europe, from Sweden to Italy. Its extension beyond that region will show whether it is sufficiently robust to show up in a wider range of cultures.

On a more speculative plane, statements have been made on the relationship of the experience of guilt to the advent of individualism, traced in Western Europe to the seventeenth century (Murphy, 1978). Within this formulation, depressive patients are not expected to experience prominent feelings of guilt unless four conditions are met: (a) internal attributions for the experience of pleasure and its opposite; (b) predictability of the operation of external forces in the environment; (c) predictability and self-control of one's own behavior; and (d) separation of mind and body as two distinct and possibly coequal agencies. This formulation anticipates the revised attribution theory of learned helplessness, which was proposed by Abramson, Seligman, and Teasdale (1980). Depressed patients are in the habit of making self-depreciating statements; they also make pessimistic statements about the prospect of help from others and are discouraged about the future (see the treatment of self-attributions by Sinha, this volume). The experience of depression in the absence of crystallized individual identity was brought forth in the subtle phenomenological analysis of Japanese depressive patients by Kimura (1965). These persons were not incapable of guilt, but, by comparison with German patients, attached it to specific acts and transgressions, fancied or real, rather than to violations of abstract moral principles. Moreover, they generally experienced themselves in relation to various interpersonal transactions rather than as autonomous individuals with a stable and permanent sense of self.

Recognizing Depression

In the light of the preceding considerations, one can conclude that the observation of depression in cultural settings other than one's own is a subtle process, subject to a great many potential biases and distortions. Psychiatrists during the colonial era in Africa and elsewhere failed to notice depression among their native clients and rushed into print to report its absence in African cultures. This experience has been repeated in psychiatrists' and psychologists' offices in the pluralistic cultural settings of this country and elsewhere. De Hoyos and De Hoyos (1965) showed that middle-class clinicians had a high threshold for recognizing depression in their Black clients, whereas they were quick to diagnose them as schizophrenic on the basis of the apparent strangeness or bizarreness of their symptoms. Another relevant finding comes from Pennsylvania and pertains to the Amish, a fundamentalist Protestant sect whose members have chosen to separate themselves from the cultural mainstream in order to preserve their preindustrial rural life-style. The Amish were studied in a genetically oriented project. An incidental finding of this investigation (Egeland, Hofstetter, & Eshleman, 1983) was the high rate of misdiagnosis of many manic-depressive Amish patients as schizophrenic. Apparently, the social deviance of the Amish and the idiosyncratic manner in which they expressed their disturbance had a multiplicative effect in the local diagnostician's minds. The result was that they assigned these doubly different people, on the basis of their culture and their disorder, to the extreme category of disturbance, that is, schizophrenia.

Depression—and in light of this research project mania as well—as it is experienced by members of culturally distinct groups is easy to miss for psychiatrists from the American cultural mainstream. Apparently, depression is primarily an internal, inconspicuous, and unobtrusive psychological state that is communicated by means of subtle, culturally conditioned signs. As the phenomenological investigators of depression have discovered, communication of depressive experience becomes a difficult undertaking, and the results of these attempts are easy to miss across the cultural gulf. The tenuous contact between the therapist, counselor, or interviewer and the depressive patient may be but a special case of the difficulty that occurs whenever depression is detected across a major social gulf. The well-known underdiagnosis of depression in the aged, the historic reluctance of the mental health community to admit the possibility of depression in children, and the low rates of diagnosed depression among lower-class patients may represent other instances of this trend.

Practical Guidelines

Therefore, the following conclusions are of practical importance for rendering mental health services. First, guilt may not be as central to depression as many clinicians believe. Especially in settings where individualism is not as developed as in the majority cultures of the United States and Canada, depression may be experienced even though guilt feelings are absent. Second, depression may assume many guises of which bodily distress is one. Third, mental health professionals should guard against the tendency to overlook depression in, and promiscuously attributing schizophrenia and other conspicuous and extreme disorders to, patients whose self-presentation and communication of distress are different from those that are culturally sanctioned. Empathy is probably the clinician's best tool in combating these tendencies, even though it is difficult to preserve it in the face of the strange and distracting cultural trappings of a patient's appearance and demeanor.

INTERIM CONCLUSIONS

At the highest level of abstraction, the above findings may be explained on the basis of variations in social distance. Social distance is increased with the width of the cultural gulf. Across such a gulf, conspicuous and dramatic symptoms of psychological disturbance are readily noticed. The subtler manifestations of distress, however, are often overlooked. This is especially true when these disturbances refer to subjective states that are inherently difficult to communicate. Such difficulty is increased as the communication is made to a person markedly different in age, gender, appearance, and social background. The clinician's prized tool for bridging these gaps in communication is empathy, and empathy may not travel well across the cultural gulf (see Draguns, 1973). The ideal for a clinician working with a culturally diverse clientele is to combine personal sensitivity with cross-cultural competence and to develop the ability to adapt quickly and realistically to new and different cultural settings (see the chapter by Bhawuk, this volume).

Cross-cultural research has amply demonstrated that the two most serious psychological disorders exist in all regions of the world and in very different cultures. Moreover, there is a recognizable, virtually identical, core of symptoms present in these two conditions at widely different sites and diverse cultures. Around this core, however, there are manifestations that can be meaningfully traced to the characteristics of the milieus in which they occur. These conclusions lend no comfort to the two extreme positions of universalism and cultural relativism. No, schizophrenia and depression are not exactly the same the world over. No, each culture does not create its own distinct patterns of abnormal behavior. Therefore, it behooves clinicians to consider culture in rendering their services. The more specific implications of this position have been spelled out above.

CULTURAL FACTORS IN ASSESSMENT

Lonner's chapter, which is devoted to psychological tests, makes a systematic consideration of testing and assessment issues unnecessary here. However, his coverage should be supplemented by briefly addressing a number of problems in the use of projective tests and inventories. The general message of this section is that the various statements on the useless and misleading nature of the major tools and formats of assessment with culturally different persons are greatly exaggerated. It is true that ample documentation exists on the many pitfalls and errors in the applications of psychiatric diagnosis across culture lines.

One of the most thorough and thoughtful studies on this subject was contributed by Cheetham and Griffiths (1981) in South Africa. These authors substantiated a high rate of errors by White psychiatrists in diagnosing schizophrenia in Black and Indian patients. Moreover, they traced these errors to their sources and suggested two workable correctives in the form of structured, objective, and standardized interviews and increased cultural sensitivity and sophistication by the White diagnosticians. Lindzey (1961) pinpointed the complexities of exporting projective techniques beyond the cultures of their origin and using them to diagnose individuals and cultures alike. This contribution effectively stopped the cross-cultural abuses and misuses of projective techniques, especially the Rorschach. In the process, research with the inkblot test or of other kinds of projective techniques by anthropologists and other cultural investigators virtually ceased in the English-speaking world. Surely this is not what Lindzey intended! His very reasonable suggestion was that within-culture norms be obtained before any test be used to describe the prevailing personality characteristics within a culture. He proceeded from the null hypothesis and was not prepared to assume that interpretive rules and principles would be applicable beyond the cultural frontiers in the absence of appropriate research.

Work in Francophone countries with the use of projective tests continued despite Lindzey's warnings (Delpech, 1971) and some of it has reached a high level of methodological and statistical sophistication. Along similar lines, the validation of the Holtzman inkblot test has been pursued on a worldwide basis. A by-product of this effort has been the recognition that test norms across cultures and countries are not as different as one might have supposed. Moreover, the same rules of interpretation have been applied in several countries and have produced very similar validity coefficients. All of these considerations are compatible with De Vos's (1976) assertion that projective tests are useful for psychological diagnosis transculturally. In developing his argument, De Vos proceeds from three cultural universals: the existence of organically based mental illness and its disruptive cognitive effects, the consistency of a social and cognitive maturational process during childhood and adolescence, and the universality of altered states of consciousness. These three characteristics should be possible to assess by means of projective tests such as the Rorschach regardless of cultural context. To this end, however, these characteristics should be separated from the cultural influences that shape and determine the patterns of social adaptation.

As De Vos (1976, p. 298) put it, "Psychological testing can be used cross-culturally. It can help us gain a glimpse into the personality structure of particular individuals, and by so doing it helps us sort out the essential differences between observable role behavior and underlying personality." These strands of evidence and conceptualization prompt me to suggest that the projective techniques be given a new lease on life as an *auxiliary* tool of cross-cultural research on clinical problems. Individual clinicians and investigators need not hold themselves back from including these techniques in their armamentarium of tests for use with culturally different clients, provided they do not forget about their cultural characteristics. That this kind of research can be useful is attested by a recent comparison by Suzuki, Peters, Weibender, and Gillespie (1987) of American and Japanese schizophrenics by means of the Rorschach. American schizophrenics were found to proceed from detail to whole responses; the opposite sequence was exhibited by their Japanese counterparts. Japanese patients tended to express their symptoms directly, whereas the Americans exercised more control over them and relied on repression in the process. Finally, the Japanese responses were on the whole more socially conforming then those of the Americans. These authors interpreted their data conservatively as indications of differences in handling impulses, conforming socially, and organizing the perceptual world. In Ireland, Scheper-Hughes (1979) was able to uncover the specific sources of guilt in her schizophrenic subjects by means of the TAT. In her words:

> Although the tendency to guilt-feelings is free floating and runs through all of the T.A.T. responses, three situations seem to be particularly guilt-provoking: all aspects of sexual behavior; failure to live up to mother's expectations (i.e., the failure and incompetency themes) and . . . negligence with regard to "old people." (Scheper-Hughes, 1979, p. 176)

With personality inventories, as exemplified by the Minnesota Multiphasic Personality Inventory (MMPI), the picture is somewhat similar. Gynther (1972) warned against applying White norms to MMPIs administered to Blacks, and these warnings have been widely heeded. The new definitive review by Greene (1987) of all the studies done with the major minority groups in the United States (Blacks, Hispanics, Native Americans, and Asian Americans) by means of the MMPI yields a somewhat more complex picture. Greene was able to show that there were virtually no main effects in the comparison of majority and minority subjects by the MMPI. In other words, the effects of minority status were limited to a clinical or demographic category and, on occasion, these effects were in the opposite directions. In any case, the effects were typically moderate and often slight. Greene's results do not argue for discarding the MMPI from use with minority subjects nor do they indicate the need for special minority norms. The MMPI, moreover, has exhibited considerable robustness in its numerous translations and adaptations that have been used around the world (Butcher & Pancheri, 1976). Basically, the same patterns of elevation were associated with the same diagnostic categories regardless of site. Moreover, very few MMPI items were found inapplicable or in need of major modification. Just as there is no need for an emic diagnostic grid, there is no justification for constructing the entire range of psychological tests starting from scratch in each culture. Of course, there is no arguing against constructing emic measures of projective or interview variety based on indigenous concepts (see Kim, this volume).

CROSSING CULTURES IN PSYCHOTHERAPY

In the available space, I shall restrict myself to the consideration of a few selected issues. First, what are the universals of psychotherapy in light of the relevant observations from around the world? Second, and of more practical relevance, must therapists and clients be matched in cultural background? Third, do members of certain cultural groups prefer directive intervention? Fourth, and somewhat speculatively, how are cultural characteristics reflected in therapeutic orientation, practice, and technique?

In reference to the first question, it may be useful to start out by taking a quick look at the modus operandi of the shamans and other indigenous healers in a variety of traditional non-Western cultures. These very different psychotherapists have been observed to achieve positive results with psychological and psychosomatic conditions by means of very different ministrations from those dispensed by modern Western therapists. Chants, dances, altered states of consciousness, and magic interventions—apparent or real—loom large in their interventions. Yet Torrey (1986) and others have been able to discern common elements in these seemingly alien techniques and the *methods* of modern psychotherapists, in the restricted sense of the word. What both kinds of therapists provide, Torrey contends, is a culturally plausible explanation for both the illness and the cure. Moreover, they are invested with the trappings of status and expertise, and they convert this status into authoritative suggestions for the alleviation of suffering and the removal of disability. A frame of reference shared by the therapist and patient is essential for bringing about these desired effects. One might add that the treatments should occur at a time and place discontinuous from the client's routine activities (Draguns, 1975). The fascination with native healers and their techniques has led to the incorporation of their services into community-oriented psychological intervention programs for various culturally distinct populations.

Jilek and Jilek-Aal (1978) have described such a collaboration with Salish Indian healers in Western Canada in which the cultural and therapeutic experience of these local specialists was effectively utilized. On the whole, however, there have been few successful blendings of indigenous and Western therapy traditions. In fact, the interest in shamans as indigenous psychotherapists has abated somewhat in recent years. Scharfetter (1985) has raised the question whether shamans are relics of disappearing culture, and whether their techniques are relevant to the contemporary clientele. The limits of shamans' effectiveness have not been established nor has a model been produced that would account for their positive results in interpersonal, intrapsychic, or physiological terms.

Within modern pluralistic cultures, must therapists and clients from the same culture be matched? The available research, mostly with dyads involving Black clients, does not substantiate a blanket preference for cultural similarity between therapist and client. The determining factor appears to be the client's attitude toward his or her own cultural or ethnic group and the stand the client is prepared to take on such options as assimilation, separation, or integration (Parham & Helms, 1981; see also Berry, this volume). In some situations, in fact, an in-group therapist or counselor evokes suspicion and distrust, because of the perceived incompatibility between in-group membership and professional status (Acosta & Sheehan, 1976). However, such attitudes are relics of the past and will no doubt be overcome. In any case, cultural discrepancy between the client and the therapist is not an unbridgeable gulf, provided the transference and countertransference issues in such dyads (that affect the feelings the client and therapist have about each other) are honestly faced, worked through, and resolved.

The third issue to be discussed here is the alleged preference by minority clients for directive interventions and closed questions. Blacks, Hispanics, East Asians of various ethnic origins, Arabs, and others have all been said to want the therapist to play an expert role, to act decisively, and to demand nothing of the client but passive compliance. Folensbee, Draguns, and Danish (1986) conducted one of the few studies to test this alleged preference with groups of female Puerto Rican and Black students and majority controls. The results were complicated and did not fit the expectations of blanket preference for direction as opposed to facilitation. My own explanation of these findings is this: Preference for directive intervention is not intrinsic to the client's culture but the result of the urgency of clinical need in the absence of a personal relationship or a basis for forming one with the therapist. The consequence of this is to cast the therapist in the role of an impersonal, but knowledgeable and powerful, authority figure. In general, the conclusion is warranted that clients in psychotherapy are more alike than different in their expectations about the helping process. Their alleged preference for the therapist as an expert is really a compromise between the need for help and the reluctance to take personal risks in an unfamiliar and often intimidating situation.

A possible solution is to orient and train the culturally different client in the rationale of psychotherapy and to articulate the expectations that the therapist would have of the client and vice versa. Goldstein (1981) has applied this procedure with good effect across class lines to poor clients with limited education. The same procedure could be extended across ethnic, subcultural, and even geographic gulfs.

The fourth and last question posed at the beginning of this section now remains to be addressed. Psychotherapeutic approaches and techniques have been alleged to differ in their prevalence in, and degree of fit with, various cultures. Yet, hard data, in the form of results from systematic comparisons, have been almost entirely lacking. Moreover, there has been a paucity of theoretical formulations, largely because few relevant cultural characteristics, with which therapeutic preferences and activities might be correlated, have been proposed.

This gap, however, has been filled in recent years, among others by Hofstede (1980), who identified four major axes along which cultures can be placed and compared. These four dimensions were derived empirically by means of multivariate statistical techniques applied to opinion statements by the employees of a multinational company active in 50 countries and three more inclusive regions. These four dimensions are individualism-collectivism, power distance, uncertainty avoidance, and masculinity-femininity. Individualism and collectivism and masculinity-femininity were reviewed by Triandis (this volume). Briefly, *power distance* refers to the preferred psychological closeness subordinates desire in relations with their superiors. High power distance in an organization is indicated when subordinates exhibit extreme deference when interacting with superiors. *Uncertainty avoidance* refers to the number of rules and regulations that people use to make decisions. With low uncertainty avoidance, people are not constrained by rules and can take risks. The challenge is to apply these four cultural characteristics to a very different domain from the one in which they were derived, that of psychotherapeutic intervention. What follows then is, at best, informed speculation. It is based, on the one hand, on the knowledge of the panorama of the empirical findings on these four constructs and, on the other hand, on information on the characteristics of psychotherapy in various parts of the world. The model for this exercise is provided in the articles by Hofstede (1986), who extended the same fourfold scheme to cultural differences in teaching and learning, and Triandis, Brislin, and Hui (1988), who focused upon the implications of individualism-collectivism for cross-cultural training.

Individualistic cultures are expected to favor insight-oriented psychotherapy, with a relatively distant "professional" relationship between the psychotherapist and the client. Themes of guilt, alienation, and loneliness would be likely to be emphasized. By contrast, in collectivist cultures, a more expressive, relatively close, and personal relationship between the therapist and the client would prevail. It may be paternalistic and directive, modeled on the powerful yet benevolent father, or it may have prominent nurturant features of which the ideal caring mother would be the prototype. In any case, alleviation of suffering, rather than self-understanding, would be the principal objective of the therapeutic experience; self-understanding and self-actualization of the client would be relegated to positions of lower importance. Similarly, the expert role of the therapist would be deemphasized.

Cultures high in uncertainty reduction would stress the "scientific," for the most part, biological, explanations of mental disorder. A generally low value would be placed on psychotherapy; it would often be criticized as "messy," unpredictable, and inefficient. Among psychological techniques of intervention, behavior modification, with its specific objectives, would be preferred. Psychotherapy, if used, may be regarded as an avenue for the transmission of scientific and medical information to the client. Legal barriers against the practice of psychotherapy by nonmedical therapists would be likely to be high in uncertainty avoidance countries. Low uncertainty avoidance would foster variety and complexity in the psychotherapy scene, almost to the point of anarchy. Fads would be embraced easily and a multiplicity of incompletely monitored options would confront a person in search of psychotherapy.

Power distance in a culture would go hand in hand with the emphasis upon the expert role of the therapist. Such variables as personal growth, self-discovery, and insight development would remain minor and subsidiary considerations, much overshadowed by the roles of behavior change, compliance with the therapist's directions and/or values, and adjusting to social expectations. Egalitarian and confrontational techniques, such as those used in encounter groups and in other forms of group psychotherapy, would be discouraged. Low power distance would spawn (a) deemphasis upon expertise, professionalism, and the differentiation of therapist and client roles, along with (b) greater prevalence of self-improvement groups and patient movements.

In masculine cultures, the therapist would be expected to represent the society's side, as opposed to the aspirations of the client. Responsibility, conformity, and adjustment would be the key concepts and, as in individualistic cultures, there would be a lot of preoccupation with guilt in therapy. By contrast, in feminine cultures, the therapist would side with the individual against the society. Central values in therapy would be expressiveness, creativity, and empathy, and the focus would be upon anxiety rather than guilt.

CONCLUSIONS

In considering cultural influences upon abnormal behavior and the role of culture in the delivery of clinical services, this chapter has steered a middle course. The notion that the psychological disturbances of each culture are unique and different has been emphatically rejected, together with its corollary that each culture must develop its own unique set of mental health services. However, the opposing stance, which maintains that the psychopathology of all cultures is identical except for peripheral trappings, is similarly refuted as is the expectation of the universal applicability of assessment and therapeutic techniques developed at specific points in space and time, usually in the West. Rather, the findings recapitulated in this chapter suggest that the manifestations of psychological disorder are culturally shaped, yet comparable. The same psychological measures can be used, albeit judiciously and cautiously, in widely different cultures. The culturally characteristic modes of therapy may appear to be overwhelmingly different at first glance, yet they are found to contain some of the same active ingredients that account for the success of psychotherapy in other settings. Thus in abnormal behavior as in other areas of psychology, we recognize both the psychic unity of humanity and the cultural patterning that suffuses all human experience.

REFERENCES

Abramson, L. Y., Seligman, M. E. P., & Teasdale, J. D. (1980). Learned helplessness in humans: Critique and reformulation. *Journal of Abnormal Psychology, 87,* 49-74.

Acosta, F., & Sheehan, J. (1976). Preferences toward Mexican American and Anglo American psychotherapists. *Journal of Consulting and Clinical Psychology, 44,* 272-279.

American Psychiatric Association. (1987). *Diagnostic and statistical manual of mental disorders* (3rd rev. ed.). Washington, DC: Author.

Ammar, S., & Ledjri, H. (1972). *Les conditions familiales de développement de la schizophrénie.* Paris: Masson.

Butcher, J. N., & Pancheri, P. (1976). *Handbook of international MMPI research.* Minneapolis: University of Minnesota Press.

Carpenter, W. T., Strauss, J. S., & Bartko, J. J. (1973). Flexible system for the diagnosis of schizophrenia: Report from WHO. International Pilot Study of Schizophrenia. *Science, 179,* 1275-1278.

Cheetham, R. W. S., & Griffiths, J. A. (1981). Errors in the diagnosis of schizophrenia in Black and Indian patients. *South African Medical Journal, 59,* 71-75.

Cooper, J. E., & Sartorius, N. (1977). Cultural and temporal variations in schizophrenia. *British Journal of Psychiatry, 130,* 50-55.

De Hoyos, A., & De Hoyos, G. (1965). Symptomatology differentials between Negro and White schizophrenics. *International Journal of Social Psychiatry, 11,* 245-255.

Delpech, B. (1971). Les techniques projectives dans l'exploration de la personnalité socioculturelle [Projective techniques in the exploration of the sociocultural personality]. *Psychopathologie africaine, 7,* 239-284.

De Vos, G. A. (1976). The interrelationship of social and psychological structures in transcultural psychology. In W. P. Lebra (Ed.), *Culture-bound syndromes, ethnopsychiatry, and alternate therapies* (pp. 278-298). Honolulu: University Press of Hawaii.

Diop, M. (1967). La dépression chez le noir africain. *Psychopathologie africaine, 3,* 183-195.

Dohrenwend, B. P., & Dohrenwend, B. S. (1969). *Social status and psychological disorder.* New York: John Wiley.

Draguns, J. G. (1973). Comparison of psychopathology across cultures: Issues, findings, directions. *Journal of Cross-Cultural Psychology, 4,* 9-47.

Draguns, J. G. (1975). Resocialization into culture: The complexities of taking a worldwide view of psychotherapy. In R. W. Brislin, S. Bochner, & W. Lonner (Eds.), *Cross-cultural perspectives on learning.* New York: John Wiley.

Draguns, J. G. (1980). Disorders of clinical severity. In H. C. Triandis & J. G. Draguns (Eds.), *Handbook of cross-cultural psychology: Psychopathology* (Vol. 6, pp. 99-174). Boston: Allyn & Bacon.

Draguns, J. G. (in press). Normal and abnormal behavior in cross-cultural perspective: Toward specifying the nature of their relationship. In J. Berman (Ed.), *Nebraska Symposium on Motivation 1989.* Lincoln: University of Nebraska Press.

Egeland, J. A., Hofstetter, A. M., & Eshleman, S. K. (1983). Amish Study III. The impact of cultural factors on diagnosis of bipolar illness. *American Journal of Psychiatry, 140,* 67-71.

Erichsen, F. (1973). Der Vater der Schizophrenen: I and II. *Zeitschrift für Psychotherapie und Medizinische Psychologie, 23,* 130-140, 169-185.

Folensbee, R., Jr., Draguns, J. G., & Danish, S. J. (1986). Impact of two types of counselor intervention on Black American, Puerto Rican, and Anglo-American analogue clients. *Journal of Cross-Cultural Psychology, 33,* 446-453.

Goldstein, A. (1981). Expectancy effects in cross-cultural counseling. In A. J. Marsella & P. Pedersen (Eds.), *Cross-cultural counseling and psychotherapy: Foundations, evaluation, and cultural considerations.* Elmsford, NY: Pergamon.

Greene, R. L. (1987). Ethnicity and MMPI performance: A review. *Journal of Consulting and Clinical Psychology, 55,* 497-512.

Gynther, M. D. (1972). White norms and Black MMPI's: A prescription for discrimination? *Psychological Bulletin, 78,* 386-402.

Hofstede, G. (1980). *Culture's consequences: International differences in work-related values.* Beverly Hills, CA: Sage.

Hofstede, G. (1986). Cultural differences in teaching and learning. *International Journal of Intercultural Relations, 10,* 301-320.

Hostetler, J. A. (1980). *The Amish society* (3rd ed.). Baltimore: Johns Hopkins University Press.

Jablensky, A., Sartorius, N., Gulbinat, W., & Ernberg, G. (1981). Characteristics of depressive patients contacting psychiatric services in four cultures. *Acta Psychiatrica Scandinavica, 63,* 367-383.

Jilek, W., & Jilek-Aal, L. (1978). The psychiatrist and his shaman colleague: Cross-cultural collaboration with traditional American therapists. *Journal of Operational Psychiatry, 9,* 32-39.

Kimura, B. (1965). Vergleichende Untersuchungen über depressive Erkrankungen in Japan und Deutschland. *Fortschritte der Psychiatrie und Neurologie, 33,* 202-215.

Kirmayer, L. (1984). Culture, affect, and somatization. Parts I and II. *Transcultural Psychiatric Research Review, 21,* 159-188, 237-262.

Kleinman, A. (1982). Neurasthenia and depression: A study of somatization and culture in China. *Culture, Medicine, and Psychiatry, 6,* 117-190.

Leff, J. (1981). *Psychiatry around the globe.* New York: Marcel Dekker.

Lindzey, G. (1961). *Projective techniques and cross-cultural research.* New York: Appleton.

Marsella, A. J. (1980). Depressive experience and disorder across cultures. In H. C. Triandis & J. G. Draguns (Eds.), *Handbook of cross-cultural psychology: Vol. 6. Psychopathology* (pp. 237-289). Boston: Allyn & Bacon.

Marsella, A. J., Sartorius, N., Jablensky, A., & Fenton, F. R. (1985). Cross-cultural studies of depressive disorders. In A. Kleinman & B. Good (Eds.), *Culture and depression* (pp. 299-324). Berkeley: University of California Press.

Murphy, H. B. M. (1978). The advent of guilt feelings as a common depressive symptom: A historical comparison on two continents. *Psychiatry, 41,* 229-242.

Murphy, H. B. M. (1982). *Comparative psychiatry.* Berlin: Springer-Verlag.

Murphy, H. B. M., Wittkower, E. W., & Chance, N. A. (1967). Cross-cultural inquiry into the symptomatology of depression: A preliminary report. *International Journal of Psychiatry, 3,* 6-15.

Parham, T., & Helms, J. (1981). The influence of Black students' racial identity attitudes on preferences for counselor's race. *Journal of Counseling Psychology, 28,* 250-257.

Perris, C., Maj, M., Perris, H., & Eisemann, M. (1985). Preserved parental rearing behavior in unipolar and bipolar depressed patients. A verification study in an Italian sample. *Acta Psychiatrica Scandinavica, 72,* 172-175.

Prince, R. (1968). The changing picture of depression syndromes in Africa: Is it fact or diagnostic fashion? *Canadian Journal of African Studies, 1,* 177-192.

Sanua, V. D. (1980). Familial and sociocultural antecedents of psychopathology. In H. C. Triandis & J. G. Draguns (Eds.), *Handbook of cross-cultural psychology: Vol. 6. Psychopathology* (pp. 175-236). Boston: Allyn & Bacon.

Sartorius, N., Jablensky, A., Korten, A., & Ernberg, G. (1986). Early manifestation and first contact incidence of schizophrenia. *Psychological Medicine, 16,* 909-928.

Scharfetter, C. (1985). Der Schamane: Zeuge einer alten Kultur—wieder belebbar? *Schweizer Archiv der Neurologie und Psychiatrie, 136,* 81-95.

Scheper-Hughes, N. (1979). *Saints, scholars, and schizophrenics.* Berkeley: University of California Press.

Suzuki, A., Peters, L. Weibender, L., & Gillespie, J. (1987). Characteristics of American and Japanese schizophrenic patients elicited by the Rorschach technique and demographic data. *International Journal of Social Psychiatry, 33,* 50-55.

Torrey, E. F. (1980). *Schizophrenia and civilization.* New York: Jason Aronson.

Torrey, E. F. (1986). *Witchdoctors and psychiatrists: The common roots of psychotherapy and its future.* New York: Harper & Row.

Triandis, H. C., Brislin, R., & Hui, C. H. (1988). Cross-cultural training across the individualism-collectivism divide. *International Journal of Intercultural Relations, 12,* 269-289.

World Health Organization. (1973). *Report of the International Pilot Study of Schizophrenia.* Geneva: Author.

World Health Organization. (1979). *Schizophrenia: An international follow-up study.* New York: John Wiley.

World Health Organization. (1983). *Depressive disorders in different cultures: Report of the WHO collaborative study of standardized assessment of depressive disorders.* Geneva: Author.

15

CROSS-CULTURAL
ORIENTATION PROGRAMS

D. P. S. BHAWUK

World trade has grown from 51.4 billion U.S. dollars in 1948 to more than a trillion in 1980; world tourism has grown manyfold in the last five decades; and the numbers of diplomatic missions, multinational companies, and international students have grown more rapidly than anyone could ever have imagined. All this has increased the probability of a person from one country having extensive interaction with a person from another country. The economy of every country depends on how well its people interact with those of other countries, be it the all-powerful manufacturing countries or the not-so-powerful, tourism-dependent countries. In view of this, it has become mandatory for the human race to rise above parochialism and be able to understand the ways of people of other countries and other cultures.

With the growth of internationalism, there is also an increased possibility of finding people all over the globe who dress alike and are fluent in more than one foreign language. This, however, should not lead to the erroneous conclusion that their value systems are also alike. For instance, it is very common to find people speaking fluent English and wearing Western-style clothes in Asia. But this should not lead Westerners to assume that they can forget the underlying value differences of the Asians (see Triandis, this volume).

As a citizen of the Third World, I have experienced a growing trend toward preservation of indigenous culture in the form of national dress, food, work habits, and social structure. It is most unlikely that the human race would drop differences to become a homogeneous entity. This growing movement toward a search for national identity, and for its preservation, makes it obligatory on our part to relate to people from different countries and cultures effectively.

Aside from this growth of internationalism, there is not one nation in the world that does not have a minority group with a different culture. Big countries like the United States, the Soviet Union, China, and India are infested with ethnic problems that demand a cross-cultural understanding of every citizen of these countries. Even in a small country like Nepal, where a number of ethnic groups live together, intercultural interactions are unavoidable. Ethnic conflicts have tortured smaller countries like Sri Lanka in recent years, whereas a country like Singapore has prospered by integrating various ethnic groups.

What becomes apparent from the above is that, because of growing internationalism as well as the desire of various ethnic groups living in any one country to preserve their cultural identities, there is no way anyone can avoid cross-cultural interaction today or in times to come. In a comprehensive literature review of the problems in cross-cultural contact, Stening (1979) has noted that the chances of misunderstanding and conflict taking place in intercultural interaction is greater than in an interaction between people of the same group, and that these conflicts are very stressful to the people involved.

In addition to the possibility of negative effects, there is a positive side to cross-cultural interaction. Intercultural relationships accrue benefits to the interacting individuals that cannot be obtained in any other way (Brislin, 1983). Cross-cultural interaction provides an opportunity to get a handle on the abstract concept of culture and a firsthand experience with "cultural relativity"—that there are other ways of living equally correctly, rationally, and meaningfully.

If cross-cultural interaction has become important due to "cultural interdependence" (Triandis, 1977), if it is not easy to handle such interactions, and if it can benefit us in ways that no other experience can, then the importance of programs preparing people for these interactions can hardly be exaggerated.

WHAT IS A CROSS-CULTURAL ORIENTATION PROGRAM?

R. Michael Paige (1986, p. 2) has defined *cross-cultural orientation* in the following words: "Cross-cultural orientation refers to those intercultural programs that are designed to prepare specific groups of learners to reside in specific target cultures for specific purposes. This includes reentry into their own culture after sojourning abroad."

Goals of Cross-Cultural Orientation Programs

I think there are two ways to look at the goals of cross-cultural orientation: first, the *end goal,* or what it is that is expected of the trainee in the interaction situation *after* the program, and, second, the *immediate goal,* the expected behavioral change in the trainee that could be measured toward the end of the orientation program. There is a general agreement on the end goals, whereas the immediate goals are still a subject of personal opinion.

The ultimate goal of orientations is to make the interaction a success. Success can be measured by using the four-part criterion suggested by Brislin, Cushner, Cherrie, and Yong (1986). Success could be attributed only if all the four parts are achieved. The first part of the criterion of success is that the sojourners feel positive about their interaction experience. The positive feelings of the sojourners reflect that they were able to relate to the new culture effectively. The second part is that not only do sojourners have a positive feeling but the hosts also have a positive feeling about the interaction. It often happens that sojourners feel good but the hosts feel otherwise, especially when the sojourners have a status advantage over the hosts that prevents the hosts from expressing their feelings freely. For any interaction to be considered a success, the hosts must also think and feel positively about the interaction.

The third part of the criterion is that the mission of the sojourners or the purpose of the interaction is accomplished (Hawes & Kealey, 1981). Students, business people, diplomats, and health workers have different tasks to perform, and their effectiveness is often judged by a third person. Evaluation by the third person makes it an objective evaluation of the performance of the sojourners. This is an important criterion because there is a possibility that sojourners do everything agreeable to create positive feelings for themselves and the hosts but do not achieve their goals—the raison d'être of their sojourn. The fourth part of the criterion, the absence of visible or invisible symptoms of stress, means that, when the sojourners complete their assignments, they do not return with stress-related or psychosomatic problems. Cross-cultural interaction can take a long-term toll in the form of increased blood pressure, stress-related problems, and the like, and we argue that those who handle cross-cultural interaction effectively do not become excessively stressed.

The immediate goals of cross-cultural training should be to (a) provide an experience so that trainees can learn how to learn, (b) enable trainees to make isomorphic attributions, and (c) enable trainees to handle disconfirmed expectancies. Each of these goals is discussed below.

Learning How to Learn

The objective of all cross-cultural orientations should be to enable the trainees to actively use their knowledge and understanding in new situations and to learn for themselves. This concept has been discussed a number of times in the cross-cultural training literature (Albert, 1986; Brislin & Pedersen, 1976), often with reference to David Kolb's experiential learning model. Hence I think it is appropriate to discuss Kolb's model, which can also be called the model of "learning how to learn."

According to Kolb (1987), the experiential learning cycle consists of four processes: experiencing something concrete (background), reflecting over the experience (knowledge), conceptualizing abstract concepts learned from the experience (understanding), and actively experimenting with the new concepts learned (behavior). These four parts of the cycle can be repeated as trainees become more knowledgeable about a topic. Because concrete experiences are so affecting in cross-cultural encounters, the first of the four processes is often the starting point for new learning possibilities. I think Kolb's learning cycle can be best explained by using the following incident.

> Helen Connor had been working in a Japanese company involved in marketing cameras. She had been there for two years and was well-respected by her colleagues. In fact, she was so respected that she often was asked to work with new employees of the firm as these younger employees learned the ropes. One recent and young employee, Hideo Tanaka, was assigned to develop a marketing scheme for a new model of camera. He worked quite hard on it, but the scheme was not accepted by his superiors because of industrywide economic conditions. Helen Connor and Hideo Tanaka happened to be working at nearby desks when the news of the nonacceptance was transmitted from company executives. Hideo Tanaka said very little at that point. That evening, however, Helen and Hideo happened to be at the same bar. Hideo had been drinking and vigorously criticized his superiors at work. Helen concluded that Hideo was a very aggressive Japanese male and that she would have difficulty working with him again in the future. (Brislin et al., 1986, p. 166)

Helen, the sojourner in the incident, has a concrete, or *background*, experience from the past as to how people behave in the situation that is facing Hideo. She observes the situation in which Hideo complains about his superiors. She *reflects* on the situation in view of her background. She probably thinks that a bar is the wrong place to discuss office work with a colleague. She also perceives Japanese people as generally complying with their superiors and not complaining about their decisions. In view of these stereotypes, she would conclude that Hideo is an aggressive man. The *abstract conceptualization* would be that every man complaining about his superior is an aggressive man and is difficult to work with. Helen would use this concept in making decisions on how to behave with Japanese individuals. Her learning from this incident with Hideo has now become a part of her *concrete experience*, or background. What if Helen knew that many Japanese always do what Hideo did? The process would be the same but the conclusion reached would be different. Most likely she would conceptualize that she should not judge people's behavior by using one standard (her own from her own culture), that there are different acceptable ways of venting off complaints in different cultures. With this idea in mind, she would proceed with experimenting with her model and soon this concept would become a part of her background.

"Learning how to learn" can be looked upon as a "meta-goal" of training. *Meta-goal* refers to the essence of a learning process that the trainees take home after the exercise and use in other situations in the future. Relating it to Kolb's model, *meta-goals* refer to the "abstract conceptualization" that the trainees acquire in the learning process and actively use in future interactions.

Isomorphic attribution. Brislin et al. (1986) have identified 18 themes, part of which most orientation programs have tried to cover. With a close look at the themes, there are two that also relate to general competencies of well-prepared trainees: " isomorphic attribution" and "disconfirmed expectancies." I think that making isomorphic attributions and handling disconfirmed expectancies are the two competencies that cross-cultural orientation programs should try to impart to the trainees. Triandis (1975) suggests that, if we can make isomorphic attributions, we can eliminate the fundamental error in attribution. *Isomorphic* and *fundamental* are two technical terms that are frequently used when attributions about behavior are discussed. If people make an isomorphic attribution, this means they make the *same* judgment about behavior as do individuals in the other culture. People do not impose their viewpoint; rather, they interpret the behavior in the same way as do members of the other culture.

What is the *fundamental* error? Consider this situation. If I am a student and I do not do well on an examination, then I would say that the reason is *not* that I am a bad student, or that I do not understand the subject, but that the teacher is bad, the test was hard, or that it was not my day. But if other students did not do well on the examination, I would think they are bad students or that they do not work hard. This tendency to ascribe situational attributes for the cause in one's personal case and to ascribe personal traits for the cause in the case of others is termed the *fundamental attribution error* (Ross, 1977). If the outcome were positive, say, if I did well on the exam, then I would attribute traits to myself—I am good, hard working, and so on—whereas if the other students do well, then I would attribute situations to be the cause of their success—the exam was easy, the professor likes them, and so forth. Let us examine the incident discussed above to appreciate how attribution errors creep into cross-cultural interactions.

Hideo was drinking and vigorously criticizing his superiors. Helen's conclusion that Hideo was a very aggressive man is a trait judgment that Helen is making about him. She has missed the situational factor, that Japanese workers often vent their emotions in a bar after office hours. One of the objectives of cross-cultural orientation programs is to enable the trainees to make the same attribution as the hosts would in a given situation, that is, to enable them to make isomorphic attributions.

Disconfirmed expectancies. The trainees should be able to identify situations where their expectations are not being met and should be able to handle them without developing a negative stereotype that would prejudice their future interactions. For example, high officials coming from Asia expect a lot of deference from people at airports. However, they are treated like everyone else in many countries, for example, in the United States, and this leads to serious misunderstanding and to the development of negative feelings. What the high officials need to understand is that, in some countries like the United States, there is less deference shown to position. When compared with the respect these high officials receive in their own countries, behavior in the United States appears to be insufficient and disrespectful. Disconfirmed expectancies remain hidden behind many concepts such as time, space, work ethics, roles, learning styles, and so on, and cause problems during cross-cultural interaction.

CURRENT METHODS

Having discussed the goals of cross-cultural orientation programs, let us now look at the current methods employed in the field.

The University Model

Orientation programs that follow the approach to teaching and learning found in universities are said to use this model. This is perhaps the most economical of all methods. Typically, a trainer lectures to a group of trainees about different aspects of another culture. This method can provide an intellectual understanding of different aspects of cross-cultural interaction. This method is also perhaps the simplest to introduce. Any organization wanting to conduct an orientation program could approach a university to develop a course. Alternatively, people who have experience living in another culture could be invited to lecture those who need to move to another culture. On the surface, the disadvantage of this method is that it transfers knowledge on the cognitive level, which does not necessarily help sojourners in their interactions with the hosts. Harrison and Hopkins (1967) have discussed at length why the university model is not very effective for preparing people for assignments in other cultures. The following are the five major arguments against this model.

(1) Source of information. In the university model, the trainees receive all the information from the experts or from printed materials. In real-life situations, one has to develop one's own network for collecting information.

(2) Problem solving. In the classroom situation, the emphasis is on solving well-defined problems using well-developed methods. In real-life situations, the trainee has to define a problem and then find ways to solve it. The emphasis is not on finding the optimum solution but on finding a workable solution that is acceptable to the hosts.

(3) "Emotional muscle." In the classroom, people are trained to look at issues rationally, giving a backseat to emotions. In effect, trainees do not learn to handle emotions well; in other words, they do not develop "emotional muscle." In cross-cultural interactions, people need a lot of emotional resilience because personally held values are challenged and one often needs to behave in ways that can be disruptive to one's personal value systems.

(4) "Paper versus people." Harrison and Hopkins point out that trainees are evaluated on the basis of their written reports in the classroom situation, whereas in the actual encounter, success is measured in terms of how effective are the relationships that are established with the hosts. Trifonovitch (1973) calls it a changing of orientation from a paper orientation to people orientation.

(5) Communication. The classroom situation demands mastery of written and, to a lesser extent, oral communication. In cross-cultural interaction, one needs mastery of oral communication along with a good sense of nonverbal communication and active listening.

Harrison and Hopkins make a good case for goal divergence between the university model and the requirements of cross-cultural interaction. They recommend the experiential model as an alternative.

The Experiential Model

There are many variations of the experiential model. One such variation is the Area Simulation Model in which the training takes place at a site that simulates the target culture environmentally. If the training was to prepare people for life on remote Pacific Islands, trainees would be required to find their own food and fresh water, come up with their own entertainment, create a waste disposal system, and so forth. The strengths of this method include the following (Trifonovitch, 1973):

(1) Affective learning is emphasized and precedes cognitive learning. Arriving at solutions through "feeling" rather than facts is encouraged.

(2) Doing is emphasized as opposed to intellectualizing. The problem has to be discovered and then solved.

(3) This method starts by removing the familiar things that the trainees are normally used to and then creating situations that add to their frustration. By doing this, it is expected that the trainees would develop an understanding about the new environment, learn to cope with stress, and learn to adjust to new situations.

(4) The attitude of accepting the cultural barriers with understanding and then learning to work with the barriers is encouraged.

(5) Above all, the trainees are not allowed to depend on the trainers. The ability to handle problems independently is crucial. Dependence on the trainer is an unwanted outcome that many orientation programs produce. This method avoids this problem.

(6) This method provides the participants with the opportunity of testing themselves during the training. The trainees can drop out if they discover that they cannot handle the overseas assignment.

(7) This method also provides feedback to the trainees as to how they should change their behavior. Hence it is possible for the trainees to learn new behaviors.

The two criticisms of this method are that it is not possible to create another culture and that the simulation ignores social, political, interpersonal, and other aspects of a culture (Gudykunst & Hammer, 1983). I think the criticisms are misplaced. No simulation can or does try to re-create the real thing. Even the simulated aircraft used for training pilots can only do so much; for instance, depressurization can be simulated but the blowing away of a section of an airplane cannot be simulated. The impact of a blown-away section is, after all, depressurization. Similarly, the site for area simulation is selected to make certain points that could only be made in that place or a similar place. For instance, Trifonovitch (1973) selected Hawaii for training Americans

who were going to Pacific Island nations because he wanted to emphasize the difference between "land culture" and "sea culture." For instance, the site provided the opportunity to reduce the trainees' dependence on clocks, and they were able to guess the time of the day by
observing the sun, the tide, and the wind direction. Area simulation
should not even try to re-create the target culture in full because (a) this
can't be done, and (b) the choices the trainers make regarding what
to emphasize and deemphasize can lead to the building of incorrect
stereotypes.

Another variation of this model is the simulation game, which provides structured exercises. The games divide the participants into two
groups and require each group to learn the behaviors of a hypothetical
culture. Once the trainees have learned their roles, they interact with
one another. The interaction involves the trainees on the affective and
behavioral levels. In many ways, the trainees experience the feelings
they will have in another culture and emotions often run high. At the
end, the trainer debriefs the trainees and a discussion of "what happened" and "why" follows. Typically, cognition follows affect. One
advantage is that there is no way the trainees could build negative
stereotypes about any real culture. Another advantage is time. The game
takes from two to four hours depending on the number of trainees. Some
of the popular simulations are BAFA-BAFA (Shirts, 1973) and the Owl
and the Albatross (Gochenour, 1977). The interested reader should read
Beyond Experience (Batchelder & Warner, 1977).

Culture Assimilator

A culture assimilator is a self-administered, programmed culture
training manual containing about 100 critical incidents. Critical incidents capture experiences people are likely to have when interacting in
other cultures (e.g., the incident with Helen and Hideo presented earlier). Because the assimilator uses short incidents describing intercultural encounters, trainees can use culture assimilators in a number of
ways. The incidents can be used for role-playing by the trainees as well
as for generating group discussions. This method emphasizes attribution training and enables the trainees to make isomorphic attributions
(Triandis, 1975).

The evolution of culture assimilators is discussed in Triandis (1975)
and Albert (1983). Albert also discusses different types of culture-
specific assimilators. This method provides a solution to the problem
of the high cost of the area simulation method and is superior to the

university model or lecture method. It is one of the most researched methods, with positive research findings supporting its use. Culture assimilators are of two types: culture specific and culture general. The only known culture-general assimilator was developed by Brislin et al. (1986). Culture-specific assimilators have been in use for more than two decades now and are available for Thailand, Arab countries, Iran, Greece, Honduras, Latin American countries, and Mexico.

Assimilators known as "specific" are required for any pair of cultures and are designed to train the sojourner to interact with hosts from a specified culture. Another assimilator would be required if the host and sojourner were to exchange their roles. An assimilator is a collection of critical incidents. An incident describes a common occurrence, a conflicting or puzzling situation, and a situation with a possible solution (Fiedler, Mitchell, & Triandis, 1971). The first step to making an assimilator is the collection of critical incidents. Incidents can be collected by examining existing ethnographies and historical records or by analyzing the subjective cultures. Another way to collect incidents is to interview returning sojourners. The incidents must address the problems that the sojourners think are critical for success in the host culture. Let us look at an incident from the Greek culture assimilator to understand how critical incidents are used (from Fiedler et al., 1971, p. 97):

> Sharon Hartfield, a school teacher in Athens, was amazed at the questions that were asked her by Greeks whom she considered to be casual acquaintances. When she entered or left her apartment, people would ask her where she was going or where she had been. If she stopped to talk she was asked questions like, "How much do you make a month?" or "Where did you get that dress you are wearing?" She thought the Greeks were very rude.
>
> Why did the Greeks ask Sharon such "personal" questions?
>
> 1. The casual acquaintances were acting like friends do in Greece, although Sharon did not realize it.
>
> 2. The Greeks asked Sharon the questions in order to determine whether she belonged to the Greek Orthodox Church.
>
> 3. The Greeks were unhappy about the way in which she lived and they were trying to get Sharon to change her habits.
>
> 4. In Greece such questions are perfectly proper when asked of women, but improper when asked of men.

Participants read the incidents and the attributions and then select the response they think is the best. Explanations to each answer could be found on a separate page or all of them could be given together on the same page, as is done here.

1. You selected one. Correct. It is not improper for in-group members to ask these questions of one another. Furthermore, these questions reflect the fact that friendships (even casual ones) tend to be more intimate in Greece than in America. As a result, friends are generally free to ask questions which would seem too personal in America.

2. You selected two. No. This is not why the Greeks asked Sharon such questions. Remember, whether or not some information is personal depends upon the culture. In this case, the Greeks did not consider these questions too personal. Why? Try again.

3. You selected three. No. There was no information given to lead you to believe that the Greeks were unhappy with Sharon's way of living. The episode states that the Greeks were acquaintances of Sharon.

4. You selected four. No. Such questions are indeed proper under certain situations. However, sex has nothing to do with it. When are these questions proper? Try to apply what you have learned about proper behavior between friends in Greece. Was Sharon regarded as a friend by these Greeks?

When trainees use the assimilator as a programmed learning tool, they go on selecting until they find the correct response. In a classroom situation, the trainer could read the incident aloud to the trainees and then ask them to vote for each alternative. Those who vote for a response are then asked to explain why they thought it to be correct. Another variation is to ask the trainees to generate attributions and then to defend their positions. Incidents are extremely useful for generating group discussions and the trainees can also share their own related experience to make the discussion more interesting.

A culture-general assimilator is developed in much the same way as the culture-specific one as far as generating incidents and attributions are concerned. The difference lies in that incidents are collected from a number of pairs of cultures. Incidents should cover all possible dimensions on which differences between any two cultures could exist. Brislin et al. (1986) identified 18 such themes that incidents could address and built the culture-general assimilator around them. An example of an incident from this assimilator was presented to explain isomorphic attribution in an earlier section (pp. 328-329).

An important aspect of long-term assimilator training is to encourage participants to write incidents from their own experience. This not only increases their involvement but also increases their depth of understanding.

Kraemer's Cultural Self-Awareness Model

Kraemer's orientation material was developed for American trainees. He offers a set of videotapes that contain 138 episodes covering 21 themes (1973, 1974). The episodes are role-played by different actors with different hosts. The trainees are required to write the underlying theme of the episodes after watching them, and they are allowed to refer to the list of themes provided as part of the orientation package. A group discussion follows with the trainer.

Kraemer based his model on the assumption that sojourners can function in a host culture more effectively if they know their own culture better. It is reasonable to assume this because culture is like the fresh air we breathe and we do not think about it unless, like air in a polluted city, it is removed. Knowing our own culture helps us understand our own attributions. By knowing their own typical attributions, sojourners can program themselves to suspend judgment when interacting with hosts. The awareness also motivates sojourners to look for the hosts' cultural biases and to compare them with their own.

Role-Playing

I mentioned role-playing when discussing assimilators. Role-playing—a tool borrowed from traditional human relations training—is one of the most powerful tools available to any trainer. People take different parts in a critical incident and act them out, sometimes modifying their typical behavior when asked to role-play someone from a different cultural background. The case method is another tool that can be used in cross-cultural orientations. A very easy way to start discussion in a homogeneous group is to ask trainees to read reports about their own culture written by foreigners. People often cannot explain their own culture but find it very easy to evaluate outsiders' opinions about their own culture (Brislin & Holwill, 1977).

Let us look at an integrated orientation program developed by Gudykunst, Hammer, and Wiseman (1977). Their model consists of three parts: perspective training (P), interaction training (I), and context-specific training (C): They have called it PIC training. They suggest using the university model and experiential model in the first phase to generally sensitize the trainees about culture and cultural differences.

In the second phase of PIC, they suggest that trainees actually interact with hosts in structured situations so that they can apply their intercultural perspective acquired in the first phase and also practice intercultural communication. In the third phase, the authors suggest a detailed culture- and job-specific orientation. Role-playing, using incidents from culture assimilators, could be used. Some in-depth lecturing may also be necessary at this stage.

A TYPOLOGY OF ORIENTATION PROGRAMS

How can we classify existing orientation programs? What are the underlying models on which various programs are built that make them different from others? The typology of orientation programs could be developed by asking the fundamental question: How can we learn another culture?

The ideal way to learn another culture would be the way we learn about our own culture. How do we do that? The answer: by interacting with our own people from the time we are born. Of course, learning another culture this way would be a very lengthy and impractical method. There are many schools of thought as to how another culture should be learned. The first school of thought includes those who believe culture can be learned in a classroom by taking a course in a particular culture. The proponents of the experiential model suggest that the only way to learn another culture is through having real-life experience in a structured situation. The major difference between these two schools of thought lies in the level of involvement of trainees, and this also includes whether the trainees are involved at the cognitive level or at the affective and behavioral levels. In the experiential school, there are two groups. One believes in training people by providing an atmosphere similar to the target culture, and the second one uses a "game" (e.g., BAFA-BAFA) to sensitize people about the underpinnings of cultures, as discussed previously.

The attribution school suggests that the way to learn another culture is to learn to make isomorphic attributions (Triandis, 1975). The behaviorists think that we can learn another culture by observing the correct behaviors of people in another culture and practicing them (David, 1972). There are still others who argue that the way to learn another culture is through self-awareness—by knowing one's own culture, its value system, its behavior patterns, and the underlying reasons for behavior (Kraemer, 1974).

With the evolution of all these schools, another issue has evolved over the years—the issue of culture-general versus culture-specific training. Some believe that cultures can be learned only one at a time and that the only way to prepare people for cross-cultural interaction is to make them conversant with a target culture—this is the school of culture-specific training. Those of the culture-general school argue that it is possible to give some tools to people so that they can go to any culture and be able to achieve their goals without excessive stress.

The culture-general orientation is superior to the culture-specific orientation along the following predictable dimensions:

(1) The culture-general orientation prepares for "learning how to learn."
(2) It provides wider experience.
(3) It is easier to go from culture-general to culture-specific training than to go in the opposite direction.

I must hasten to add that there is no research finding to support the assertion that the culture-general has these benefits over the culture-specific method. The major criticism of this approach is that the trainees would be completely on their own in a new culture if they were to be given only this kind of orientation (Rhuly, 1976). I would argue that people trained to work independently would go and do some research on their own to prepare themselves for the particular culture, assuming that they have the time to do so. I do not think the other criticism, that culture-general training takes more time in preparing trainees, is valid. In any case, I am of the opinion that cross-cultural orientations cannot be done in a short time.

A culture-specific orientation can be significant to those people who are going for very important negotiations. In such cases, it would be important that one is impeccably conversant with the particular culture, and general awareness would not be enough. In situations where the sojourners are going to stay for two or more years, a focused culture-specific program may amount to creating other disadvantages like building unwanted stereotypes and rote learning of facts with the omission of underlying concepts. Others have also criticized the culture-specific approach along similar lines (Rhuly, 1976).

In view of the above, let us look at some of the typologies developed by researchers in this field. Triandis (1977) has suggested a seven-part classification on the basis of whether the emphasis of the orientation is culture specific or culture general and whether the focus is on cognition, affect, or behavior. A cross between culture specific and general on the one hand and cognition, affect, and behavior on the other gives six types and the seventh is Kraemer's self-awareness model. Gudykunst and Hammer (1983) have developed a four-part typology that distinguishes orientations on the basis of whether the method used is didactic or experiential and whether the content of the training is culture specific or culture general. Brislin (1989) has developed a comprehensive typology on the basis of trainee involvement (low, moderate, and high) and the objective of the orientation (cognitive, affective, and behavioral). This leads to nine cells, and different training methods can be placed in each.

Having argued that the goal of orientation programs should be to make a sojourner successful, I do not think there is only room for cognitive orientation programs. Also, to bring about any affective or behavioral change in a trainee, the program must involve the trainee at least moderately, though I prefer nothing short of high involvement. Hence I suggest a framework for classifying orientation programs that could be differentiated on three axes: trainee involvement varying from low to high, trainer involvement varying from low to high, and content of the orientation program varying from narrow focus to broad focus, that is, culture specific to culture general. This framework can be looked upon as an extension of that of Gudykunst and Hammer. I am suggesting that the didactic-experiential axis suggested by them be split into two axes—trainee involvement and trainer involvement—to avoid the apparent confusion that, if the student is involved highly, trainer involvement has to be low, which is false. In experiential exercises, trainers have to be completely involved for them to be able to debrief the trainees and to ensure that the underlying message of the exercise has been communicated. Because "trainee involvement" pretty much covers the "cognitive, affective, and behavioral aspects," I argue that trainees should be experientially involved. The framework also provides room for accommodating such programs as on-the-job orientations that have not been given sufficient consideration in the cross-cultural orientation literature.

Let us look at the framework (see Figure 15.1). I am looking at the eight points of the cube formed by the three axes—trainee involvement, trainer involvement, and cultural content. The points are at the low or high end of the axes. The low end of cultural content is culture specific (CS) and the high end is culture general (CG). I have also used numbers in parentheses—one for low and nine for high, one for CS and nine for CG. LOW, LOW, CS (1, 1, 1) means low trainee involvement, low trainer involvement, and culture specific.

LOW, LOW, CS (1, 1, 1). This point characterizes such orientation programs that are so brief in duration that there is only time to talk about

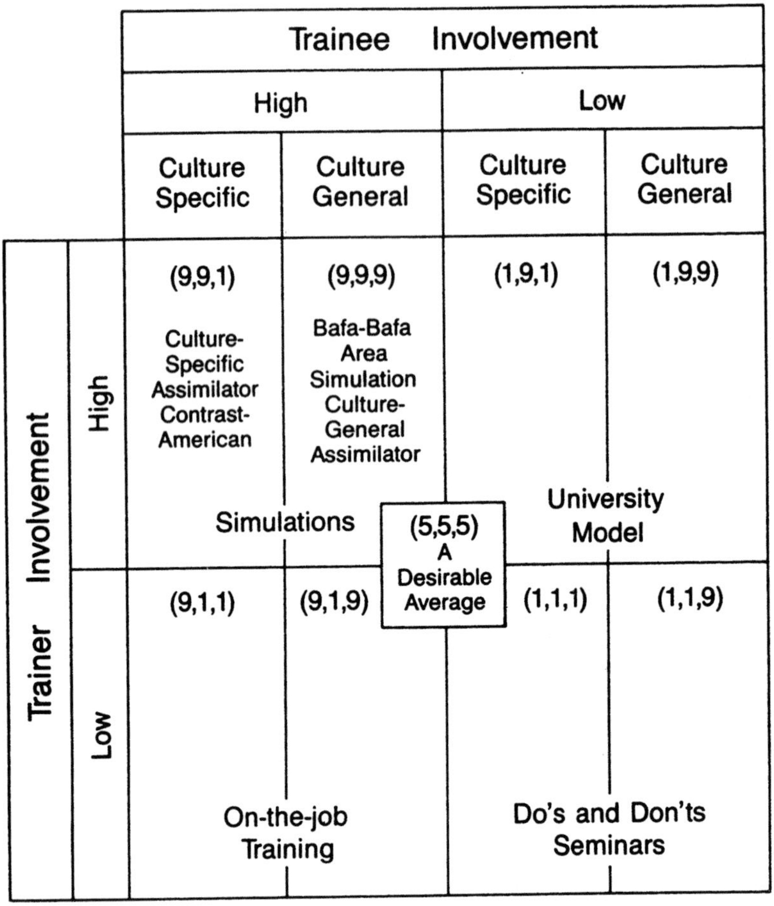

Trainee Involvement				
	High		Low	
	Culture Specific	Culture General	Culture Specific	Culture General
High	(9,9,1) Culture-Specific Assimilator Contrast-American	(9,9,9) Bafa-Bafa Area Simulation Culture-General Assimilator	(1,9,1)	(1,9,9)
Trainer Involvement — High / Low	Simulations		University Model	
	(5,5,5) A Desirable Average			
Low	(9,1,1)	(9,1,9)	(1,1,1)	(1,1,9)
	On-the-job Training		Do's and Don'ts Seminars	

Figure 15.1. Framework for Classifying Orientation Programs

the "do's and don'ts" of the target culture. There are advantages to such information sharing when it comes to advising people on such things as "how to take a bus." I have myself profited from detailed advice on how to take a bus and how to buy a ticket from a machine in West Germany. In such orientations, typically, the trainer may be embarrassed (I wish I could share more with you!) and the trainee is too stressed or preoccupied with so many other things (passport and visa details, for example) to be receptive. Even if orientations last for a few days, they would still fall in this category if the objective of the seminar is only to transfer information. The orientation program given to participants of the East-West Center on their arrival at the center would be one such program—very useful (e.g., how to keep visas up to date) but not directed at preparing sojourners for intercultural interaction.

LOW, LOW, CG (1, 1, 9). One target group of people who may qualify for this kind of orientation would be diplomats or business people who can be posted to more than one possible place. The typical scenario would be like the previous one except that the trainer would be giving generic "do's and don'ts" such as—do not form stereotypes; you will experience culture shock wherever you go; you have to be people oriented or relationship oriented to succeed in Asia; and so on.

HIGH, LOW, CS (9, 1, 1). I would call this "learning on the job." The trainee is highly motivated and involved but the trainer is typically unclear about his or her contributions. A typical situation would be business people learning the ropes from colleagues who have other responsibilities, a problem commonly faced in organizing on-the-job training. Another situation familiar to most trainers is their personal experience of learning the tricks of cross-cultural interaction without much help from anyone. And this should also cover the first time a person from one culture is going to another, when no ethnographies are available or there is literally no one to tell "war stories" about a particular culture.

HIGH, LOW, CG (9, 1, 9). This is a tricky slot in the matrix to fill. One scenario that I can imagine is that of a person highly motivated to become world-minded, anticipating extensive travel in the future, picking up a structured exercise book prepared for training people for more than one culture (Brislin et al., 1986), and training him- or herself using a lot of introspection combined with reading and doing practical exercises.

The two types that we have just discussed would accommodate all those programs that could be used at a computer terminal (there are none available at the moment), structured for individual learning at home. There is reason to expect such a package in the near future, given that most training materials of this type in other fields (for example, management) have only recently appeared. This category should be prominent in the field of cross-cultural orientation because the objective is to make a trainee learn how to learn, if the exercises have the force to disturb the trainee so as to create mild frustration that is normally produced in cross-cultural interaction. In turn, the mild frustration leads to motivation to learn more about the other culture.

LOW, HIGH, CS (1, 9, 1). This is the frequently criticized university model in which the trainee takes the role of the audience. The trainers have a great responsibility in this situation, because the burden of transfer of knowledge falls on them. The content of the lecture is culture specific—the target culture. The lecture usually encompasses the history, religion, culture, political system, and so on of the target culture. We must note that, despite the unpopularity of the university model, lecturing is still a part of most cross-cultural orientation programs, and I do not think this will change in the near future.

LOW, HIGH, CG (1, 9, 9). The university model for the culture-general approach—this is similar to the previous one except that the content is not any particular culture but culture at large. This situation could appear in the training of diplomats or business people who are not trained for one particular country. At the East-West Center, the faculty conducted a weekly seminar for the participants from Asia, the Pacific, and the United States, with the objective of providing a culture-general orientation. Because the participants were highly motivated and many of them were cross-culturally sophisticated, it was thought that they would profit from learning the abstract concepts underlying cross-cultural interaction. The first three weeks were devoted to lectures on underlying concepts (Brislin et al., 1986), followed by a discussion of two to three incidents of the type reviewed previously. The faculty invited comments from the participants and there was always a lively discussion—participants shared their personal experiences. The participants were more excited in the following weeks when they broke up into small groups and then assembled again to share the group reports in the plenary session. The seminar was a mixture of lectures (also guest speakers) and group exercises. The sessions in which lectures and incidents were presented appear to be closer to the university model than any other and, despite the fact that some of the speakers were truly charismatic, the students still preferred group exercises.

HIGH, HIGH, CS (9, 9, 1). This is the alternative to the university model—the experiential learning model. When people talk about this model as the opposite of the university model, I get the impression that the student is involved but the trainer is not involved. This, however, is not at all true. The trainer and the trainee are both involved when the experiential method is used. There is a lot of planning for the trainer before starting the training, and a lot of monitoring work, without being obtrusive, during the orientation. The content of the program would address a specific target culture.

HIGH, HIGH, CG (9, 9, 9). This is identical to the preceding part of the typology except that the content of the program is not focused on one particular culture. An orientation program could be developed to train people from the United States to go to different Pacific Island countries. Though every island has its own language and culture, it is still possible to pick up a few themes that are common to the islands that could be contrasted to the American culture. We shall discuss this in more detail shortly. Various simulation programs like BAFA-BAFA and the Owl and the Albatross belong in this category.

I must suggest that the point (9, 9, 9) is not necessarily the "best." A desirable target point on this three-dimensional matrix should be the one that takes advantage of all the methods. That point would be (5, 5, 5) on the matrix, *as an average,* for a long program. Sometimes both the trainers and the trainees would be highly involved in exercises and sometimes only one of them would be actively involved while the other takes the role of an observer. This would be required to avoid keeping the trainees "up" all the time to the point where fatigue interferes with training. There is general agreement supported by research findings that the best orientation program involves the trainees on all levels—cognitive, affective, and behavioral (Gudykunst & Hammer, 1983).

EVALUATION OF ORIENTATION PROGRAMS

Having looked into various methods of training, it is glaringly obvious that we must evaluate every orientation program if we want to ensure that we are meeting the objectives outlined at the outset of the program and, more important, that we are not obtaining negative, unintended outcomes. Brislin and Pedersen (1976) have devoted a chapter on evaluation in their seminal book on cross-cultural orientations. They give three reasons for evaluating orientations:

(1) The organizers can improve their programs further.
(2) The merit of the program can be proved.
(3) Others can learn from the experience.

Many researchers have advocated "formative" as well as "summative" evaluation (Triandis, 1977). In formative evaluation, one frequently evaluates programs and finds ways of improving them, whereas, in summative evaluation, the program is evaluated in its totality and is judged as successful or not. Decisions about improving the program are often the result of formative evaluations. Decisions to continue or to discontinue funding are often a result of summative evaluations. Cross-cultural orientation programs are highly suited to formative evaluation because the programs could be continuously improved to the benefit of the organizers.

Triandis (1977) has discussed the role of various independent variables in cross-cultural orientation and strategies for evaluating their effect on the dependent variables. Research in this field is limited but that should not discourage trainers from carrying out evaluation studies. There is evidence that people like to take part in evaluations (Aronson & Carlsmith, 1968). One important point to keep in mind is that trainers and evaluators must be different to have objectivity in the evaluation.

THE FUTURE OF CROSS-CULTURAL ORIENTATION

The inevitability of cross-cultural interaction and the importance of orientation has now been accepted. However, cross-cultural orientation has yet to reach all who need it. For example, I know there are no cross-cultural orientations offered in the field of aviation and I would except many more such fields where people are not aware of cross-cultural training.

The future of cross-cultural orientation is promising. There will be self-help training materials available in the future, most likely on computers. Some think there will be a time when people will look for "culture brokers" to guide people on how to achieve their goals in another culture. Others think that cross-cultural interactions are going to enable people to know themselves better and that cross-cultural orientation would help people in achieving those goals. I think cross-cultural orientation should become a part of the school curriculum in the future so that students are prepared to interact effectively in multi-cultural settings. As they become more skilled, trainers can take on highly complex tasks like training people from cultures that are going through dramatic changes (e.g., Hong Kong, as it reverts back to mainland China). Concepts presented in various chapters throughout this book (e.g., acculturation, development) should be useful in creating such innovative programs.

REFERENCES

Albert, R. D. (1983). The intercultural sensitizer or culture assimilator: A cognitive approach. In D. Landis & R. W. Brislin (Eds.), *Handbook of intercultural training: Vol. 2. Issues in training methodology.* New York: Pergamon.

Albert, R. D. (1986). Conceptual framework for the development and evaluation of cross-cultural orientation programs. *International Journal of Intercultural Relations, 10*, 197-213.

Aronson, E., & Carlsmith, J. (1968). Experimentation in social psychology. In G. Lindzey & E. Aronson (Eds.), *Handbook of social psychology* (Vol. 2, 2nd ed., pp. 1-79). Reading, MA: Addison-Wesley.

Batchelder, D., & Warner, E. G. (1977). *Beyond experience*. Brattleboro, VT: Experiment Press.

Brislin, R. W. (1981). *Cross-cultural encounters: Face to face interaction*. New York: Pergamon.

Brislin, R. W. (1983). The benefits of close intercultural relationships. In S. H. Irvine & J. W. Berry (Eds.), *Human assessment and cultural factors*. New York: Plenum.

Brislin, R. W. (1989). Intercultural communication training. In M. Asante & W. Gudykunst (Eds.), *Handbook of international and intercultural communication* (pp. 441-457). Newbury Park, CA: Sage.

Brislin, R. W., Cushner, K., Cherrie, C., & Yong, M. (1986). *Intercultural interactions: A practical guide*. Beverly Hills, CA: Sage.

Brislin, R. W., & Holwill, F. (1977). Reactions of indigenous people to the writings of behavioral and social scientists. *International Journal of Intercultural Relations, 1*(2), 15-34.

Brislin, R. W., & Pedersen, P. (1976). *Cross-cultural orientation programs*. New York: Gardner.

David, K. (1972). Intercultural adjustment and applications of reinforcement theory to problems of culture shock. *Trends, 4*, 1-64.

Fiedler, F. E., Mitchell, T., & Triandis, H. C. (1971). The culture assimilator: An approach to cross-cultural training. *Journal of Applied Psychology, 55*, 95-102.

Gochenour, T. (1977). The owl and the albatross. In D. Batchelder & E. G. Warner (Eds.), *Beyond experience*. Brattleboro, VT: Experiment Press.

Gudykunst, W. B., & Hammer, M. R. (1983). Basic training design: Approaches to intercultural training. In D. Landis & R. W. Brislin (Eds.), *Handbook of intercultural training: Vol. 1. Issues in theory and design*. Elmsford, NY: Pergamon.

Gudykunst, W. B., Hammer, M. R., & Wiseman, R. (1977). An analysis of an integrated approach to cross-cultural training. *International Journal of Intercultural Relations, 1*, 99-109.

Harrison, R., & Hopkins, R. L. (1967). The design of cross-cultural training: An alternative to the university model. *Journal of Applied Behavioral Science, 3*, 431-460.

Hawes, F., & Kealey, D. J. (1981). An empirical study of Canadian technical assistance: Adaptation and effectiveness on overseas assignment. *International Journal of Intercultural Relations, 5*, 239-258.

Kolb, D. (1987). *Learning style inventory*. Boston: McBer.

Kraemer, A. (1973). *Development of a cultural self-awareness approach to instruction in intercultural communication* (Report 73-17). Arlington, VA: HumRRO.

Kraemer, A. (1974). *Workshop in intercultural communication* (Report). Arlington, VA: HumRRO.

Paige, R. M. (1986). *Cross-cultural orientation: New conceptualizations and applications*. Lanham, MD: University Press of America.

Ross, L. (1977). The intuitive psychologist and his shortcomings: Distortion in the attribution process. In L. Berkowitz (Ed.), *Advances in experimental social psychology* (Vol. 10). New York: Academic Press.

Rhuly, S. (1976). *Orientations to intercultural communication*. Chicago: Science Research Associates.

Shirts, G. (1973). *BAFA-BAFA: A cross-cultural simulation*. Del Mar, CA: Simile 11.

Stening, B. (1979). Problems in cross-cultural contact: A literature review. *International Journal of Intercultural Relations, 3,* 269-313.

Triandis, H. C. (1975). Culture training, cognitive complexity, and interpersonal attitudes. In R. Brislin, S. Bochner, & W. Lonner (Eds.), *Cross-cultural perspectives on learning.* Beverly Hills, CA: Sage.

Triandis, H. (1977). Theoretical framework for evaluation of cross-cultural training effectiveness. *International Journal of Intercultural Relations, 1,* 19-45.

Trifonovitch, G. (1973). On cross-cultural orientation techniques. *Topics in Culture Learning, 1,* 38-47.

AUTHOR INDEX

Abbey, D., 228, 300
Abbott, R., 286, 298, 299
Abelson, R., 54
Aberle, D., 16, 33
Abramson, L., 312, 322
Acosta, F., 319, 322
Adler, P., 168, 183, 224, 228
Agarwal, A., 86, 94
Agarwal, D. K., 81, 84, 94
Agarwal, K. N., 81, 84, 94
Albert, R., 328, 333, 344, 345
Ali, F., 225, 228
Allen, V., 95, 96
Allport, G., 113, 119
Alston, J., 210, 212, 218, 228
Altbach, P., 162, 183, 184
Althen, G., 167, 175, 176, 185
Altman, I., 254, 265, 266, 269, 271, 274,
    275, 276, 277, 299
American Psychiatric Association, 302,
    322
American Public Health Association, 282,
    298
Ammar, S., 307, 322
Amoh, K., 167, 183
Anastasi, A., 57, 58, 74
Andrews, J., 226, 229
Angyal, A., 129, 139
Annis, A., 267, 276
Annis, R., 236, 242, 246, 253
Ardrey, T., 265, 274
Aronson, E., 344, 345
Asai, M., 40, 54, 55, 290, 301
Asant, M., 345
Athos, A., 213, 230
Austin, L., 206
Azuma, H., 119, 147, 152, 154, 158, 159,
    160
Azumi, K., 187, 206

Bacon, M., 257, 275
Bagby, J., 61, 74
Bagur, J., 225, 228
Bahuchet, S., 241, 253
Bailey, K., 171, 172, 183
Bain, D., 288, 300

Bakan, D., 129, 130, 139
Banks, J., 118
Barber, E., 170, 173, 176, 183, 184, 185
Barker, R., 258, 259, 274
Baron, R., 261, 274, 275
Barry, H., 257, 275
Bartko, J., 304, 322
Bartlett, K., 37, 54, 285, 299
Barwick, C., 251, 252
Bass, B., 186, 204, 206
Batchelder, D., 333, 345
Baum, A., 254, 262, 267, 270, 271, 275,
    277
Beeson, W., 287, 288, 300
Befu, H., 154, 158
Behera, H., 88, 96
Beiser, M., 251, 252
Bekman, S., 132, 135, 140
Bell, P., 254, 261, 274, 275
Bellack, A., 159
Benjamin, R., 222, 228
Bennett, M., 167, 183
Benton, A., 225, 228
Bergman, A., 125, 140
Berkel, J., 288, 298
Berkowitz, L., 54, 345
Berman, J., 323
Bernstein, B., 84, 94, 122, 139
Berry, J., 9, 20, 21, 22, 30, 33, 38, 42, 54,
    58, 60, 62, 72, 73, 74, 75, 76, 123, 139,
    140, 147, 150, 152, 158, 161, 163, 167,
    232, 236, 239, 241, 242, 243, 244, 246,
    247, 249, 251, 252, 253, 278, 284, 299,
    300, 319, 345
Bhatia, B., 94
Bhawuk, D., 19, 32, 60, 103, 113, 116, 168,
    227, 237, 315, 325
Bhogle, S., 82, 95, 97
Bilsky, W., 57, 76
Black, J., 272, 275
Blanchard, D., 299
Blankenship, E., 173, 183
Blaugh, M., 172, 183
Blauner, B., 15, 33
Bloom, B., 94, 95
Bochner, S., 301, 323, 346

Bond, M., 141, 200, 206, 208, 223, 229, 289, 298
Bontempo, R., 39, 40, 43, 53, 54, 55, 290, 301
Booth, A., 268, 275
Boring, E., 142, 158
Boski, P., 147, 158
Boucher, J., 59, 76
Boulding, K., 146, 158
Bowser, B., 120
Boyanowsky, E., 261, 275
Brahe, Y., 144
Brazelton, T., 134, 139
Brewer, M., 35, 54
Brideau, L., 261, 275
Bridge, T., 299, 300, 301
Brigham, J., 119
Brislin, R., 9, 10, 20, 33, 43, 44, 55, 58, 61, 73, 74, 76, 102, 117, 119, 146, 150, 175, 184, 185, 208, 228, 251, 253, 256, 274, 285, 299, 301, 320, 323, 324, 326, 237, 328, 329, 334, 335, 336, 339, 341, 342, 343, 345, 346
Brislin, T., 24, 33
Bronfenbrenner, U., 129, 139
Brouwers, P., 300
Brown, D., 260, 275
Brown, K., 171, 183
Brown, R., 148, 149, 158
Bruni, J., 187, 207
Bujaki, M., 244, 253
Bullard, L., 285, 300
Burger, W., 218, 228
Burrisch, M., 73, 74
Burton, I., 263, 275
Butcher, J., 70, 74, 317, 322
Byrnes, D., 114, 119

Calhoun, J., 267, 268, 275
Calvert, J., 261, 275
Campbell, D., 35, 54, 62, 74
Campbell, N., 225, 228
Carlsmith, J., 344, 345
Carment, D., 223, 229
Carpenter, W., 304, 322
Carroll, W., 58, 75
Carter, W., 293, 300
Carvioto, J., 135, 139
Casey, T., 200, 207
Cashmore, J., 123, 139
Cavalli-Sforza, L., 241, 253
Cawte, J., 296, 300

Chance, N., 309, 324
Chazen, M., 84, 95
Cheetham, R., 315, 322
Chemers, M., 254, 265, 266, 269, 274
Cheng, B., 195, 200, 206, 208
Cherrie, C., 33, 102, 119, 228, 251, 253, 327, 345,
Child, I., 257, 275
Ching, C., 147, 158
Chiu, L., 104, 119
Cho, Y., 230
Chorover, S., 153, 158
Christian, J., 268, 275
Chung, C., 301
Ciborowski, T., 33, 120
Clack, F., 40, 55
Cohen, A., 16, 33
Cohen, J., 300
Cohen, R., 58, 67, 75
Cohen, S., 290, 299
Cohler, B., 129, 139
Cole, M., 100, 110, 120
Cole, R., 188, 206
Colligan, R., 69, 75
Colomb, E., 84, 95
Cook, R., 219, 220, 230
Cook, S., 116, 119
Cooper, J., 304, 305, 306, 322
Copernicus, N., 144
Cox, T., 84, 95
Crashaw, R., 262, 275
Cronbach, L., 58, 73, 75, 142, 158
Cross, D., 179, 183
Cummings, L., 226, 228, 229
Cummings, W., 273, 276
Cushman, D., 223, 228
Cushner, K., 9, 10, 12, 19, 20, 22, 23, 25, 28, 33, 98, 116, 119, 152, 167, 228, 240, 251, 253, 327, 345

Dalal, A., 97
Dana, R., 69, 75
Danish, S., 319, 323
Dansereau, F., Jr., 200, 206
Danzinger, K., 142, 158
Darlington, R., 92, 95
Darwin, C., 144
Das, J. P., 84, 87, 96
Das, U. C., 95
Dasen, P., 33, 76, 84, 95, 122, 139, 140, 146, 148, 150, 152, 158, 253, 299, 300
Dash, A. S., 83, 85, 87, 96

Dash, U. N., 83, 85, 87, 96
Dauderis, H., 187, 189, 190, 207
David, K., 337, 345
Davidson, A., 40, 54
Davidson, L., 262, 275
Davis, A., 16, 33
Davis, H., 189, 207
Davitz, J., 293, 299
Davitz, L., 299
de Boer, C., 187, 188, 206
De Hoyos, A., 313, 323
De Hoyos, G., 313, 323
de Lacey, P., 241, 253
De Vos, G., 316, 323
de Waard, F., 288, 298
Delpech, B., 316, 323
Deregowski, J., 61, 75
Deutsch, M., 78, 83, 97
Dhanamitta, S., 134, 135, 140
Diaz-Guerrero, R., 40, 54, 70, 76
Dickenberger, M., 221, 229
Dickson, W., 119
Dien, D., 17, 33
Diop, M., 311, 323
Dohrenwend, B. P., 306, 323
Dohrenwend, B. S., 306, 323
Doi, T., 154, 158
Donahue, R., 286, 299
Donohue, W., 228, 298
Doo, L., 223, 228
Draguns, J., 9, 19, 31, 33, 69, 75, 175, 176,
    185, 278, 289, 296, 300, 302, 306, 314,
    318, 319, 323, 324
Drenth, P., 58, 73, 75
Dresch, S., 172, 173, 183
Druckman, D., 225, 228
Dunnette, M., 207, 208
Dusek, J., 88, 95
Dyal, J., 72, 75
Dynes, R., 262, 276

Eagly, A., 50, 54
Egeland, J., 313, 323
Ehrlich, A., 273, 275
Ehrlich, P., 273, 275
Einstein, A., 144
Eisemann, M., 312, 324
Ekstrand, G., 129, 139
Ekstrand, L. H., 129, 139
England, G., 193, 206
Enriquez, V., 146, 147, 158
Epstein, Y., 277

Erelcin, F., 128, 139
Erichsen, F., 307, 323
Erickson, B., 229
Erickson, F., 111, 119
Ernberg, G., 304, 309, 323, 324
Eshleman, S., 313, 323
Ewen, R., 187, 206

Feeley, M., 230
Feinleib, M., 300
Felstiner, W., 216, 218, 228
Fenton, F., 310, 324
Fiedler, F., 334, 345
Fisher, J., 254, 275
Fishman, P., 171, 183
Fiske, D., 61, 62, 74, 75
Fleming, R., 262, 275
Folberg, J., 215, 218, 229
Folensbee, R., 319, 323
Fonnebo, V., 288, 299
Fraser, G., 288, 300
Freeman, D., 146, 159
Freeman, H., 84, 95
Freeman, J., 268, 275
Freud, S., 144
Friedland, N., 221, 229
Friedman, H., 289, 299
Friedman, J., 293, 301
Friend, R., 88, 95
Fritz, C., 263, 275
Fry, G., 174, 183
Fry, P., 88, 95
Fu, V., 129, 139
Furstenberg, F., Jr. 127, 139

Galanter, M., 218, 229
Gale, J., 172, 183
Galilei, G., 144
Galle, O., 268, 275
Galler, J., 81, 95
Gallimore, R., 150, 151, 160
Gallo, R., 10, 33
Garcia-Palmieri, M., 282, 299
Gardner, H., 65, 66, 75
Gavin, J., 187, 206
Gay, M., 301
Geboers, J., 291, 301
Geyer, S., 129, 139
Ghiselli, E., 196, 206
Ghosh, R., 88, 95
Gibson, J., 142, 159
Gillespie, J., 316, 324

Gladwin, T., 213, 299
Glaser, R., 289, 299
Glaser-Kiecolt, J., 289, 299
Glenn, E., 224, 226, 229
Gluckman, M., 216, 217, 229
Gochenour, T., 333, 345
Goldberg, L., 68, 75
Goldstein, A., 214, 229, 319, 323
Goldstein, G., 74
Gonzales, L., 73, 76
Good, B., 324
Goodenough, W., 277
Goodman, N., 174, 184
Goodnow, J., 122, 139
Goodwin, C., 181, 184
Gordon, T., 282, 299
Gorn, G., 187, 189, 190, 207
Gorsuch, R., 70, 76
Gove, W., 268, 275
Graen, G., 200, 206
Graham, J., 225, 226, 228, 229
Graumann, C., 147, 159
Graves, T., 233, 253
Green, C., 212, 230
Greene, R., 317, 323
Griffeth, R., 187, 206
Griffiths, J., 315, 372
Griffitt, W., 267, 275
Grove, C., 167, 184
Gudykunst, W., 228, 332, 336, 339, 343, 345
Gulbinat, W., 309, 323
Gulliver, P., 216, 228, 229
Gynther, M., 317, 323

Habicht, J., 84, 95
Hackman, J., 208
Haga, W., 200, 206
Haire, M., 196, 206
Hakuta, K., 27, 33, 119, 158, 159, 160
Halisch, F., 139
Hall, E., 52, 54, 265, 266, 275
Halpern, R., 92, 95
Hamilton, H., 284, 299
Hammer, M., 332, 336, 339, 343, 345
Hamouda, R., 167, 184
Hanna, J., 260, 275
Hanna, M., 129, 139
Hansen, F., 263, 276
Hanvey, R., 116, 117, 119
Hardin, G., 273, 274, 275
Harkness, S., 282, 299

Harnett, D., 226, 228, 229
Harrison, R., 331, 345
Hartup, W., 76
Hatand, G., 119
Hawes, F., 327, 345
Hawkins, J., 174, 184
Hayashi, T., 301
Hays, D., 275
Heberlein, T., 272, 275
Helms, J., 319, 324
Hendrick, C., 276
Henslin, J., 139
Herbert, T., 189, 207
Heron, A., 33, 120
Hersen, M., 74, 159
Herskovits, M., 12, 33, 233, 253, 255, 275
Hertenberg, R., 92, 96, 132, 133, 140
Hess, R., 86, 87, 95, 106, 153, 156, 159
Heuman, L., 265, 275
Hewstone, M., 89, 95
Hilliard, A., 103, 119
Hinkle, D., 129, 139
Hirschman, A., 216, 229
Ho, D., 147, 157, 159
Hoff, B., 167, 184
Hofstede, G., 39, 42, 49, 51, 54, 190, 191, 192, 200, 206, 223, 229, 320, 323
Hofstetter, A., 313, 323
Holdern, J., 273, 275
Holloway, S., 119
Holwill, F., 336, 345
Hom, P., 187, 206
Hood, M., 181, 184
Hoopes, D., 113, 119
Hope-Simpson, R., 261, 275
Hopkins, R., 331, 345
Hostetler, J., 323
Huges-Weiner, G., 103, 119
Hui, C., 13, 22, 25, 28, 29, 43, 44, 54, 55, 131, 175, 185, 186, 192, 196, 206, 223, 320, 324
Hulin, C., 186, 208
Hunt, R., 120
Hwang, K., 197, 200, 206, 207
Hymes, D., 159

Ibrahim, F., 58, 71, 75
Ikle, F., 226, 229
Ilola, L., 9, 20, 22, 23, 24, 31, 118, 175, 261, 278
Inkeles, A., 126, 139, 163, 185
Irvine, S., 58, 62, 73, 75, 76, 345

Jablensky, A., 304, 309, 310, 323, 324
Jaccard, J., 40, 54
Jackson, S., 84, 95
Jacobson, L., 87, 88, 96
Jain, H., 187, 189, 207
Jain, U., 89, 96, 267, 271, 276
Jalali, F., 103, 119
James, L., 187, 207
Jandt, F., 230
Jensen, A., 95
Jilek, W., 318, 323
Jilek-Aal, L., 318, 323
Joffe, R., 300
Johnson, K., 301
Jolbert, A., 225, 228
Jolly, 135, 139
Jones, A., 187, 207, 288, 300
Joossens, J., 299
Jordan, C., 20, 33, 106, 120
Joseph, G., 88, 95
Juan, M., 173, 185

Kagan, A., 282, 284, 286, 299, 301
Kagan, J., 84, 95, 104, 120, 124, 139
Kagan, S., 120, 139
Kâgitçibaşi, Ç., 13, 18, 19, 22, 23, 25, 28,
    33, 60, 85, 87, 108, 121, 124, 127, 128,
    129, 130, 131, 132, 135, 139, 140, 147,
    152, 157, 174, 179, 184, 191, 283
Kahn, H., 203, 207
Kalin, R., 249, 253
Kalleberg, A., 187, 207
Kameda, N., 211, 230
Kamin, L., 64, 75
Kannel, W., 282, 299
Kantor, M., 253
Kanungo, R., 187, 189, 191, 207
Kao, H., 127, 128, 141
Kaplan, R., 58, 75
Kashima, Y., 53, 55
Kashiwaga, K., 119
Kates, R., 263, 275
Kato, H., 284, 299, 301
Katz, D., 114, 120
Katz, I., 95
Kaur, B., 96
Kazin, A., 159
Kealey, D., 327, 345
Keller, L., 70, 74
Kelly, D., 162, 183
Kemble, E., 143, 144, 159
Kendall, L., 186, 208

Keniston, K., 129, 140
Kepler, J., 143, 144
Kesteloot, H., 299
Keyes, J., 127, 140
Kiesler, C., 273, 276
Kim, H., 152, 159
Kim, S., 209, 229
Kim, U., 12, 15, 19, 20, 23, 25, 28, 29, 85,
    122, 142, 149, 157, 159, 174, 242, 244,
    247, 249, 251, 253, 274, 317
Kimura, B., 312, 323
King, S., 223, 228
Kirmayer, L., 311, 324
Klein, R., 84, 95, 134, 139
Klein, T., 229
Kleinman, A., 293, 300, 311, 324
Klugman, E., 139
Koch, S., 142, 159, 160
Kochan, T., 210, 215, 229, 230
Kodama, K., 301
Kohlberg, L., 16, 17, 18, 33
Kohn, M., 42, 54, 123, 140
Koike, R., 193, 206
Kojima, H., 154, 159
Kolb, D., 328, 329, 345
Komin, S., 203, 207
Kornadt, H., 125
Korten, A., 304, 324
Kotchabhakdi, N., 134, 135, 140
Kraemer, A., 336, 337, 339, 345
Kressel, K., 219, 229
Krishnamurthy, K., 93, 95
Krishnan, L., 223, 229
Kroger, R., 149, 159
Kulkarni, S., 56, 58, 75
Kuulasmaa, K., 301
Kuzma, J., 287, 288, 300, 301
Kwon, T., 147, 159

LaFrance, M., 226, 229
Lagerspetz, K., 159
Lagunes, I., 139, 140, 141
Laing, A., 84, 95
Lambert, W., 33, 123, 140, 276, 277
Lamy, S., 178, 184
Landis, D., 184, 344, 345
Landy, F., 29, 33
Lane, H., 300
Lantz, H., 127, 140
Lasch, C., 218, 229
Lasky, R., 134, 139
Lazar, I., 92, 95

Leary, D., 142, 159, 160
Lebra, T., 156, 159
Lebra, W., 323
Lechtig, A., 134, 139
LeCompte, M., 105, 120
Lefcourt, H., 72, 75
Leff, J., 306, 324
Leslie, C., 295, 299
Lesthaeghe, R., 126, 140
Leung, K., 19, 22, 30, 40, 43, 54, 55, 118, 191, 209, 221, 222, 223, 229
Leung, V., 161
Levine, R. V., 37, 54, 285, 299
LeVine, R. A., 123, 140
LeVine, R. C., 154, 156, 157, 160
LeVine, R. T., 35, 54
Levy, M., 16, 33
Levy, S., 289, 296, 299
Lewin, K., 256, 276
Lewis, M., 96
Lichton, I., 284, 300
Liebrand, W., 223, 229
Lien, N., 81, 95
Lifton, R., 262, 276
Lin, E., 293, 300
Lincoln, J., 187, 207
Lind, E., 214, 215, 221, 222, 229, 230
Lindzey, G., 315, 316, 324, 345
Ling, W., 195, 207
Linton, R., 233, 253
Lippitt, G., 189, 207
Locke, E., 188, 207
Logue, J., 263, 276
Lolb, D., 102, 120
Lonner, W., 11, 26, 27, 33, 56, 58, 59, 60, 71, 74, 75, 76, 101, 118, 148, 175, 185, 253, 267, 276, 290, 296, 300, 301, 315, 323, 346
Loomis, R., 254, 275
Lotz, T., 287, 300
Lowell, W., 81, 95
Lucca, N., 40, 54, 290, 301
Lulat, G., 162, 183
Lushene, R., 70, 76
Lynch, J., 118

Mabey, C., 99, 120
Macfarlene, A., 126, 140
Mack, R., 214, 230
MacLean, C., 301
MacMahon, S., 286, 298
Mahanta, J., 84, 96

Mahler, M., 125, 140
Maj, M., 312, 324
Malhotra, M., 260, 277
Malpass, R., 279, 300
Maretzki, T., 296, 300
Marmak, A., 159
Marmot, A., 284, 299
Marsella, A., 33, 120, 175, 184, 310, 323, 324
Martin, J., 181, 184
Martin, S., 149, 159
Marty, G., 178, 184
Matthews, R., 267, 276
Mawhinney, T., 253
Maxwell, G., 226, 230
Mayo, C., 226, 229
McCall, G., 159
McClelland, D., 130, 140
McDermott, J., 296, 300
McDevitt, T., 119
McGee, D., 300
McGregor, D., 199, 207
McGurk, H., 96
McMillan, C., 187, 206
McPherson, J., 268, 275
McReynolds, 76
Mead, M., 146, 159
Meissner, H., 225, 228
Mercer, J., 64, 74, 75, 76
Merry, S., 220, 230
Mestenhauser, J., 169, 171, 178, 184
Meyer, K., 81, 95
Michelson, W., 269, 276
Miller, A., 286, 287, 300
Miller, D., 301
Miller, G., 32, 33
Mills, P., 288, 300
Minde, T., 251, 253
Minuchin, S., 125, 140
Mirsky, A., 299, 300, 301
Mischel, L., 33
Mishra, R., 84, 95
Misra, G., 78, 84, 86, 89, 96, 277
Misumi, J., 157, 159, 190, 195, 196, 207
Mitchell, T., 334, 345
Miyake, K., 119
Moch, M., 187, 207
Mok, D., 251, 253
Montague, P., 58, 67, 75
Moock, J., 174, 184
Morales, M., 40, 54
Moran, R., 225, 230

Morris, R., 169, 184
Moscovici, S., 147, 159
Moss, H., 104, 120
MOW International Research Team, 190, 205, 207
Murgan, R., 170, 173, 176, 183
Murlidharan, R., 81, 83, 96, 97
Murphy, H., 249, 253, 306, 308, 309, 312, 324
Myers, R., 92, 95, 96, 132, 133, 140, 184

Nacht, M., 181, 184
Nader, L., 217, 230, 231
Nadkarni, M., 93, 95
Nagand, S., 119
Nagar, D., 264, 267, 268, 269, 270, 271, 276
Naidu, N., 82, 97
Nathanson, L., 58, 67, 75
Native Hawaiian Health Research Consortium, 296,300
Neale, J., 88, 95
Negandhi, A., 199, 201, 207
Neki, J., 128, 140
Nevis, E., 189, 192, 207
Newman, L., 272, 277
Newton, C., 299
Newton, I., 144
Nichaman, M., 284, 299, 301
Niemi, P., 159
Nissinen, A., 291, 300, 301
Normand, J., 187, 189, 207

O'Connell, M., 207
O'Donnell, C., 150, 159
Offord, K., 69, 75
Okuwaki, N., 220, 221, 230
Olmeda, E., 236, 253
Olson, E., 262, 276
O'Reilly, C., 187, 207
Osborne, D., 69, 75
Oskamp, S., 273, 276

Padaki, R., 204, 207
Paige, R., 9, 20, 29, 161, 169, 171, 174, 178, 184, 185, 326, 345
Pallak, M., 273, 276
Palomba, K., 140, 141
Pancheri, P., 317, 322
Panda, K., 84, 87, 88, 95, 96
Pandey, J., 12, 22, 31, 75, 118, 207, 254, 264, 268, 269, 270, 271, 276, 277

Pareek, U., 86, 96
Parham, T., 319, 324
Pascale, R., 213, 230
Paulus, P., 267, 269, 270, 271, 275, 276
Payer, L., 292 300
Pedersen, J., 75, 175, 184, 185
Pedersen, P., 296, 300, 323, 328, 343, 345
Pelto, P., 49, 54
Perris, C., 312, 324
Perris, H., 312, 324
Peters, E., 189, 207
Peters, L., 316, 324
Peterson, R., 211, 213, 230
Pettengill, S., 122, 140
Pettigrew, T., 115, 120
Phares, E., 72, 75
Phillips, R., 287, 288, 300, 301
Piaget, S., 144
Pialorsi, F., 172, 183
Piha, T., 291, 301
Pine, F., 125, 140
Platt, J., 274, 276
Poortinga, Y., 139, 140, 141, 147, 150, 152, 158, 279, 300
Popp, G., 189, 207
Popper, J., 286, 299
Porat, A., 224, 230
Porter, L., 196, 206
Porter, R., 183
Power, S., 244, 253
Prasad, J., 262, 276
Price, G., 119
Prince, R., 310, 324
Pross, S., 299
Pruitt, D., 219, 229
Puhan, B., 56, 58, 75
Pulsford, R., 296, 300
Puska, P., 291, 300, 301
Pye, L., 226, 230

Quarantelli, E., 262, 263, 276, 277

Rajalakshmi, R., 95
Ramirez, A., 119
Ramsey, F., 81, 95
Rao, S., 84, 96
Rapoport, A., 264, 269, 276, 299
Rath, R., 83, 85, 86, 87, 96
Rawson, G., 288, 296, 301
Read, M., 296, 300
Redding, G., 186, 200, 207
Redding, S., 200, 208

Redfield, R., 233, 253
Reed, D., 284, 286, 298, 299, 300, 301
Reid, J., 184
Renwick, G., 212, 225, 226, 230
Resch, J., 301
Rhoads, G., 284, 286, 299, 301
Rhuly, S., 338, 345
Ricciuti, H., 80, 82, 96
Richardson, S., 81, 96
Roberts, K., 187, 207
Rodin, J., 270, 276
Roehl, J., 219, 220, 231
Rogler, L., 269, 276
Rogoff, B., 109, 120
Rohner, R., 121, 122, 140
Ronen, S., 186, 204, 208
Rosenberg, L., 173, 185
Rosenblum, L., 96
Rosenfeld, H., 52, 54
Rosenham, D., 87, 96
Rosenthal, R., 87, 88, 96
Ross, L., 329, 345
Rotter, J., 71, 76, 87
Ruback, R., 270, 277
Rubinow, D., 289, 300
Russell, J., 254, 258, 277
Ryckman, D., 84, 96

Saal, C., 129, 140
Saccuzzo, D., 58, 75
Sahu, S., 84, 96
Salazar, J., 92, 96
Salonen, J., 301
Sameshima, Y., 293, 299
Samovar, L., 183
Samuda, R., 58, 76
Samy, J., 147, 159
Sano, Y., 225, 229
Sanua, V., 307, 324
Sartorius, N., 140, 253, 299, 300, 304, 305, 306, 309, 310, 322, 323, 324
Sasaki, H., 301
Scharfetter, C., 318, 324
Scheper-Hughes, N., 317, 324
Schieffer, K., 181, 184
Schiffman, J., 282, 299
Schkade, J., 267, 276
Schmidt, K., 225, 230
Schmidt, S., 210, 230
Schmitt, D., 226, 230
Schmitt, R., 268, 277
Schultz, M., 127, 140

Schwartz, S., 57, 76
Scribner, S., 100, 110, 120
Sechrest, L., 160
Segall, M., 147, 150, 152, 158, 229
Seligman, M., 312, 322
Sells, S., 187, 207
Senechal, C., 241, 253
Serpell, R., 65, 76
Seta, J., 267, 276
Shamgar-Handelman, L., 140, 141
Sharma, M., 86, 96
Sharma, R., 88, 89, 96
Sharma, S., 104, 120
Sharma, V., 260, 277
Sheehan, J., 319, 322
Sherif, M., 115, 120
Sherrell, B., 284, 300
Shimada, E., 53, 55
Shimada, J., 211, 213, 230
Shimizu, Y., 301
Shirts, G., 333, 345
Sigel, I., 104, 120
Silin, R., 201, 208
Sills, D., 275
Simons, L., 288, 300
Sindell, P., 253
Singer, J., 254, 275
Singh, A., 83, 84, 85, 97
Sinha, D., 22, 23, 25, 26, 27, 56, 76, 77, 84, 86, 87, 97, 101, 126, 127, 128, 130, 140, 141, 147, 152, 157, 159, 256, 262, 263, 277, 283, 295, 300, 312
Sinha, J. B., 130, 131, 141, 195, 196, 208
Sinha, Y., 89, 97
Sirowy, L., 163, 185
Sit, V., 202, 203, 208
Slavin, R., 115, 120
Slocum, J., Jr., 189, 208
Smedslund, J., 147, 159
Smilansky, M., 132, 140
Smitasiri, S., 134, 135, 140
Smith, P., 186, 208
Snarey, J., 16, 17, 33
Snyder, R., 214, 230
Social Science Research Council, 233, 253
Soga, N., 164, 185
Solimano, G., 81, 95
Sommer, R., 265, 277
Sommerlad, E., 243, 253
Sowder, B., 276
Spearman, C., 63, 76
Specter, S., 299

Spielberger, C., 70, 76
Squillace, K., 300
Steegman, A., 260, 277
Steele, S., 179, 185
Steglitz, E., 178, 184
Stemmermann, G., 286, 301
Stening, B., 326, 346
Sternberg, R., 66, 76
Stevenson, H., 119, 153, 154, 158, 159, 160
Stevenson, K., 224, 229
Stewart, L., 228
Stogdill, R., 194, 208
Stokols, D., 254, 267, 271, 274, 275, 277
Stonequist, E., 245, 253
Storer, D., 128, 140
Strauss, G., 200, 208
Strauss, J., 304, 322
Strawser, R., 189, 208
Struening, E., 263, 276
Sue, D., 175, 185
Suedfeld, P., 260, 261, 277
Sullivan, J., 211, 222, 230
Sunar, D., 132, 135, 140
Sundberg, N., 73, 76
Sundstromm, E., 267, 277
Super, C., 282, 299
Suresh, J., 84, 97
Surkyn, J., 126, 140
Sussman, N., 52, 54
Suttle, J., 208
Sutton, F., 16, 33
Suzuki, A., 316, 324
Swenson, W., 69, 75
Swerdlik, M., 58, 67, 75
Symes, S., 300

Tamir, P., 111, 120
Tanabe, K., 222, 230
Tanaka, H., 218, 230
Tannenbaum, A., 194, 208
Taylor, A., 215, 218, 228
Taylor, D., 249, 253
Taylor, R., 207
Taylor, V., 263, 277
Teasdale, J., 312, 322
Teddlie, C., 266, 277
Temoshok, L., 290, 301
Tharp, R., 20, 33, 106, 120, 150, 151, 159, 160
Thibaut, J., 221, 230
Thomas, K., 167, 175, 176, 185

Thorndike, R., 58, 64, 74, 76
Thornton, A., 126, 140
Tietjen, A., 17, 33
Tillotson, J., 284, 299, 301
Ting-Toomey, S., 228
Tjosvold, D., 195, 208
Tobin, J., 293, 301
Todd, H., 217, 230, 231
Tognoli, J., 264, 265, 277
Tomasic, R., 230
Torbiorn, I., 167, 184
Torrey, E., 305, 318, 324
Toulmin, S., 142, 160
Toynbee, A., 257, 277
Triandis, H.C., 12, 13, 18, 21, 25, 26, 32, 33, 34, 39, 40, 43, 44, 53, 54, 55, 57, 75, 76, 103, 107, 113, 120, 124, 166, 175, 185, 186, 190, 192, 198, 206, 208, 211, 222, 223, 224, 230, 255, 274, 276, 277, 278, 285, 290, 301, 320, 323, 324, 325, 326, 329, 333, 334, 337, 338, 343, 344, 345, 346
Trifonovitch, G., 331, 332, 346
Trimble, J., 59, 75, 76, 175, 185, 236, 253, 296, 300
Tripathi, H., 104, 120
Tripathi, K. K., 86, 94
Tripathi, L. B., 78, 84, 86, 96
Tripathi, R. C., 88, 89, 96, 277
Trommsdorf, G., 122, 140
Tronick, E., 134, 139
Tseng, W., 296, 300
Tuomilehto, J., 291, 300, 301
Tyler, T., 214, 215, 221, 230
Tyler, V., 74, 75, 76, 118

Upadhyay, S., 81, 84, 94

Valins, S., 254, 270, 275
Valyasevi, A., 134, 135, 140
van de Koppel, J., 241, 253
Van Deusen, J., 295, 301
Vaskaran, A., 260, 277
Vazir, S., 82, 97
Veitch, R., 267, 275
Vernon, P., 63, 76, 152, 153, 160
Villareal, M., 40, 53, 55, 196, 206, 290, 301
Vogt, L., 106, 107, 120
von Mehren, A., 230

Walker, L., 221, 230

Walsh, F., 139
Walter, I., 213, 229
Wang, J., 162, 183
Ward, L., 254, 258, 277
Warner, E., 333, 345
Warwick, D., 207
Weaver, G., 167, 185
Weber, M., 191, 208
Webster, I., 288, 296, 301
Weibender, L., 316, 324
Weigal, R., 272, 277
Weil, S., 129, 140
Weiner, B., 88, 97
Weiss, H., 129, 139
Weissbach, T., 119
Welch, S., 268, 275
Wells, L., 228, 230
Wennergren, E., 173, 185
Werner, E., 81, 83, 97
Wheeler, L., 75
White, L., 255, 277
White, M., 154, 156, 157, 160
Whiteman, M., 78, 83, 97
Whiting, J., 257, 277
Whyte, W., 212, 230
Wicker, A., 258, 259, 277
Widen, R., 299
Williams, L., 212, 230
Williams, P., 172, 183, 185
Winichagoon, P., 134, 135, 140
Winick, M., 81, 95
Winter, D., 130, 140
Wintrob, R., 253
Wiseman, R., 336, 345
Witkin, H., 72, 76, 241
Witmeyer, D., 224, 229

Wittkower, E., 309, 324
Witty, C., 215, 218, 219, 220, 224, 231
Wober, M., 59, 65, 76
Wohlwill, J., 254, 274, 276, 299
Wong, G., 186, 200, 207
Wong, S., 198, 202, 203, 208
Woods, L., 149, 159
Worchel, S., 266, 277
World Health Organization, 280, 281, 301, 304, 305, 306, 309, 324
Wright, H., 258, 274
Wright, J., 120
Wu, D., 17, 33
Wu, P., 19, 22, 30, 209
Wundt, W., 142
Wyon, J., 282, 299

Yamamura, Y., 154, 160
Yang, C., 127, 128, 130, 140, 195, 206, 208
Yang, K. S., 130, 140
Yano, K., 285, 286, 298, 299, 300, 301
Yarbrough, C., 84, 95
Yin, Y., 298
Yngvesson, B., 217, 231
Yong, M., 10, 33, 102, 119, 228, 251, 253, 327, 345
Young, J., 261, 275
Young, M., 244, 253

Zavalloni, M., 57, 76
Zawacki, A., 207
Zhang, H., 56, 64, 74, 76
Zigler, E., 139
Zikopoulos, M., 164, 185
Zollinger, T., 288, 301
Zukowski-Faust, J., 172, 183

SUBJECT INDEX

Ability testing, 63-66
Abnormal psychology. *See* Health, mental
Abstract conceptualization, 103
Acculturation, 18, 21, 30-31, 101, 113, 150-152, 153, 161, 167-168, 182, 232-252, 284, 344
Achievement, 25, 28-29, 47, 51, 86, 89-90, 91, 92, 93, 105-106, 126, 130, 136-137, 150, 153-154, 156, 189, 270, 344
Acquaintance potential, 115-116
Active experimentation, 103
Adjudication, 214-216, 221, 227
Affective disorders, 309-314
Africa, 310-311
AIDS, 9-10, 289-290, 296
Alcohol use, 285-286, 287-289, 291-292
Alzheimer's disease, 289
Amae, 154-155
Anxiety, 68, 70-71, 86, 247, 263, 321; *See also* Stress
Arbitration, 214-216, 218
Assertiveness-control, 193
Assessment. *See* Testing
Asian-Americans, 12, 99, 128, 293-294
Attitudes, 47, 116, 186-194, 210-211, 243-246, 251, 256, 271-274, 290-292; *See also* Values
Attributions, isomorphic, 19, 36, 53, 329-330, 337
Attribution theory, 19, 87, 88-90, 113, 156-157, 227-228, 263, 273, 310-311, 312-313, 329-330, 333-336, 337
Authority, 22, 86, 200, 319; *See also* Superior-subordinate relations
Autonomy, 23, 25, 106-108, 124-125, 130, 136-137, 154-155, 189, 205
Avoiding, 216

Bargaining, 209-228
Behavior and health, 282-289
Behavior settings, 258-259
Berlin Wall, 17-18
Biculturalism, 100, 237, 245, 294
Blacks, 99, 189, 228, 313, 315, 319
Blocking behavior, 211-212
Blood pressure, 24; *See also* Heart

Brain drain, 174
Bribes, 46
Built environment, 263-265
Business people, 9, 22, 28-30, 45, 186-205, 209, 212-213, 225-226, 325-326, 341; *See also* Superior-subordinate relations; Work

Canada, 22, 232-252, 318-322
Cancer, 286-289, 297
Cardiovascular. *See* Heart
Case studies, 134-138
Caste, 265
Catharsis, 52
Change, 232-252; *See also* Interventions into poverty
Child care. *See* Socialization of children
China, 17, 56, 126, 128, 165, 168, 174, 189, 192, 193, 195, 196-205, 223, 311, 344
Chinese familism, 195-206
Cigarette use, 283-292, 296
Classification, skill of, 110-111, 143, 158
Climate, 36, 260-261, 264
Clinicians, 302-322
Cognition, 28, 78, 83-87, 92, 94, 108-112, 131-138, 147-148, 181, 205, 224, 251, 256, 278, 313, 333
Cold climate, 260-261
Collectivism, 192-193, 274; *See also* Individualism-collectivism
Communication, 35, 36, 43, 123, 167, 227-228, 237, 241, 263, 266-267, 273, 297-298, 311, 331; *See also* Contact across cultures; Negotiation
Community organization, 93, 135-137, 218-219, 263, 274
Competence-performance distinction, 151
Complexity, cultural, 36-39, 42
Concrete experience, 103; *See also* Experiential
Conflicts, 30, 43, 44, 52, 118, 129-130, 157, 170-172, 209-228, 263; *See also* Dispute resolution
Conformity, 67-68, 86, 155, 168, 321
Confrontation, 225-226

Confucianism, 203
Concession, 226
Contact across cultures, 9-10, 18, 26-27, 30, 34, 54, 98, 100, 113-118, 205, 232-252, 266, 313-314, 325-344; *See also* Acculturation
Contact-no contact cultures, 52
Context, 43, 66, 104-105, 110, 121, 122, 137, 142-148, 205, 258-259, 264-265, 314; *See also* Family
Cooperative learning, 25, 106-108, 113-116, 148, 150-152, 155, 194, 203-204, 290
Coping, 86-87, 247, 269, 270-271, 289-292, 331
Cost-benefit analysis, 48, 273; *See also* Economic factors
Counseling, 161, 175-176, 252, 294, 295-296, 302-322; *See also* Cross-cultural training; Health, mental
Courts, formal, 19, 30, 64, 209-228
Creativity, research, 73, 234
Cross-cultural training, 26-27, 32, 44-49, 50, 116-117, 168, 227-228, 237, 295, 314-315, 325-344
Crowding, 259, 266, 267-271
Cultural differences, 14-15, 16-18, 136-137, 166-168, 186-193, 205, 209-212, 221, 224-227, 232, 239-240, 250-251, 261, 265, 270-271, 296-297, 308-309, 316-317, 322
Cultural relativism, 64-66, 122-123, 146, 189-191, 252, 326; *See also* Attributions, isomorphic
Cultural sensitivity, 65, 101-102, 106-108, 131, 138, 227-228, 252, 313-314, 325-344
Cultural syndromes, 37-50
Cultural transitions, 52-53
Culture, definitions/explanations, 10-18, 23-24, 27, 36, 138, 143, 145-146, 227-228, 245-256, 279, 296-297, 302-303; subjective, 12; *See also* Subjective culture
Culture assimilators, 116-117, 333-336
Culture general/culture specific, 20-22, 31-32; *See also* Emics-etics
Culture of schools, 104-108
Culture shock, 101-102, 106-108; *See also* Cross-cultural training
Culture, subjective, 12; *See also* Subjective culture

Cumulative deficit phenomenon, 83
Curriculum, 98-118, 178-180, 344

Decision making, 9, 46-47, 203, 204; *See also* Leadership
Deficit. *See* Difference-deficit distinction
Democracy, 13, 14-15, 17-18, 23-24
Demography, 30, 98-99, 163-165, 233-236, 238, 239, 247, 264
Density, 267-271
Dependence, 136-137, 154-155
Depression, 260, 263, 304, 309-314
Description, 143, 153-158, 258-259
Deviance, positive, 135
Diagnosis, 26, 310
Diet, 257, 284-289, 296; *See also* Nutrition
Difference-deficit distinction, 24-26, 44, 62, 150-152, 199
Disasters, natural, 254, 261-263
Disconfirmed expectancies, 330
Disease. *See* Health, physical
Dispute resolution, 19, 30, 209-228
Diversity, 125-127
Divorce, 128

Ecology, 30, 36, 123, 124, 138, 152, 157, 232, 233, 279; *See also* Environment
Economic factors, 30, 36, 42, 77-78, 92, 130, 138, 166, 170, 172-174, 182, 234, 239, 261-262
Education, 9, 11, 12-13, 15-16, 18, 19, 20, 26, 27-29, 98-118, 131-138, 178-179, 203, 234, 240, 251, 270, 283, 290-292, 330-331, 341-342
Emics-etics, 20-22, 65, 69-70, 138, 146-147, 149, 296-297, 304-305, 309-310
Emotional control-expressiveness, 51-52, 104, 128-131, 186, 343
Empathy, 113, 116; *See also* Cross-cultural training
Environment, 31, 78, 83, 94, 100, 103-104, 118, 123, 132, 152, 168, 254-274, 279, 296-297
Equal status contact, 114
Equity-equality, 45, 48
Equivalence, 60-61, 70-71; *See also* Measurement
Ethnic affirmation, 53, 244-245, 246
Ethnicity, 122-123, 187, 242-246, 250, 287-289, 325-326
Ethics, 17, 203
Ethnocentrism, 18-20, 21, 24-25, 26, 34-54

Etiology, 279, 283, 290, 294, 298, 305-306
Evaluation, 343-344
Exercise, 296
Expectations, employee, 188, 204-205; teacher, 87-88, 99, 117; *See also* Work
Experiential, 66, 103-104, 251, 269, 328, 332-333, 339, 342
Extended families, 128-129; *See also* Family
Extension to society, 86, 274

Face, 44
Family, 22-24, 25, 28, 39, 45, 47, 85, 93, 94, 100, 105-106, 121-138, 150-152, 154-157, 180-181, 196-205, 245-246, 264-265, 304-305, 307
Field dependence-independence, 38, 72
Finland, 290-292
Flexibility, 115
"Foreign TA Problem," 170-172
Formality, 45
Fundamental attribution error, 329-330; *See also* Attribution theory

g factor, 63-64; *See also* Intelligence
Genetic factors, health, 283-285, 287-289, 298, 307
Geography, 36, 259-260, 273, 278-283, 302-303; *See also* Ecology
Gifts, 46
Global education, 112-118, 178-181; *See also* International thinking
Glossary, health, 261, 297-298
Goals, 40, 152, 210-211, 344
Government intervention, 14, 23-24, 92, 182, 228, 232-233, 237, 244, 271-274, 280-283, 290-292
Graduate education, 176-177
Greece, 203-204
Groups, 44; *See also* Family; Individualism-collectivism
Growth of children, 80-83

Hawaii, 20, 24, 25, 106-108, 150-152, 157, 283-285, 296, 306, 332-333
Head Start, 90-91
Healers, 293-295, 303, 318-322
Health, Mental, 9, 20, 30-32, 52, 68-70, 78, 182, 246-252, 260, 278, 293, 302-322; physical, 9, 20, 22, 23-24, 30-32, 78, 79, 92, 118, 129, 134-135; 175, 268, 270-271, 278-298, 327

Heart, 261, 283-289, 290, 292, 295-297
Helper roles, 31-32; *See also* Counseling; Leadership
Hierarchies, 41; *See also* Superior-subordinate distinction
History, 30, 100-102, 142-145, 294, 305
Hmong, 290, 294
Home-based interventions, 131-138; *See also* Family
Homelessness, 27
Homes, 255, 264-265
Hong Kong, 209, 344
Hot climates, 260-261

Identity, 198, 325; *See also* Individualism-collectivism; Self
Ideology, 43, 249
Immigrants, 9, 22, 26, 27, 30, 101, 176-177, 209, 232-252, 278, 293; *See also* Acculturation
Imposition, 147
Independence-interdependence, 123-125; *See also* Individualism-collectivism
India, 17, 56, 77-94, 131, 165, 255, 261-262, 264, 266, 270, 310
Indigenous psychology, 25, 28-29, 122-123, 142-158, 174, 317
Individual differences, 11, 12-13, 77, 102-104, 232-236
Individualism-collectivism, 13, 17-18, 19, 20-22, 25, 26-28, 39-49, 53, 103-104, 121-138, 154-156, 175, 191-193, 196-205, 222, 250, 285-287, 289-290, 314, 320-321
Industrialization, 25, 28, 30, 42, 113, 126-127, 138, 224, 262, 304
Ingroup outgroup, 34, 39-41, 44, 113-118, 169, 196, 197-205, 217, 223, 237-240, 319; *See also* Ethnocentrism
Initial position, 226
Inquiry method, 111-112; *See also* Curriculum
Intelligence, 11-12, 26, 39, 59-60, 63-66, 80-81, 83, 85, 90-91, 92, 122-123, 147-148
Intensity of conflict, 212-213
Internalization, 14, 234, 310
International education, 112-118, 173, 178-181
International law, 220-221
International students, 9, 20, 29, 161-182

International thinking, 20, 29, 112-118, 170-172, 176-180, 182; *See also* Cross-cultural training

Interventions, family; 19, 22-24, 28, 121-138, 344; *See also* Family

Interventions into poverty, 9, 22, 25-26, 27, 77-94, 121-138, 282-283, 295-296, 344

Iran, 179

Japan, 12-14, 15, 20-21, 28-29, 43, 49, 53, 106, 126, 152-157, 165, 174, 190-193, 193, 201, 210-211, 212-213, 220-221, 222, 225-226, 283-287

Job satisfaction, 186-194

Korea, 12, 122, 126, 149

Language, 107-108, 170-172, 235, 244, 325; *See also* Linguistic skills

Latin America, 91-92

Law, 218-220; *See also* Courts, formal

Leadership, 29-30, 66, 131, 193-206

Learning, 100-106, 108-112, 167-168, 179-180, 327-330, 341; see also Education; Family; Schools

Learning styles, 102-108, 118, 147, 327-330

Lebanon, 220

Legal aspects, 166, 169-170

Levels of analysis, 233-236

Life-style, 20, 77, 92, 287-289

Linguistic skills, 25, 61, 66, 84, 94, 99, 100, 107-108, 123, 148-149, 151-152, 170-172, 245; *See also* Education; Schools

Litigation, 218; *See also* Dispute resolution

Locus of Control Scale, 68, 71-72, 86-87

Lumping, 216

Malaysia, 211-212, 225

Malnutrition, 79, 80-83, 93, 94, 134-135; *See also* Diet; Nutrition

Managerial behavior, 186-205; *See also* Work

Marginality, 49

Masculinity-femininity, 50-51, 223-224, 320-321

Maslow need hierarchy, 189

Mathematics, 105-106, 143-145, 152-157

Measurement, 43-44, 57-58, 70-71, 262, 269, 280-281, 292, 303, 315-317; *See also* Testing

Mediation, 215-216, 218-220

Memory, 109-110

Mexico, 135, 269

Migration. *See* Immigrants

Minnesota Multiphasic Personality Inventory, 68-70, 317

Modal personality, 67

Modernization theory, 126-127, 304

Modes of conflict resolution, 214-216, 222-223

Modesty, 45, 218-220

Moral development, 16-18, 195-196

Motivation, 85-87, 94, 108, 189; *See also* Achievement

Multiculturalism, 100, 101, 112-118, 178-179, 209, 249, 295; *See also* Acculturation

Multinational corporations, 186-205, 209

Multiple intelligences, 65-66

Multiple methods, 62, 63, 101, 146; *See also* Research methods

National character, 67

Native peoples, 242-246

Natural environment, 257-263; *See also* Environment

Negotiation, 209-231

Neighborhood Justice Centers, 218-219

Nepotism, 200

Networks, 27

Nonformal education, 131-138

Nonverbal behavior, 226-227, 265-271; *See also* Time

Norms, 12, 115, 190, 239-240, 317

Nurturance, 51, 131, 194-195, 320-321

Nutrition, 22, 25, 80-83, 93, 133, 134-135, 280-281, 282; *See also* Diet

Obesity, 287-289; *See also* Diet

Obligations, 272

Onchocerciasis, 281-282

Organizational culture, 11, 196-205

Outcomes, work, 193; *See also* Work

Overmanning-undermanning, 259

Parent to child behaviors, 106, 121-138, 154-155; *See also* Family; Socialization of children

Participative decision making, 204
Particularism, 67-68
Perception, 61, 109, 193, 218, 251, 263, 270, 292-295, 307, 310, 313-314, 315-317
Personality, 67-72, 85-87, 257
Persuasion, 47, 224-225, 273
Philosophy, 17-18
Physical environment. *See* Environment
PM leaders, 195-196
Policy, 65, 144-145, 178, 182, 228, 237, 238, 243-244, 249
Politics, 25, 30, 77-78, 85, 92, 182, 239, 241, 244, 342
Poverty, 31, 77-94, 264, 269, 271-274, 280-283, 290-292, 295, 304-305; conceptualization, 77-80; impacts, 80-90, 269; *See also* Interventions into poverty; Socioeconomic status
Power distance, 148-149, 200, 320-321
Prejudice, 15, 35, 113-118, 152-153, 179-180, 227-228, 237, 243-245, 249, 252, 265; *See also* Ethnocentrism
Privacy, 46, 266-267, 269
Procedural preference, 216-218, 221
Process control, 221-222
Process in change, 234-240
Production, 195-196, 258-259, 271; *See also* Work
Projective tests, 315-317
Pronoun use, 148-149
Protestant ethic, 191
Prototypes, 11
Providers, health, 295-296
Proxemics, 266-267
Psychology, history, 142-145
Psychopathology. *See also* Health, mental
Psychotherapy, 318-322; *See also* Health, mental
Public health, 278-298
Push-pull factors, 235-236
Pygmalion effect, 87-88

Raven's matrices, 63
Reentry culture shock, 168, 181-182
Reflective observation, 103
Refugees, 242, 245, 252; *See also* Acculturation; Immigrants
Reinforcement, 86-87, 273
Rejection, 122

Relationships, 30, 44-45, 51, 66, 219, 225-226, 241, 244, 266-267; *See also* Social support
Religion, 20, 191, 241, 290, 306
Research methods, 240-242, 292, 303, 315-317; *See also* Emics-etics; Testing
Resource conservation, 273-274
Response sets, 61
Rivalry, 201
Roles, 162, 169-170, 180-181, 213, 295, 308, 336-337

Schizophrenia, 19, 304-309, 315
Schools, 11, 13-14, 22-23, 25, 27-29, 41, 78, 83, 85, 93, 94, 98-118, 131-138, 150-152, 178, 245-246, 344
Science, assumptions, 142-145
Science education, 111-112; *See also* Mathematics
Self, 41, 66, 115-116, 135-137, 168, 191-192 263, 290, 321, 336; *See also* Individualism-collectivism
Self-fulfilling prophecies, 87-88
Seventh Day Adventists, 287-289, 296
Siblings, 133
Simple-multiplex distinction, 216-218
Skills, 94, 104-105, 118, 181, 203, 218, 247, 344; *See also* Cognition; Linguistic skills; Motivation
Sobriety, 203; *See also* Alcohol use
Social environments, 265-271; *See also* Context
Socialization of children, 10, 12-14, 20, 29, 38, 42, 82, 87, 93, 105-106, 121-138, 150-152, 153-157, 193, 217, 238-239, 250, 257, 280-281, 295-296, 304-307, 312-313; *See also* Family
Social skills, 13, 20-21, 66, 148, 250
Social structure, 216-218, 224, 246-252, 304-305
Social support, 268-269, 285-287, 289-292, 308-309; *See also* Individualism-collectivism
Socioeconomic status, 78, 79, 83-84, 89, 104-105, 108, 114, 121, 123, 171, 249, 250, 265, 280-281
Sojourners, 162-163, 168, 242-243, 327
Somatization, 31, 293-294, 311-312, 327
Specificity-diffuseness distinction, 38
Stages, 16-17

State-Trait Anxiety Inventory (STAI), 68, 70-71
Status, 45-46, 48; *See also* Power distance; Superior-subordinate relations
Stereotypes, 35, 226-227, 333
Stress, 28, 30-32, 246-252, 263, 269-270, 285-287, 289-292, 293, 302, 308, 327
Stroke, 285-287; *See also* Heart
Subjective culture, 12, 36, 211, 255-256; *See also* Culture, definitions/explanations
Success-failure attributions, 88-90; *See also* Attribution theory
Superior-subordinate relations, 22, 29-30, 45, 47, 48, 62, 113-114, 148-149, 169, 189, 197-205
Superordinate goals, 115, 117
Support groups, 32
Sweden, 43, 67, 225

Tacit knowledge, 66
Taxonomies, 145, 337-343
Teacher expectations, 25, 87-88, 151-152, 170-172, 320; *See also* Pygmalion effect
Technology and its transfer, 173-174, 181, 188, 210-211, 218, 257-258, 262
Tertiary education, 161-181
Test administration, 73; *See also* Testing
Testing, definition, 57-58; major issues, 58-63; purpose, 57
Thailand, 134-135, 203, 310
Theory X-theory Y, 199
Third world, 56, 77, 127, 130, 131, 145, 180, 188, 325
Time, 37-38, 48-49, 86, 212-213, 225, 257-258, 285-287, 294

Tight-loose cultures, 49-50
Training, 219, 227; *See also* Cross-cultural training
Translation, 61, 69, 70
Triarchic theory, 66
Trust, 199-200, 201, 212, 219, 223
Turkey, 124, 128, 135-137, 152, 217-218

Uncertainty avoidance, 49, 320-321
United States, 90-91
Universality, 17, 59-60, 64-66, 67-68, 145-149, 189, 318-322, 338; *See also* Emics- etics
Urbanization, 18, 28, 30, 42, 113, 138, 219, 240-241; *See also* Industrialization

Validity, 138; *See also* Testing
Value of Children Study, 124-125, 127, 138
Values, 14-15, 37, 57, 189-193, 204, 212, 221, 224, 290-292, 325
Verbal/visual tests, 61; *See also* Testing
Vertical dyad linkage, 201-202
Violence, 214

Win-win thinking, 30, 210, 214
Women, 180-181, 295-296; *See also* Family
Work, 22, 28-30, 39, 131, 186-205, 210-211, 240, 271
Work ethic, 126-127, 190-191, 203

Yielding, 216

Zero sum, 210

ABOUT THE AUTHORS

John W. Berry was born and raised in Quebec, Canada. He was educated there and at the University of Edinburgh (Ph.D., 1966). After three years at the University of Sydney, working on projects with Aborigines (cognition and acculturation), he settled in at Queen's University (Kingston, Canada), where he is now a professor of psychology. His interests center on cross-cultural psychology including the role of ecological and cultural factors in development, the psychology of acculturation and ethnic relations in plural societies, and cross-cultural research methods. He is a past Secretary-General and a past President of the International Association for Cross-Cultural Psychology; Associate Editor of the *Journal of Cross-Cultural Psychology*; and a member of the editorial board of the *International Journal of Psychology*.

D. P. S. Bhawuk is an alumnus of the East-West Center and is now Manager, Management Training, Royal Nepal Airlines Corporation, Kathmandu. He has a degree in mechanical engineering from the Indian Institute of Technology and also a management degree (M.B.A.) from the University of Hawaii. He has trained maintenance and frontline personnel for 10 years. He has been a workshop leader for the East-West Center's Summer Workshop for the Development of Intercultural Coursework. He received the Distinguished Service Award for the year 1989, the highest honor conferred on participants and fellows by the East-West Center.

Richard W. Brislin is Research Associate at the Institute of Culture and Communication, East-West Center, in Honolulu, Hawaii. He attended Pennsylvania State University and received a Ph.D. in psychology in 1969. Since coming to the East-West Center in 1972, he has directed programs for international educators, cross-cultural researchers, and various specialists involved in formal programs that encourage intercultural interaction. One of these programs overlapped with a conference to develop the *Handbook of Cross-Cultural Psychology* (1980; Harry Triandis, senior editor), of which he is a coeditor. His other books include *Cross-Cultural Research Methods* (1973, with W. Lonner and R. Thorndike); *Cross-Cultural Orientation Programs* (1975, with P. Pedersen); *Cross-Cultural Encounters: Face to Face Interaction* (1981); the three-volume *Handbook of Intercultural Training* (1983,

363

coedited with D. Landis); and *Intercultural Interactions: A Practical Guide* (1986).

Kenneth Cushner is Assistant Professor of Education and Associate Director of the Center for International and Intercultural Education in the College of Education at Kent State University. He has been a degree scholar with the Institute of Culture and Communication at the East-West Center and has written in the areas of cross-cultural training and international education. He is coauthor of the textbook *Intercultural Interactions: A Practical Guide*. He has worked extensively with educational programs for teachers and youths on five continents.

Juris G. Draguns is Professor of Psychology at Pennsylvania State University, University Park. He received his Ph.D. at the University of Rochester. He has held visiting appointments at the Johannes Gutenberg University in Mainz, Germany, the East-West Center in Honolulu, Hawaii, and the Flinders University of South Australia. His research interests in cross-cultural psychology include personality, psychopathology, and complex social behavior. He is the author of numerous publications in psychological, psychiatric, and interdisciplinary journals, and coeditor of the *Handbook of Cross-Cultural Psychology, Volume 6, Psychopathology* and of *Counseling Across Cultures.*

C. Harry Hui, who received his Ph.D. from the University of Illinois, is a member of the Psychology Department, University of Hong Kong. In addition to research interests in industrial psychology, he has published a number of scholarly papers on the topic of individualism and collectivism. Some of his work has been integrated into formal training programs to prepare business people to work in cultures other than their own.

Lisa Marie Ilola was born in England to a Japanese American and a Finnish national. She lived and/or attended school throughout the United States, in Maryland, California, Alabama, Florida, and New York. Her first two years of college were completed in England and the final two years of the Bachelor of Theology were completed while attending the Seventh-Day Adventist Theological Seminary, Far East, in the Philippines. She earned a Master of Public Health from Loma Linda University, California, and a Ph.D. in Educational Psychology from the University of Hawaii at Manoa. She worked in health education in Finland from 1982 to 1985. She is currently Director of the

Division of Educational Services, University of Illinois College of Medicine at Peoria.

Çigdem Kâgitçibaşi is Professor of Psychology at Bogaziçi University, Istanbul, Turkey. She received her Ph.D. from the University of California, Berkeley; she taught there and at Columbia University, and was a visiting scholar at Harvard. She was involved in a nine-country cross-cultural study on the value of children. Her numerous publications include her edited volumes *Sex Roles, Family and Community in Turkey* (Indiana University Press, 1982) and *Growth and Progress in Cross-Cultural Psychology* (Swets, 1987), a selected papers volume from the 8th International Congress of Cross-Cultural Psychology (IACCP), Istanbul (1986). She is the Deputy Secretary General of IACCP.

Uichol Kim was born in Korea. His family emigrated to Canada in 1968. As an undergraduate at the University of Toronto, he majored in psychology and Korean studies. He pursued his graduate training in cross-cultural psychology at Queen's University. His cross-cultural research has focused on cultures of East Asia, especially Korean people living in Korea and abroad. His research interests include topics such as acculturation, ethnic relations, individualism and collectivism, indigenous knowledge, quality of life, and sociohistorical analysis of scientific psychology. Currently, he is Assistant Professor at the Department of Psychology, University of Hawaii.

Kwok Leung (Ph.D., Illinois) is Chinese by birth and teaches psychology at the Chinese University of Hong Kong. His research interests include distributive and procedural justice, conflict resolution, cultural collectivism, and organizational psychology.

Walter J. Lonner is Professor of Psychology and Director of the Center for Cross-Cultural Research at Western Washington University, Bellingham (Washington 98225, U.S.A). He is founding Editor and currently Senior Editor of the *Journal of Cross-Cultural Psychology*. From 1986 to 1988 he served as President of the International Association for Cross-Cultural Psychology. He is coauthor of *Cross-Cultural Research Methods* (1973, with R. Brislin and R. Thorndike) and is coeditor of the *Handbook of Cross-Cultural Psychology* (1980).

R. Michael Paige is Associate Professor of International and Intercultural Education in the Department of Curriculum and Instruction, and

Associate Director and Head of the Education and Training Division in the Office of International Education at the University of Minnesota. He received his Ph.D. in International Development Education from Stanford, served as a Peace Corps Volunteer in Turkey, and has worked in Indonesia, Thailand, and the Philippines as a professional cross-cultural trainer and educational researcher. He is the editor of *Cross-Cultural Orientation: New Conceptualizations and Applications* (1986).

Janak Pandey (Ph.D., Kansas State University) is Professor at the Centre of Advanced Study in Psychology and is also currently Dean, Faculty of Arts, Allahabad University. He has published extensively in scholarly journals on social influence processes and on contemporary social and environmental issues (e.g., poverty, crowding) that are relevant to socioeconomic change in developing societies. Recently, he edited a three-volume set, *Psychology in India: The State-of-the-Art* (Sage, 1988). Earlier, he served as the Deputy Secretary General and at present is a member of the Executive Committee of the International Association of Cross-Cultural Psychology. He developed and taught cross-cultural psychology courses at Wake Forest University in the summer of 1984 and again in 1986-1987 as a visiting Fulbright professor.

Durganand Sinha, educated in Patna and Cambridge universities, has taught at Patna University, Indian Institute of Technology, Kharagpur, and established the Department of Psychology in Allahabad University, which was later upgraded as a Centre of Advanced Study in Psychology. He was Director of ANS Institute of Social Studies, Patna, for over five years. He was a National Lecturer and National Fellow of the University Grants Commission, and has just retired as the ICSSR National Fellow. He has been President (1980-1982) of the International Association for Cross-Cultural Psychology, member of the Executive Committee of International Association of Applied Psychology (1972-1986) and International Union of Psychological Science since 1980. His current research interests are human development, cross-cultural psychology, and psychology in developing countries.

Harry C. Triandis is Professor of Psychology at the University of Illinois. He is a Fellow of the American Association for the Advancement of Science, a past President of the International Association of Cross-Cultural Psychology, two divisions of the American Psychological Association, and the Interamerican Society of Psychology; he is President Elect of the International Association of Applied Psychology.

He received an honorary degree from the University of Athens, Greece, for his cross-cultural work. He is the senior editor of the *Handbook of Cross-Cultural Psychology.*

Pei-Guan Wu earned his B.A. at Zhongshan University, Guangzhou, People's Republic of China, and is currently pursuing a master's degree in psychology at the Chinese University of Hong Kong. He is interested in values, intergroup bargaining, and work motivation.